I0160636

Author's Note: Though the incidents recalled in this book are as true and accurate as my memory can make them, I have taken great pains to change the names of most of the folks involved to spare their privacy. It is not my intention to offend or defame, just to tell my story the way I lived it to the best of my recollection and to remember those guys. I hope their memories of me are as fond as mine are of them.

I owe a special thanks to David Yeager, who was there and proofed my manuscript; thanks to "Gunny" Joe Muccia, whose tireless work to tell the real Grenada story was of great help in correcting my "worm's eye view" of the battle on several points. I eagerly look forward to your book as being the final – definitive account of the entire battle from our point of view.

Thank you, Elyse, for helping me realize the dream.

And of course, thanks to God, without Whose help nothing is possible.

Cover photo: 250-foot towers at the Jump School at Ft. Benning, Georgia, taken by Elyse Wood

1

"The sky, even more than the sea, is unforgiving of the slightest mistake."

Sign over the 82nd Airborne Division Jumpmaster School at Ft. Bragg, NC.

CONTENTS

Forward

It was a difficult thing to write this book; it took years and several re-writes. I'd ask myself what to put in and what to leave out. Many chapters were typed and deleted. It makes you thankful for computers.

Writing is cathartic. I heartily recommend it as an emotional purge.

Having done the writing, the question comes to mind, who would want to read a book about me? It has always seemed to me egotistical to write an autobiography. I am not famous; I do not consider myself a hero (nor, do I think should anyone else). But I served, like millions of other men and women, during a period called the Cold War. During that period the American people often believed we were at peace, blissfully unaware of the sacrifices being made on their behalf so they could remain blissfully unaware of the sacrifices being made on their behalf. Maybe by telling my story I hope I can somehow pay homage to my buddies – the Cold Warriors, who had their lives interrupted when they were drafted to give two years of their lives to their country, or later, when the draft was abolished, for whatever reason, raised their hands and volunteered to serve when military service wasn't too popular.

At the same time, my experiences have left me with a profound faith. There have been many "coincidences" in my life that I choose to call the result of what George Washington called "Divine Providence." Even the doctors who tended me have said the very fact I am here today, much less able to type this story, could be called a miracle.

I fought with myself over which stories to include, or even whether to limit this book to a particular period of my military experience. Again, I am thankful for computers. I leave the reader to decide whether I made the right decision to include my time in Germany as well as at Bragg. Both served to make the man I am today.

I wish to thank my fellow paratroopers both whom I've met recently and with whom I've managed to re-establish contact over the last two years or so. Shooting the breeze and re-living old memories has been a blessing in clarifying dusty recollections and correcting misconceptions. Again, it is out of respect for their privacy that I do not call them by name. It was one of the highest honors of my life to serve alongside my "Brothers of the Silk." I hope this book reflects that.

Wayne Wood

Introduction
The Legend of Private Tuffy, the Airborne Trooper

One of the enduring stories among paratroopers is the story of Private Tuffy, the Airborne Trooper. Few paratroopers make it past the first week of Jump School without being told about him. No one knows how the story originated; it is one of those timeless myths handed down from trooper to trooper, generation to generation.

Tuffy grew up in a rough neighborhood where one had to be tough to survive. He was probably like most kids early on. It was only as he grew older that he began to be separated from the crowd. While his classmates in school grew to full adult height as they blossomed into manhood and womanhood, Tuffy stopped growing. He topped off at about armpit height for the average adult man.

Now, when you're a little guy in a bad part of town you learn fast that if you're going to survive you have to do one of two things. One, you can learn to run fast; or two, you get tough.

Tuffy got tough.

Gradually his reputation grew until people began looking him up to see how tough he was. He made his living fighting; he took on all comers and whipped them all. He became known as "Tuffy." Soon, folks forgot his real name. This went on for years until he had beaten everyone and no one wanted to fight him anymore.

Driven by an obsession to prove to himself and the world he was as good, if not better, than anyone else, he began seeking other ways to stand out. Tuffy took up any challenge brought to him. He climbed mountains, swam raging rivers, hunted wild animals, roamed wild forests, taking any chance he could until finally, he ran out of new challenges. He had done it all. One day he found himself sitting on a street corner, despondent. Life had lost its meaning, there was nothing more to prove.

An acquaintance happened by (Tuffy had few friends, people like Tuffy seldom do). He noticed Tuffy's dejection and sorrow.

"What's wrong, Tuffy?" he said, "You look like you've lost your last friend."

"There's nothing left to live for." Tuffy said dejectedly.

"What do you mean?" the acquaintance said, sitting down next to Tuffy.

5

"I've done it all. There are no new challenges. I've climbed every mountain, swam every river-no one wants to take me on anymore. What's there left to live for?"

"I see." said the acquaintance sympathetically. The two sat for a few moments in silence.

After a moment, the acquaintance brightened, "I know!" he said, "Tuffy, have you ever thought about becoming a paratrooper?"

"A paratrooper?" Tuffy said, perking up with interest. "What's that?"

"Paratroopers are just the toughest outfit in the Army."

"What do they do?"

"Man, they jump out of airplanes behind enemy lines and fight off the enemy until ground troops arrive."

Tuffy thought about it for a minute, letting it sink in.

"That sounds tough..." he said.

"It is! Not everyone who volunteers makes it in the paratroopers."

"That's it!" Tuffy said decisively, "that sounds like just the outfit for me! From now on call me 'Private Tuffy, the Airborne Paratrooper! Where do I sign up?"

When Tuffy marched into the Army recruiter's office he created quite a stir. He marched right up to the recruiter's desk and proudly announced, "I'm going to be a paratrooper!"

The recruiter, glad to see someone sign up for what was then considered a suicide outfit, said, "Sure! What's your name, son?"

"Private Tuffy, the Airborne Trooper!"

"Okay, what's your real name?"

"Private Tuffy, the Airborne Trooper!" Tuffy showed him his birth certificate and, lo, indeed, he'd had his name legally changed to "Private Tuffy, the Airborne Trooper."

The recruiter shook his head sadly, obviously this guy was a nut case, but, who else would volunteer for the paratroops? He signed him up.

It didn't take long for Tuffy to make a name for himself. In basic training he wore out the drill sergeants who tried to wear him out. He took every punishment, every form of harassment with the same boundless energy and enthusiasm he took every task to which he set himself. He had a new goal, a new purpose in life. All the pushups, low-crawls-on-your-belly-through-the-mud, and indignities heaped by the sergeants trying to break him down and recreate him in the Army's image were just grist for his mill. He was going to become a paratrooper. What was more, he excelled in every way. He broke all records for PT[1]; he ran faster, did more pushups, sit-ups and any other exercise than any soldier before. When the drill sergeants dropped him for pushups, he'd pleasantly ask, "Which arm?"

At first, they thought him a smart aleck. Then they realized he was just eager to please. He was so eager that he mastered all the basic soldiering skills in half the time it took normal soldiers. Seeing no need to keep him in basic training (and worn by his energy) he was graduated early and sent on to Jump School.

Jump School is supposed to be a three week course, divided into three phases of one week each. The black hats,[2] warned about Tuffy by the drill sergeants, were waiting for him. Like the drill sergeants, they too, tried to break Tuffy, but found they couldn't. Tuffy passed through every task in Ground Week[3] in one day. Sent on to Tower Week, in spite of the best efforts of the Tower Week instructors, who were in a contest with the Ground Week instructors to see who were the toughest blackhats, Tuffy passed Tower Week with flying colors. In two days Tuffy managed to fly through one of the most challenging and demanding schools in the Army. The only task left was the final exam – successfully jumping from an aircraft while in flight five times – and walking away from the experience.

On Wednesday morning he found himself reporting to Lowry Field at Ft. Benning, Georgia, to make the five jumps, which would qualify him to wear the parachutist's badge and become a fully-fledged paratrooper. His dream was about to come true.

He sat impatiently through the pre-jump briefing and eagerly ran to the parachute shed to don his chute. He endured rigging and JMPI,[4] and, finally, found himself aboard a C-47 aircraft, flying toward Fryar Field, the Drop Zone (DZ), where he would make the first of his five jumps. He could barely contain his excitement as the jump sequence began. These were the series of commands, which would get the jumpers in the aircraft ready to make a safe exit from the aircraft.

Everything was going fine until the command came to hook

---

[1] PT- Physical Training.

[2] Black Hats- Airborne instructors. Their name comes from the black baseball caps they wear.

[3] Ground Week- the first week of the three week Jump School course. Each will be explained later.

[4] JMPI- Jumpmaster Physical Inspection. A final check by jumpmasters to ensure the jumper has donned his/her equipment properly, and to ensure there are no discernable deficiencies in the equipment.

up the lines that would pull their parachutes from their packs. When that command came, everyone hooked their static line anchor hooks to the static line anchor cable that ran the length of the aircraft at a height of about six feet - except Tuffy. Tuffy, being barely tall enough to get in the Army, couldn't reach it, try as he might. Tuffy jumped up and down, trying to reach the cable suspended agonizingly close, but just out of his reach. As he was in the back of the stick, no one noticed his plight. He was too proud to ask for help.

Finally, the green light, signaling the plane was over the drop zone, came on and the line of jumpers made their way toward the doors to leap into the sky. Tuffy, in back, moved along with the line, still trying to hook up.

Finally, it was his turn to jump. Still unhooked, but determined to make his jump, he shrugged, handed the jumpmaster his unattached anchor line cable hook, and jumped. The sergeant could only stare in horror as Tuffy leaped into the back blast of the aircraft's engines without hooking up.

Down Tuffy plummeted, 1250 feet to the drop zone. On the edge of Fryar Field there were gathered several hundred high ranking officers and government officials, who had heard about Tuffy and come to see this "supersoldier" make his first jump for themselves. They watched in helpless horror as he plummeted to the ground, without even attempting to open his reserve. They saw him hit the ground with a mighty thud.

When they got to the place he landed all they saw was a monstrous crater. They peered into the darkness of the hole trying to get a glimpse of Tuffy. Seeing none, they stood in mournful silence for a moment. Then, one general broke the silence.

"What a waste," he said sadly.

"Yes," said another wistfully. "If we could have learned what made him tick, we'd have had an army of supermen..."

"Oh well..." said another as they all turned to walk away.

Then, out of the hole came a low murmuring. The murmuring increased to a grumbling and cursing. They turned in amazement as two hands appeared at the edge of the crater. Their amazement turned to shock and disbelief as they watched Tuffy drag himself out of the crater.

They watched in astonishment as he stood there a moment, oblivious to their presence, dusting himself off and cursing under his breath. Then, he noticed he was not alone. He looked up, saw all the stars and miscellaneous brass gathered about him and, as any good soldier, snapped to attention and saluted.

"SIRS!" he shouted. "Private Tuffy the Airborne Trooper reports! But I'm telling you something..." he said as they stood there with their mouths dropped open in amazement.

"...if this training gets any tougher - I'm gonna quit!"
AIRBORNE!

Chapter 1
The Jump – Gallant Eagle 82

C-130 rolling down the strip
Airborne Daddy gonna take a little trip
Stand up, hook up, shuffle to the door
Jump right out and count to four.
If I die on the old drop zone,
Wrap me up and send me home.
Pin my wings upon my chest,
tell my girl I did my best.
Pin my wings upon my chest,
bury me in the leaning rest.
*(*Anonymous Airborne Running Cadence)

If you ever get the chance to jump out of an aircraft flying over the Mojave Desert at an altitude of eight hundred feet with over one hundred pounds of equipment strapped to your body into a fifty-knot to seventy-knot crosswind, take my advice.

Don't.

It's not as much fun as it sounds. I know. I've tried it.

Of course, this wasn't something I did intentionally. It's not like I woke up that morning saying, "Hey! I think I'll jump out of a plane into a fifty-knot to seventy-knot crosswind!"

As a paratrooper in the 82nd Airborne Division, I may have been crazy (and there are those who hold that opinion), but I didn't think I was stupid. The whole thing was supposed to be just another jump except for the fact it was to be the largest airborne operation since World War II.

Here's what it was all about; the troopers of 2nd Brigade, 82nd Airborne Division, and selected support elements (of which my battalion, 1/320th FA[5] was one), were to fly across the Continental United States and conduct a simulated assault onto five different drop zones (DZs) at Ft Irwin, California. Over twenty-five hundred troopers and their equipment, ranging from their personal weapons to tanks and artillery pieces, would load onto almost two hundred aircraft for the trip. The drop would be followed by two weeks of intense desert warfare training. The operation was called Joint

---

[5] The official designation of my battalion was 1st Battalion (Airborne (Abn)) 320th Field Artillery Regiment.

Training Exercise (JTX) Gallant Eagle 82.

It would be my first jump with "The Division," as we troopers fondly (and sometimes not so fondly) referred to the 82nd[6]. It was to be my thirteenth jump from an aircraft while in flight (fright?). I don't know if there is any significance to that number. I am not, by nature a superstitious man. I wasn't thinking about any of that anyway on the morning of March 29, 1982 anyway. I had other things on my mind.

I had kissed my wife goodbye that morning and told her I would see her in a couple of weeks. I hoped to be back for Easter, though I knew that was doubtful. The exercise would end only a few days before the holiday and old timers in the Division informed me that while most of the personnel would be back within a day or two after the end of the exercise, vehicles and heavy equipment sometimes took weeks to find a bird (aircraft) home. As I was the S-3, Operations Section, vehicle driver I would come home with our section's "gamma goat,"[7] or just plain "goat," for short.

I hadn't seen much of my wife and kids these last few months I had been with the Division. Since I had transferred into the unit, I had spent most of my time out in the field. It was tough, but it seemed better than the alternative at the time - an all expense paid vacation for one year on the Soviet border in Turkey without my wife and kids.

When I walked into the S-3 office that morning SFC DuPont[8], who was going to be the Battalion Operations NCO[9] for this operation, was looking at aerial photographs of the DZ with SSG Robertson, the Battalion Chemical Warfare NCO.[10]

"Take a look at these shots, Wood," SFC DuPont said with a grin, "you're going to have to be careful coming down, you might get hung up on one of the mountains."

I looked at the picture of the drop zones. There were two, side by side. One was labeled "Silver," the other "Gold." The boundaries of the drop zones were superimposed on the pictures for

---

[6] As if the other fifteen active combat divisions the Army had at the time didn't exist.

[7] The "gamma goat's" proper nomenclature was Truck 1 1/4 Ton, M561; a six-wheeled all-terrain vehicle that was supposed to be amphibious as well, though I've never seen one I would trust to float.

[8] For the sake of privacy, I have changed the names of most of the guys I served with.

[9] NCO - Non-Commissioned Officer: the official designation for a Sergeant. SFC DuPont would be the ranking sergeant for the exercise in the field headquarters.

[10] Official designation- NBC: for Nuclear, Chemical, and Biological Warfare.

reference. The DZs ran from east to west across a flat stretch of the Mojave at the base of a range of mountains. A valley between two peaks opened up on the western end of the drop zones. A dirt road ran between the two DZs. I was told there would be a couple hundred reporters waiting for us along the road. A scale at the bottom of the picture told me the drop zones were each over three miles long.

"That's a lot of drop zone." I said quietly.

"'An awful long drop time," SSG Rob said doubtfully. "A lot can happen..."

"Well, at least we won't have to worry about running out of drop zone," I said.

"Naw," DuPont jibed in. "'Just getting hung up on some mountain top!"

Rob and I continued to study the photos. The more I looked at them the queasier I felt. I've had some interesting experiences jumping in off-post exercises, that is, away from Ft. Bragg. There is always a risk jumping into a strange place with unfamiliar terrain but that is what made OPTs (Off-Post Training Exercises) such great training. After all, if we were ever to go to war we would be jumping into unfamiliar terrain.

I don't want to sound super *macho* here, but risk was part of the turf - a part of being a paratrooper. The Army let us wear silver wings and the maroon beret to set us apart from the rest of the Army. They also paid us extra pay; jump pay, for throwing our bodies out of aircraft. A few months before, enlisted paratroopers got their jump pay raised to one hundred and ten dollars a month, double what it had been when I first went on status – unchanged from $55 a month since World War II.[11] Still...

What folks who aren't airborne don't understand is jumping out of an airplane is inherently risky business, but it is a calculated risk. I looked over at Rob's face and could see that something was eating at him, too.

Rob looked at me with that Georgia Cop look he always got. "This is your first jump with the Division, ain't it, Wood?"

"Yeah, Chief." As stated before, I had been on jump status with the XVIII Airborne Corps. With seven jumps since graduating from Jump School, I wasn't quite an "old-timer," but I wasn't a "cherry" or novice jumper, either. But jumping with the 82nd was

---

[11] Jump Pay – officially hazardous duty pay was $55 a month for enlisted and $110 a month for officers from World War II through 1981 when the DoD finally raised enlisted pay to $85 in a step-process to equalize pay with officers. Shortly before Gallant Eagle Jump Pay was equalized at $110.

different than jumping with a Corps unit. The Division had quite a reputation at that time, the year was not quite three months old and already three Division troopers had been killed in parachute accidents.

I smiled at the concern in Rob's eyes. SSG Robertson was a sort of mother hen to the enlisted men in the section. He was older than the average NCO in the unit. He had originally enlisted in the sixties, during the Vietnam conflict. During his first hitch in the Army he had seen combat in both Vietnam with the 101st Airborne Division and in the Dominican Republic with the 82nd. Toward the end of his hitch he learned that he was about to come down on levy for Vietnam again. He opted to get out of the service when his time was up rather than re-enlist and go to Nam again. It seemed to him that someone in Washington had something against him. Even if this were not true he had spent about eighteen months out of his first three years in the Army in combat. If he re-enlisted he could look forward to another twelve months as a grunt beating the bush. The odds in favor of his dying in bed were decreasing.

After his discharge, he spent the next ten years as a deputy sheriff in South Georgia. Then, for some reason, he decided to go back into the Army. In the course of time he worked his way back up through the ranks, even managing to get out of the infantry to become a chemical NCO, a specialist in chemical and biological warfare. As such, he was assigned to our battalion. In the S-3 shop Rob was a pillar, even the Battalion Commander respected his wisdom and experience.

"Don't worry about it, Wood," he said with a shrug. "Greater minds than ours have thought this up."

"That's what scares me."

I went back to my desk, where my gear was sitting, rigged for jumping. According to Division regulations, my ALICE (or field pack) was loaded with at least one change of uniform, a couple changes of socks and underwear, wet weather gear (yes, Virginia, it has been known to rain in the desert), my shaving kit, various other personal and military equipment, and a day's worth of C-rations, which was to feed us until we could get supplied out in the field.

In a real combat situation I would also be carrying a couple hundred rounds of ammunition for my M16A1 and any other equipment and special gear, depending on the mission and location of the mission. This might include ammunition for the section's M-60 machine gun, claymore mines, a Light Anti-Tank Weapon (LAW) or two, hand grenades - whatever might be needed to sustain us in combat for three days. Three days is the time an airborne task force is expected to be able to hold out, surrounded, against a superior enemy force. That's when the ground forces ("legs" in airborne terminology) are supposed to break through and relieve us. My pack now weighed around fifty pounds. With a full combat load it might weigh upwards of a hundred pounds.

"Come here and give me a hand with this, will you, Wood?"

I looked up and saw the Battalion Communications Officer (CESO) grinning at me. He was a young first lieutenant. I was told he had graduated near the top of his class at West Point. Right now, he was undoing the rigging on his equipment. He had a large field pack, the type we called a "mountain ruck." It was about twice the size of the field pack we were normally issued, being reserved for units required to sustain themselves for extra long periods of time behind enemy lines or away from normal support, such as Rangers or Special Forces. Of course, one could always buy a mountain ruck, as the CESO had.

He was having a hard time stuffing a case of C-rations into his pack. The old C-rations were packed into cans, twelve meals to a case. They could get quite heavy. I got a look into his pack and saw that he was carrying a portable field radio (an AN-PRC-77, or "Prick-77", or just "the Prick" for short) stuffed in there.

"They left the Cs off the goat and we're going to have to eat..." he explained. "I'm taking the Prick with me for commo in case the Colonel's jeep burns in. We'll need commo."

I saw that he had also packed extra batteries for the radio. Adding together the weight from the radio, the C-rations, the batteries, and his personal gear, I figured he had well over one hundred pounds of gear in his pack. Then I noticed he had a pack frame, but wasn't using a lowering line[12] I tried to diplomatically point this out to him.

"I don't need a lowering line, I'll ride it in," he said with a grin.

"That's a heavy ruck sir, you'll hit like a ton of bricks."

"Naw, I've done it before, it'll act as ballast."

"I'm not using my lowering line, sir, you can use it..."

"Naw, it'll be okay."

So I shrugged and helped him put the attaching straps around his pack that would be used to attach his field pack to his parachute.

---

[12] A lowering line is a fifteen-foot strap that hooks from the parachute harness and any item of equipment deemed too heavy to land with. This is used to lower equipment before landing, reducing the risk of injury.

By the time we finished it was time to go to pre-jump training.

Every time an Army Airborne unit jumps it is a requirement for that unit to conduct "pre-jump" training within 24 hours of "drop time." Pre-jump consists of the jumpers being broken down into "chalk order" and "stick order." Chalks being an aircraft load of troopers and "Sticks" being the lines of jumpers going out the door of the aircraft. Once broken down and organized each aircraft's jumpmaster and safety (who assists the jumpmaster in the aircraft) brief the mission, using aerial photos and/or diagrams – pointing out possible obstacles and dangers on the drop zone – discussing rally and rendezvous points. Then jumpers rehearse every action in the aircraft required for the jump, from hook-up procedures through exiting the aircraft; they practice actions in controlling one's parachute, and PLFs (Parachute Landing Falls) from platforms around six feet high. Everything is rehearsed again and again until done right, for the sky is unforgiving of the slightest mistake and every action must be instinctive – if you have to think about what to do you've taken too long.

Pre-jump is serious business. Even though the troopers get tired of doing and re-doing the same thing over and over each jump inside they realize its importance.

On that March 29 though, there was an almost festive air to the proceedings as we went through the drills. Never before or since have I seen so many jumpers prepping for the same jump. The excitement in the history we were making with the presence of the media added to that atmosphere. I remember folks with cameras filming us as we trained. While waiting to mount the platform to practice PLFs couple of us had a conversation with the first jumper of our stick – a cameraman from a major network. He was a veteran photographer who shot skydiving competitions for his network. The plan was for him to exit my bird first and take video of the jump from the air.

This was to be the first field test of the Joint Rapid Deployment Task Force. Gallant Eagle 82 was to be a real media event. We were told there would be some 200 reporters waiting for us on the DZ.

It seemed to many of the folks I knew the US had been taking it on the chin time and again in the seven years since the fall of Saigon. That pummeling from all quarters culminated in the fall of our embassy and hostage taking of fifty-two US Embassy personnel in Tehran, Iran on November 29, 1979.

For Jimmy Carter, the hostage crisis was the final nail in his Presidency's coffin. He had ordered the JRDTF formed to deal with any future acts against US interests around the globe. A new President, Ronald Reagan, promised the world there would be no more Irans. He had supported its development from theory into reality. The US was about to show its enemies that no place was safe from the military might of the US Armed forces. There was no place to hide where couldn't come get you – land, sea or air.

It was 2200 hrs, 10:00 PM civilian time. The call came for us to gather our equipment and move out to our aircraft. This was it.

We had been in "lock down" for the past several hours waiting for the time to board our aircraft. This was Standard Operating Procedures (SOP) for an actual alert, which we were simulating. The atmosphere in the containment area had been more like a party than one of getting ready for a combat operation.

The mess hall had brought us a fried chicken dinner, which the troopers from our battalion wolfed down picnic style around the area. After chow we'd gone into the old World War II era barracks and relaxed till it was time to go. Most of the guys in my barracks had spent the time watching the NCAA basketball championships on a TV someone had brought in. Our "home" team University of North Carolina (UNC) was playing Georgetown (UNC won). I idly wondered what they'd do with the TV when we pulled out.

I saw our Battalion Command Sergeant Major, CSM Cross, come into the barracks, toss his gear on the floor next to a bunk frame and lie on the bare metal supports. All the mattresses had been taken. I offered him my bunk, but he refused, saying he'd slept on worse. I remember him watching the guys huddled around the TV set with a smile. I wish he'd taken me up on my offer of a bunk with a mattress.

I remember taking a couple aspirin from a bottle I'd gotten from the medics and washing it down with a swig of water from my canteen. I told myself I'd better remember to refill the thing before we moved out. After all, we were jumping into the desert. I had been fighting a fever and chills all evening. It was a reaction from a shot given me that morning when a records check[13] revealed I needed a Yellow Fever/Typhoid shot. I remember thinking it took a genius to think of giving us shots before a major jump.

---

[13] These were called "PORs," short for "Preparation for Overseas Redeployment." They were held periodically in Division, usually before going on "Mission Cycle", which I'll explain later. The purpose is to prepare us for no-notice callout to any place in the world in case of emergency. Needed shots are given, wills are updated, etc.

I must have dozed for the next thing I remember we were being hollered out to the marshalling area where we'd break down into "chalks" or aircraft loads for the trip to California. My fever must have broken as I was damp from sweat and the night now seemed cold. I washed a couple more aspirin down with some water from one of my canteens and headed out to the formation in front of the building. I don't remember now if I ever refilled my canteen or not.

We were marched from the holding area where we had been staying to Green Ramp on Pope Air Force Base, where we boarded our aircraft. There, we were broken down further into our chalks, or planeloads. The jumpmasters called out chalk numbers so the jumpers could get on the right plane. I was on chalk thirteen.

I saw Sergeant Rob standing alone amidst the hustle. He was staring into space, seemingly unaware of his surroundings.

"Have a good one, Chief." I said.

He started, "Yeah, you too, Wood," he said, but it seemed to me his mind was still a million miles away.

"Chief," I said.

"Yeah?"

"It's a lovely day to die."

"Yeah," he said. I had meant it as one of those morbid jokes that only paratroopers find funny. That night, it wasn't funny even to me. I shook off my misgivings and ambled over to where my chalk was gathering. People have asked me why I jumped if I felt that way. The answer is simple. I was ordered to.

The flight to California was estimated to take about six hours. The personnel birds would take off from Ft. Bragg and join with the equipment birds, which had been pre-loaded and would take off from other airbases, somewhere along the way. The equipment birds would go in first and heavy drop the equipment ahead of the personnel drop.

In the meantime, we had hours to kill as our C-141A made its way across country in formation with the vast air armada. The ride was made bumpy by turbulence caused by the other aircraft. It would get worse when we dropped altitude two hours out to approach the drop zones flying "nap-of-the-earth," that is, flying low to the configuration of the terrain to avoid enemy radar. We spent the time sleeping and teasing each other to dispel our nervousness.

The Air Force crew got into the spirit of things during our flight safety briefing. While the pilot gave the briefing over the intercom the Air Force crew chief hammed it up by imitating airline stewardesses as they went through the motions of donning oxygen masks and showing us where the exits were. The Division troopers showed their appreciation with wolf whistles and cheers.

One young trooper, Morales, from B (Bravo) Battery, had just gotten married before going to jump school and coming to the Division. He had spent the majority of his married life in the field. Now he was being sent to California for Gallant Eagle. Everybody wished him a happy honeymoon. A sergeant sitting next to me playfully reprimanded him for not putting his wife in his duffle bag so she could come along. It was discovered that his wife was expecting their first child and that he had gone to jump school for the extra $55 a month Jump Pay.[14] This would be his sixth jump - his first jump out of jump school, and - like me - his first jump with the Division.

Next to him was a major of the engineers. I later learned this was his first jump with the Division, also. He had recently reported as the Division's Engineering Officer. I remember him smiling at the good-natured kidding among the NCOs and enlisted men. He seemed like a nice guy.

About halfway through the flight we were served a boxed lunch which we gulped down gladly. A soldier never refuses food. I popped a few more aspirin as my fever was up again and dozed off.

The next thing I knew, it was time to put on our chutes. On shorter flights we would have chuted up at Green Ramp. As this was a longer flight we conducted in-flight rigging. Paratroopers use the two man "buddy system" to don their equipment. SFC DuPont would help me put on my equipment, and then I would help him. I was sick and really having trouble with my equipment. SFC DuPont impatiently brushed my hands away and told me to let him rig me. After I was rigged I did what I could to help him, but I wasn't thinking clearly. He JMPI'd[15] me and OK'd me as ready to go. Before he sat me down so he could inspect other jumpers he looked me straight in the eye, "Wood, are you sure you're okay to make this jump?"

"I'll be okay, Chief, my fever is breaking. I'll be all right."

"Are you sure?"

"Yeah, I'll be okay," I hoped I sounded convincing. "I'll pop a couple more aspirin and I'll be okay."

---

[14] See previous note on Jump Pay.

[15] JMPI- Jumpmaster Physical Inspection. This is a final check of the rigged jumper by a jumpmaster-qualified individual. The Jumpmaster quickly, and meticulously, inspects the chute assembly for defects, both visually, and physically, ensuring proper rigging.

"All right," he said doubtfully. "But if you don't get any better I'll sit your behind down and you can catch up with us on the ground. You don't need to be jumping if you're sick."

"I know. It'll be okay."

I sat down and hoped I was right because the fever had given way to chills; those shots were really hitting me hard. I knew I had no business jumping if I wasn't feeling one hundred percent. Only a fool takes a chance like that. My concern wasn't only for my own safety, but for the safety of other jumpers who might be around me.

On the other hand, I sure didn't want to sit out my first jump with the Division. It was a matter of pride. It's hard to explain, but once a trooper is manifested, chuted up, and on the plane, he wants to go out that door. I had been in this plane for almost six hours. Unless I was dead, I was going to put my knees to the breeze.

Finally, the twenty-minute warning was given. We watched as the jump warning lights, three lights, red, amber, and green, set at various points around the aircraft shifted from red to amber. This began a series of jump commands, which would get us hooked up to our static lines and out the door. At this command everyone put their helmet back on, buckled their chinstraps, made last minute equipment checks, and undid their seatbelts. One could almost cut the tension in the air with a knife.

"TEN MINUTES!" came the ten-minute warning. The loadmaster, the jumpmaster's liaison with the pilot, whispered something in the jumpmaster's ear, "WINDSPEED FOUR TO SIX KNOTS!"

A cheer went up in the aircraft; conditions were almost perfect for our jump.

"GET READY!"

"OUTBOARD PERSONNEL, STAND UP!" came the command from the jumpmasters. This was the command for all personnel sitting along the outer wall, or "skin" of the aircraft, to stand up. In a fully loaded C-141, personnel are loaded in C-141s in four rows of seats, set two along the outside facing in, and two down the middle facing out. The inside seats had been removed and replaced with pallets of equipment and a jeep rigged for airlanding. This had made our air trip somewhat more comfortable as we had more space. In a bird fully loaded with troopers we would have been face to face, knees almost interlocking with the middle rows with our rucksacks and weapons cases making conditions even more cramped.

I couldn't hear the commands firsthand because I was in back of the stick, at the front of the plane. Jumpers repeated the commands so everyone got the message. We stood up.

"HOOK UP!" We hooked our static lines to the static line anchor cables that ran the length of the aircraft at a height of about six feet.

"CHECK STATIC LINES!" We checked our static lines from the static line snap hook snapped on the static line anchor cable, to the point where it disappeared over our shoulders. From there, the jumper behind us checked the static line to where it criss-crossed the pack tray of the parachute, held in place by rubber bands; our inspection ended at the piece of cotton cord, called quarter-inch cotton webbing, which tied our static line to the apex loop of our parachute canopy. This was done to ensure there were no cuts, frayed edges, or tangles in the line. Anything such as this might cause the static line to break before it could pull the chute out of the pack tray. SFC DuPont, being the last man in line, turned so I could check his static line. I tapped his hip "Okay."

"CHECK EQUIPMENT!" This was a final equipment check to make sure every snap was snapped and every buckle was buckled. Again, once we checked ourselves, we checked the jumper in front of us to make sure nothing was misrouted or twisted, which could cause a death or injury.

"SOUND OFF FOR EQUIPMENT CHECK!" Each jumper, starting with the man in the back of the stick, slapped the jumper in front of him on his thigh while giving him an oral "Okay!" The signal proceeded up each line of jumpers until the front jumper pointed to the jumpmaster and shouted "ALL OKAY, JUMPMASTER!" This told the jumpmaster that everyone in his stick was hooked up and ready to jump.

"STAND BY!" As we were in a C-141 the first jumper in each stick moved up to the edge of the door to await the next command. In a C-130, the command would have been "STAND IN THE DOOR!" and the first jumper in each stick would take up a door position and wait for the command to jump. Every eye in the bird was now fixed on the sets of jump lights situated throughout the aircraft, watching the amber light.

"Are you sure you're all right?" SFC DuPont's worried voice came over my shoulders again.

"I'm fine, Chief, the fever's broken."

He moved forward a bit to check my eyes, satisfied, he nodded.

The amber light flicked off and the green light flicked on. This was the pilot's way of notifying us that we were over the drop zone and could jump.

"GO!"

Every trooper on the aircraft began to inch toward the door. We had to climb over some of the equipment as we made our way to the door. Personally, I wanted to get out of that bird and into the open sky. My fever had broken for the time being, but I still wasn't feeling all that great. It seemed to me we had been standing an awful long time. I figured they had given us a premature time warning. My equipment was getting heavy.

As I always did before a jump, I began reciting the Lord's Prayer, "Our Father, Who art in heaven..."

I could see daylight through the open door and hear the deafening roar of the wind blowing in. There were four jumpers ahead of me, three, two, one- my turn. The klieg light of a news camera hit me straight in the face as I made my final steps to the door, temporarily blinding me. I gave the camera a thumbs up, made my half-turn, stepped out into the back blast of the jet engines, and was sucked out the door.

The world spun about as I was caught in the wind, all sense of direction and gravity was lost as I fell through the sky. There is no way to describe the exhilaration experienced in these few seconds as I began my count,[16]"One thousand...two thousand-" my count was halted by the sudden violent shock of my chute opening.

I looked up quickly, afraid that something might have gone wrong; the chute had opened too early and too violently. I felt that my navel must have been jerked up into my throat. Could I be a towed jumper?[17]

I was greatly relieved to see a fully opened chute over my head. I began to look below and around me for other jumpers. Most airborne accidents are caused by carelessness such as jumpers not keeping an eye out and colliding with other jumpers.

Suddenly, I was whipped around in a complete circle. Once more I looked up, afraid I had blown a panel or worse. I was puzzled to see a full chute over my head- relieved, but puzzled. What on earth could make my chute act that way?

---

[16] When a jumper exits the door in static line jumping he gives a "four thousand count." "One Thousand - Two Thousand -" etc. If his main parachute doesn't open by the time he reaches four thousand, he immediately goes back into a tight body position and pulls his rip cord to his reserve. At eight hundred and fifty feet he has already lost four hundred feet in the count and it will take his reserve another four hundred feet to deploy.

[17] Towed Jumper- This occurs when the jumper doesn't separate from the aircraft and is towed behind the aircraft by his static line. The jumper has three choices when this happens: to be cut away and land using his reserve, be hauled in, if possible, or land behind the aircraft on a foamed runway.

WINDS!

"Oh brother," I thought. "This is going to be a no-kidder!"

I looked down again. Fortunately, there were no jumpers near me, so I didn't have to worry about a mid-altitude collision. At the same time I remember thinking it was strange. On a jump this big I expected to see the sky full of chutes. Off in the distance I saw a jumper hit the ground, watched his chute begin to collapse, only to be caught by the wind and take off, dragging the unfortunate man along behind. He was boogying. I figured the poor guy was traveling at least fifty miles an hour. Closer, I saw another jumper get slammed into one of the vehicles waiting on the DZ. He was smashed pretty badly, literally ripped in half. Later, I learned it was Morales. He had been killed instantly.

I don't mean to sound callous, but at the time I didn't have time to react to seeing Morales killed. I was having problems of my own, trying to avoid his fate. I was descending in a spiraling motion and the closer I came to the ground the faster my descent. If I didn't do something quick I was going to hit like ten tons of bricks. There was a danger of being knocked out or breaking something. If that happened I would be completely helpless against whatever waited for me on the ground. Getting to the ground was only going to be the beginning of my problems. Remember, all this only took a few seconds, but those seconds seemed like an eternity.

I reached up behind me and grabbed the risers[18] opposite the direction of my descent to allow the canopy to catch as much air as possible and slow my descent. I pulled the risers down as low as I could; it seemed I brought them at least to my waist, if not my knees. I kept a steady watch on the ground, checking my descent. The stunt I was about to pull would require split second timing.

At the last second I let go of my risers, allowing the chute to pop up. The popping of my chute pulled me up right before I hit the ground. This softened my landing. I still hit the ground hard, but not as hard as I would have otherwise.

I immediately grabbed my risers again. I was congratulating myself on having gotten myself out of another tough scrape as I took hold of my canopy release to disconnect it and deflate my chute. The riser was violently jerked out of my hands as the wind caught my chute and began to carry it across the desert, dragging me behind.

I struggled desperately with my equipment, trying to reach

---

[18] Risers are the straps which connect your parachute harness to your parachute suspension lines, which in turn are connected to your parachute canopy. On the T-10 parachute the risers are used to steer the chute.

the canopy releases and get them to open. I had the old T-10 harness that used a pinch-type release system. One pressed on two button-like devices on either side of the assembly and it was supposed to come loose. Unfortunately, the tension on the assemblies made it impossible to depress the buttons. I grabbed my risers above the releases trying to take pressure off the assemblies in hopes of getting them to work. It was no good. Every time I got a good grip on the risers I would hit a rock or bush and my hands were knocked loose. They were getting bloody from the beating they were taking. Even when I did get a good grip it wasn't enough to alleviate the pressure on the assemblies.

I was being dragged across the desert at a speed exceeding forty miles an hour, possibly closer to sixty. People who have never been to a desert usually think of sand dunes when they try to picture a desert scene. There are dunes in the desert, but most of a desert is made up of rocks and brush, and rocks, and cactus, and rocks, and gullies, and rocks. There are even pieces of petrified wood out there, who knows where they come from - and there are more rocks. I was getting a first hand, worm's eye look at desert terrain. The dust being stirred as I was dragged along was choking me to the point I could barely breathe.

I reached down and tried to undo the quick release buckle on my T-10 harness. If I could get it undone, three of the four leg and shoulder straps would come undone and I would just slide out of my equipment. At least, that was the idea. However, I couldn't even reach my quick release buckle, as my harness had been pulled up on my body by the drag. My reserve chute, usually situated at about the level of my solar plexus, had been pulled up to my chin. I tried to unhook my reserve from the D-ring attachments to which paratroopers connect their equipment (pack, weapon's case, reserve, etc.), but was prevented on the one side by the snap hooks of my pack and weapons case, and on the other by a safety pin which was designed to prevent the reserve from coming accidentally unhooked. This pin had been used so many times that it was crooked. I'd had a difficult time inserting it when I rigged. On a normal jump, in good weather conditions, it wouldn't have made a difference. Now, as I was being dragged along the desert floor at an excessive speed, the jerking of my equipment, caused by being pounded by rocks and other obstacles, made it difficult to extract the bent pin from the snap. This was made even more difficult by the other snap hooks attached to the D-ring.

I wished I had a knife to cut myself loose from this mess. I had almost bought one before the operation but had held off. Good knives were expensive and I had a wife and two kids. Going off for three to four weeks I hadn't wanted to spend money on a knife that my family might need for milk and bread.

"Oh Lord," I prayed. "Help me, Jesus, to get out of this..."

At about that time I tangled with another jumper as he was dragged across my path. This guy was cursing with all the imagination at his disposal.

We were tangled for a moment, and then either broke, or were cut, apart. I had no room to judge him. At that time, my mouth could be as foul as the worst reprobate. But I remember thinking that I'd hate to stand before the Lord with such blasphemies as my last words on this earth.

It was then that the truth of my predicament hit me. I had done - and was doing - all I could do to get loose of my equipment and none of it was working. The very safety devices that had been built into my equipment to preserve my life were hindering all my efforts to save it. Unless the wind died down I was going to be dragged to death on this DZ.

What was worse, I knew that if I died right then, I was going to hell. I had been playing cat and mouse with God for the last eight years. You think you've got the rest of your life to make it right with God. Then you find out the rest of your life is only seconds.

"Oh Lord," I said. "I'm going to die. Please take me. I don't want to go to hell."

And there, on that drop zone in the middle of the Mojave Desert, the Lord reached down and cut through all the religious confusion that had stood between us. There were no preachers, no deacons, and no manmade dogma. There was no one there to tell me I had to hold my nose a certain way or say this or that prayer. It was just the two of us. And in my situation I had no room for pride or fear. I cried out to my Savior and He heard me.

"I've got you," came a still, small voice in the back of my head. *"It's all right."*

I wasn't convinced. Years of religious confusion still tried to stand in the way, "But Lord, I've never been baptized!"

"It's all right child, I have you."

I still wasn't convinced. I wanted to believe, but could I?

. I began arguing with God, giving objections as to why I couldn't be saved. Many times I had prayed the sinner's prayer, but because I had never met this denominational requirement, or that qualification, or met certain standards of holy behavior I never thought it had "taken."

"I know your heart."

For the first time in my life I felt it, or should I say, felt *Him* - *that* peace that passes all understanding. I knew the Lord had me in His arms. It was going to be all right. And that's the last thing I remember before I died.

Chapter 2
The Aftermath of a Disaster

The days he lived and loved and laughed kept running through his mind,
He thought about the girl at home, the one he'd left behind,
He thought about the medics and he wondered what they'd find.
HE AIN'T GONNA JUMP NO MORE!

Gory, gory, what a terrible way to die!
Gory, gory, what a terrible way to die!
Gory, gory, what a terrible way to die!
He ain't gonna jump no more!
("Blood Upon the Risers" an old Airborne song, author unknown)

I now remember hearing two guys (medics?) talking about me. One guy, evidently, was checking me over. I don't know, I don't remember anything but the sounds of their voices.

A disembodied voice, "He's dead, man."

"Wait a minute!" Another voice.

"Man, he's got no vitals. Look at him. Let's go help someone who needs it!"

The next thing I remember[19] is feeling extremely cold. I was lying in a ravine or a ditch. I could hear the wind whistling overhead. Off in the distance, men urgently shouted instructions to one another. I could also hear moans and shouts for help. The roar of helicopters flying over was constant.

I was alive. Thank God. I was alive.

I knew I was hurt, though I could feel no pain - yet. It was more of a knowledge that something was drastically wrong with me. I decided I wasn't going be carried off that drop zone on my first jump with the Division. I might have to report to the medics later, but I would walk off this drop zone under my own strength. I had been banged up on jumps before, but I always managed to leave the DZ on my own two feet. I tried to get up, but couldn't, I was too weak.

---

[19]I have reconstructed the events of the next few days as accurately as possible. Some of my memories came back slowly, months or even years after the accident. Some of my information came from talking to others who were there. Even now, a bit or piece of memory falls into place occasionally and adds to my picture of events.

I was able to move my hand and saw it for the first time. It was covered with blood.

"Oh Lord," I moaned weakly, "I'm hurt bad, please help me. Don't let me die here, after all this..." I began to black out and fought to retain consciousness. If I passed out right now I might never wake up. I mustered all the strength I could, "Somebody help me!"

"We're coming!" came the reply from what seemed to be a long way off.

"I'm hurt!"

"Everybody is!"

"I'm hurt bad!"

"We're coming man, hold on, everybody's hurt bad!"

I lay back and felt waves of nausea sweep over me from the exertion of talking. Again, I fought to retain consciousness. I prayed and waited for my strength to return so I could once more call for help. I didn't know how long I could hang on.

I don't remember how many more times I called for help or even whether or not I blacked out before a face appeared over the edge of the ravine, I later learned the man was SP4 Joe Cress, of the 2/325th Infantry[20], "Oh boy!" the man said, "Are you okay?"

"No, I'm hurt!"

He slid down the ravine and took my hand, patting it and feeling for a pulse, "You'n' everybody else! They really messed this one up... there's guys stretched out all over the place. We thought *you* were dead! Hey!" he shouted, "Get over here quick! I've got somebody over here who's hurt!" he looked down at me and said reassuringly, "It'll be okay, man."

From over the hill came the reply, "Everyone's hurt!"

"Man, you don't understand!" he yelled with growing frustration, "This man is HURT! Get over here NOW!" he looked back at me, "It'll be okay man. I'm hurt, too. I messed up my knee on the jump, they wanted to medivac me, but I figure I'm a medic and there's guys a lot worse off than me out here who need me - *WHAT ON EARTH IS TAKING YOU GUYS SO LONG? GET YOUR HEADS OUT OF YOUR BUTTS AND GET OVER HERE, I'VE GOT SOMEONE HURT*" he looked back at me, "Don't worry man, it's gonna be okay."

"What on earth is all the yelling about, for crying out loud?" I heard another voice come from over the rise, getting closer, "Man, I - oh man! That guy's dead!"

---

[20] Joe's real name. After some 25 years through the miracle of the internet I've finally been able to make contact with him and thank him for saving my life.

"He ain't either, man, he's alive, but he won't be if someone don't medivac him out of here, for crying out loud, will you get off your dead butts and move?"

More shouting. More commotion.   Finally, a litter was brought to me and I was gently put on it.

"Man, we thought this guy was dead..."

"Careful with his head, geez, what a mess..."

"Will you idiots shut up? He can hear you!"

I was wrapped in blankets and carried to the medivac point. There was a commotion on the way, something about photographers. I heard someone swear and tell someone else not to let them get a shot of my head. I was set down to wait the next chopper. I faded out...

I learned what happened next only several years later from my mother. She was told the medical personnel lost me again. I didn't respond to the emergency procedures available at the site, so they set me aside. Cress came half-limping, half-crawling back to the medivac point and saw me laid out, ready to be zipped up in a body bag.

"Aw, no..." he went over to me to check me out, "Ma'am," he said to an Air Force nurse, a CPT McConnell, from March AFB, who had volunteered to help out with the disaster, "This guy ain't dead."

"Now, Specialist, he's gone..."

"No Ma'am," Cress said excitedly." I saw him move! Please Ma'am, check him out..."

"Specialist, there are hundreds of men..."

"Ma'am, he ain't dead!"

At about that time, I am told I moaned, "Oh, mama... oh, Jesus..."

I was put on the next medivac chopper out of there. I remember being lifted onto the chopper, and feeling safe, secure, warm...

My memories of the next day or so are in bits and pieces, vague reflections of the surgeons at the MASH hospital set up in the desert for the operation frantically attempting to sew my head together. I was told later I kept the surgical team well entertained with my one-liners while they were working on me. Nothing like a near fatal injury, massive loss of blood, and the resultant traumatic shock to get one's sense of humor started.

I was rushed from the evacuation hospital to the Intensive

Care Unit at March Air Force Base Hospital. When they wheeled me in, there were about a dozen or so people working on me. They tried to take my blood pressure, but couldn't. I had second and third-degree friction burns on both my arms. The nurse in charge, CPT McConnell from the DZ, told the orderly to take it from my legs. The guy pulled back the sheet, "Uh, oh!" he said.

"What now?" CPT McConnell asked, wearily.

"Look at these legs- they're huge! We'll never get the cuffs around them!"

"We're going to have to get some special cuffs."

"Man, they're solid as rocks, too. What do they do to you guys?" he asked me.

I was semi-conscious. "We usually run from four to eight miles a day before breakfast... depends on how Top feels..." I slurred.

"All these guys are in excellent condition," CPT McConnell said. "It's probably what's kept them alive..." I sank off into La-La Land again.

"I spent the next day or two like that, zoning in and out. They had smeared some kind of junk all over the burns on my arms to alleviate the pain and help them heal. I later learned the stuff was called silvadene. To prevent the scarring which results when burns are allowed to heal by themselves my nurses would come in and scrub my burns to allow the wounds to heal evenly, from inside out. I have never before or since felt such pain as when they scrubbed my arms. In spite of the fact the doctors had me on morphine, then Demerol, for pain, I would cry like a little baby during the entire ordeal. As soon as they finished, I would whimper my way back into oblivion.

One time, I woke up to see our Battalion Executive Officer, Major McCall standing in my room. I had always liked him; he seemed like a warm and caring individual. I remember there were tears in his eyes as he looked down at me. I didn't know it at the time, but they had lost heartbeat and respiration on me twice in the previous twenty-four hours and didn't expect me to live through the night.

"Hello, sir," I mumbled. There was something wrong with my tongue.

"Hello, Wood, how are you?"

"Okay, I guess. Was I the only one hurt?" I was worried about that. How embarrassing it was, to get hurt on my first jump with the Division. In my confusion, I had forgotten everything that happened on the DZ. I had forgotten being told about all the injuries.

I only remembered later.

    "No," he choked.

    "How many got hurt?"

    "Hundreds."

    Tears began to fill my eyes. "'Anyone get killed?"

    "Yes."

    That's when I learned that the CESO and Morales from our battalion had been killed on the jump, along with three others. The Major from the Engineers was listed in critical condition along with several others. Our Battalion Commander, LTC Andrews had broken his collarbone on the jump and had been medivaced back to Bragg. Major McCall was acting Battalion Commander. Our B (or Bravo) Battery had lost over half its troops to injury. My battalion had suffered seventy-five casualties. What caused it all? Winds.

    At the time I didn't remember seeing Morales die. It came back to me one night in a dream a few months after I returned home. I was reliving the jump as I did every night. Every detail came through so vividly; I could even feel the cold wind blow against my face as I stepped out the door. I was checking my descent when I saw a guy get slammed into one of the trucks heavy dropped ahead of us. I watched in horror as the guy was literally ripped in half. When I woke up, I realized it wasn't just a dream. I was reliving things I had forgotten.

    I lay there watching Major McCall as he told me what he felt I could handle. I saw the pain and concern on his face. At that moment, I loved the man for his compassion. I wished I could help him in some way. Then I nodded off again.

    When I came to it was dark in my hospital room. This struck me as strange as I was in the Intensive Care Unit and there was normally a light on. The Division Chaplain[21] was standing at the foot of my bed with his head down, praying silently. There were tears in his eyes. He was popular with the Division troopers as he made a point of greeting each new bunch of troopers to the Division. He would always open his talk with the story of Private Tuffy.

---

[21] Later on I worked with a guy who said he was in Nam when the Division Chaplain started out told me a story about the Chaplain. According to this guy, the Chaplain once received a Bronze Star for Valor and a Letter of Reprimand the same day for the same incident. He had gone out on a patrol with some of the guys he ministered to. It was ambushed and the leaders were killed. Instead of aborting the patrol, which evidently was of some importance to HQ, the Chaplain took charge, successfully completing it. This earned him the Bronze Star. But, as Chaplains are supposed to be non-combatants, and the Chaplain had violated the rules of his office by leading the patrol, the Division Chaplain had no choice but to give him a letter of reprimand. Again, this is just barracks rumor and I never got to see the Chaplain in his dress uniform to see if he wore a "V" clasp on his Bronze Star.

He looked so sad standing there, fumbling with his beret with his hands, I actually felt sorry for him. I wanted to cheer him up, "Hello, Chaplain."

I must have startled him because I thought he was going to hit the ceiling, he jumped so.

"Hello Wood," he said, almost cautiously. "How're you doing?"

"Okay, I guess," I said. "But I'm going to tell you something."

"What's that?"

"If this training gets any tougher, I'm going to quit!"

He looked at me, "You're going to quit?"

There was a brief moment of confusion as he tried to figure out if I had said what he thought I said. Then his face broke into a broad grin, "Oh, you've heard me tell the story..."

"Yes, sir."

He laughed at that. Later on, he told me he knew then I was going to make it. One of my troops who came in after the jump told me the chaplain mentioned what I said in intensive care when he told them the Tuffy story.

I was famous.

What I didn't find out until much later was that right before I spoke to him they had lost vital signs on me. I suppose that's why the Chaplain nearly jumped out of his skin when I spoke. He had been in a room with a dead or dying man and the dead spoke.

My periods of coherence became more frequent as time went by. My doctor came in and examined me. I asked him exactly what was wrong.

"You tell me," he said. Right off, I didn't like him. I mean, let's not be coy. I know I'm pretty banged up. I'm in intensive care with all sorts of tubes running in and out of me. Just about every bodily function I have has been wired for sound. I've got an army of nurses and orderlies running in and out of my room every time I cough. And he wants to play head games?

Oh well, let's play. There wasn't much else to do, "Well, there's something wrong with my tongue."

"Yes, you almost bit it off."

That was nice. No wonder my speech was slurred. Strangely enough, it didn't hurt too much. I felt around in my mouth, "I've got a tooth missing."

"Yes, he said, pleased. He reminded of a teacher with a precocious child who had just successfully passed an intelligence test.

"And my head's hurt," I was tiring of the game.

"Yes," he said.

"How bad?" I wanted to know, but he wouldn't tell me. This irritated me more. After all, it was my head. Didn't I have a right to know? I suppose, looking back now, he was trying to save me from the trauma when I was weak. Perhaps he was afraid if he told me the full extent of my injuries it might throw me into shock and kill me. It was a genuine enough fear. At the time, it just made me mad. I wanted to know what I had to deal with so I could deal with it.

I knew something serious had to be wrong with my head. After all, they had it wrapped tighter than King Tut's, but he's telling me I've had an "injury." No kidding. It was nothing to worry about. Right! That was why they had me in the ICU.

My wife called from North Carolina. I tried to soothe her as she was near hysterics. She told me the Army had been ready to fly her out to California to be with me (a sure sign things were serious) but had backed out at the last minute. My condition had been upgraded from "critical" to "stable." I smelled a dead fish there. If I was doing so well, why was I still in ICU? I said nothing. Of course, at this time I still didn't know I had lost it all three times and that my prognosis for the first thirty-six or so hours had been less than fifty-fifty for my survival. The fact was, as I saw it later, they didn't see the sense in flying her out to California if I was going to die. She'd be on her way west; I'd be heading east in a body bag. We'd pass each other in the air. Even at this time, the odds against my full recovery were slim to none. There was a good chance of some permanent brain damage. As far as the doctors were concerned, my career was over, forget about my ever jumping again.

I talked to my kids. I said the usual Daddy things to them, I suppose. Then Debbie came on the phone again to tell me my mother was flying down from Alaska to find out just what was going on. She was going to catch a military hop[22] down to the Continental United States and then fly commercial to California.

I lay in my bed during this period and tried to figure out who to blame for this mess, who to hate. There were some NCOs and

---

[22]Military hop- One of the benefits we used to get in the military was free, space available air travel on military aircraft. If you could find a seat going where you wanted to go, you could fly. It could be interesting, as you could end up on just about any kind of military cargo aircraft. It could also be risky. When my family flew space available back to Germany in 1975, they spent almost a week in Air Force terminals on the east coast, trying to catch a flight with enough seats for all of them.

officers from the Division Public Affairs Office who came in and visited me just about every day. I talked about jumping again and they just looked at me sadly. I asked them about the jump and what went wrong. They told me the winds had come out of nowhere and funneled through the same valley between the mountains we had looked at in the photos back at Bragg.

I had lived in the desert before. My family had been stationed at Ft. Carson, Colorado while I was in high school and I spent some time in Nevada after graduation. I had seen these high winds. They called them "Chinook" or "devil" winds in Colorado[23]. You could be standing in your front yard on a nice sunny day and one of these winds would come tearing through at speeds exceeding seventy miles per hour. It would tear up houses and yards across the street, blowing trashcans and anything not bolted down all over the place. Standing in your yard, out of its path, you wouldn't be touched. Then, as quickly as it came, it would be gone. I understood desert winds and figured there was no one to blame. No one to hate. Even if there were, it would have been a waste of time and energy.

Somehow, the accident caught everyone totally off guard; in spite of the fact NASA had moved the landing of the space shuttle from Edwards AFB to Texas earlier that week because of foul weather along the west coast. I've heard more than one trooper comment bitterly that it was too risky to land the shuttle but safe enough to drop the 82nd Airborne!

I learned I must have lain in that ravine for over two hours before coming to. On a normal jump of this magnitude one allows for one to two percent casualties, so the medics had been prepared to treat between twenty-five and fifty jumpers. The typical jump injury is a sprained ankle from a poor landing, maybe an occasional broken leg or arm. In spite of the inherently dangerous nature of parachute jumping, deaths are rare and seldom the fault of equipment malfunctions. Usually, death or injury is caused by carelessness and mistakes on the part of the jumper.

The Army medical facilities had been overwhelmed by hundreds of troopers lying smashed up on the western end of Gold and Silver DZs, where the majority of the injuries and deaths occurred. The other three drop zones only suffered the normal casualties. There had been reluctance on the part of the Army to accept help offered from other services. One could chalk it up to interservice rivalry, or initial ignorance of the actual severity of the

---

[23] The name comes from the Chinook Indians.

accident at higher headquarters. CPT McConnell told my mother she had been part of a team the Air Force put together to help when word of the catastrophe first got out. They waited over two hours after the accident before the Army requested their assistance. She had watched me be put on the helicopter and seethed with anger that we had to lie out in the sun for all that time without assistance. The Air Force always tends to be critical of how the Army treats its people and this incident did little to improve our image.

I had finally gotten help, and I was thankful. Had I not come to when I did and not been able to call for help, I would have bled to death in that ravine. That is, if shock or my head wounds hadn't killed me. As it was, I lost a great deal of blood. My records state I had to be infused with two whole units of blood at the MASH and that's not counting the plasma the medics pumped into me on the trip from the DZ to get me to the MASH.

One day I looked up and there was Mom. She stopped for a split second at the door, appearing to catch her breath. Years later, Mom told me she hadn't recognized me when she first saw me. She said it was only when I smiled at her that she knew me.

Mom caused quite a stir among the brass. They were learning she could be a force of nature. The Division Public Affairs people (PAO) were jumping through hoops trying to keep her happy and away from the press. There had been enough bad press already. One injured trooper's wife, who was living in California, had come to see her husband. The reporters made sure her hysterics in the hospital lobby after her visit got on the evening news. They didn't need another trooper's mother giving interviews.

Hospital personnel had tightened security on the patients. Several reporters had been caught trying to sneak in to the several hospitals to which we had been parceled out trying to get an interview. CPT Ross, our Battalion S2, had saved the press the trouble by holding an impromptu and unauthorized press conference in his hospital lobby. The reporters got quite a story before my buddies from the PAO arrived on the scene. I understand he received quite a chewing out over that one. On the one hand I was touched by the care the Division gave my mother. On the other hand the people from the PAO were understandably concerned about one of the most seriously injured trooper's mother being let loose to speak with the press.

We got a kick out of the PAO people trying to "take care" of my mother. She was treated like a queen. When they discovered she didn't check into a motel before coming to see me it was arranged for her to have a room at the guesthouse free of charge. They provided her with transportation to and from the guesthouse.

One morning Mom got up early and decided not to wait for her Division-provided ride. She took a cab to the hospital. She had been there about fifteen minutes when the Division PAO, a major, practically ran into the room. The relief on his face when he saw Mom was classic. It was hard not to laugh, in spite of my pain. He acted as if his feelings were hurt because they had gone through all the trouble to arrange a ride and she had gone off on her own, wasting money on a cab. Mom explained she didn't want to be a bother and was used to being independent. When the major left, Mom rendered her verdict, "They're scared."

"They have reason to be." I agreed.

It was understood we troopers were not to speak to anyone about the operation until Division investigators had debriefed us. On any fatal jump accident there is an investigation to determine whether or not negligence was involved.

There was little or no chance of my speaking to anyone anyway. I was well guarded. Even my stepmother couldn't get a call through to me. She had called while my mother was there and identified herself as my mother. The staff, not knowing my parents were divorced, thought she was a reporter trying to sneak an interview or get some information. She later told me they had been quite rude to her. They thought they were doing their job. When I first heard about what happened it didn't dawn on me who might be calling.

There were, of course, the denunciations from quarters both within and without the Division of a cover-up. There usually is that sort of thing. As far as I could tell at the time, the major reason the Division and the Army was being quiet was the simple reason that for the first few days after the accident they weren't sure about what, exactly, had happened.

It did look bad. The 82nd's track record hadn't been good in the year of 1982. Two rookie troopers (called "Cherries" in the Division) had collided in mid-air during a mass tactical night jump shortly after New Year's Day. It seems they had not yet mastered their MC1-1B steerable parachute and steered right into one another, causing their chutes to collapse. Shortly thereafter, a letter came down from Division Headquarters stating the 82nd would no longer use the MC1-1B parachute on tactical or night jumps, using only the T-10 parachute.

The first (and to my knowledge, so far the only) woman to

be killed in a military parachute accident died later on the same month when she collapsed in the door of her aircraft and stumbled out into the blast from the C141's jet engines. As she was probably unconscious, and therefore limp, the wind caught her body and blew it back against the aircraft. My neighbor was in the bird with her that night, said he heard the "thud" of her hitting the "skin" (or outer wall) of the aircraft. Her chute got twisted up by the twisting of her body and she "streamered in." 82nd history was made.

As with any fatality, rumors abounded. There were accusations the jumpmaster had pushed her out the door when she collapsed in his arms. It is expressly forbidden for a jumpmaster to intervene with a jumper in the door. The legendary helping boot out the door is supposed to be a thing of the past. My friend told me they had been standing in the aircraft too long waiting for the green light. In spite of the fact the jump took place in the winter, it was hot in the aircraft and the weight of the equipment acted with the heat to cause her to pass out. It looked to him as if she stumbled in the door. The jumpmaster moved to help her to her feet and get her out of the way as it was obvious she was in no condition to jump. When the jumpmaster got her to her feet she pulled away from him and went out the door. If this were so, the jumpmaster was not at fault. Of course, no matter what an investigation finds in such a situation, there will always be that ten percent who will believe the worst.

There were many who blamed the increase in accidents on the prevailing attitude of the chain of command. The Commanding General of the 82nd, Major General James Lindsay, upon assuming command of the Division a year before, had instituted a policy by which all training and proficiency jumps were to be conducted at night and in full combat gear. His reasoning, which seemed sound to me from a purely military perspective, was if we were ever to jump into combat (and that's what we were supposed to be about anyway) it would most likely be at night. Day jumps without equipment ("Hollywoods"), while useful in allowing troopers to get used to their chutes and overcome their fear of jumping, accomplished little in preparing for the mission. Many units had gotten so spoiled doing Hollywoods, except when absolutely required for tactical exercises, many of their troops were forgetting how to properly rig for a full combat equipment jump. As a result, there was an increase in injuries due to poorly rigged equipment in masstacs.

There were other stories, which filtered through Ft. Bragg, about guys getting banged up jumping in high winds against Army regulations. There was talk about a major in one infantry battalion who took wind readings with his helmet. According to regulations, winds were supposed to be measured with a delicate instrument called an anemometer. Any reading over 13 knots was unsafe and would cancel a jump. This major would hold the helmet over his right toe and drop it. If the helmet hit his toe, he declared the winds safe enough to jump.

Whether this major really existed or not, there seemed to be a lot of liberties being taken with the safety regulations laid out in the ASOP. I was in the emergency room at Womack Army Hospital with my son one night when fifty troopers from one of the infantry battalions were brought in. They had been blown into the trees by high winds during a CAPEX (Capabilities Exercise) given to show off for some brass in from Washington. No one had wanted to scrub the jump because the brass wanted to see a show and it would have been embarrassing to cancel it. I suppose it was much better to have the battalion blown into the woods and mangled. I remember seeing one trooper, who'd landed in the trees, sitting patiently in the hallway with a tree branch stuck through his leg.

The Division people came in to debrief me while Mom was still there. I told my story, what I could remember of it at the time. My mind was still hazy, but I guess I gave them enough to satisfy them.

After everyone had gone and left us alone, Mom and I were finally able to talk, "The Lord spared me." I said.

"I know."

"I knew it was all over and I knew I was going to hell. I asked Him to take me. I really wasn't concerned about whether I lived or died. I just didn't want to go to hell."

"Maybe that's why He didn't let you die."

"But why me and not those other guys?"

"Maybe He has a work for you to do. Remember years ago you felt the call? You've never answered it."

"I guess it's time to stop running." I thought a moment, "I need to get baptized. It hit me before I blacked out I have never been baptized. He let me go this time. I might not get a second chance."

Mom had to leave the next day. I was out of the woods and the talk was I'd be taken out of ICU in the next day or two. After that, it wouldn't be long before I would be flown back to wherever they were going to send me. There wasn't much more Mom could do for me in California. She had three boys in Alaska who needed her more than I, and her money was running short. I felt terribly lonely after she left, but she had been there when I needed her. The very fact she had flown down was a boost to my spirits.

One of my younger brothers just recently told me that after going "home" to Ft. Richardson, having been strong for me, she cried. He said she cried a lot.

I was going to require some sort of surgery on my head. The Air Force people wanted to do it. They didn't seem to trust the Army folks too much. The Army was fighting the Air Force people for me, and the Army doctors were fighting among themselves for the privilege of putting me back together. I felt special.

The next day I was wheeled out of ICU to have some tests done on me. They X-rayed my head again, ran an EKG to check my brain waves, and ran a check on my mouth, where my tooth had been knocked out. Years later an Army dentist accidentally discovered a hairline fracture in my jaw when he was putting a bridge where the tooth was missing. No matter how much anesthesia they pumped into my mouth it never quite deadened the nerves where the tooth had been knocked out. After new X-rays and a careful examination of the pictures he found it. Evidently, the fracture severed the nerve connection from the base from the base of my jaw to the tooth. Of course, having been discovered several years later, it was never officially attributed to my jump injuries.

What was important about my excursion that day was it was the first chance I got to get a good look at myself, the new me. I knew I must have been a mess from the way people kept staring as I was wheeled through the hallways in my wheelchair. I'll never forget a small boy, about eight or nine. He just stared at me with that look of unmitigated awe and horror that only a child that age can manifest. His eyes popped open to about the size of silver dollars and his little mouth flopped open. I thought he was going to scream.

"Don't worry, babe," I said, trying to make him feel better, "I don't bite."

His mother got on to him for staring. I told her it was all right, and I apologized for scaring him. My curiosity was now aroused. What kind of mess was I? There was full-length mirror at a turn in the corridor. It was a decorative thing with smoked designs on it. There was enough clear glass for me to get a good look at myself. I had the orderly pushing me stop. I wasn't prepared for what I saw.

Where to begin? Well, for one thing, my head was encased in an enormous bandage, which came down over my ears and around my neck. I had known that, I could feel it. What I wasn't expecting was what the exposed portion of my face looked like. There was dried blood all over my face in a weird, web like pattern. I couldn't tell how much of the blood was from tiny scratches or whether it was all just blood from my head wound which had been allowed to dry on my face. Why hadn't they at least washed my face? Both my eyes were severely bloodshot with dark black rings around them. This is called "raccoon eyes" and is caused by concussion. My whole face seemed weirdly swollen and distorted beneath it all.

I was reminded of a guy named Bates I'd punched out in Germany. *"As ye sow..."*

No wonder the kid had freaked out! He had come to the hospital expecting a routine visit and had run into the Frankenstein monster. Looking at myself I could understand the shock my mother had tried so hard to conceal. I could barely recognize myself. I wondered what my wife would say.

When I was returned to my room I asked for a washcloth.

The time finally came for me to leave ICU. I had grown fond of the folks there. I know they were doing their job, but these people had gone the extra mile for me and for that I am grateful.

I was taken to a four-man room on a regular ward filled with jump casualties. When they discovered I was the guy in ICU their joy in seeing me still makes my eyes water. Other casualties of the jump were down the hall. As I was semi-ambulatory I was allowed to limp down the hall to visit them and swap stories. As with my ward, most of them had heard about me and seemed as happy to see me as I was them. Even though we didn't know each other we were brothers. They had been pulling for me.

It was somewhat therapeutic for me to hear some of the other guys' stories. One of the guys had seriously cut himself up with his own knife while trying to cut his risers as he was being dragged. "I couldn't cut the lousy risers for being banged around by all the rocks and everything," he said. Every time he would get a grip on the risers and be about to cut he'd hit a rock or a bush or something and it would cause him to cut himself. It might not have done any good to have had a knife after all.

I talked to another trooper who had been dragged almost as far as me. He had been skinned up pretty bad. He told the story of a network cameraman who followed him as he was being dragged across the drop zone. The cameraman ignored his cries for help as he continued to shoot, getting the whole grisly scene on tape.

I don't really recall how long I was on the ward before they sent me back to Bragg. While I was there, SSG Rob and SFC DuPont stopped in to see me. It was great to see them again. They filled me in on what was going on out in the field.

They told me that after everything got sorted out on the Drop Zone, what was left of the battalion moved out to continue on with the maneuvers. After all, the whole purpose of our going out there in the first place had been to conduct desert training at the National Training Center (NTC) at Ft. Irwin, California.

Our Battalion had suffered around seventy-five casualties on the drop. Two men had been killed, our CESO and SP4 Morales from Bravo Battery, the newlywed on the plane. The contingents from our Bravo (B) Battery and Headquarters and Service Battery (HSB) had suffered the majority of the casualties. They had landed on Silver DZ, which bore the brunt of the winds. Charlie (C) Battery had only fared slightly better, having landed on the western end of Gold DZ, immediately next door to Silver. It was no picnic over there, either. Bravo had been left in such a shape that only one or two men manned the majority of its six guns, rather than the six to eight normally assigned to a 105mm howitzer section.[24]

Poor SFC DuPont had been left alone for the first day of the operation in the Battalion Tactical Operations Center (TOC), which functions as the *de facto* battalion headquarters out in the field. Everyone else assigned to the TOC for that operation had been scraped up pretty badly and were in the hospital. Our CESO, as already mentioned, had been killed. Our S-2 Officer, CPT Ross had banged up his knee and, as mentioned before, was holding press conferences in the hospital lobby. The S-2 NCO and Sergeant Rob had been medivaced because the dust kicked up while they were being dragged had temporarily blinded them. They had suffered some pretty nasty abrasions from the drag but had been able to rejoin the unit after the medics flushed their eyes for a day or so.

DuPont should have been medivaced. When he landed on the DZ his risers had somehow gotten twisted around his neck. It was a wonder he hadn't died from strangulation. As it was, he had pulled several muscles in his neck. Even now, a week later, his neck was badly bruised and he still had problems turning his head. He later told me that he and I had tangled for a moment while being dragged. He had been the guy I'd heard cussing on the DZ. He told me he had cut some of my suspension lines, too. That may have helped slow my drag and lessoned my injuries. Rob told me later

---

[24] We were authorized ten men per howitzer section but I never recall seeing it happen in real life.

guys from the Battalion Fire Direction Center (FDC) had to come over and help him get up in the morning and lay down at night. He had refused medical treatment, after all, if they evaced him, who would man the TOC?

They told me the Division had been kicking behinds out in the desert. They had come back from the disaster with a vengeance. Actually, all we had out there was a little bit more than a brigade (the Second Brigade, three battalions of the 325th Infantry with its supporting elements from other units), less than a third of the actual Division strength. Our opponents in the war games were a National Guard armored division and the OPFOR Brigade. A few days into the operation some of our infantry had managed to lure the majority of the tankers into a valley. The rest of the Division task force had dug in along the cliffs overlooking the valley and were waiting for the signal to open up with everything they had. In an actual combat situation the National Guard Division would have been wiped out. The Commanding General of the Division had raised his hand, when he lowered it the 2nd Brigade of the 82nd Airborne Division would open up. Our weapons had been fitted with laser training devices to score hits against the enemy. There would be no doubt as to the effectiveness of the fire. Before he could lower his hand the chief controller stopped it. He couldn't wipe out the tanks now; the operation had to last at least another week.

As I listened to them talk I couldn't help but feel proud of my new Division. I wondered if there was any other organization of fighting men in the world who could come back from such a trauma in such a way.[25] I was proud to wear the patch on my shoulder, the beret on my head, and the wings on my chest. All I had to do now was recover so I could continue to wear them.

---

[25] In retrospect I have to admit there were others that probably would have come back just as well as we did. But you'll have to pardon military people of all branches for thinking they are somehow better than everyone else – particularly in the elite outfits. How else would they continue doing the things they are called upon to do? That is the magic of *Esprit de Corps*.

Chapter 3
An Army Brat During Vietnam

Vietnaaaaam, Vietnaaaaam
Late at night while you're sleeping
Charlie Cong comes a'creeping
All arou-ou-ound...
(Vietnam era marching cadence (to the tune of "Poison Ivy"))

It's not everyone who can say they've died for their country; though I didn't realize at the time that dubious distinction belonged to me - in an offbeat way. I was aware that something special had happened to me. In some way I had been spared.

As I lay in my room staring at the ceiling, dozing in and out, I had time for reflection. Nothing makes you take stock of your life and its direction like almost losing it. I realized I had gotten into the predicament I was in because I was running. I was also trying to prove something. I was trying to prove I was as good, if not better, than anyone else.

I could blame all the deacons and preachers and church people who had hurt my feelings as a child for my spiritual state when I faced death on that drop zone in 1982. It's true these people will bear some responsibility for their actions. After all, the Word says it would be better that a millstone be bound about one's neck and be cast into the deepest part of the sea, rather than cause a child to fall (I'm paraphrasing Mt. 18:6).

Ultimately, though, we hoe our own row in the garden of life and can blame no one else for all the weeds that crop up. When I faced eternity that day I was going to hell. I knew it. What's more, I knew I deserved to go to hell. I had been disobedient to God's call in my life. I could blame no one but myself for my disobedience.

Just recently, I was sitting in a recording studio waiting for my turn to record. We were listening to the final touches being put on a sound track from a "Judgment House" being put on by one of our local churches. They were doing the sound effects of hell.

It was pretty gruesome. The youth pastor of the church, whom I suppose was in charge of the project, was chuckling as he described how they were going to make it the most realistic depiction of hell ever. I listened to the moans and groans, the screams and sounds of chains jangling. "Yeah," I thought."' Pretty scary."

Then, I heard something that just hit me wrong. A voice screamed out, "It's not fair! It's just not fair!"

Before I thought, I spoke, "That's not right."

"What isn't right?" the young minister asked.

"What that guy just said."

"What do you mean?" he asked, perhaps, a bit offended.

"What that guy said about it not being fair. You won't hear that in hell."

The guy grinned at me skeptically, "Oh no?"

"No." I said, "Everyone in hell will know exactly why they're there. And they'll know it's just."

"How do you know that?"

"I've been there. I've seen it."

He looked at me like I'd just climbed out of a space ship. I guess I can't blame him. Maybe I shouldn't have spoken. Maybe it didn't make a whole lot of difference what was on that tape. Then again, maybe it did.

God is just. God is merciful. That is why I believe it's important to understand, that everyone who ends up on the wrong side of eternity will know why they are there. For me, one of the worst parts of my revelation on that drop zone was the knowledge I deserved what I was getting. There were no excuses.

I had always been confused about "religion." It's little wonder, considering my religious upbringing.

On my mother's side, I came from four generations of Pentecostal/holiness preachers. My father's family was fundamentalist Baptist. Don't tell me God doesn't have a sense of humor.

I've often wondered whether my mother and father's religious differences added to other tensions present in my parents' marriage. They divorced when I was two years old. Religion wasn't by any means the only reason for the split, but it probably was a contributing factor.

Mom used to drive me over to my father's parents' house to spend the weekend every so often. I loved my grandparents. We called them "Mom and Dad Wood." If my Grandma Phelps had a problem showing affection it wasn't so with Mom Wood. She lavished love and attention on me, spoiling me.

It was the same with Dad Wood. I always liked to read comic books when I was a kid. Mom Wood told me later when Dad

Wood heard I was coming to visit he would say, "I'd better go buy some 'funny books' for Wayne. You know how he loves those funny books."

Of course, they gave the same love and attention to all their grandkids, but they always made me feel special. That was the way they were. I remember sitting in the front room of their little house in Cahokia, Illinois playing with my toy soldiers. Mom would be crocheting; Dad would be sitting in his rocker, reading the paper. Then, I'd hear a soft snoring; Dad had drifted off to sleep.

If it were possible, Mom would let me visit my grandparents on Memorial Day weekend so I could lay a wreath on my Uncle Ralph's grave. Ralph Lee Wood had been killed in France in 1944 fighting the Nazis. The family received the telegram on Thanksgiving Day.

We would go to the Memorial Day service held in downtown Cahokia where Mom Wood would be honored as a "Gold Star Mother." After the ceremony, we would drive across the old Jefferson Barracks Bridge to the Jefferson Barracks Military Cemetery. There, amid the row upon row of white crosses and occasional Star of David, we would find Ralph's grave and lay our wreathes.

Afterward, we would re-cross the Mississippi River and go home. Sometimes we would eat out. I remember eating in silence. Mom and Dad would be lost in their memories and grief over the baby they had brought into the world, raised into young manhood, and sent across the ocean to die at the age of nineteen.

I remember lying in the big feather bed in their guest bedroom and looking at his Army picture, sitting on the dresser with the high school pictures of my other aunts and uncles. There were my father's and Uncle Verne's Navy pictures. Ralph was the last member of the Wood side of the family to serve in the Army. Until me.

I was born, and spent most of my younger years in East St. Louis, Illinois, across the river from St. Louis, Missouri. In the course of growing up, we moved around a lot. One year, I attended three different schools. This was common in East St. Louis at the time. The city was deteriorating and the folks who could, found themselves moving further and further out of the inner city to the outskirts. It wasn't until we moved to Edwardsville, Illinois my fifth grade year that I learned there were kids who were born and raised in the same town, even the same house, and had gone to the same school all their lives. To these kids I was an outsider, a new kid, in spite of the fact that I had begun the year at the school. In East St. Louis, you were only "new" if you came in late in the year.

I find it amazing it was in Edwardsville that I began having my first schoolyard fights. All those years in the "slums" of East St. Louis, I had never been in one fight. I don't recall anyone ever picking on me at school before. I didn't really know how to fight at first. It was when I moved into the so-called nice towns, where I was an "outsider" I began having troubles. Go figure that one.

It was here I encountered a problem I would face most of my life BC (Before Christ). I am not a very physically imposing person. Being short and stocky, with glasses to boot, it seemed there was always someone who wanted to pick on the new kid. Threats and tough talk didn't sound convincing coming from me so I'd always have to fight. With no father around and an older brother who wasn't much of a brawler (that's not necessarily a bad thing); I had to learn the art of battle through OJT (On-the-Job-Training). After the fifth grade, each move meant new battles.

Mom married Ron when I was ten. When I was twelve Ron, who had done a stint or two in the Navy some years before, decided he'd had enough of civilian life and went back into the military. This time he joined the Army. From then on, we lived all over the country, even the world. We went to Europe twice, first to Belgium, then to Germany. In the States, we were stationed in Florida, Alabama, Colorado, and returned to Illinois in between tours, waiting to join Ron, or, as when Ron was in Vietnam, we couldn't go with him. It was probably the best thing that happened to our family.

But it was the time of Vietnam War.

Though I never went to Vietnam myself, as an Army brat of the Vietnam era I have my own memories and maybe a few emotional scars from the conflict. Of course, they are nothing like those of the guys who went and fought, but they are real just the same.

In the dependent schools I attended just about every kid had a dad or a brother who was either over there, had just returned, or was going. My best friend in the 9th Grade in Belgium had to fly home to the States with his family to bury his brother, killed in Nam. As the war dragged on, seeming without end, many of us figured when we graduated it would be our turn to go.

I watched my mother's hair turn gray as first my brother, and then my dad, did their tours. My brother was home barely a month when Dad began his tour. Army policy prohibited close family members from serving in the same theater of war. We felt relief when Dad got stationed in the south, in a relatively quiet sector.

We got a letter a few months into his tour. "I'm moving up to a place near the border, Lang Vie, folks say it's real quiet." The next thing we heard on the evening news the South Vietnamese Army (ARVN) had invaded Laos in an effort to clean out North Vietnamese and Viet Cong strongholds there and stop traffic on the Ho Chi Minh Trail. The jump off point was Lang Vie, Firebase #5.

We watched the evening news every night as the firebase at Lang Vie and the old Marine stronghold at Khe Sanh was shelled twenty-four hours a day by mortars. We looked for a glimpse of Dad or a familiar face. One night we saw one. Dad's old supervisor in Belgium, SFC Percy, was standing behind a war correspondent reporting from Khe Sanh during an attack. We watched in horror as a rifle bullet hit him. The correspondent droned on while a few steps behind him a drama of life or death unfolded. Soldiers rushed to SFC Percy's side picking him up and carrying him off. We later learned he had been wounded in the shoulder and survived.

But there was no word from Dad.

To make matters worse, Mom's letters to him began coming back stamped "Addressee Unknown." This was what usually happened before a wife was notified her husband was killed or missing in action. Mom had just given birth to the twins, we wondered if they would ever see their daddy. Still, she wrote him every day, hoping he was still alive and one of the letters would reach him. Every day she would walk the twins in their twin stroller to the post office and bear the sad looks of the postal workers when there was no letter.

Finally, after a month, we got a letter. Dad was all right. He was going to be able to come home for R & R (rest and rehabilitation leave), to see his sons.

I often look back and think how nice it would have been to have had even e-mail back then.

I've had people tell me they wouldn't have served in Vietnam; it was a dirty war. I can understand a true conscientious objector, but I don't understand that mentality of being unwilling to serve. I was waiting my turn to go. I was raised to believe it was my duty. Whatever else I did with my life, I figured if my country was at war it was my duty to enlist and help fight that war. Then I could think about going to college or whatever else it was that life held for me. That is what the male members of at least my mother's family always did. We have had a member of the family in every war this country has fought, back to before the Revolution.

Then the war ended. You might say I was left without a plan.

I often tell my students I wish I could go back and grab the seventeen-year-old kid that was me by the hair of his head and shake him. I had no direction, no real goal in life. It's true, the Lord had called me to preach, but I was avoiding that.

My stepfather told me the night I graduated from high school he wanted me to go to college. He would send me if he had to take out a GI loan to send me (at that time it could be done). I truly appreciated the offer because I knew he meant it.

I couldn't accept his offer. He had three other kids to raise on a sergeant's salary. That wouldn't be fair to them. I didn't even know what courses I would take if I were to go to college. I was faced with the big question- "What do you want to be when you grow up?"

I could picture myself being a schoolteacher, maybe. But, what would I teach? To which college would I go? I had often thought about the Army as a career, it seemed a natural choice having been an Army brat. I remembered thinking when I was a kid that being a soldier was one of the highest, noblest callings a man could answer. Even in my senior year I had serious thoughts about enlisting. I had always wanted to be a general. But to become a general, one must first be a lieutenant, captain, major, and so on... Then I thought who wanted to be a lifer?[26] Now that the war was over, there didn't seem to be much point enlisting or being an officer. I knew that the military would be downsizing. Promotions are slow in peacetime armies; times are tough. Was there really a future in the military now?

But I think in the back of my mind I felt it was my duty to serve at least one tour of duty in some branch of service. I believed we owed our country that much even in peacetime. I never considered enlisting in any other branch of the military except the Army.

College first? Later? I knew I didn't want my folks to be out anything. I didn't know the first thing about getting into college anyway. The guidance counselors at the schools I attended didn't seem to go out of their way to help kids go to school. I suppose if one wanted help from them they had to go see them. I look at the counselors at the school at which I worked and see how they went

---

[26]Lifer- a slang term for career soldier. One who is in for life.

47

out of their way to help kids get financial aid and know which tests to take and wish someone would have helped me. But then again, having attended five high schools (some more than once) didn't lend itself to getting involved in a college prep program – or any of the activities that assisted one in getting a scholarship. As it was, in spite of having a solid B+ - A- GPA (don't remember now, been a looong time) I moved at least twice my junior year as a result of Dad's transferring from Ft. Carson to Germany. In each move, I lost a course due to scheduling problems and different curriculums. I finished my junior year in Illinois waiting to join Dad, who was already in Germany. I'd lost my math and science classes, as well as my language class – the school in Illinois didn't have German. I almost didn't graduate because of the different requirements at the school I ended up at – Frankfurt American High School – in my senior year. I had to drop all electives to take some required courses.

As it was, I never felt I was a good enough student to get a scholarship, though representatives from both West Point and the Army ROTC program had interviewed me. Looking back, had I no hope of getting in they would have never interviewed me in the first place, after all, they had looked at my scholastic records and aptitude scores. But I was discouraged. I told them I didn't want to be a "lifer."

You've got to be a "lifer" at something.

After graduation, I returned "home" to Illinois and the St. Louis area.

I stayed there about six months. It didn't seem anything was going my way. The economy was in a slump. Later on, I would learn it was a recession caused by the end of the Vietnam War and the Arab oil embargo of 1973.

I tried to get a few gigs playing music but there wasn't much demand for live music in the area in which I was living – at least not a lone guitarist doing Dylan, Simon and Garfunkel, and Denver. I worked a couple of dead end jobs. I got laid off from one so the boss could hire his son, who'd gotten thrown out of school for swinging at his high school principal.

Then my mom's brother Earl came to town to watch my back while I took care of a couple of the young town toughs who'd been itching for a fight. The folks had bought a house about sixty miles from the St. Louis metropolitan area in a small farming town. The nearest I could figure was word had gotten out about me being a brown belt in Judo and someone wanted to see how tough I was.

One of the guys had gone so far as to swerve off the road to hit my brothers' dog. The problem was, every time I went to do something about it they always had their friends around to help them if I started getting the better of the fight.

So Mom called Earl and asked if he knew of someone who could watch my back while I took care of business. A few nights later, my uncle showed up on his motorcycle. With my friend Joe, we walked downtown to see if we could stir something up and sort things out.

My uncle stood fifteen or so guys in their late teens and early twenties against the wall promising to lay out at least four of them if they budged. No one wanted to be one of the four. With my back watched I was able to make short work of their leader, who was considered the toughest dude in town and we went home. End of troubles.

Shortly after that Earl offered me a job with his company. For me, it was like a dream come true. Earl, one of the original Navy Frogmen in the Pacific during World War II, had always been a hero to me. He had run off to join the Navy at fifteen, got discovered, then tried again and succeeded the next year, using his dead brother's birth certificate. At the end of the war he had fought in just about every major campaign in the Central Pacific but was still too young to drink a toast to the victory.

After the war, he was never able to settle down. He lived a life most only dream about – and envy. He had dated Hollywood starlets, lived just about everywhere, and done just about everything. When I was in the Army we'd have called him an adrenalin junky. Today, they'd say he had PTSD.

I worked for Earl about a month as a mobile janitor; he began teaching me the art of window cleaning. When he asked me if I wanted to help him move his business out to Las Vegas, I jumped at the chance. I had the family worried I was going to be my generation's hellion.

I remember sitting at my grandmother's kitchen table the day we left for Vegas. Earl was out taking care of some last minute business. She reached out across the kitchen table at me and with such concern in her eyes begged me not to turn out like Earl.

I remember reaching out and taking her hand in mine and assuring her everything would be all right. I realized then how much Grandma really did love us all – she just had problems showing it.

When we arrived in Las Vegas that fall of 1974 we walked

into a mess. When Earl had been in Vegas ten years before he and his partner had fallen out. Earl said he'd been stealing from the company. When he went to confront his partner Earl had lost his temper, "I saw him standing there in a silk bathrobe smoking a big three dollar cigar and I lost it."

Earl had thrown the guy down to the floor and stomped him. Earl had been wearing cowboy boots with taps on the heels. The guy carried the scar of Earl's heel print on his forehead to the day I saw him ten years later; probably to the day he died. In the ten years Earl had been gone, the partner had become a wealthy man with friends in high – and low – places – if you get my meaning. For some reason he objected to Earl trying to move back to Vegas and start a competing business. A little over a month later I was back in St. Louis, barely having enough money for a plane ticket home; flat broke, and a broken guitar (which I took as a "goodbye" from Uncle Earl's "friends") with even fewer options that I'd had before. Looking back, though, it was a wild ride I don't really regret taking.

I toyed with the idea of taking my guitar and heading off to New York as Bob Dylan had fifteen years before. That was stupid. Times had indeed changed and I was no Bob Dylan.

I realized I had been avoiding the obvious. Deep down inside I had always wanted to be a soldier. When other kids were building '57 Chevys I had been building King Tiger tanks. I could recite the entire chain of command of both the European and Pacific Theaters in World War II. Living around Army bases and soldiers the past seven or eight years had done nothing to dampen my love for the Army.

The war in Vietnam was winding down, all ground troops were home, and our advisors were packing their bags. Had the war still been going on I wouldn't have procrastinated as long as I had. As it was, within the month I was reporting to Ft. Leonard Wood, Missouri for Basic Combat Training. I would serve my country as the men in my family had done for generations; after all, the country needs soldiers in peacetime, too.

Chapter 4
The Making of a Soldier – Basic Training

Everywhere I go... there's a drill sergeant there.
Everywhere I go...there's a drill sergeant there.
Drill sergeant...drill sergeant...
Everywhere I go

When I sleep at night... there's a drill sergeant there...
When I brush my teeth...
When I'm on the street...
When I go to eat...
(Anonymous Marching Cadence)

During the mid-to-late 70s all of the armed services, and particularly the Army, were going through a period of self-examination and soul-searching; a rethinking of their purpose in a post-Vietnam world. This was the period of the unfortunate "The New Army Wants to Join You!" advertisements. The Army was trying to overcome the anti-military bias held by society at the time and lure young men (and more increasingly, women) to fill the ranks of the New Volunteer Army (VOLAR).

I could still be (and was) called "Baby Killer" in an airport as late as 1977. Most of my unit's NCOs (Sergeants) and several senior enlisted men were Vietnam veterans. Some were alcoholics. Many fought numerous other personal demons.

America's soldiers had fought valiantly on the battlefield, had won every major battle in the war, yet Saigon fell. I remember sitting in my unit dayroom at Ft Sill, Oklahoma watching the news reports of the North Vietnamese takeover of South Vietnam in 1975. Some of the guys going through Artillery training with me were prior servicemen, Vietnam veterans. There were tears in the eyes of many as they watched the South Vietnamese Army retreating because they had no ammunition to fight. It seemed to me then, and did for years, that it was at that point that all the effort, all the American lives lost in the conflict, became vain.[27]

---

[27] My mind was changed recently while listening to a call-in radio program. The host made the comment that the Vietnam War and its veterans' sacrifices had not been in vain. After all, for over ten years the Vietnam veterans had held the line against Communist expansion. Imagine how far the Communists would have gone had we not held them in

At the time we chalked the fall of Vietnam up to the cowardice of the ARVN.[28] Later, I learned our Congress had refused to live up to the Paris Peace Treaty by refusing even money to buy ammunition for the South Vietnamese Army to allow them to defend themselves. Some of the soldiers defending Hue city had as little as two rounds of ammo in their weapons. What do you do when you only have two bullets in your rifle?

You fire them and run for your life.

Vietnam still affected those of us who came in after the war's end. Vietnamese GI Army slang became part of our vernacular; *beaucoup* (*boocoo*) meant a lot, a crazy person was dinky *dow* – a *really* crazy person was *boocoo dinky dou*. When we wanted to leave a place we *didi mao'ed. Sin* (or *xin*) *loi*, sorry about that. I never served a day in country, but those words are in my vocabulary to this day. But then again, I was also a brat...

The Army still hadn't quite figured out how to train men for a peacetime environment without relaxing discipline too much, or adversely affecting our combat readiness. As a result, the first generation of VOLAR soldiers was a messed up bunch. We were trained and conditioned one way, then told to behave in a totally different manner later.

I used to wonder why we were so crazy back then. It seemed every one of us in the Army during that period was a fight waiting to happen. It took a few years of chewing on it to come with a satisfactory solution. I finally figured we were the result of the mental conditioning the Army gave us in training.

The Training and Doctrine Command (TRADOC, for short) had been set up at the end of the Vietnam era. Its primary purpose was to ensure Army wide standardization of training. Changes were being made to adapt to a peacetime status. In the basic training companies, however, the drill sergeants were still doing their job of preparing young men mentally and physically to go to war.

The process of turning a young kid off the street into a soldier the Army used back when I came in has always amazed me. The drill sergeants had to take us apart and put us back together again. They had to strip away at least eighteen years' worth of old values which would get us and our buddies killed in a combat environment and replace them with instinctive reflexes which would

---

Vietnam for so long. When I think of the fifteen or more countries that fell to communist aggression in the years between Vietnam and Reagan's election I see the merit to that point of view. In that respect, in light of the overall Cold War, Vietnam becomes a limited strategic victory, if a tactical failure.

[28] Army of the Republic of Vietnam

save our lives and win wars. The battlefield is no place for what we recently called "sensitive, enlightened 90's type of guys." Such men could not take the rigors and horrors of combat.

The drill sergeants would take fat boys and make them into lean men. They would take skinny kids and make them muscular soldiers. They would take selfish, mama's boys and "rugged individualists" and teach them to think, act, and work as a team. They did this all in eight weeks.

Civilians and even younger soldiers often have a hard time believing some of the stories I tell about what we went through in basic training. When I tell them about some of the "games" the drill sergeants played with us in basic I hear folks say, "I don't know how you put up with that."

To someone who hasn't lived through it, I know it all sounds horrible. They wonder at how we veterans can laugh about the misery we were in. All I can say is it isn't so bad when you're in it. I guess you don't have the time to think about it. I can also say this about my basic training and drill sergeants: for the most part our drill sergeants were professionals. I saw some things I thought then, and still do, that were cruel. But I don't remember personally going through anything, no matter how stupid or cruel it seemed at the time, that didn't have a purpose. I've learned nothing the military does is without a purpose. You may not know the reason, and once you learn it, you may not agree with the logic, but there is a legitimate reason for just about everything the Army does. It took me years to realize what all the harassment, the punishments, the grass drills, and the humiliations were all about.

They were trying to make us angry.

They succeeded.

How do you get someone who has been raised by the Ten Commandments to squeeze a trigger and blow someone away? You have to build up anger inside that person so that, given the chance to channel that anger, killing isn't so hard. The hard part comes later, in living with yourself after you've done your job.

I remember hearing guys coming back from the rifle range joking about how they were able to hit their targets. All they had to do was imagine the silhouette outline of a man they were shooting at was their "favorite" drill sergeant.

Sometimes it backfired. The week before we went to the hand grenade range a recruit killed his drill sergeant. When you throw your live hand grenade you're in a concrete bunker with a drill sergeant to help you. The kid pulled the pin, brought the grenade back to throw it and dropped it behind his back. He jumped over the concrete wall, leaving his drill sergeant behind. The sergeant was blown to pieces. Nothing happened to the recruit because they couldn't prove it wasn't an accident.

When it was our turn to go to the hand grenade range they still hadn't repainted the bunker. We marched past the gore on our way to our own bunkers. Our Drills were real nice to us for a couple of days before we went to the grenade range. I ended up in a bunker with probably my least favorite Drill Sergeant in our company.

It was my chance for some passive aggressive revenge with the live grenade. I had an unconventional way of throwing a baseball (and thus a hand grenade), the instructors kept trying to get me to throw it the regulation way, but I couldn't quite get the hang of it in our one day at the range. Eventually, I was able to get it down by throwing a lot of rocks, but it's hard to break a lifetime habit.

On that day, though, I took advantage of the opportunity fumbling with it a bit – even getting him to offer to throw it for me before I gave it a pretty good lob in my own style. I think he realized then I'd been having him on. I figured who cared what my form was if I hit the target.

Bayonet training reinforced the aggressive instinct they were trying to instill in us. During bayonet drill we would be asked by our drill sergeants, "What's the spirit of the bayonet?"

"Kill! Kill! Kill!" we would reply, shouting our lungs out.

As we would attack the practice dummies we would shout "Kill!" as we stuck our bayonets into the padding, twisted the bayonet, and pulled it out. It was all part of our mental conditioning.

My older brother told me about a kid who complained to his drill sergeant about having to shout, "Kill!"

"Does it bother you that much, son?" the sergeant asked not unkindly.

"Yes, Drill Sergeant, it does."

"Well, I don't care if you shout 'love!' as long as you shout something!"

So the kid had to scream "love!" at the top of his voice as he plunged his bayonet into the dummies.

At about the time I came in TRADOC announced they were shortening Basic Training to six weeks. We were one of the last classes (or "cycles") to go through an eight week cycle. Even then, we were informed of shortcuts being taken as the training command was adjusting to the new curriculum. We were told the Army was eliminating a lot of the "archaic" techniques and skills being taught soldiers. One of these things was bayonet training. The explanation was you'd probably never need it in real combat, anyway. I believed then it was a mistake.

Later on, in the eighties, TRADOC reconsidered their move and reinstated bayonet training, claiming it instilled a basic aggressiveness needed in a combat soldier. I applauded what I considered one of their few pronouncements that made good sense to me.

Our indoctrination was total. We had one drill sergeant who, at bedtime, would often lead us through a parody of the twenty-third psalm:

> *"Yea, though I walk through the valley of the*
> *shadow of death*
> *I will fear no evil,*
> *For I am the meanest, toughest, roughest,*
> *[blankety-blank] in the valley!"*

Then he would say, "Good night, fourth platoon."
"Good night, drill sergeant."
"Pray for war!"
There was another purpose behind our conditioning. It was discipline. Lack of self-discipline will get you and your buddies killed in combat. From the first day we arrived at our company the discipline started.

They always waited till Friday afternoon to ship new companies to begin Basic Combat Training. Your first week or so in the Army back when I came in was spent at what they call reception station. Your purpose in life at reception station is to get processed into the Army. We were issued uniforms, training and field gear, given some of our shots, issued dog tags, and accomplished numerous other minor administrative tasks to further our transition from civilian life to the Army.

I was put in charge of a platoon, or roster, at reception station, though I didn't realize it at first. We had left St Louis in the late afternoon on a bus for Ft. Leonard Wood, Missouri. We arrived late in the evening, were given a welcome briefing, and taken to our barracks. Other men, who had arrived earlier in the day, were already in bed as it was after lights out. A Sp4[29] with a flashlight led

---

[29] Specialist 4, now just called a Specialist (SPC)

us to our bunks in the dark. Everyone got a bunk except me. The Sp4 looked at me, "What's your name?"

"Wood, roster number 50."

"Oh yeah, come with me."

These were old wooden World War II barracks. He led me through the bay to a small room with a single bunk. "This is yours."

I put my stuff in my locker and got ready for bed. As I lay there, listening to "Taps" sound, I was thinking to myself, "What have I got myself into?"

Some of the guys who had ridden the bus with me came into the room, "How come you got a room to yourself, are you some sort of captain or something?"

"Naw, man, they just ran out of bunks." I said.

"I bet he's a captain..."

The next morning I found out I was the roster leader, responsible for getting the fifty men in my barracks to wherever they were going. "See, I told you you were a captain!"

Life in reception station was pretty much a picnic. We got a small advance pay with which to buy necessities from a list we had been given at the PX down the street. It was then I learned first-hand the truth of the old Army song which said, "They give you a hundred dollars and take back ninety-nine!"

After duty hours we were even allowed to go to a small theatre next door to the PX. The only time we saw any drill sergeants was during formations, or if they wanted to see an individual for a specific reason.

The drill sergeants got a kick out of our roster because I had started teaching the guys how to march. I had taken JROTC my senior year in high school – I'd only had a semester because it was one of the classes I'd had to drop to take a required course. Because it was a new program at my high school I was made a squad leader. I'd learned the Army's Manual for Drill and Ceremonies, FM 22-5, by teaching it to my squad of underclassmen. I figured I'd put the training to good use. While the other rosters moved to the formation area like a mob, our platoon marched. I figured we get a head start on basic training.

I remember the sergeants in their shack pointing and grinning out the window as I dressed my formation and got them in line and faced properly to report.

The guys found out I was an Army brat and began asking me what to expect when we got to our company. I told them what I knew from what my dad and brother had told me. "Pure hell."

For that reason, I was pretty lenient on the guys. After all, I was just one of them. Some of the guys suggested I ought to get tough on some of the "players." I figured to let them enjoy their last few days of relative freedom. Once we started basic all fun would be over for at least eight weeks.

On Friday afternoon they loaded us and our baggage on "cattle cars" and "shipped" us to our companies. I'll never forget the looks on everyone's faces when we pulled up to the company area. It was Bambi in the headlights. The doors opened to reveal a drill sergeant in full dress uniform with bloused spit-shined jump boots, "What are you standing there looking at, dummy? Get your behind off that truck before I kick it into next week!" he screamed. Then, he picked the nearest kid up by the collar, duffel bags and all, and slung him off the truck. The kid slid across the ice (It had snowed the day before, melted, and froze over again) into another drill sergeant, who was waiting for him.

"You lowly piece of [dirt]![30] You messed up the spit-shine on my boot!" the drill sergeant picked the kid up and began boxing his ears.

"What are the rest of you waiting for, an invitation? Move!" the first drill sergeant screamed.

I'd been warned about what our welcome would be. I paused for just a second to size the situation up. There were two lines of shouting, cursing drill sergeants marking our path to a place behind the barracks. They were making sure the sheep didn't go astray. I noticed anyone who got within arms reach of a drill sergeant got nabbed. I picked my path dead center between the rows of drill sergeants where I'd be out of anyone's reach. Army drill sergeants invented the concept of "reach out and touch someone." Safe, I made my way behind the barracks where names were being shouted to divide us up into platoons.

After that, we were taken to our barracks and assigned bunks. Our platoon sergeant gave us a few words of greeting. He wasn't like most drill sergeants. He spoke in a low tone, reasonable. In my mind that made him even more threatening than the screamers. He told us that as long as we came in best in everything we didn't have to worry, the moment we came in second... well, the implied threat was enough. Our platoon managed to pull honor platoon for most of the cycle. Honor platoon marched at the head of the

---

[30] Again, I am sanitizing the language used here. You've probably heard it before and if you haven't, you don't need to hear it or read it here, right?

company and had the honor of carrying the company guidon.[31] When we finally lost it more than halfway through, our drill sergeant told us it wasn't our fault, the Company Commander was trying to raise the morale of some of the other platoons. We were just happy we didn't catch it for losing the guidon.

After he finished we were again formed up as a company and marched over to a classroom where we received our welcome to the unit by our Commanding Officer, Basically, he told us he had better never, ever, see any of us individually because that meant we were in trouble. As he hated every one of us, he'd make us sorry we ever messed up in his company.

Then, our Senior Drill Sergeant came up. He was the same drill sergeant who had greeted us upon our arrival. Standing up on the platform addressing us, he now seemed a reasonable man. He lay out the basic rules by which we'd live the next eight weeks: there would be no walking in the company area, we'd move at a double time, no talking in the mess hall, etc. etc. He explained the reasons for each rule, so there'd be no misunderstanding. Then he told us there wasn't a single man in the company who couldn't make it through basic training if he tried. He also told us the drill sergeants were there to help us become soldiers, and not to take anything a drill sergeant said personally, as he was doing his job. Then we were told to go back to our barracks and get them straight.

We were awakened next morning and sent to have a nice breakfast. Our battalion was blessed to have an excellent mess hall. It had been awarded the Kelly Award as best mess hall in the Army for two years in a row. And I imagine the food was great, had we time to taste it. There wasn't much time for that, as the entire company of some one hundred and forty or so men had only thirty minutes for any meal from the time the first man hit the door until the last man was to leave. The motto in basic was, eat it now, chew it later (except on Sundays, when we were given more time to eat), taste it the rest of the day.

I ate a great breakfast that morning. I would live to regret it. We had all walked down to the mess hall that morning in little clusters of two and three. We sat at the table talking about the craziness the night before, laughing about how scared we'd been. We were barely aware of our drill sergeants standing in the corner sipping their morning coffee ("Lifer Juice") and watching us carefully, nodding their heads knowingly. We had a lot to learn.

---

[31] Guidon- A small swallow-tail flag; the Company banner carrying its unit designation.

After breakfast the company formed. The Senior Drill Sergeant (SDI) stood on his little platform box speaking at us through a bullhorn. He began by telling us it was obvious some folks didn't believe fertilizer stank, fire burned, and the Senior Drill Sergeant meant what he said when he said, "Don't talk in the chow line, and don't walk in the company area." It was time to learn basic lessons in life. The first, most important, was, this is the Army, not home. Your sergeant is not your mother, when he tells you to do something, you don't talk back, you don't shrug it off- you do it!

He backed us off the sidewalk where we were formed up in PT (Physical Training) formation on the nice, muddy slope behind our barracks. There he had us do squat thrusts until we had dug holes up to our knees in the mud. Then, they moved us so we could do more. We were moved like that at least three times until we had torn up the entire area. All the while the SDI[32] was shouting our multitude of sins over the bullhorn. When the DIs got tired of squat thrusts we were taught how to do the low crawl. We low crawled through the mud back and forth. After all, we had to smooth out the mess we'd made with all our squat thrusts.

They soon became bored low-crawling, so they began to run us around the company area. Around and around we ran, till, soaked with mud and our own sweat, guys began to drop out. When a man dropped out of the run, the drill sergeants would jump all over him, making him do pushups, sit-ups, some more squat thrusts. After a little bit, they put the men at parade rest alongside of the building to wait for the rest of us to drop. The realization of what was going on hit me.

"Okay," I thought to myself, "the longer we run, the longer this is going to last." I was exhausted, my legs and arms felt like rubber. More guys were beginning to fall from exhaustion. I decided I'd make one more lap to make it look good and fall out, which is what I did.

After the drill sergeants finished putting me through what I now realize were "cooling down" exercises I stood and watched the others keep running. There were a couple of guys whom I thought were going to die from stroke, but they kept running. I didn't know whether to feel sorry for them or not. Why didn't they figure out what was going on? On the other hand I had to admire their guts and stamina, their refusal to quit. Finally, the last guys were told by the drill sergeants to stop running and we were told to go inside and prepare for an inspection in thirty minutes. Of course we failed.

---

[32] SDI- Senior Drill Instructor, or Senior Drill Sergeant

More punishment.

Later on, I learned this little ritual was called "hell Saturday." It was part of every soldier's welcome to the Army until 1979 or 1980 when two recruits from the same Company at Ft Jackson, SC, dropped dead on the same day. An investigation later discovered both men had heart murmurs, had received their physicals at the same induction center by the same doctor, who had scratched off their heart problems as unimportant. Two drill sergeants, career NCOs, professionals, were court-martialed for the men's deaths. The Department of the Army issued an order stopping the practice of hell Saturdays. The Army is good at killing a cow because a gallon of its milk went sour.

In my opinion it was the doctor who had failed to note these soldiers' heart problems who should have been burned. The drill sergeants were only doing their job. They had no reason to assume they were dealing with anything but young men in the finest of health. Why should they have been punished?

Nothing done to me in basic training really hurt me. To the contrary, I believe basic training made a better man out of me. Better than anyone else? Not necessarily, but better than I was before.

There was one evening when we were doing grass drills in our protective (gas) masks as punishment. We did more grass drill than any other company in our basic training battalion. As a matter of fact, we found out from some of the guys from Bravo Company we were called "Grass Drill Charlie." We took a perverse pride in that.

Anyway, we had been out there for at least an hour. The guy next to me had gotten sick in his mask and was gagging on his own vomit. One of the drill sergeants started screaming at him for messing up his mask.

The senior drill sergeant always liked to get us at the end of the training day, while we were waiting our turn in the chow hall. After all, what else did we have to do before we ate? We were on our bellies in the mud and I looked up to see one of the guys from my platoon walking past us on the sidewalk in his dress greens uniform. He was going home on a medical discharge, bad knees. As he walked by, grinning at us in our misery, I almost hated God for making me so healthy.

A few weeks later, when we marched back from graduation. I thanked God for helping me get through it. It was one of the proudest days of my life. I had made it when so many had failed.

Some of the guys couldn't take the stress. They cracked. The system had a way of ferreting out the weak ones. There was AWOL Anderson. He had been in my barracks at reception station. He had come to me the day we shipped to talk to me about his personal problems. It had something to do with his ex-wife. We were just getting into his problems when the call came for us to load up and ship out.

The poor guy ended up in the platoon of the most sadistic drill sergeant in the Company, SSG Godwin. One of his favorite pastimes were making soldiers who fell asleep in class sit on invisible chairs, or do the "dying cockroach." To do the dying cockroach, one lies down on the ground with his legs and feet in the air at about a forty-five degree angle. Usually, the "cockroach" is placed in a doorway or entryway. When someone else enters or exits the doorway, the cockroach says, "I am a dying cockroach, somebody please step on me and put me out of my misery." If you aren't "kind" to the cockroach you could end up down there with him.

He also liked to make troops sit in an imaginary chair. This could be agonizing.

Drill sergeants had ways of getting a trainee into a no-win situation where no matter how you answered a question your were wrong. A case in point: a guy dozes off in class. The drill sergeant hones in like a lion on a wounded gazelle.

In a soft, kindly voice, "Are you tired, son?"

Now the soldier knew he was cooked. If he answered "no," the drill sergeant would scream, "THEN WHY ARE YOU SLEEPING IN MY CLASSROOM?"

If he said "yes," the drill sergeant would then give him some rest by putting him in the "front-leaning-rest" or pushup starting position – and making him stay there until the drill sergeant got tired.

Drill sergeants were masters at asking you questions for which there was no right answer. For instance, you would be at attention and a drill sergeant would be chewing on the guy a couple troops down the line from you. Remember, at attention head and eyes are supposed to be directly to the front. But it takes a lot of discipline to look straight ahead when someone is being chewed out to your right or left. The sergeant would notice you were looking over at him chewing out the other guy.

"What are you looking at? Are you in love with me or something?"

Now there is NO good answer for that question. If you say, "No, Drill Sergeant!" it's, "What's the matter am I not good enough for you?"And you didn't want to say yes – not back then.

If you hesitated, you were often treated to, "'You wanna marry me? 'You wanna have my children?"

Then the entire platoon would be treated to a detailed description of your honeymoon night that was graphic, explicit, and usually hilarious.

But you'd better not laugh.

What an exercise in discipline.

Godwin was a master at these games.

Godwin got a bead on Anderson and began making his life miserable. Every time Anderson messed up, Godwin was there to catch him and harass him. Two weeks into basic training Anderson went AWOL. His entire platoon was punished for letting him go AWOL. They lost all privileges and had to do, as a platoon, sixty-four thousand squat-thrusts that weekend. They started on Friday evening and did squat-thrusts until lights out. In the morning they started after breakfast, quitting for lunch. After lunch, they exercised until supper. After supper they exercised until lights out again. They completed their squat-thrusts late Sunday evening.

Anderson headed straight for home. When he got there, his mother, learning that he was AWOL, turned him in for his own good. When he got back to Ft. Leonard Wood, Godwin and his platoon were waiting for him. I heard they gave him a blanket party that night. The next morning Anderson was gone.

This time, he was gone a little more than a week. His mother had turned him in again. I saw him in the chow line; he was totally withdrawn from the world. I tried to whisper something to him to encourage him, but he seemed not to notice. Then again, we weren't supposed to talk in the chow line, maybe he was afraid of getting in more trouble.

The last time I saw Anderson was on a payday.[33] We were in line waiting for pay call, standing at a stiff parade rest. We were lined up on the sidewalk- outside the barracks, as an entire company. Anderson walked by; he was awaiting a discharge for failure to adapt to military life so I guess he didn't get paid that day (then again, as he had been AWOL during most of his time in the Army, he probably hadn't earned any pay). As the sidewalk was taken up by the Company, he stepped off the sidewalk and made his way on the

---

[33] We were paid in cash that day. A unit – usually company sized - lined up in alphabetical order to report and receive pay from the unit pay officer.

grass,

"Anderson!" It was Godwin.

Anderson was right by me, though I was at parade rest and couldn't turn my head to the right or the left, I could catch what transpired next out of the corner of my eye.

I saw Anderson stiffen; he shivered like a babe in the cold. "Anderson, what are you doing walking on the Army's grass?"

"I'm sorry, Drill Sergeant," Anderson answered in a weak, pathetic voice; I wanted to cry for him.

"Don't apologize to me, Anderson, you didn't step on me. Apologize to the grass!"

"What?" Anderson asked, incredulously.

"You heard me, apologize to the grass!"

Anderson looked down at the grass for a moment, swallowing hard, "I'm sorry I stepped on you, grass." he said, softly.

"You don't sound like you mean it, Anderson, get down on your knees and let the grass know how sorry you are!"

Anderson got on his knees and began petting the few blades of grass left on the winter lawn, "I'm really sorry, grass, I am so sorry I stepped on you, please forgive me."

"That's better, Anderson, now get up and get your sorry hide out of the sight of these soldiers!"

Anderson obeyed Godwin's order. He stood up, turned around, walked out into the middle of the street, and flagged down a post taxi. In front of Godwin and everyone he got in and rode off. I learned later he rode it to the main gate. He was gone again. They caught him, again, of course, but he never came back to the company. I often wonder if he got straightened out. I hope so.

There was pride mixed with pity at that moment. Godwin had called us soldiers! It's the first time I remember ever being called a soldier. Heretofore we had been referred to in terms that are unprintable. In my mind, it marked the beginning of the second phase of our conditioning. For four or five weeks we had been torn down, stripped down to nothing. Now, began the rebuilding, the molding us into soldiers. We were given pride in ourselves as soldiers, pride in our unit, pride in the Army. We were proud to serve; after all, not everyone made the grade to be called "soldier."

In the eighties, the Army (TRADOC again) made a decision to start calling trainees "soldiers" from their first day in the Army. I believed then, and still do, that this is a mistake. I wasn't a soldier when I entered the Army, in spite of the fact I had been raised around the Army. No, I became a soldier sometime, somewhere, at Ft.

Leonard Wood, Missouri. It wasn't a title given to me by some officer or sergeant. I earned it on the ten-mile forced road marches, the PT field, the rifle ranges, the grass drills- the crucible that was Army basic combat training. I don't mean to sound melodramatic here, but what I'm saying here is there is more to being a soldier than the uniform. Anyone can put on a uniform, not everyone can be a soldier.

As much as I felt sorry for Anderson, and still do, I had to admit, it was better for him to crack at Ft Leonard Wood, Missouri, than in some jungle in Southeast Asia or some desert hole in the Middle East. There, he might not only get himself killed but his buddies as well. As cruel as Godwin was, I could somehow understand his motivation. He just seemed to get so much pleasure out of his work.

Anderson hadn't even left the Army when Godwin started on Brooks. Brooks was a young National Guardsman from Mississippi. National Guardsmen (we called them "Weekend Warriors" back then) were considered by our drill sergeants to be the lowest form of life next to a draft dodger. Brooks was a nice kid, but he wasn't too bright. Godwin set his sights on Brooks and soon had the whole platoon ragging him.

Things got worse when the platoon broke out in body lice (crabs) and Brooks got blamed for it. Brooks was the recipient of several blanket parties. I felt bad about the whole situation because I knew Brooks hadn't been the one who spread the lice. Again, at reception station, a guy in my barracks, who later was assigned to Brooks' platoon, came to see me about his problem. I told him to go on sick call and get some medicine for it before he spread it to the rest of us. I don't know if he ever did. He made me promise not to tell anyone.

When word got out about Brooks and the infestation, I knew the truth. A day or two later I was supervising the chow line and the guy passed me. We were both at parade rest, and couldn't speak. All I could do was glare at him. He flushed red. He knew I knew the truth. But I had given my word to keep his secret so I was in a bind. Later on that day, during a break in training, I managed to get a word to one of the guys in the platoon that Brooks wasn't at fault without breaking my word. I don't know if it helped or not. After all, Godwin had his victim. His platoon had to have the record on blanket parties on Ft. Leonard Wood. But Brooks made it through basic, and he did it without losing that innocent smile of his. I was especially proud of him.

We didn't have blanket parties in our platoon. The closest thing to it was when marijuana seeds were found in one of our latrines. Our Drill Sergeant gave us until the next morning to find out who'd been smoking pot in our latrine or the whole platoon would pay. We got the name of one guy involved. We trainee leaders took turns sitting up all night with the guy, one on one, in an attempt to "persuade" him to tell us what happened.

I told the guy if he wanted to hit me back to feel free, he didn't. Before the night was over we knew who the culprits were and the platoon was not punished. I have to say I'm not proud of that night.

I learned some of the wisdom behind Jesus' instructions to turn the other cheek that night. There is nothing so demeaning as to strike someone who will not fight you back. It's been over thirty years since that night and I still feel bad about it. To the kid's credit, he never seemed to hold hard feelings against us in spite of everything. I respect him for that.

The Army back then wanted its soldiers to be fighters. Though there was a strict disciplinary code, certain things were given a wink - if perpetrated by a good troop. Soldiers were expected to be heavy drinkers, great lovers, and, more important, hard fighters. From the songs we sang while marching, to the war stories our drill sergeants told us in relaxed moments, it was John Wayne all the way. By the late seventies to the early eighties, the Army began to about-face on some subjects and crack down on drinking and fighting. As a Christian, I can applaud the better morality. As a soldier, I can only shake my head when an organization destroys a man's career - his life- for behaving the way that organization taught him to behave.

At Ft. Leonard Wood, we were housed in three-story red brick barracks, in six man rooms. My platoon, 4th platoon, Charlie Company took up most of the first floor of our building. There was a plywood wall built to separate us from Bravo Company, which had a couple rooms at the other end of the hall and a stairwell to the second and third floors. One end of the second floor housed a part of our 3rd platoon. The rest of the building housed Bravo Company.

One night, one of our guys, Zack, got drenched by a couple of guys from Bravo Company, who emptied a cigarette butt can of water on him. Angered, he charged up the steps to Bravo Company's barracks. When I heard what had happened, I followed him up there. Altogether, I figure there were about eight of us from Charlie

Company fixing to take on Bravo Company. At the time it seemed like a fair fight.

To get to where we had to go, we went up the stairs past the second floor, climbing a barricade to get to Bravo Company's barracks on the third floor. Reaching the third floor, we stormed down the hall to the stairs on the other end, running down them to the second floor. I remember the panic we caused in Bravo when we were recognized by the Bravo guys, "Get the Drill Sergeant, it's Charlie Company!"

Finally, we got to the room on the second floor, where the water came from. We had squared off in the room and were about to mix it up when the Bravo Company Charge of Quarters (CQ), a drill sergeant, came in and broke it up.

While Zack was explaining what happened another buddy and I slipped quietly out of the room. If there wasn't going to be a fight, there was no point in hanging around. We were both squad leaders and had taken off our acting sergeant stripes before ascending the stairs. There was no need in having them permanently removed.

We were about halfway down the hall when a Bravo Company guy hollered out, "Hey! Here's two of them!"

I looked at him, and then glanced at his nametag meaningfully, "I'll remember you, Turkey!" I whispered.

Three of us got caught. We were marched down to the CQ office while Charlie Company's CQ was summoned. It was Drill Sergeant Campbell, 3rd Platoon Sergeant. When he came in, he was taken back to see two of 4th Platoon's squad leaders involved. All he said was, "I might have known it was you, Wood!" he shook his head, "What's going on?"

While Zack was explaining what happened, I was figuring out my story. Zack finished and Drill Sergeant Campbell turned to Murdock and me, "What's your stories?"

Murdock got the jump on me, it seemed as if two great minds had come up with the same thought, "Well, Drill Sergeant, when I heard men from Charlie Company were going up to take on Bravo Company, I figured it was my duty as a trainee leader to try and stop them..."

"Why didn't you come get me?" Campbell asked.

"Well, Drill Sergeant," I broke in, "I guess we were hoping we could handle it without anyone getting in trouble."

Campbell looked at us through squinted eyes. He looked at my bare sleeve meaningfully. He knew we were shooting a line. I almost thought I saw a half-grin. The Bravo Company drill sergeant was shaking his head, "You two are squad leaders?"

"Yes, Drill Sergeant," I said, "We were trying to take care of our men."

I could tell he wasn't buying it either.

Oh well, you couldn't blame a guy for trying, could you?

"You two go on back to your barracks." Campbell finally said, "The next time there's trouble, you get a drill sergeant, 'hear me?"

"Yes, Drill Sergeant!" Murdock and I left. I looked over at Zack as I was leaving. He gave me a look that told me he understood. When you got caught like we did it was every man for himself.

When we got back to the barracks everyone was waiting for us. We swapped stories with the guys who'd gotten away. Several had climbed out the window and walked along the ledge to our 3rd platoon's barracks. There, they'd gotten stopped by Krauthammer, a kid from 3rd platoon who kept asking them what they were doing on the ledge.

"I'm freezing my buns off you idiot! Let me in!"

It took them several minutes to get him to finally open the window for them. All the time, they were hanging out on the ledge freezing, hoping no one came by and caught them. Before that, a couple of guys, cold and desperate, jumped off the ledge into the snow below.

Zack returned shortly afterward. When Drill Sergeant Campbell got back, he called us in and gave us a dressing down. Other than that, nothing happened to us. I did get a nickname from it. After that, Drill Sergeant Campbell always addressed me as "Slick-tailed Wood."

I saw the kid who turned us in the next day in the mess hall. I was controlling discipline in the chow line, as was my duty as squad leader, when I saw him.

"Man, look!" he whispered to the buddy next to him, "it's one of the guys from last night. He's a squad leader!"

"No talking in the chow line!" I snapped, "Or doesn't Bravo Company have to obey the rules?" This brought his drill sergeant over on him. I just watched and grinned at him as he received his chewing out and pushups.

They stopped issuing entrenching tools for a while after a platoon cleaned up one of the enlisted men's clubs on post with theirs. One of their guys had gotten beaten up in the club parking lot. He went back to his barracks to get some help. About fifty guys from his company hit the club swinging their tools. We were told dozens were hospitalized before it was over.

We were taught to "make things happen." For instance, one evening our drill sergeant noticed there was no sugar for the coffee maker in his office. We trainee leaders were allowed to use the coffeemaker when we stood our watch at night.

"There's plenty of sugar in the mess hall." was all he said.

The next morning, there were seven sugar dispensers sitting on his desk in a formation - one for each of the squad leaders and assistant squad leaders in his platoon, except for Myers. He was a Christian and we didn't expect him to steal.

As I said before, years later, reflecting on how we were trained, I figured one of the reasons we troops were so wild in the seventies was not only a reflection of the times in which we lived, but the mental conditioning to which we had been subjected. And they wondered why we caused so much trouble.

Toward the end of the seventies, when I was getting short, I think the Army got the message. They were beginning to tone it down a bit. I read articles in *Soldiers*[34] and *The Army Times* about how TRADOC was changing this and ending that practice. We began to get troops in who were less apt to brawl. I also noted they'd had less of the "block" taken out of them.

By the mid-eighties, I was getting troops at Fort Bragg who told me they had been disappointed in their basic training. They had actually hoped it would be tougher than it was. One kid told me his basic training was a joke. Trainees were actually told to fill out report cards on their drill sergeants after graduation. I wondered how tough the Drill Sergeants were on their troops knowing they were going to be evaluated by them later?

I felt sorry for the kids coming in. They wanted to be challenged. They wanted to be tested. I was glad I was put through a mill. I would not take a million dollars for the experience. By the same token, you couldn't give me a million dollars to go through basic training - or jump school- again.

---

[34]The Army's monthly magazine, distributed to units for free.

Chapter 5
Welcome to Germany, 3rd Armored Division

My Country's mad at me
They sent me to Germany
To see the King.
His name is Daffy Duck
He drives a garbage truck
On every mountainside
Let garbage be.
(Barracks song, author unknown, to the tune of "My Country 'tis of Thee)

Sad to say Basic Training was the high point of my first hitch. My first disappointment came when I received my orders for my next phase of training (Advanced Individual Training, or AIT). I had gone through Basic thinking I was going to be an Airborne Infantryman. I was preparing myself for the Infantry School, which at that time was at Fort Polk, Louisiana. When I read my orders for Artillery School at Ft. Sill, Oklahoma my jaw dropped.

I went to my drill sergeant, "Drill Sergeant, there's been a mistake in my orders. They have me going to Ft. Sill."

The drill sergeant gave me a quizzical look, "So?"

"That's artillery school; I'm supposed to be an infantryman."

He raised his eyebrows, "Let me see your orders." He read them over. I was leaving in the morning. "Wood," he said, not unsympathetically. "It looks like you're going to be a cannon cocker."

You would think that as an Army brat who grew up in the system I would have been able to do better for myself. But the plain fact of the matter was the Army was going through so many changes between the demobilization from the Vietnam War and the move from a draftee Army to VOLAR, all the policies were in flux.

With the anti-military sentiment prevalent in the States at the time the Army of all the branches was having difficulties enticing young men into the service. The fact the country was going through the post-Vietnam recession helped a bit. The Army was still toying with the system trying to find the right formula that would attract qualified recruits into the MOSes (Military Occupational Specialties)

69

they needed. The concept the Army came up with was to give the recruit as much of what he/she desired as was possible, considering the needs of the Army. Things had changed from the Vietnam Army where you went where they told you and took the job they gave you. You had a choice of assignments.

I was aware of that when I walked into the recruiter's office, but I'd been in Illinois, away from the Army for over six months. Dad was in Germany where he couldn't advise me on what to do. A lot had changed in that time.

When I decided I wanted to enlist I knew right away what I wanted to do for my time in the Army. I wanted to follow a dream I'd had since childhood. I wanted to go into the Special Forces and earn a green beret.

I was told one could not enlist for Special Forces but had to volunteer from within the Army. Unable to get my "dream assignment" of Special Forces straight off the block, it became a matter of finding something that would be a step on the road to the Special Forces. After much discussion I opted for Airborne Infantry.

The Army at that time was pushing a new bonus program for combat arms (Infantry, Armor, Artillery, and some Combat Engineer specialties) enlistees. If one enlisted for four years in any of the combat arms he could be guaranteed a station of choice (for at least a year Stateside) anywhere the Army had troops in that specialty, his choice of combat arms branch, and receive a $2,500 bonus upon completing his AIT.

I didn't like the idea of signing up for a four year hitch. It seemed like too long if I discovered I didn't like being in the Army. Also, I knew that once one accepted a bonus, he was stuck in that job. I didn't want to limit my options.

In my head I was really in a bad bargaining position. If I had been willing to have waited awhile before reporting to basic training I might have done better; but once I had decided to go into the Army I wanted to go quickly. I really didn't see as I had much choice. Mom was due to rejoin Dad in Germany at any time and I couldn't see myself going back over there with them. A guy had to grow up sometime.

With a three year enlistment the best deal I could get was to enlist for three years in the Combat Arms, with unit of choice Ft Bragg, 82nd Airborne Division. They said they couldn't give me a guaranteed MOS without a bonus at the time, but I requested Infantry school. My contract read Combat Arms, Infantry preference.

So, I ended up at Artillery school after Basic, cursing my

stupidity and the Army's warped sense of humor. I mean, if a guy *wants* to be an infantryman, who's going to argue? Only the Army.

As a result, I always had a love/hate relationship with the artillery. I felt I'd been tricked or cheated into being a cannon cocker.

Then I washed out of Jump School.

I'd totally screwed up the tendons and ligaments in my ankles escaping from German railroad personnel during my senior year in high school (there are strict laws against crossing railroad tracks in Germany and there were a set of tracks separating our housing areas in the Pioneer Kaserne area of Hanau – for teenagers, it took too long to go to the overpass – the legal route – when we had holes in the fence). I spent several months on crutches because the docs would say I was healed, I'd get back on the Judo mat or just step wrong and the thing would go out again. For some reason they didn't want to operate and fix it, preferring for the ankle to heal itself. That took time. One guy said it might never heal properly – always prone to give away at the worst moment.

I finally thought the thing had healed. I'd been over a year without incident when I enlisted. I'd developed tendonitis in my ankle and Achilles tendon (the area I injured in high school) the first week in Basic; the docs put me wearing low quarters (dress shoes) for a couple weeks and put some inserts in my combat boots and I was good to go. I was behind in PT but was able to catch up in no time. And I hadn't had trouble with my feet since. But something happened in Jump Training. I don't know if it was the PLFs, the Swing Landing Trainer, or all the above. I was still able to walk, but with great pain and couldn't hide the limp. The blackhats[35] are always on alert for injuries. My airborne career was over – at least temporarily.

I was pretty screwed up in a lot of little ways. I had an infection on my chest from where the quick-release buckle of the T-10 harness jammed the middle button of my fatigue shirt into my chest, rubbing it raw. I still carry the scars on my chest. We spent hours in parachute harness while going through the 34 foot towers; the leg straps had rubbed my inner thighs raw. In the heat of the summer the blackhats ran us through showers to prevent heat injury. Then, wet, we returned to training practicing PLFs in sawdust PT pits or practicing exits from the towers; skin became raw and inflamed from the heat and sweat, infection set in. Many of us

---

[35] Blackhat – airborne instructors, so named for the black baseball caps they wear; more on them later.

suffered the same ailments. Like most of the others I had been ignoring the problems rather than report on sick call and get recycled. Now, "busted" with the ankle, I was able to get attention for the other problems.

It was at the replacement detachment (called a "repple depple", or just "repo") at Ft. Benning, after I'd healed up a bit and was waiting to find out my fate that I began to feel ashamed of myself for not finishing. The detachment was made up of men who had gotten hurt in Jump School and were waiting to heal and finish the course or had quit, otherwise washed out, or were too screwed up to finish and were waiting reassignment. There were two platoons, as I recall; one was the Medical Hold platoon, the other was for guys to be re-assigned. I got stuck in the second one. I was told there had been a lot of MedHolds and I was overflow.

Don't worry, they told me, it doesn't mean a thing.

Famous last words.

In the meantime, I was in a platoon with those for whom our chain of command had nothing but disgust. One morning our platoon sergeant spelled it out for us. He was giving the entire platoon a dressing down for some reason or another, "You guys are the duds of the Army trying to get your act together."

It was true, there were many in repo who had plain quit because they couldn't, or wouldn't take the harassment of the blackhats. They just didn't want it enough. Some discovered a fear of heights. One guy, who stood six-foot-six, had problems doing the chin-ups properly because the chin-up bars were too low for him to fully hang without his feet hitting the ground. There were kids who had been injured in training. Some had valid health problems that disqualified them from training.

The sergeant's words stung. I came out of the daze I had been in since I left the Airborne Training Company. I may have been many things, but I was no dud! I mentally recounted my accomplishments my first six months in the Army. I had been an acting sergeant in basic training and had been among the tops in my class in artillery school. I was a good soldier. I had been in the Army less than six months and had already received several letters of commendation for my performance.

But I learned a valuable lesson in both the Army and life: before you start something, count the cost. Less than five percent of all Army personnel are airborne qualified. No one (except paratroopers) really thinks less of the other 95% who aren't "airborne." There is no shame in not wanting to be airborne. But if

72

you try to join the elite units and fail there are consequences for your career in every one of them except the SEALs.

When I went through jump school, fully a third of each class and sometimes almost half failed to graduate with the class with which they started. These are marked as "the duds of the Army." The personnel records of quitters are marked with "permanently disqualified from airborne training due to lack of motivation (self-imposed withdrawal)." This will follow a soldier throughout his military career. If everyone could pass through Jump School and be a paratrooper, where would be the sense of accomplishment?

Even if they make it through jump school, that's only the beginning. They then have to cope with life in an elite airborne unit. There, the attrition rate continues. Troopers have been known to "burn out" in the 82nd and terminate their jump status, that is, request to be removed from jump status. That is another road of no return. If a trooper hasn't completed a full tour of duty in a jump unit (at least three years) he can lose the wings he worked so hard for.

Life in an airborne unit is demanding. They make you earn your beret. As a sergeant at the 82nd Replacement Detachment told us, "You will be expected to march longer, run farther, carry a heavier load, and do more - because you are a paratrooper. For the 82nd Airborne, excellence is the norm!"

I've passed through several "Repple Depples" in my time. I have to say the one at Benning was the worst. I've already spoken to the attitude of the cadre towards the troops. Every morning, it seemed there were guys being written up on report. I still can hear the First Sergeant standing in front of our formation when he announced someone had missed a formation or committed this or that infraction. His favorite refrain was, in his thick Puerto Rican accent, "Mark him down as A-WOL, we take some money out of his pay check." He always had a wide grin on his face as he said it.

Every day we were parceled out on details according to our physical limitations, if there were any.

They sure didn't want to do any of us any favors at the Repo Depo - after all, we were duds. I came down on orders for Ft. Hood, Texas. I knew there must have been some mistake; after all I was on MedHold. The guys at personnel didn't even want to entertain the idea there was a mistake. After all, I was in the 2nd Platoon... And there wasn't time to lodge a formal complaint, I had, for all intents and purposes cleared Ft Benning while at Repo, so if I remember right, I was due to ship the next day and only had three days until I reported to Ft. Hood. No time to get the orders changed or a hold put in those pre-internet days. And, there was no apparent desire on the part of the guys at Repo to do anything that might be done. They didn't even want to give me leave to go home to see my family before they returned to Germany.

It took the personal intervention of the First Sergeant to make the personnel sergeant give me a PCS leave.[36] I was up and around now, though still favoring my ankle. I had been put on his personal detail the last week of my stay, cleaning up the company area for the annual general inspection. He had liked the job I had done for him. When he overheard me arguing with the personnel sergeant over getting a leave, he stepped in and ordered the sergeant to type up my orders.

So I got home in time to say goodbye to my folks. Dad had flown home to take the family back to Germany with him. As they were flying a "military hop[37]," they needed to get back to the east coast to catch a flight. It looked like I would be spending my three-week leave alone. At the last minute I decided to hop in the car and ride with the family to New Jersey.

While I was in New Jersey I made a visit to the Pentagon. From the Pentagon, I hopped a shuttle bus over to Fairfax, Virginia, the home of the Army Personnel Center. I had been thinking. The Second Armored Division at Fort Hood was organizing a new unit called "Brigade 76," which they were sending to Germany for a six-month rotation. I figured that's where I was going to end up. If I was going to Germany anyway, why not go over there the right way?

I said the five magic words, "My dad's stationed in Germany," and got my orders changed. Back then, the Army tried to keep families together unless it was wartime. It took less than fifteen minutes to have my orders changed. I hopped a bus back to Jersey. A week later I flew out of MacGuire AFB, actually ahead of my family, who'd been waiting for a "hop" to Frankfurt for over a week.

I'd spend the rest of my enlistment overseas. Unless I re-enlisted there was no chance of my ever going to jump school again. It would be difficult enough to go as it was, having failed once.

I arrived in Frankfurt almost a year to the day from when I left. It was good to be in Frankfurt again, seeing the familiar sights. As they took us by bus through the city I had a feeling of coming home.

---

[36]PCS- Permanent Change of Station: the Army's technical term for transfer. Leave is routinely granted in conjunction with transfers.

[37] Military Hop- Military personnel and their dependents under certain circumstances can fly free of charge on military aircraft on a space available basis.

Back then; they took new arrivals to Gutleut Kaserne in the heart of downtown Frankfurt, about a block from the Hauptbahnhof (Main Train Station), on the border of one of the most infamous red light districts in Europe. We were confined to the *kaserne*. I supposed they were trying to protect the new soldiers from the evils of downtown Frankfurt. I found this amusing in my case, as I had already experienced Kaiserstrasse, the main drag in the district. As a senior in high school, my buddies and I would often cut class to tour the sites of Frankfurt. Of course, knowing what I did about the *strasse*,[38] I knew full well what a dangerous place Kaiserstrasse could be to an unsuspecting GI, away from home and lonely.

There were the downtown strip joints, which preyed on such innocents. While the strippers danced other beautiful women would help lonely men run up huge bar tabs that they either paid or got their heads busted. After the beating, the poor soldier would be arrested for disorderly conduct. What the soldier didn't know was there were two menus with two brands of the same liquor. The menu on the table had reasonable prices, the other, hidden behind the bar was expensive. The soldier bought looking at the cheap menu but was charged by the expensive one.

The strip joints aside, the *strasse* abounded with every kind of sleazy con artist, free-lance prostitute, and crook one could imagine. The commander of the replacement detachment at Gutleut decided to spare his mostly young charges the risk until they could be properly briefed as to the dangers of the *strasse*.

Gutleut Kaserne itself was interesting. It was a forbidding structure made of black stone. It looked like an old medieval fortress; which it was. During the Nazi regime it had been Gestapo headquarters for the Frankfurt area. In the basement, where we stored our bags, there were still rings set in the wall to which prisoners were once chained. In the *kaserne's* courtyard was a wall, which evidently had been used to execute prisoners. One could still see where bullets used to strike the wall. Welcome to Germany.

As we only stayed at Gutleut one day, I guess the accommodations didn't matter much. I managed to get assigned to Third Armored Division, which was headquartered in Frankfurt. From there, I was able to get assigned to an artillery unit in Hanau, the town where my folks were assigned.

I was assigned to Battery B, 1st Battalion 40th Field Artillery.

---

[38] *Strasse*- literally German for street. Pronounced strassa in German, Americans dropped the last syllable, "strass." GIs used the word as a slang term for the rough part of town, much like "the hood," or "the block."

At the time we were the best howitzer firing battery in 3ʳᵈ Armored Division. As a reward we were the 3ʳᵈ Armored's Salute Battery. Our trophies were four old WWII era 75mm howitzers, called "pack 75s" because they used to be able to take them apart and pack them on mules for mountain warfare. They also were used in the first airborne divisions as their main artillery pieces. The pack 75s were the salute guns of the division. I was in a good unit in a good duty station.

My first year in Germany was about the best anyone could have. After all, I was stationed in the same town as my parents. Upon reporting to the battery, I was greeted by SFC Frankie Peters, the Chief of Firing Battery (or Chief of Smoke). I had taught his son Judo two years before, when I was still a dependent. Of course, he didn't recognize me without my hair and beard – if he did he didn't say anything. I didn't say anything, I didn't want the other troops to think I was brownnosing. He gave me one of the best pieces of advice I had ever been given about doing well in the Army, or anywhere else, for that matter.

"Be where you're supposed to be, doing what you're supposed to be doing, stay off drugs, and you'll get along fine, Wood."

My Battery Commander was Captain Kowalski, for whom I had worked during the Hanau Military Community's People's Expo the summer before – between my graduation and return to the States. He didn't recognize me at first, he just kept staring at me for a week or so as if I seemed familiar but he couldn't place me. Then, one day in the Orderly Room, he exploded.

"I know you!" he exclaimed triumphantly.

"Yes sir."

"People's Expo 74! I knew you looked familiar! I just couldn't place you." He looked over at Top Flick, "Top, this man's worked for me before. He'll do just fine."

My unit was preparing to go to Grafenwoehr, or Graf, one of the major combat training areas in Germany. The units in Germany were spread out over the countryside in small bases, called *kasernes* (barracks). *Kasernes* could be large enough to house an entire mechanized brigade with its supporting artillery battalion, such as at Gelnhausen, Kirchgoens, or Friedburg (where the three brigades of 3rd Armored Division were stationed), or small enough to house one battalion or company sized unit, such as ours, which was the 3rd Armored's 8-inch, or general support artillery battalion. The name of our *kaserne* was Francois; off Lamboystrasse in Hanau am Main (Hanau on the Main (River)). Hanau had one of the largest concentrations of American troops in Germany, with five *kasernes* scattered across the city.

Training therefore had to be conducted either in the countryside, which was useful, as it was where we would have to fight if "the balloon went up;" or at one of the three major training areas. If we trained in the countryside we had to be careful to keep destruction of private property to a minimum. According to the "Status of Forces Agreement," the treaty that lay out the rules by which we kept our troops in Germany, the US Army was liable for any damage done to civilian property. Such damage, called "maneuver damage," could be quite expensive. Running over a chicken, for instance, could cost the government (or the driver, if he was held personally liable) as much as two hundred US dollars (these are, remember, 1975 dollars).

According to the status of forces agreement, the "complete" value of the chicken had to be taken into account. Things such as the age of the chicken at the time of its death, its estimated lifetime, how many eggs it could have laid in that lifetime, how many chicks might have hatched out of those eggs, etc., etc., were tallied down to several generations. A tree - even a sapling - was even more expensive. Don't even think of running over a cow.

We trained in the countryside; after all, as I said, we had to familiarize ourselves with our potential battleground. We were outnumbered ten to one by the opposing Soviet and Warsaw Pact Forces; we needed every advantage we could get. Knowledge of terrain would be invaluable in combat. But if we wanted to do proper get down and dirty training, we had to go to a specially designated area for such. For one thing, to actually fire our weapons safely, an "impact area" is needed. This is especially true in the Field Artillery, which requires a place to land high explosive rounds without danger of hurting or killing anyone. My unit was an 8-inch howitzer battalion, which fired the biggest conventional round in the US Army's arsenal. We needed a large impact area to do proper training. The training areas at Wildflecken, Hohenfels, and, later, Baumholder, just didn't provide the facilities we needed. Occasionally, though, we would venture to Wildflecken where we could use one position and fire rounds into a limited "box."

We would go twice a year, in the spring and fall to Grafenwoehr, the largest tactical training area in Germany. There we could shoot, move, and communicate, the three basic functions of the field artillery, with relative freedom. As moving the big self-propelled howitzers to Graf was a major operation requiring rail transportation; we would go for anywhere from thirty to forty-five days at a time. We're talking thirty to forty-five days at Graf, spending four or five days in the field at a time, coming in only to clean up and repair equipment just to go out again.

The training schedule at Graf ran seven days a week. Sunday was just another day on the calendar. Somehow, we always managed to be at our spring Graf during the Easter holiday. I spent more than one Easter out in the field. Of course, if we were in the field on a Sunday the chaplain was supposed to come out and hold services for us in the field. I never remember the chaplain coming out to see us in the field once during the entire two and a half years I spent in Germany.

In the field we practiced the three primary functions of a Field Artillery unit: Shoot, Move, Communicate. As a self-propelled/mechanized Field Artillery unit we did RSOPs (Reconnaissance Setting Of Position) - a planned deliberate movement of a firing battery into position. An advanced party was sent out ahead of the rest of the battery to "occupy"[39] the position. The advance party team consisting of BC, First Sergeant, each gun section's "advance party man" or scout, members of the communications section (Commo), and in Germany, the Survey/Recon Section, moved into the selected position sweeping the area, locating and eliminating any enemy presence. Once the area was secured, the job of preparing the position for the arrival of the "main body" began. Each gun section advance party man marked the place for his gun to set up. Commo established telephone communications throughout the area, from Fire Direction Control (FDC, the nerve center of the battery) to the guns and to the other sections on the perimeter. The BC set up the M2 aiming device to establish the azimuth (direction) of fire of the battery in relation to grid and magnetic north. That done they waited for the arrival of the battery, holding the position against any attempt by the enemy to recapture it.

When the main body arrived, it was all knees and elbows. We had minutes to get the battery "laid" for azimuth (direction) of fire, and ready to shoot. The advance party men for each section would wait at the edge of the road or tank trail for their guns to arrive. Seeing their guns they would signal their guns (at night colored lenses on flashlights helped distinguish sections) and run ahead of the gun following a pre-arranged path to the location of the

---

[39] The command given by Jesus to occupy is a military term and is actually an aggressive command to take ground and hold it until relieved.

78

gun position.

As soon as the gun stopped the artillery crewmen would hop off and go about their business of getting the guns ready to fire.[40] First order of business was planting the gun so it wouldn't move when it fired. While two cannoneers were doing this, the gunner and assistant gunner were "laying the gun" for azimuth of fire with the magnetic aiming device (M2 Aiming Circle). This was getting the guns aligned so they would all be firing in the right direction to grid north.[41] Once the battery was set up for firing, "position improvement" began, camouflage nets were erected over the guns, disguising the outline of our equipment, foxholes were dug- in other words, we began making ourselves at home.

We also did "hip shoots," or emergency missions. We'd be driving down the road when a call for fire would come in from an infantry unit. The battery would have to exit the road at the best nearest location and set up within minutes and fire the mission. The artillery doesn't have the luxury of telling the infantry or tankers, "Wait, we're on our break."

If they're calling for fire, it means they're in trouble; it's our job to support them. So the hipshoot is an all out haul heinie operation to get off the road and shoot as fast as you can.

And of course, there was the tactical nuclear option. My 8 - inch unit had the capability of firing the tactical nuclear round. So we had to be up on that.

To save ammunition, usually only one gun – Base Piece - fired most missions. Even in combat FDC usually wants to "register" before firing for effect from a new position. In layman's terms[42] registration was a way of ensuring accuracy by figuring out where the rounds were actually landing from a given firing position. When you are shooting large amounts of high explosives at unseen targets over the heads of friends miles away you want to be as careful and as accurate as humanly possible. The FOs would call a round, see where it landed, and from there adjust until it was on target.

Base Piece was usually a center gun in the battery position, either gun two or three in the four-gun 8-inch battery. In a six-gun

---

[40] In a "towed" howitzer the troops would jump off the back of the truck towing the gun and unhook it from the truck – or "prime mover."

[41] Grid north is north on a map, as opposed to magnetic north, which is where a compass needle points, as opposed to "true north" where the North Pole is. Artillery men use grid north to point their guns, azimuth, directional fire commands are always given off in relation to grid north.

[42] And I am trying to keep these explanations simple. My apologies to my fellow cannon cockers.

battery (105mm or 155mm) base piece would be either gun three or four. It is generally considered the best functioning crew in the battery because when the Forward Observers and Fire Direction Center are zeroing in on a target it is Base Piece that fires those bracketing rounds. Once the FOs and FDC have zeroed in the target, then it is time for the rest of the battery to join in with "Fire for Effect."

So for most gun sections, the days were spent moving the guns and "following" the missions given to Base Piece while waiting for our turn to fire. Because if there is one thing artillerymen love to do it's shoot those big hawgs we manhandled into position.

On a typical day in the field, the battery moved between three and four times a day. There would be a morning occupation (RSoP), we'd set up and stay put, firing a few missions. We would often have "noon chow" (lunch) at that position. After chow, we would move again and occupy another position. We'd fire some more and stay there until "evening chow" (dinner). Then we'd do a night move. During those moves we might practice hip shoots or a number of different tactical situations.

When we were in the rear there wasn't much to do. One could go to the movie down at main post. Usually, the movies arrived at Graf a couple of months after they had played Hanau, so we had probably already seen then. Or one could avail himself of the entertainment at one of the two clubs on post, the Fifty Staters or the Pinewood EM/NCO Clubs.

I never figured it out, myself. Here you have at any given time some ten to twenty thousand combat arms soldiers confined to post for anywhere between thirty and forty-five days. They're away from families and girlfriends, working twelve-hour days and more, out in the field. What do you give them for entertainment in their off time? Bikini and topless go-go dancers! And then the brass wonders why just about every night the soldiers tear up the clubs brawling!

I remember my first brawl at Graf. I was out with a bunch of guys from the battery. A pretty English redhead was up on the stage dancing in a bikini. It was kind of sad. She was obviously self-conscious about being up there on the stage with all the guys howling and shouting at her. Every now and then some guy would shout something particularly suggestive and she would flush red and get a look on her face that was a mixture of anger and embarrassment. I felt sorry for her on the one hand; on the other I reflected she was definitely in the wrong business. After all, if you don't want a bunch of losers ogling you don't get up on stage half-naked in front of several hundred drunk and lonely GIs...

One of the guys I was with, Sellers, had ordered a *schnitzel* sandwich[43] right before the kitchen had closed. When the waitress brought the sandwich another guy began teasing him, trying to take it from him. The next thing I knew, fists were flying as Sellers went after the teaser. I tried to break the two up and the next thing I know I've got some guy from another table lunging at me with a broken beer bottle. I turned just in time, but was nicked right under the chin by his bottle. I palmed him across the face, breaking his nose. I've still got a scar, right under my chin, from the cut.

By this time, MPs were flooding into the joint. I figured I'd better make myself scarce. I remember stepping through the broken plate glass window in front of the building. I was crossing the parking lot when the guy with the bottle, holding his broken nose, fingered me out to an MP.

"Hey you!" came a voice from behind me. I froze, "Were you involved with this?"

"Not really," I explained, "I was at the table, but I tried to break it up."

"How'd this happen?" the MP asked, pointing to the guy with the nose.

"He came at me with a beer bottle." I said, pointing to the wound under my chin, which was bleeding pretty freely and beginning to sting.

"Get out of here before someone else busts you, man."

"Thanks!" I said. That had been close. I was about halfway back to my battalion area before I realized I'd left my field jacket back at the club. It was the only one I'd brought to Graf. Oh well, there was no way I was going back after it that night. One close call was enough. Maybe I'd go back and get it the next day.

When I got back to the barracks the entire place had gone wild. CPT Kowalski was having a busy night. Two guys from our battery survey section had gotten busted trying to steal a spare jeep tire from another unit's motor pool. They had somehow managed to get over the concertina (a type of barbed wire) wire surrounding the place and stolen the tire, but had gotten hung up trying to get the tire out over the fence.

---

[43]Schnitzel is probably one of the most famous, yet least understood German dish to Americans. Most Americans, having heard of Wiener Schnitzel, think it's some sort of sausage. Actually, the Wiener refers to the city of Vienna, the W is pronounced "'v'" in German Therefore, Viener Schnitzel is Vienese Schnitzel. Schnitzel itself is a breaded pork, beef, or veal steak which is deep fried and served with several variations, such as Jaeger Schnitzel, which is "Hunter's schnitzel," which is schnitzel with a mushroom gravy, etc.

Let me take a minute here to tell what happened when poor CPT Kowalski got the two thieves in his office. The two guys, Weaver, and Miller, were legendary drunkards in the battery. I could write a whole chapter on their antics. They might have gotten away with their crime if they hadn't been so wiped out drunk. They might have thought to toss the tire over the wire before trying to climb it themselves. They might not have tried stealing the tire.

As it was, the BC (Battery Commander) got them back into his office. Now, when you're in the Commander's office for any reason, you should stand at attention or parade rest unless told otherwise; particularly if you're in trouble. Weaver was doing his best to present some sort of military demeanor, even though he was weaving (no pun intended) back and forth. Miller, on the other hand, made himself at home. He found a folding chair, sat down, and, reaching into one of the pockets of the cold weather parka he was wearing, pulled out a beer, opened it, and took a swig.

"Give me that thing!" the BC snapped, grabbing it from Miller.

Miller, taken aback by the BC's action, just stared at him with a glazed eye for a moment. Then, he shrugged his shoulders, reached into his other pocket, and pulled but another beer.

Before CPT Kowalski could react, the phone rang. Sellers and several others from the club brawl had been arrested and he needed to pick them up, "I'll take care of you two when I get back!"

I had made it back to the barracks and was talking to Powers, who'd just been released, by the time Sellers came in, crazy mad. He grabbed Powers by the hair of the head and began beating his face in. Then, he threatened me; he'd take care of me later, he said, after he finished with Mitchell. I was standing there, wondering how I got involved in the mess when Singletary, the Executive Officer's (XO) driver, came up and began picking a fight with Watson, a guy in my section.

Singletary had been giving me a hard time since I arrived in the Battery. He was short, close to going home, so I had been hoping to avoid trouble with him until he left. When he shifted his attention from Watson to me I lost my temper. He began taunting me and daring me to hit him. So I did. Before I knew it I had thrown him to the ground and was on him.

I had gone into a total rage like none I had ever before experienced. What made it worse was the fact that the more I beat on Singletary, the more he cussed me. I'd hit him; he'd just spit blood and cuss me worse, making me angrier.

If it hadn't been for two or three guys pulling me off him I might have killed him. Singletary was a mess. There was blood all over him. I looked down at him and gave him a kick in the stomach, "I told you!" I was still shaking with rage.

A couple of guys carried Singletary off. Now that the beating was over, he was silent. He seemed dazed. I was dazed. Later that night they drove him to the dispensary to have his nose fixed. He was having problems breathing.

After all that, we had to go out to the field the next morning. I've always believed the BC took us out a day earlier than planned to keep us out of trouble. I never did get my field jacket back.

I got my first glimpse of the damage I'd done to Singletary's face as I was coming out of the mess hall. I was going to the arms room to draw my M16A1. He was walking away from the arms room with his weapon. His face was one big bruise. I heard a guy ask him what did he do, run into a tree? Then the guy laughed at the pun. Singletary just glared at me, "That's okay," he said, "I've got a buzz saw!"

I couldn't believe it; the guy was still talking trash. Top Flick came up to me out in the field, "Did you do that to Singletary, Wood?"

I dropped my head. I was in trouble now, "Yeah, Top, I did."

"Boy, you did a number on him!" Top chuckled, "'Messed 'im up!" he walked off, "That's one to be proud of, Wood!"

I watched Top walk off. I couldn't believe I wasn't going to be busted for messing the guy up so bad. Top thought it was funny! So, apparently, did the rest of the battery, including the Battery Commander. I didn't think it was funny. And I wasn't particularly proud, either. I was ashamed. And I was kind of scared. I had never gone off like that before. I could have killed him. What's more, I would have enjoyed it.

We returned to the rear a few days later to rest and repair our equipment for our test, or ARTEP.[44] That was when Sellers (from the Club) and his buddy Van Dorne got into trouble. I've already told you a bit about Sellers. Let me tell you about Van Dorne. I was told later he had gone to Vietnam as a Private First Class (PFC), E-3. He

---

[44] **ARTEP – Army Readiness and Training Evaluation Program** -If I recall correctly, this was the first year we called our tests ARTEPs. It was supposed to be a new improved method of evaluating a unit's combat readiness. Pardon me if I just think it was another case of re-inventing the wheel.

came home three years later as a Sergeant First Class (SFC), E-7. After six months at home he was a PFC again. It seems he couldn't adjust to peacetime garrison soldiering. Over the next three years he went up and down through the ranks several times. Once, he even made it back up to Sergeant (E-5) before a brawl got him busted back to Private (E-2). He was constantly in trouble for drinking and fighting.

My number had come up on the duty roster for KP (Kitchen Police).[45] I had it pretty easy working as Dining Room Orderly (DRO), making sure the tables were wiped.

I heard a commotion outside. Someone shouted, "All For One!" That was our unit motto. It was also the battalion distress signal. Whenever a guy from the 1/40th FA got in trouble, if he yelled, "All For One!" the guys in the battalion would come running.

I came out the door of the mess hall to see a big pile of guys moving slowing toward our battalion cantonment area from the snack bar between us and a tank battalion's area.

Van Dorne and Sellers had managed to sneak off to the Post Class VI Store (Alcohol and Tobacco Sales) an get a bottle of hard liquor, which they consumed. Fired up they went into the snack bar, which was full of guys from the tank battalion and began to hurl a series of slurs and epithets guaranteed to start a fight. Soon they were fighting the snack bar. Realizing they were slightly outnumbered they began trying to move the fight back to our battalion area where they could get some help.

Every so often someone would fall out of the crowd to lay on the ground unconscious. By the time I got to the brawl the mob was surrounded by NCOs and officers trying to break the fight up. When they got to the bottom (center?) of the pile they found a bruised and battered Van Dorne and Sellers (from the Club) still wanting to brawl.

They got Sellers quieted down but Van Dorne was too far-gone. He had flashed back to Vietnam. He mistook our Battery Executive Officer (XO), who was Japanese, for a Viet Cong and attacked him, calling him all sorts of "Charlie blankety-blanks." None of his nouns or adjectives were complimentary.

---

[45] When I first enlisted there were still two ways one could end up on KP- one was on a regular duty roster. After all someone had to wash the dishes and mop the floors before the Army hired civilians to do it all. The second was to get in trouble and have the First Sergeant put you on punishment KP. Other than the long hours you worked, regular KP wasn't too bad. You got to eat all you wanted. A soldier didn't want to get stuck on punishment KP; those guys got the nastiest jobs. It was a great tool for discipline without hurting a guy's record before the gurus in Washington took it away because of abuse by some.

By the time it was over, there were over one hundred counts of assaulting a superior officer, assaulting an NCO, disrespect to an officer, disrespect to an NCO, simple assault, aggravated assault, assault with intent to commit grievous bodily harm, assault with intent to kill, disobedience of a lawful order, and a myriad of other charges. You get the picture...

Several NCOs managed to wrestle him down. He was strapped down to a cot with pistol belts. He should have been taken to the nearest mental ward. I guess the Battery Commander wanted to keep everything in the family. They put him in a room by himself all night with at least one NCO sitting there to guard him. My sleeping quarters were in the next room and all night those of us in the room listened to him as he would hallucinate, imagining himself back in Nam. Sometimes he would come to his senses, realize what trouble he was in, and begin crying over what a wreck his life was. He would doze awhile just to wake up screaming. The whole cycle would begin again.

CPT Kowalski was a good fellow. He understood Van Dorne's problems and didn't really want to "burn" him. He was always pretty good to us if we were good soldiers. We may have been hellions, but we were good in the field. More than once, he or the First Sergeant had gone into town after a wild Saturday night and talked the proprietor of a destroyed bar into dropping the charges if we would pay for the damages done to his property.

"I'll see you payday – or I'll see you payday," he was fond of saying.

After that, we would be left at the mercies of Top, the First Sergeant. We would be on the "honor roll," doing whatever "chores" he had for us after duty hours. It was better than losing a stripe and having a bad mark on our record.

The BC gave the guy as much of a break as he could within Army Regulations. He got the Army Prosecutor (Army lawyers are called Judge Advocate Generals, or JAG Officers) to drop most of the charges if Van Dorne would agree to an Article 15[46] and expeditious discharge for the good of the service. Faced with the alternative of couple hundred years in prison if convicted of the charges (which he would have been, there were just too many witnesses), the fellow took the discharge. The last I heard of him, he was trying to get back in the service.

---

[46] Article 15- Nonjudicial punishment administered in lieu of a Court-martial for relatively minor infractions of military regulations. The accused admits to guilt and avoids having the stigma of a federal conviction on his record.

I came down with a case of bronchial pneumonia after that and was on quarters with a fever when the battery took its ARTEP. I wasn't there when we lost our Packs.

The guys told me later that everything had been going smoothly. Then orders came down for a 3200 mil (180°) shift. This called for the battery to turn completely around and fire in the opposite direction. As the guns were being turned around, data started coming down for a simulated nuke mission.

When protests started coming from the gunline that the data was unsafe,[47] FDC waved the protests away.

"Safe by FDC," came the reply.

The guns loaded the round and were ready to fire when the order, "Checkfire" came across the phone.

Later on I learned there'd been an argument in FDC over the mission. Joe Dickson had been our Fire Direction Computer (FADAC) operator at the time. When the data came in for the mission he knew something was wrong. He tried to warn our Battery Fire Direction Officer, a young second lieutenant straight out of West Point, the data was unsafe.

"It's all right, Dickson, I've got it," was the reply.

"But sir, did you account for the shift?"

"I have it all under control, finish your comps."

"But, sir!"

"Specialist, do what I tell you. I'm an officer; I know what I'm   doing."

Joe shrugged and went on. He finished his computations, "Sir, I wish you'd-"

"At ease, Specialist. Give the data."

I thank the Lord there was an evaluator in the FDC at that time (there usually is during an ARTEP, I was glad he hadn't taken a break). He let the lieutenant get us to the point of giving the order to fire when he stopped us.

Joe said if the battery had fired the mission, a simulated nuclear round would have been fired into downtown Vilseck, a village outside the training area.

The lieutenant was sent to another outfit. I imagine he was given some important job like making sure there was toilet paper in the latrines at Division Headquarters. Joe Dickson was allowed to

---

[47] As an added safety precaution, FDC issues a "Safety T" to gun chiefs that lays out the limits of fire for a gun in a given position. When data comes down that falls out of the boundaries on the Safety T, it is the gun chief's duty to alert FDC lest an artillery round falls on friendly heads.

make corrections and the Battery Executive Officer took over FDC until a new FDO could be sent from Battalion. We passed the ARTEP but the points we lost on the nuclear mission- the most important of an 8-inch battery's missions - cost us our place as "Best by Test." We lost our Pack 75s because of one man's arrogance.

Chapter 6
A Bad Dude

They say that in the Army the pay is mighty fine
They give you a hundred dollars and take back ninety-nine

Chorus: O how I want to go, but they won't let me go
O how I want to go ho-o-o-o-o-o-o-ome – hey!

They say that in the Army the coffee's mighty fine
Good for cuts and bruises and tastes like Iodine

They say that in the Army the biscuits mighty fine
But one rolled off the table and killed a pal of mine
(Anonymous Army marching cadence)

Have you ever had one of those times in your life when, if you had the chance to live something over again, you'd do it differently? One of those times came in the spring of 1976, though I sure can't figure out how I'd have done it differently – well, maybe I can. That's when I ran afoul of a major black marketer in the battalion, a SSG Phillips. I was a PFC (E-3) at the time.

Phillips had been busted a few months earlier on hundreds of counts of black marketing loan sharking, forging ration cards[48], assault, and just about every illegal act imagined except murder. There's no doubt in my mind that he and the folks he hung around with were capable of that.

Maybe they'd just never been caught.

At the time, I really had no idea of who the guy was until I tangled with him. Oh, I'd heard about him when he got busted, but I couldn't have picked him out of a lineup. He worked over in the battalion motor pool as a parts sergeant. I had probably seen him before, but paid little or no attention to him.

---

[48]Ration Card- as American cigarettes and liquor sold in American military exchanges weren't charged an import tariff in Germany and were highly desired by the German people. To help prevent the illegal sale of these items (black marketing), cigarettes and liquor were rationed. Each soldier and dependent over a certain age was issued a ration card which allowed that person to buy so many bottles of hard liquor and so many cartons of cigarettes from the "Class VI" stores on post. It was permissible to give an occasional carton of cigarettes or bottle of liquor away as a gift, to a prescribed limit it was illegal to sell untaxed liquor or cigarettes to Germans.

I got to know him too well when I got on to his eighteen year old son for bullying my twelve year old brother. I was nineteen at the time, only a year older than Phillips' kid. He stood at least a head taller than me. I figured he had no business picking on my kid brother. No one picked on my kid brothers. I had never had anyone to stand up for me when bullies picked on me growing up. I was determined no one would bully my little brothers. The problem was I was in the service and classified as an adult. The Phillips kid was, in spite of his age, a dependent and considered a child.

I didn't want to hurt him; I wanted him to stop bullying my brother. I went to Cardwell Gym across from our housing area where he had pushed my brother down when Larry was playing basketball. I got there he was still playing ball. I told him to leave my brother alone and he smarted off to me and left the gym with his friend. I followed behind, with my brother and a friend of his. Somewhere along the line as I was making threats as to what would happen if he didn't leave my brother alone he turned around to face me; it looked to me like he was going to come at me. I tossed him to the ground with a leg sweep and slapped his cheek, "That's how tough you are, punk. Leave my brother alone."

In my nineteen year old mind I could have done much worse.

When I finished with him, he ran home screaming like a stuck hog. The older Phillips came out of his apartment ready for a brawl. I saw him coming and figured it would be better to meet him on my home turf. I headed up to my parents apartment to wait for him.

He tried to force his way into my parents' apartment. My mom, all five feet four inches of her, blocked his path. He began blasting threats at me. I didn't really want to fight the guy; he stood 6'3" and weighed in at over two hundred and fifty pounds. Had I known that in his younger days he had held both the USAREUR[49] boxing and wrestling titles several times, I would have definitely had second thoughts about tangling with him.

But, he had intruded in my mother's house, had actually pushed her aside, and threatened to get me sooner or later. No one messed with my mother if I could help it, either. Also, as my Uncle Earl used to say, when you're in for a whipping, you might as well get it over with and save the anxiety of waiting.

I knew if I didn't fight him that day I would have to deal with

---

[49]USAREUR- United States Army, Europe- the controlling command of all U.S. Army forces in Europe.

him sooner or later. I'd be walking down the street one night, there'd be a tap on my shoulder and he'd be there. I might not even get the benefit of the tap. It was better to fight now, when I was ready.

And at that stage in my life I had come to the decision to never allow myself to be intimidated or to back down again.

So I went down the stairs with him and we had it out. My dad finally stepped in and broke it up. In my opinion, the fight was broken up before it was finished. I didn't want to fight, but once I got into it I wanted to finish it - one way or another.

The next day, a CID[50] agent came by to persuade me to press charges against the guy for assault. I didn't want to. I figured the trouble was between him and me. We'd had it out; that was that. It wasn't to be that simple.

It turned out the CID had been using some of the apartments in my parents' building to take pictures of Phillips hauling black market items in and out of his apartment. Some of the pictures had been taken from my parent's apartment while the previous occupants lived there. Others had been taken from our neighbors' apartments and they were scared out of their minds that he was going to come after them next. He had already intimidated twenty-two witnesses out of testifying against him.

It all began to make sense. I suspected I had been set up. I felt so stupid! The Phillips kid had picked on my brother trying to provoke us - or me- into doing something like I did. It must have looked suspicious to Phillips. I get assigned to his battalion, my parents move in across the yard, he gets busted, and some of the pictures came from our apartment building. He figured he'd set up a brawl with me, flushing me out. Maybe he could even intimidate the family and me out of testifying against him. That's how the CID figured it, too. Well, April Fools on him. April Fools on us.

Now, the CID wanted us to press charges against Phillips. The prosecution's case was disappearing. The CID man explained to me they needed to get him off the street before he could intimidate more witnesses. His attack on me was the first excuse he had given them to get him. But I had to press charges.

I still didn't want to. It went against the grain to bring the law into a personal matter. When I said that, our neighbor, who had brought the CID man over, told me if I didn't press charges against Phillips, he would press charges against all of us for disturbing the peace. After all, my dad had stepped in and broken up the fight. I thought about the impact that would have on my dad's career and

---

[50] CID- Criminal Investigative Division- The Army's undercover cops.

agreed to press charges. Phillips was picked up that day.

Phillips countercharged that I had assaulted his son. That was expected. I was picked up and charged. I explained that it looked to me like Phillip's son was hauling back to swing at me when I took him down. I also explained that, other than his pride, I hadn't hurt the kid. That wasn't my point; I just wanted him to lay off my brother. After some MP Sergeant gave me a hard time in the basement of the MP headquarters I was released.

The next six months of our lives were interesting. They put the guy back in Mannheim;[51] which was the point of my pressing charges. We had to testify at the preliminary hearings, which determined whether or not there was enough of a case to justify a full court-martial.

I've heard civilians talk about how one-sided military courts are. After going through the Phillip's trial I learned why. By the time a case comes to actual trial, it has been through so many stages of determining the strength of the evidence and the case against the accused, it is practically open and shut. The Army doesn't waste time and taxpayer money on frivolous court cases.

When our case reached trial I was more than ready. We had received numerous death threats. My little brothers, about four at the time, were playing outside one day, when a German man came up and told them if I didn't leave well enough alone something very bad would happen to me. That about killed my mother; she knew all of us were in danger. Something awful could just as well have happened to my brothers.

I was followed home on several nights. Someone even lit a bonfire in the stairwell outside my parents' apartment. The implication was not lost on my folks.

It turned out to be basically for nothing. Phillips plea-bargained in exchange for dropping some of the more compromising charges. All that was left was for a hearing to be held to determine sentencing. I never even got to testify. No, that's not exactly right. I was sworn in and asked a question by the prosecutor. Before I could answer, Phillips' lawyer, an American civilian attorney on retainer by the black market, was up and objecting to this line of questioning. As Phillips had already pled guilty, my testimony was irrelevant.

The JAG[52] officer was apologetic. This was the best deal he could get under the circumstances. In the face of all the witnesses being scared off by the terror tactics and intimidation of Phillips and

[51]Mannheim was the main U.S. Army prison in Germany at the time.

[52]JAG- Judge Advocate General, an Army lawyer.

some of his buddies, the prosecutor figured at least this way he'd get a conviction.

After I was dismissed, all the defense witnesses paraded into the courtroom and told the jury what a great guy the defendant was. He had been assigned to the battalion motor pool. The only time any of them knew of him doing anything underhanded with the alcohol or tobacco ration was to trade for needed spare parts for the battalion from German employees of the US government. This didn't explain the hundred cartons of cigarettes and fifty plus bottles of booze they found in his basement and the trunk of his car when they busted him. I bet he got a lot of oil filters for them.

As far as my part of the case (the JAG office had thrown the assault charges in with the black marketing charges, a mistake on their part, I still believe), Phillips' lawyer handled that superbly. He produced the results of a medical examination given him the day after our brawl when he was taken to the military prison at Mannheim. These disclosed quite a bit of internal damage from blows I had dealt him during our fight. I had punched kicked, gouged, poked, grabbed, and even bit him everywhere I could, trying to stop or slow him. At the time of the fight I didn't think I had fazed him.

The report said he had been passing blood in his urine from my kidney punches. Mom told me she had seen him limping around the day after the fight - before the MPs came for him. He saw her watching him from the kitchen window and tried to straighten up, but she could tell he was in pain. Lord forgive me, but I have to admit I took more than a little satisfaction in knowing I had at least hurt him a little bit in our fight. I guess he was like a mad grizzly that day, you can shoot one and he'll kill you before he realizes he's dead.

After the lawyer produced this medical evidence and contrasted it with my condition after the fight. I had only received a cut on my cheek from a peculiarly sharp ring he was wearing when he landed the first blow (I had to let him have the first blow - assaulting an NCO is a court-martial offense). Then, he brought out the fact I was the Judo instructor at the local Dependent Youth Association (his boxing and wrestling history was never brought out, either by the defense or the prosecution). I became the bully in the story. After I heard this I began to understand the funny looks several of the jury members gave me when I walked into the courtroom. As I've said before, I'm not a particularly intimidating looking guy.

Considering all of this, and the fact he had over nineteen

years of loyal, exemplary service (according to his chain of command), the jury slapped his hands. He was sentenced to reduction in rank to PV1 (E-1), jail time served, and a general discharge. Somehow or another, he was allowed to finish out the sixty days he needed to retire. With his discharge, he would collect his retirement pension. The reduction in grade would make no difference to his pay, as at the time his pension would be based on his highest rank.

I thought of young soldiers who'd had the book thrown at them when they were caught trying to sell a few cartons of cigarettes to pay their rent. I couldn't believe this guy had gotten off so lightly.

And things were just going to get better, too.

The next morning, when I walked into our battalion mess hall, Phillips was there. He had been reassigned to HHB (Headquarters and Headquarters Battery) 3rd Armored Division Artillery while awaiting discharge. That was only across the street, on Hutier Kaserne. It became Phillips' habit to come to our mess hall in the morning so he could sit at the Sergeant Majors' table and glare at me as I ate breakfast. When I would walk to my Judo class over across from Pioneer Kaserne, Phillips would be at a small *trinkhalle*[53] on my way, sitting on the corner, glaring at me as I passed. I knew he wanted me to say or do something, but I wasn't giving him an opening. If he wanted to finish our business, let him start it.

Finally, Phillips retired, to the relief of many in the area. A little over a year later, I heard Phillips died of stomach cancer. It was a tough way to go. I wondered about his kids, particularly his youngest son, he was about my brother Larry's age. I had always liked him. I always felt bad he got hurt over the mess.

My folks went home that summer instead of extending as originally planned. With all the nonsense going on they had the safety of my three little brothers to think about. As for me, I still had a year and a half to do in Germany by myself.

My "buddies" at the JAG office and with the CID offered to get me transferred someplace where I'd be "safe." I thought about it, but I didn't like the idea of running. At the same time, I knew if the black market wanted me, they'd find me no matter where I went. At least in Hanau I'd be on guard, watching for something. In Friedburg, or even Baumholder, I might develop a false sense of security and let my guard down. I declined the offer.

---

[53] *Trinkhalle*- Literally, drinking hall. These are little open beer stands on the sidewalks in Germany where one can have a beer as one passes by or stop and shoot the breeze. They also sell cigarettes, candy, etc.

I saw my parents and brothers off at the airport that August of 1976 and returned to a changed – and changing unit. We'd lost our packs. There was a change of command ceremony; CPT Kowalski was replaced by CPT Hendrickson, who had been Phillips' OIC (Officer in Charge) at the Battalion Motor Pool when he was busted.

He was the only member of Phillips' chain of command who didn't appear at his trial to vouch for him. I've often wondered if that had something to do with what happened to CPT Hendrickson – and Bravo- later. Maybe I'm just suspicious. But remember, all because you're paranoid-schizophrenic doesn't mean the little green men aren't really out to get you.

It was about a year later, the next spring or summer (1977) that anything unusual happened. I was walking home (to the barracks) one night from downtown Hanau. I had just turned onto Lamboystrasse and was crossing the Kinzig River when a Turkish national approached me.[54]   It was late, and this guy approached me and asked if I had a light for his cigarette. Now, this was an old trick muggers used over there on GIs. One guy would come up and ask you for an American cigarette or a light. While you were giving him the cigarette or lighting him up, a friend or two would get you from behind. Every so often you'd hear of a GI getting stabbed or clubbed and robbed this way – if he lived to tell the tale.

So I was suspicious of the guy when he asked me for a light. I didn't smoke (never have) so I normally didn't carry matches unless I was out in the field. I told him I didn't have a light.

By this time he'd moved in and was in my comfort zone. I could smell the sickly sweet aroma of hashsish – somewhere in the brief instant I had to think I recall thinking the guy had "done a bowl" getting courage up to do the deed. Then in the darkness I caught him glance behind me. I turned with my arm in a sweeping motion in time to brush a knife his buddy was bringing up to my side away. My first Judo instructor (Sensei) at Ft Carson always told us that you never went up against a knife or gun if you could avoid it.

---

[54] There were a lot of Turkish workers and folks from other countries who came to Germany to take advantage of the manual labor shortage caused by Germany's booming economy. Some found ways of making extra money in illegal activities. A year or so before this incident INTERPOL and the CID had busted a Turkish-owned bar that was being used as a way station in a human-trafficking ring that was taking teenaged European girls from as far north as the Netherlands and Denmark down to the Middle East. The slavers had made the mistake of grabbing the daughter of an American colonel, thinking she was a German national. INTERPOL was tracing the path of this particular "shipment" of girls hoping to find the head of the gang. The colonel wasn't about to allow his daughter to spend any more time in the slavers' hands than she already had and raised a stink until the police caved in and did the raid, saving her and about twenty other girls from a fate worse than death.

But if you had to go against a knife, expect to get cut. The problem was to get cut where it would do the least damage. I'd had experience at this in Vegas before I enlisted.

I came out okay – by sheer chance. The sharp edge of the knife caught the back of my hand – causing a lot of bleeding but doing no real harm. It turned out there were three of them. My movement startled them long enough to allow me to take the initiative. Another key to fighting more than one is to not stay still and allow them to bring their numbers to bear. Eventually, I had two out of the fight and it was me and the original guy (I think). He took off, leaving his two buddies behind.

I was kind of dazed, but I remember walking down Lamboystrasse trying to get back to the relative safety of my kaserne. I remember reaching down the front of my shirt and grabbing hold of my t-shirt underneath. I pulled at it tearing enough out to make a pseudo-bandage for my cut and bleeding hand. I was about half-way back to my barracks when I started hearing the honking noises of Polizei sirens; I watched one Polizei car zoom past, siren honking and blue light blazing. Then a few minutes later I watched it – or another like it – zoom back the other way, totally ignoring the lone GI shuffling back toward the US Army kaserne down the street.

I remember nodding to the guard at the gate, a buddy of mine, and crossing the blacktop quadrangle to my barracks that faced the street. The CQ on the desk was a buddy; who'd made sergeant. He looked at my bandaged hand, "Another wild night, eh, Woody?"

I kind of laughed, "Shoulda been there." And went to bed.

I almost slept the day away the next day – it was a good thing it was a weekend. When I finally pulled myself out of bed I went over to the small PX on post and got some gauze and tape to put on my cut. I think I got some peroxide or alcohol to clean the wound. I hoped it wouldn't need stitches. I didn't know what shape those two dudes were in I left on the street and sure didn't need hassles with the German authorities. GIs in Germany soon learned that where a GI and German authorities were concerned the GI was always wrong.

Monday morning Top told me my old buddy the Army prosecutor needed to see me. He really didn't say it in that way; he hadn't been in Bravo when the Phillips thing was going on. I can't say I was surprised to hear from JAG. I had been wondering if the Phillips thing and my being jumped were connected. I had been half expecting something to happen for some time; I was wondering why they took so long – I figured they were waiting for me to let my guard down. They were patient.

When I walked in the JAG officer noticed my bandaged hand and I think (maybe it was my imagination) I saw a slight smile. He told me to sit down.

"I have some news that I thought you might find interesting, Wayne," he looked at a file on his desk. "There was some excitement over in your neck of the woods... Yeah, German police said they found two Turkish nationals laid out on Lamboystrasse – over by the Kinzig River. A witness, a German lady who says she heard a disturbance and made the call saw a fellow who looked like a GI fighting three guys. Apparently, they tried to mug the GI and got their clocks cleaned."

He paused a moment, but I wasn't about to open my mouth. I didn't know if I was in trouble or not; I could have been wrong about his smile.

When I didn't say anything he continued, "I thought you might be interested. 'Turns out the two guys they found at the scene had a several ounces of hash and cocaine on them when they were taken to the hospital – just enough to make it more than simple possession. You know how hard the Germans are on drugs. When the docs are finished patching them up they're going to do some time. The Germans have been looking for a reason to pick them up for some time. They've done errands for some mutual friends of ours."

"That's interesting," I said. I was trying to give anything away.

The JAG smiled at that. Then his smile faded, "Are you okay? How are you doing? That looks like a nasty cut on your hand."

I thought about it for a long moment before I answered that question. I knew all I had to do was say the word and I was out of the unit and Hanau, gee, I might even be on my way to a stateside post. Unlikely but a nice fantasy – even if it only lasted a brief moment.

"I'm all right."

He nodded, "By the way, that GI doesn't have anything to worry about from the German authorities. The description could have matched any one of a thousand guys – short to medium height, stocky build, dark hair... It was dark. Considering who these guys are I don't think anyone's going to be looking too hard for the mugging victim. I know we won't."

"That's nice to know," I said. "Thanks."

I was never bothered again. By the Black Market. That I know of.

Chapter 7
Drugs and the Pee Man

Once I owned a Chevrolet, now I'm marching everyday
Once I drove a Cadillac, now I carry on my back
Used to have a girl at home, ran off with Jody now she's gone
Once I thought I was the man, now I work for Uncle Sam
(Anonymous Marching Cadence)

Drugs were a major problem in the post-Vietnam Army in Germany.[55] It was the seventies and the drug counterculture was alive and well. Most of us grew up listening to songs glorifying drugs, ignoring the fact that many of the idols who sang of the virtues of "mind expanding" chemicals had fallen victim to their own gods and died by overdose. I was stationed about twenty miles from Frankfurt A/M, which was one of the stops on a main drug supply route from Turkey and the other middle eastern drug producing nations, and the nations of Western Europe and the U.S.

Many GI's, away from home for the first time, were caught off guard by the sheer high potency of many of the drugs available on the street in Europe as compared to the U.S. This is because, as a general rule, the dope in Europe had passed through fewer hands than the dope bought on the street in America and had been "cut" (diluted with other substances to increase profits) fewer times.

One poor soldier from the 23rd Engineer Battalion across the street from my kaserne bought himself a hit of heroine and shot up in his room in the barracks. He had just enough time to put his jacket on, leave his barracks, and get out the front gate of his kaserne. He turned blue in the middle of the street and fell in front of an oncoming truck. When the autopsy report was returned, it was discovered the dope he had shot up was eighty per cent pure. The doctors didn't know which killed him first, the truck or the dope.

My kaserne was situated right in the middle of town. The street outside the post was one of the worst sections of town. Lamboystrasse was lined with the litter of society- all catering to the baser wants of young men with money in their pockets and away from home for the first time.

---

[55] Actually drugs were a problem in the entire Army throughout the war and afterwards

There were strip-joints, *schnell-imbisse* (fast food places), pawnshops; clothing stores that would sell a GI clothes on credit, providing he made out an allotment (deduction from his paycheck) directly to the store. One place, Marco's would give you one thousand dollars worth of clothes immediately if you took out a twelve-month allotment of a hundred dollars to his store. [56]

The saddest part of the *strasse* to me was the sight of streetwalkers plying their trade to support their drug habits. Prostitution is legal in Germany and is supposed to be strictly regulated and zoned. One can go into the red light district of Hamburg, Frankfurt, Nuremburg, or Munich, and can see, do, or buy books depicting any degrading or perverted thing the human mind can imagine. When folks start talking about getting rid of laws against "victimless" crimes I recall what I saw in Europe. I just can't buy it.

In the brothels, prostitutes were licensed and had to submit to weekly health inspections. The hookers on Lamboystrasse were, for the most part, unlicensed.

I've seen beautiful young girls appear on the *strasse* looking for excitement. Disco was popular at the time and many a young German girl was attracted to the discothèque on a side street off Lamboystrasse where the music blasted every night. Before long they would get in with the wrong crowd, who were also attracted to the music – and the girls the music attracted. The next thing you know they'd be on drugs and into prostitution and selling drugs to support their habits. Within a few months, they would be walking skeletons, shadows of the people they had been, with pale skin, hollow eyes, rotting teeth. They were dead but hadn't realized it. It would break your heart if you let it. In order to survive, one had to harden one's heart to it. It was something I was never quite able to do. It was always difficult for me to see the "zombies" walking the street. I couldn't get the fact that they had once been beautiful girls, someone's darling little babies, out of my mind. I put on a hard face, but it bothered me inside. Sometimes their faces still haunt me.

If one couldn't "score" drugs on Lamboystrasse one could always go down to the city parks in Hanau or Frankfurt where pushers and dealers would sell you everything from hashish to

---

[56] An allotment is a given amount of money a soldier wants set aside, or allotted to a person, or person. Usually, allotments were sent by the Army to a soldier's family (spouse, parents, etc.) for their support. The advantage to an allotment was that the Army could not touch a soldier's allotment for any reason, unless the soldier forfeited all pay and allowances. Many businesses took advantage of this regulation. To stop it, the Army stopped allowing soldiers to make out allotments to businesses.

heroin, depending on your desire. One kid even bought a kilo of camel dung from a Turkish dealer. He'd gone to Frankfurt to make a "big score" of hashish.[57] He came back to the barracks and bragged too much about it to his buddies. The Battery Commander (BC) found out.

A "health and welfare" (shakedown) inspection of the barracks was ordered. Of course, the command knew what they were looking for and where to find it. The guy really thought he was in trouble; after all, a kilo of an illegal substance is a lot of dope. The stuff was sent to the lab for verification. I don't know if the kid was more relieved or embarrassed when he found the Turk had switched the black Lebanese hash he had paid for with a kilo of camel dung. I do know one thing; he never lived it down. Till the day he left he was the butt of countless toilet jokes.

It would be a safe bet to say that most of the GI's in my unit used some sort of illegal drug or another-usually hashish - on the weekends or after duty. A few smoked as part of their daily routine. One guy I knew would get up in the morning and "smoke a bowl"[58] while he was getting dressed. He would work all morning and smoke another bowl during lunch. Of course, he would smoke another one before walking over to the mess hall to eat his dinner at night, and would usually get totally stoned in the evening so he could pass out on his bunk.

In 1977 one fellow got nabbed on his way home. When he was shipping his "hold baggage," that is, personal belongings he couldn't take on the plane with him, customs officials were intrigued by his photo album. He had scores of pictures of just about every guy in the unit, including some of the younger sergeants, getting high. There were pictures of guys smoking bowls in the barracks, out in the field, in 5-ton trucks, in pup tents; just about everywhere soldiers go. Top called all the NCOs to the day room to look through the album, some of them looked real sheepish when they saw themselves in some of the pictures grinning stupidly at the camera, glassy-eyed, obviously stoned.

There was quite a commotion in good old B Battery for a while. They had to hide the kid to whom the album belonged. He had been detained in Germany while the JAG Officers went over the book and tried to figure out whether or not to press charges. Word had gotten out that some of his old dope-smoking buddies wanted to

---

[57] A product of the resin of the cannabis – or marijuana plant; usually sold in small lumps or larger "bricks." More common in Europe than marijuana and popular among the GIs.
[58] Bowl- pipe, hashish is smoked in a pipe, or "bowl."

kill him. I told a couple of the "heads" (what we called dopers) I didn't understand why they were so upset at the kid. After all, he didn't force them to smoke the dope and they seemed pretty happy to pose for his pictures.

In the end, no charges were pressed. After all, no one could prove what the men in the pictures were smoking.

I wasn't too popular with the dopers in the battery. Early in my career, my chain of command discovered I could type, which was, and still is, a valuable skill in a line unit. I've already explained how I went from being a "gun bunny" to a "survey dog." When I was put in survey our assistant section chief had an additional duty in garrison as the unit Training NCO. The training NCO at that time was responsible for typing and publishing the battery's weekly training schedules and keeping records on all individual training conducted by the battery personnel. With my typing skills I was put in the training room to help him.

An additional duty given the Training NCO was the care and handling of the unit's drug abuse prevention program. I helped there, too. The Training NCO went home to Oklahoma on leave for Christmas, 1976. I remember telling him not to worry; I could hold things down until he came back.

"I keep telling you – I'm not coming back!"

He didn't. He reported to Ft Sill, Oklahoma, requesting a compassionate reassignment. They never replaced him. The job of Training NCO fell upon me, a PFC. And I held the job – along with all the others almost until the day I left Germany.

In spite of the fact I held four different titles and was in charge of five major areas of responsibility in the battery (I also became at one point, by time in grade, the assistant survey chief) I became infamous as the urine man. I was in charge of conducting random urinalysis drug abuse detection tests for the unit. When a soldier came up positive for drug abuse I handled the administrative details of his rehabilitation program and, acted as a counselor and point of contact within the battery.

Most of the dopers looked upon me as some sort of narc, a bootlicker, the enemy. Of course, I didn't consider myself that at all, I was just a guy with a job to do. I tried to help guys with a drug problem that wanted help. When they got caught on a positive urinalysis test, I would call them in and tell them exactly what was facing them. Then, I would ask them if they really wanted help, or if they were merely trying to get out of the Army. I lost count of the guys who intentionally got caught doing drugs through urinalysis because they thought it was an easy way to get out of the Army.

Back in the seventies, one of the quickest ways to get out of the Army ahead of time with an honorable discharge was to get caught doing drugs. The way the Army's drug control program was run back then, once a guy was put on the program, he was entered into an "exemption" program that exempted him from further punishment for drug abuse charges. A soldier was then given a certain amount of time to show progress in kicking his drug habit. During this time, he underwent counseling at both the unit level, and at the Drug Abuse Clinic. If, after this time, the soldier showed no sign of improvement, or came up with repeated positive urinalysis tests, he was discharged honorably from the service with full benefits. Many guys, having enlisted, figured this was the easy way out. Unfortunately, by the time they were declared rehab failures and discharged it was too often too late, they had a king-sized monkey on their back. This regulation was much abused and I felt it needed changing. Eventually, it was.

In the meantime we had to live with the regs we had. There was one kid who joined the Army because his wife was pregnant. He stayed in just long enough to get his baby born in an Army hospital and get GI Bill benefits – six months. When he came down positive he was absolutely pleased. He was gone in about two months, with a baby, a discharge, GI Bill benefits, and a habit. I wonder if it would be as easy kicking it as he thought it would be. Of the many guys I processed he's one who sticks out in my mind.

Maybe it's the baby.

As I said, when a guy came down positive the first thing I usually asked them was if they really wanted help or were trying to get out. I didn't want to waste time on losers who were stupid enough to pick up a habit (there were no tests for THC – the active ingredient in marijuana yet) and I sure didn't want to trust my life to a junky, so I tried to concentrate my attention on guys who had screwed up and wanted to be straight. The other guys were going to continue what they were doing until they'd had their three strikes and within a couple weeks they'd be out. I don't know how many guys I had to put out of the Army.

One of the rottenest things pulled on anybody in Europe while I was over there was the spiking of someone's drink with overdoses of LSD, or acid. The hallucinogenic drug in massive doses can cause brain damage or even death. The first publicized case was when somebody put several "hits" of acid in the coffee urn at a mess hall someplace in Germany. Several people had to be hospitalized when the effects of the drug hit them. It hit the front page of "The Stars and Stripes," the official newspaper of the armed forces overseas.

The next thing you know, there were copycats all over Europe. I knew of several cases where young female soldiers would be overdosed with acid by some of the guys in their units when they refused to have sex with them. It happened to a buddy of mine's girlfriend, a WAC[59] from a maintenance unit when guys in her unit got mad because she was dating a cannon-cocker. She was shipped home on a mental discharge.

When I first entered the ministry years later, we had a fellow in our church to whom this had been done. It had been twenty years, and he still suffered from paranoid-schizophrenia from the trauma of it all. LSD never leaves one's system, flashbacks can occur at any time for the rest of one's life.

LSD keys on your emotional state, if you're in a good mood, and happy you'll have a good trip. However, if you're in a bad mood, if there are any hidden fears or anxiety, it will find them and give you a living nightmare from hell. This is what happened to Sigrid, my buddy's girlfriend. It's what happened to Allen, a kid in my unit.

Allen was a good kid. He was from West Virginia. He didn't talk much, but I got the impression his family was poor. He was a Christian, who read his Bible every day. I respected that. The only thing he ever wanted was to be a good soldier. His uniform was always starched, his boots always spit-shined. I imagine you could go into his locker at any time of the day or night and find it prepared for inspection. He didn't drink, never caused trouble. I guess that was too much for the dopers he was stuck with in the barracks.

For over a year after it happened the only thing I knew was that he was in his room in the barracks and someone, somehow, slipped an overdose of LSD in his coke one night. He flipped out. His section chief, SSG Hildebrand, asked me to drive him to the 97th General Hospital in Frankfurt so we could admit him to the mental ward. As we drove in my car to Frankfurt I could see his eyes looking back at me through the rearview mirror. The sight haunted me. He had calmed a bit, but I could see the paranoia at every noise. The headlights of the onrushing vehicles spooked him.

We got him into the ward and assured him everything was going to be okay. His eyes, looking back into mine seemed empty,

[59] WACs- Members of the Women's Army Corps, i.e.; female soldiers. An obsolete term as the Women's Army Corps was officially disbanded in late 1975.

103

yet haunted. I remember looking back as we walked out of the ward and seeing him sitting in a straight-backed chair in the middle of the ward, looking so young, so scared, and so alone.

I drove SSG Hildebrand back to Hanau in silence. There were tears in his eyes. I had always thought him a good man. I kept thinking about Allen. I wondered who had done such a thing to him. I promised if I ever found out they'd pay. It was a lousy thing to do to a buddy.

I asked around trying to find out who did such a lousy thing to the poor kid. It could have been anybody in the room that evening. At least one of Allen's roommates was a notorious head and his buddies had been in and out of the room all night. Either no one knew or no one was talking. It took me over a year to find out what happened to Allen and who did it.

There was a guy named Wilson in my battery. He came to the unit shortly after I did on a two-year enlistment. It didn't take him too long to endear himself with the "old-timers" in the battery. For one thing, he bragged about being in Vietnam. He told all these war stories about "the Nam." Most of the guys, thinking he might be prior service, spared him the usual harassment meted out to "crutes," at first. He looked young, but, hey, looks can be deceiving. Then, we found out he had gone to Vietnam all right, but on a business trip with his father when he was a kid.

The guy had a big mouth. He was constantly smarting off to everyone. Within two months of reporting to the unit, just about everyone in the battery had beaten him up except me. One night, two of the "old timers," Pagan and Meyers, got into an argument over who was going to whip him that night. Finally, they flipped a coin. Meyers won. They walked into his room. Wilson was in bed. Meyers picked him up by the hair of the head and punched him in the face four or five times.

"Good night, Wilson." Meyers said, as they left.

"It's my turn tomorrow night, Wilson." Pagan said.

This might have gone on indefinitely. Wilson never seemed to learn to shut up. Then Wilson crossed Thompson, the biggest guy in the battery. We called him "Big T."

Big T was an easygoing fellow usually. But when you got him drunk or riled he was dangerous. One day Wilson mouthed off to him in the motor pool. T just smiled and shrugged it off. That night, Wilson ran into T coming in from one of the bars. Big T was coming up the stairs in the barracks, Wilson coming down. Wilson smarted off.   T told him to shut up.   Wilson came back with his favorite comeback, "Freedom of speech is a right not a privilege!"

Big T slugged Wilson, catching him right on the nose, and knocking him off his feet.

Wilson came back swinging. His mistake.

Big T caught Wilson right under the chin and sent him flying down two flights of stairs. Everyone thought Wilson was dead. They rushed him to the dispensary, it turned out he merely had a mild concussion. He spent the next two weeks wearing a huge bandage around his head. Everyone called T the mummy maker after that.

T didn't think it was funny. After messing up Wilson so badly, he stopped brawling. I think it scared him to come so close to killing someone.

Wilson rubbed me wrong during the entire eighteen months I knew him. After Thompson had almost killed him he still didn't shut up. I guess we all figured if a brush with death didn't shut him up nothing would. As for me, I had a slow fuse. I did most of my brawling and Cain raising away from my unit. As my "Uncle" Busch used to say, a good dog never messes up his own yard. I was always reluctant to punch out a guy I had to live and work with. Every so often I'd have to punch a particularly obnoxious guy out just to let everyone know there was a line not to cross.   For the most part, I tried to live in peace within my own unit.

But Wilson kept gnawing at me. He got hooked up with the dopers. The dopers back then all thought they were cool - smarter than those of us who didn't do dope.   Wilson was the kind of guy whom you could agree with, but still want to punch out. He was always trying to stir something up with the guys in the unit. Like the time we were out in the field and the chow truck was several hours late.   Before you knew it, he was trying to incite the guys to strike, "If we don't get fed, we don't work!" Good old Wilson, leader of the people!

I was hungry, too, and angry over the foul-up that caused our mess hall truck to be diverted to the wrong place.   Everyone probably was, but I could see a bunch of guys didn't like Wilson's instigating any more than I. I told him to shut his face.

Wilson used to like to needle me, I'd heard guys warn him not to get me riled, but he didn't take them serious. One day, after he'd made another sarcastic remark, I looked at him and smiled, "How long do you have left over here, Wilson?"

"Five months, fifteen days, and a wake up!"

"Getting short then, eh?"

"Yeah, Lifer!"

"Good!" I said, "Give you heart to God, Wilson, because before you leave here your butt belongs to me."

"Am I supposed to be scared?"

"No, Wilson, you're not smart enough for that."

After that, things got worse, he'd needle me every chance he got. I'd just smile and tell him he wasn't gone yet.

It all came to a head about ten days before he left. It was around May 1977. There had been an argument between Top and one of the guys pending a drug discharge. This guy had messed up and overdosed on heroin, passing out and turning blue at a battalion party. It was from the same batch that had killed the guy from the engineers a week or so before.

I was really mad at the guy for messing up. First, I had warned the battery about the bad dope on the street in a class the week before. Second, I'd warned him he was coming under scrutiny for urinalysis tests in the coming weeks. He'd been on the drug abuse program but because of a bureaucratic foul-up he hadn't been taking enough urinalysis tests to ensure he was staying clean. He was going to have to make them up now.

I had warned him to stay clean; he'd be donating samples three to four times a week for the next month. Then he went and did something stupid like overdosing in front of his entire chain of command!

Top had been dressing him down. In the course of the argument, Top called him a dirt bag and a waste of his parents' efforts, and useless to the Army. "Look at your uniform; it looks as if you pulled it out of your laundry bag! Your boots look like they've been shined with a chocolate bar and a brick!"

At this, the soldier tried to get me involved in the argument. I refused to get involved. I had liked the guy as a person, but Top was fairly accurate in his description of his worth as a soldier. And if asked I'd have no choice but to tell the truth concerning the conversation – though I didn't really think he had a legitimate complaint against anything Top had said. But in any case I wasn't going to get involved in this argument. He began calling me a traitor and a sellout.

Wilson came in later, after the smoke had cleared. I was alone in the office. He began calling me a sellout. He was the last guy I wanted giving me lip. I told him to get out of my office and I was about to remove him when Joe Dickson stepped in. We had never been close. I guess he still held the night I'd busted his nose during my first Graf against me. He was a sergeant now. So it surprised me when Joe said, "Don't do it, Wood, he ain't worth it. Get him later."

Again, I told Wilson I'd see him before he left Germany. His crack about me selling out particularly angered me as I made a point to do my job without becoming a narc. As a matter of fact the BC, Captain Holloway had been questioning my integrity at about this time because I refused to "narc" on my buddies.

Just a week or so before the new BC, CPT Holloway had called me in to his office and asked me why more men hadn't been coming up positive on our random urinalysis tests when he knew there were guys in the battery doing drugs.

He wanted me to catch more people on random urinalysis testing. The inference was I was somehow covering up for the drug users in the battery. I resented that. I explained to him I ran a clean program, and that, occasionally, a man would come up positive. But I wasn't going to be a narc and go hunting anyone in particular. That could get a guy killed. I don't care how tough you are, or think you are, there is always someone tougher and you've got to sleep sometime.

The BC told me from now on he'd give me the people to be tested. Fine. It was his prerogative. That was the way the program was supposed to be run anyway. I resented the implication that I couldn't be trusted. I had run a clean program and had suffered ostracism by many of my peers because of it.

After that, we began getting positives left and right. Someone was fingering the dopers. Some suspected me, though most knew better. But who was it? I began to hear talk of threats against me from some of the dopers.

I began sleeping with one eye open, I almost decked a CQ runner when he tried to wake me one morning and made the mistake of touching me. I had him stretched out over the bed with me on top, ready to take his throat out. Fortunately, I realized who he was before I followed through. After that, runners would just crack open my door and say my name to wake me up.

Now Wilson was accusing me of narcing on all the guys getting busted.

I almost went after him again; he was taunting me, "Come on Lifer – let's get it on right now."

"No, Sergeant Dickson's right." I said regaining control, "How long do you have left in Bravo, Wilson?"

"Ten days and a wake up, Lifer!"

"Well, give your heart to whatever god you pray to because before you leave Germany your butt belongs to me!"

"I said let's get it on now, Lifer!"

"No, but soon."

It was a week or so later, on a Friday night. Vinnie and I were sitting at the rod and gun club, listening to the band with some guys from the unit. I was thinking about saying goodbye to Wilson. He had been baiting me all week (no pun intended); we'd pass in the hallway of the barracks and he'd snicker or grin that grin that had gotten him punched out so many times when he first arrived in Bravo. I got to thinking. He was leaving Monday. I wondered aloud if he had done the smart thing and spent his last weekend with a friend off post.

Mueller interrupted my musings, "You really want him, don't you Woody?"

"I promised him I'd say goodbye," I said. "I always liked to keep my promises."

"Somebody ought to get him." Mueller said, "It's a shame they didn't get Rabbi after what him and Wilson did to Allen."

My antenna perked up.

"Allen?"

"Yeah," Mueller said, "it was Rabbi and Wilson that slipped the acid to Allen that made him flip out."

That settled it for me. Allen's face came to mind. After Allen got out of the hospital he was given a convalescent leave. While home he checked into Walter Reed Army Hospital. We never heard from him again. For all I know he might still be there – or in a psych ward at a VA hospital somewhere.

I had about given up on finding out who'd dosed him. Rabbi Smith had left months before on a junkie discharge. I couldn't get him.

But I could still say goodbye to Wilson.

Vinnie and I made it back across town to the barracks. When I got there I found a buddy of mine on CQ, Norman Flood. "Hey Norm, is Wilson home?"

"He sure is."

"Good, I want to say goodbye to him.'

"Please be discreet."

"Discretion is my middle name, Norm."

Vinnie watched the door while I went in to Wilson's room. I

108

won't go into the gory details of what happened. I don't remember much, really, I blacked out into a fury. I remember seeing Allen's face in front of me each time I hit Wilson. The next thing I remember is I had Wilson on an empty bunk; I was on top of him, beating his head against a radiator pipe. He was begging for me to stop before I killed him.   Suddenly, I saw Wilson's blood spread over the mattress. I snapped out of it. I still believe it was the grace of God that stopped me before I killed him. I looked around and saw Bate's blood everywhere.

I was still on top of him. I looked down into Wilson's eyes, they seemed clear. He was terrified.

"Are you okay?" I asked him.

He nodded his head.

"This is between you and me, okay? No one else needs to get involved."

He nodded again.

I put my hand out. Somehow, he reached up and shook it.

"God," I kept thinking, "I almost killed him! I could have killed him!" I left him in his room. I was stunned. I had come so close...

Wilson was as good as his word, I'll give him that. He went to the dispensary that night to get his head sewed up, but he didn't tell anyone what had happened or who had done it. It was all over the battery by Monday what had happened. All weekend guys went to the room to see the blood on the mattress.

On Monday, Top asked me if I had done that to Wilson.

I had to admit that I had.

He grinned, "Boy, you really messed him up!"

I saw Wilson one more time. It was right before he flew home. He was in his dress uniform. There was a bandage around his head. He was wearing sunglasses to hide his two black eyes. There was a bandage over his nose. Someone told me his jaws were wired. I couldn't believe he was going home like that. I couldn't believe the Army would let him.

I shook his hand again. I wished him well, "and Wilson, watch your mouth before it gets you killed." I wonder if he ever learned.

That was late May or early June 1977. As for me, I have never since let myself go as I did that night. I have been tempted, but I have never since allowed myself to hit another man in anger. I guess I owe Wilson for that.

Oh yeah, the guy in trouble for drugs got a Chapter 16, drug abuse discharge, three days after is actual ETS.[60]

Chapter 8
Adventures in the Fulda Gap

This is the Soviet Soldier. The cold winter does not bother him for he has grown up in the frozen wastes of Siberia. He is inured to hardship by the deprivations of the communist system. He is extremely disciplined. When a Soviet officer or NCO gives him an order he snaps to attention and responds, "I Obey!"

What would you do if you ran into the Soviet Soldier on the battlefield?
(The caption on an Army Training poster in barracks during the Cold War showing a Soviet soldier standing in a snowy forest holding an AK assault rifle (from memory))

I will kick his [behind]!
(Scribbled by a GI under the above caption by a GI – with edit)

Between 1946 and 1991 the border between what was then West Germany and what was then East Germany and Czechoslovakia was known as the Iron Curtain. One could tell where the border was because the communists marked it clearly.

They marked the border with a solid line of barbed wire and storm fences that extended along the entire border between East and West. In most places there were two lines of fences. The area between the fences was sewn with land mines and other obstacles. At intervals all along the border the Soviets and East Germans had set up guard posts with soldiers armed with searchlights and machine guns.

Some countries put up fences along their borders to keep folks out. The communists put up the Iron Curtain to keep folks in.

If the Soviets and their allies ever decided to come across the border there were three likely areas of approach, in the British Sector across the North German Plain, through the Danube River Valley in Austria to the South (considered unlikely), or across the Fulda Gap northwest of Frankfurt. This was in the US Sector. Hanau a/m was in the direct path between Frankfurt and the Gap.

The Fulda Gap was named after one of the two German cities that lay in its valleys. The Gap was actually two valleys that offered a path through the Vogelsberg Mountains from the east to the west (or west to east, I suppose).

I grew familiar with the area. As a member of the battery survey section, I was required to go out with the section to the border every three months to do reconnaissance of our forward fighting positions. We would locate and survey good positions so if war broke out we'd be ready. We'd spend a week out there with the other survey sections in the battalion. It wasn't too bad. We'd work all day, returning to our base camp at night, where we'd party all evening with refreshments bought in town. These trips were called "Sector Recon."

We were given a weeks worth of C-Rations – which we supplemented with great German food and beer from the local restaurants or Gasthauses – usually free as the Germans living in the shadow of the Iron Curtain rarely allowed us to pay for anything – and for us luxurious camping gear, a large tent for the crews with gas heaters and electric lights powered by a gas generator. Things those of us in line batteries rarely got to see in the tactical field environment – where light and noise discipline were the rules. It was like a campout away from the most of the stuff that usually got on the average GI's nerves – even in the field. Of course there had to be an officer along – the Battalion Survey Officer. Usually he was a junior lieutenant and only had the vaguest notion of what we were doing. I realize now, that was what he was there for – to learn that aspect of Field Artillery.

I remember hearing from the Headquarters Survey Section about how the DivArty commander came out to observe the crews at work during one Sector visit. He approached the Survey Officer, who was watching the HHB (HQs Battery) section working and asked, "Lieutenant, what's the crew up to?"

The lieutenant gave the obvious answer without missing a beat, "They're doing a survey, Sir."

The guy telling me the story said the LT was obviously pleased with his answer (it wasn't really wrong); and the DivArty commander was either satisfied or saw no point in pursuing the matter, for he said, "Carry on." Then he left to go inspect other units.

We had one officer who would drive us crazy with his questions. He was a super intelligent guy, and a really nice guy, but he was one of those guys who was so smart he often had problems relating to "normal" people. I realized one day while I was being grilled over my job that his questions were out of a genuine curiosity and desire to know everything he could discover about Artillery Survey and his questions were intelligent well-reasoned questions when you thought about them.

He later became our Battery XO. The troops nicknamed him "Goofy Grape" after the cartoon character because of his laugh. I thought that was mean even then. He was a good guy. But even I had to laugh when he got a 50 gallon trash can of water on his head on chilly afternoon when entering the back door of the barracks. This had to be late 76 or early 77.

This had become a fad in the barracks and one never knew when one was going to get it. One afternoon, Vinnie and I almost got it. The windows in the old German-built barracks were large and low. There was a fire escape above the door. We'd opened the door when all of a sudden we heard, "FIRE IN THE HOLE!"

We were barely able to get inside the barracks before the deluge fell. We got our revenge on the guy later. The barracks were equipped with both CO_2 and refillable water fire extinguishers that made great squirt guns. I leave the rest to your imagination.

The poor LT wasn't fast enough and got the full dose. I'd never seen him so angry before. He reported it to the First Sergeant and announced he was going to his office to dry off (I think I would have gone home and changed...) so no one would seem him wet. It didn't dawn on him his office was by the back entrance to the barracks and everyone could see him sitting stock still behind his desk as they entered and exited the building. The door was busy that afternoon.

Everyone knew who'd done it, a guy I'll call Hokey the Wolf, but no one could prove it. We knew he was the guy who'd gotten the Staff Duty Officer the last 4th of July – the nation's bicentennial. The SDO, a captain, told the CQ he was going to change his uniform but the CQ was not to let anyone pass by his desk until he got back. He was going to put every man in the barracks on report.

Word got around somehow.

No one passed the CQ desk but the fire escapes and first floor windows in the Day Room were busy. When the SDO returned the barracks was empty of everyone but the Battery Commander's driver, who was taking a nap.

Hokey even got one of our First Sergeant's eleven or twelve year-old son, who had a habit of coming to the battery and telling the guys we all worked for his dad. Sweet kid. Hokey got him.

Top brought Hokey into the Orderly Room and I thought I might have to pull him off my buddy. I didn't blame him for being so angry – even though I didn't like the kid either – but I did have the greatest respect for Top. It would have been the end of his career.

Hokey just stood there blank-faced through it all and Top got control of himself as he threatened to rip off Hokey's head and spit down his neck (among other things) and called him things I don't think Hokey's mother ever dreamed of. But eventually, Top knew he couldn't prove anything – more frustrating – and had to let Hokey go with a warning he'd better not even scratch his nose wrong from here on out.

Fortunately for Hokey, and unfortunately for Bravo, that Top left to take over the newly created Personnel Actions Center at battalion shortly after and we got a new Top.

But I digress – back to Sector Recon on the Fulda Gap.

The Germans at the border were much friendlier on the whole than those back at Hanau. I believe this was at least partly because they weren't used to American soldiers and our bad habits. At the same time, we often could see the frontier outposts of the iron curtain as we worked. We could see the barbed wire, the armed guard posts, and the anti-tank obstacles that marked the border of the free world. Sometimes, at night, we could even hear gunfire and sirens from afar off. If we went outside out tents and searched the eastern sky, we often could see the glare of spotlights from beyond the horizon. We knew someone was trying to make the break to freedom. It was moments like these the whole reason you were in Germany came home to you. It also made you appreciate how blessed you were to be an American. The Germans on the border were reminded daily of why we were over there and appreciated us.

When our military vehicles would rumble through the villages on the border the German children would come out of their houses and stand by the roadsides flashing us "V" signs with their fingers, for victory. I imagine more than one GI got dust or something in their eyes seeing those kids. Most of us were homesick. There were times we'd be so disgusted with life in the peacetime Army over there we would have done almost anything to go home. As I've pointed out before, many did. But, I could think of those little kids standing by the roads with their rosy cheeks and big smiles with their fingers up in the air. It made it all seem worthwhile.

The kids. Some of my fondest memories of Germany are of being in the field, either or Recon or sometimes when the entire unit would go out to train in the German countryside. If we were near a town as soon as school let out our position would be overrun by curious schoolchildren wanting to see the GIs and our equipment. For the most part we allowed them to satisfy their curiosity – while making sure of their safety, allowing them to touch our M-16s and howitzers (had to keep them from climbing on the vehicles, though – that was sometimes dangerous for us). I remember pulling road guard in a village one morning, directing a convoy. Before I knew it I was swarmed by kids waiting for their school bus. I let about everyone of them hold my M203 combination M16 and grenade launcher before the bus came. They got a kick out of that as I showed them how the thing worked. Of course, the weapon was unloaded – I didn't even have blanks on me for that trip.

Sometimes the crews would do their field work, measurements and such in the morning; doing up to three or four positions, making sure our section recorder got everything down. Then we would repair to a gasthaus in a nearby village and have a good meal while we did the computations and paperwork in a nice warm – and friendly environment. Because the proprietors seldom let us pay for our food we rarely went to the same place twice, which was sad if the food was particularly good and the waitresses pretty, and we left BIG tips, so as not to abuse the German hospitality.

We also took care to make sure our vehicles were parked out of the way in case someone with no sense of humor (such as the Division or DivArty Commander) drove by checking on the troops in the field. It was fear of getting caught the led our chief, SSG Romanelli to be less willing to allow us to enjoy the hospitality of our host nation than the other chiefs in the battalion were. But occasionally even he got tired of C-rats.

Interesting things happened so close to the border. There was a 1 Kilometer Zone that ran all along the Iron Curtain – it was a sort of de-militarized zone to keep incidents between Soviet and US troops at a minimum. Every so often and along every road headed east there was a sign that warned in several languages one was entering the "1K Zone" and all US Armed Forces Personnel were to turn back or face punishment under the UCMJ. It was clearly marked.

That's what makes what happened to O'Leary so crazy.

Everyone out on Recon that week heard about it; our NCOs

and officers told us the story as a warning to be careful as we often worked real close to the border and 1K Zone (which brings to mind another story, but maybe later). Anyway, as I heard it from some buddies in the DivArty Survey Section (Vinnie had an old buddy from the block with DivArty Survey) O'Leary was driver for the 3rd Armored Division Artillery (DivArty) Commander's - a colonel.

One day the DivArty Commander decided to make a trip to the border and see what we were up to. Being a colonel and a very important and busy man, he couldn't waste all the time it would take to drive to the border so he arranged for O'Leary to drive up to where we were; the colonel would fly up in a Huey helicopter and meet him in a designated field, do the tour, and return to Hanau in the chopper while O'Leary drove back in the jeep.

All things went well until O'Leary got lost trying to find the field and ended up in the 1K Zone – in spite of all the warning signs! What's worse (as I was told), O'Leary drove up to a Soviet border checkpoint to ask for directions! The guys told me (and I saw O'Leary back in Hanau when we returned a few days later and he was pretty bruised) that the Soviets pulled him out of the jeep and worked him over before letting him loose so he could go back west, where he eventually linked with the colonel.

For some reason he didn't get busted or lose his job. That happened a few months later when a beautiful refugee Czech model showed up on the Strasse and picked out this peach-fuzz-faced nineteen year-old Midwestern farm boy over all other would-be suitors for her boyfriend and turned out to be a communist spy. At least that's what I was told. And I know just about every troop on Lamboystrasse got shot down trying to pick her up when she first showed up at the American Legion across Chemnitzerstrasse from our Kaserne. And those of us who knew O'Leary and that she picked him up every evening after duty and dropped him off in the morning in her Mercedes smelled a rat somewhere. But, then again, maybe we were jealous and O'Leary had charms which we just didn't appreciate?

But I imagine O'Leary, being the DivArty Commander's driver was a load of intelligence that was of interest to the communists. He probably knew stuff he wasn't aware he knew. One could picture her rubbing his back and asking him how his day went. There was no telling what experts could glean from his driver's accounts of driving the colonel around and comparing her notes with others. On the day he drove across the 1K Zone I was told he had the commander's map case with all his maps and our projected unit dispositions in time of war. If only one of the guards had thought to look in the back seat of the jeep…

It may have been during that trip I had a meaningful contact with a Soviet border guard myself. As I remember it, we had driven right up to the edge of the 1K Zone to find a survey control point to gain control on this field we needed to survey. Our chief, SSG Romanelli had gone to another control point to mark it so our instrument operator could get an azimuth (direction) so we could start our survey. It's complicated. Anyway, I'm with the instrument operator waiting for him to "shoot the azimuth" with his T-16 Theodolite (used to measure directions and angles) and got bored.

We were right on the edge of the 1K Zone; there was a warning sign not too far from us. I used to have a picture of it but it has disappeared over the years, though I still have a picture of the field and village where this happened.

With nothing to do, I dug around in our jeep trailer where we had loaded the BC Scope. The telescopic device we used when we were calling in field artillery missions. Our operator was busy peering into his instrument lens waiting for Romanelli's signal – a long survey post with a light attached – so he could take the measure and I record it. So he wasn't paying too much attention to me.

So I set up the Scope and began studying my surroundings, the village, in which I could see no sign of life that morning. I followed the road leading east through the village to what we called the "Iron Curtain." There was no border crossing point here. Here the road came to an abrupt halt where someone had dug a trench where the road had once been. I recall concrete anti-tank or vehicle devices laid out in front of what I estimated to be a twelve foot storm fence. There were actually two fences, but at my angle of view I couldn't tell you how far apart they were. And then there was the guard post.

I zeroed in on that and could see the soldier inside staring back through big binoculars. We were told the Soviets took great interest in our activities when we showed up on the border. I could see him watching us intensely. I could see his breath in the bitter cold. I remember it being so cold that day. That morning when we were having our C-rations for breakfast, my Beef with Spiced Sauce had frozen in the can. I was able to pull it out of the can on my mess kit fork like a Popsicle. Then I had to put it back in so I could heat it and make it half-way edible.

It occurred to me that the Soviet soldier wasn't so different from me. We were about the same age, we were both a long way from home – but I was a volunteer and he had been drafted. So I did a no-no.

I waved at him.

He didn't know how to respond to that so I waved again. It took three times before he very cautiously waved back.

Then, maybe I realized he was the enemy and I might have to kill him one day; maybe I thought about the nights on the border we had heard machine gun fire from these same guard posts – had he squeezed off on some poor folks just trying to get to freedom?

I flipped him off.

Evidently he understood the gesture because he picked up the field phone – snitch – and began talking.

I looked over at the instrument operator and asked him if he had the azimuth.

"Yeah, he's marking it now. Prepare to copy."

So he read the azimuth, read it off to me, I wrote it down, and suggested we get out of there. I never told anyone but Vinnie what had happened. He was really the only one I could trust.

In May of 1977, we got called out to the border for a "five day war." Out in the field we discovered every combat unit in Germany was on the border for "maneuvers." In the gap or corridor near Fulda, was the US V Corps, consisting of the 3rd Armored and 8th Infantry Divisions, with supporting units. The US VII Corps, consisting of the 1st Armored and 3rd Infantry Divisions, with their supporting units weren't far away. Each Corps' units would face off against each other maneuvering back and forth while not moving too far from their assigned sectors if real war broke out.

We had established our position in the Fulda Gap when CPT White called the battery together for a briefing. We stood in battery formation in the woods.

"Gather around me men," he said, "I don't feel like yelling."

We gathered around him and he climbed on his jeep to address us.

"My orders were to tell you men only what I felt necessary about this operation, but to use discretion. I've been giving it a lot of thought and I think it's only fair that you know what's going on.

"About two weeks ago the Soviets moved three motorized divisions to the border. G-2 (Intelligence) didn't pay much attention to the movement at the time as the Soviets routinely rotate their border guards every six months. They move three divisions in; they move three divisions out.

118

"This time, they didn't move the divisions being relieved to the rear. They've doubled their force on the border. We don't know exactly what this means, but USAREUR doesn't want to take any chances. They devised this little maneuver to get in the maximum readiness posture without causing undue alarm back home. At the same time, the Soviets will see us out here and get the message we're ready for them."

He let his words sink in. All of us knew the odds against us if the Soviets came across the border. We all knew their tactics. The Soviets used chemical weapons as standard operating procedure. When artillery rounds came in, we knew to automatically mask, as Soviet doctrine called for every tenth round to be a chemical round. It would be a nasty war. For those of us in Germany, when the Soviets came over, it was a no win situation. We knew we were in Germany as a deterrence measure. We would be little more than a speed bump in an actual war.

The Soviets weren't so much afraid of the US military actually in Europe as the thought of confronting all of the US military might when stirred. We also knew that unless we were given enough warning to get substantial reinforcements before the shooting started, we would in all likelihood be wiped out. Our only ace in the hole was the threat of using tactical nuclear weapons, which could be shot from our howitzers. They were capable of obliterating large areas, destroying everything within their range.

This gave us artillerymen little comfort, for those of us who were let in on the nuclear surety program knew the truth about the nuclear round. When one compared the range of the M110 howitzer at that time[61] with the blast radius of the nuclear round, one found it was well within range of the initial blast of the round, with only seconds until it hit. Whenever we went on a simulated nuclear (or "snake") mission, we practiced "march ordering," that is tearing down and moving the gun, as soon as the round went down range. But we knew this was an exercise in futility. The best we could hope for was to be down the road a bit before we were hit in the back by the blast.

Even if we did survive using the nuclear round, if we used tactical nuclear weapons, there was the danger of the war escalating into total thermonuclear war. It was not a pleasant thought.

---

[61] Shortly after I left Germany, our howitzers were finally fitted with long promised longer barrels (or "tubes"), making our guns M110A1s. This greatly increased their range. Perhaps the new tubes made it safer to fire the nuke round.

CPT White went on to explain that our battery ammunition section had gone to the 3rd Armored ammunition depot outside of Friedburg to draw our basic combat load of ammunition. They were camped about a mile away from us, ready to issue our ammo if we needed it.

I had seen this before, from a different angle, when I was a kid. In 1968, when the Soviets crushed the democratic revolution in Czechoslovakia, USAREUR went on full alert. My older brother, who was in Germany at the time, recalled spending almost a month on the border, waiting either for orders to go over to rescue the Czechs, or for the Soviets to come across.

In 1973, when I was a senior at Frankfurt American High School, the entire world stood on the brink of war over the October 1973 Yom Kippur War. My dad went on alert. We were told to pack our bags and be ready for evacuation in case the Soviets came over. Then Nixon and Kissinger stepped in and brokered a deal for a ceasefire while we replaced the Israeli losses from the Arab sneak attack.[62] Total nuclear war was barely avoided, Dad came home, and everyone stood down.

Now the Soviets were playing their games again, testing our resolve and it was my turn to go to the border.

So there we were in our stomping grounds near our sector and Romanelli got the idea for he, Vinnie, and I to get in the jeep and take a ride and see if we could go to some of our positions and make sure our markers hadn't been moved by some German farmer wanting to plow his field.

It seemed like a good idea to me if for no other reason that a good chance to get away from the battery and all the nonsense that went on. The BC, CPT White, agreed – after all, we were in an admin phase at the moment and the "war" wasn't scheduled to start until 0001 (12:01 a.m.).

So we took off, the three of us, my chief had the map and was giving me directions as I drove; Vinnie in the back seat enjoying the ride. To make a long story short we made a wrong turn (it may seem self-serving if I state here I tried to warn him) and ran off the map we had. When Romanelli tried to get us back on the map we just got more lost.

Finally, as it was late afternoon, we all agreed the best

---

[62] I think I can safely say this is when the radical muslim jihadists turned some of their hatred toward us. The Arab leaders didn't tell their people we had saved them from thermonuclear holocaust. All the people knew was we had helped Israel. We became terrorist targets. As they say in the Middle East, "The friend of my enemy is my enemy."

course was to head toward the sun; eventually we were bound to hit something familiar, get our bearings, and find the battery. At least we wouldn't end up like O'Leary.

We were in some hilly country and we topped a rise and before we knew it there was a village spread before us in the valley like out of a postcard. It was filled with US troops and vehicles. They were all "enemy" vehicles. By the time we realized it (they were taping the "OPFOR" signs on the sides of their vehicles and putting white armbands on as we drove past the first checkpoint) it was too late we were in the middle of town – surrounded by the "enemy." We had breezed right past the checkpoint and no one bothered to even stop us.

I figure we had stumbled into the middle of at least an armored brigade. And they were gearing up for an attack.

Remember, Romanelli's nerves were shot from Nam. He was freaking out, not only at the thought of being captured, but also at the embarrassment of the Survey Chief getting lost. Vinnie was (as was I) laughing at the whole thing, I figured the best way we could get through this was to play it off and act like we owned the place. So I started waving at folks like I was returning home, to Romanelli's horror and Vinnie's and my amusement – the "enemy" soldiers started waving back. I'll never forget the look on one lieutenant's face, on top of an M60A1 Main Battle Tank who was grinning and waving at us when he noticed we didn't have an "enemy" sign on our vehicle, maybe he saw the 3rd Armored patch on our shoulders or the unit stencils on the bumpers of our jeep.

At about that time someone must have realized they had been "infiltrated" because I saw an MP jeep barreling up the road behind us as fast as they safely could with all the personnel crowding the road. I put the gas on just a bit - not so much to alarm anyone. There was a field to my left – the other guys were using it to park some choppers. I figured they weren't worried so much about maneuver damage. I seriously considered four-wheeling it across the field to escape the village, but up ahead I could see the edge of town and another road block/checkpoint. The guards there had just been alerted to our presence and were moving to close us off but I managed to pedal it and get through in the nick of time.

Vinnie and I were laughing so hard it was difficult for me to drive. This seemed to make Romanelli even angrier. But we had escaped and no one seemed to care enough about us to follow us, so we were good. We suggested that this was a great opportunity to "wipe out" a brigade and maybe win the war at the start. We had a radio; we could call in a fire mission once we got to the top of the hill. Romanelli nixed it. He didn't want the battery to know how far off the beaten path we had gotten.

One good thing, though, we recognized the name of the village we had just driven through and were able to get our bearings back so we could rejoin our battery. I did warn our Chief of Firing Battery about a platoon of enemy M551 Sheridans we'd seen slinking through a logger trail not far from our battery.

Nothing was done.

We got over run that night – almost immediately after the exercise went tactical. One of the Sheridan's tracks rolled over inches from my head, waking me out of as sound a sleep as I got in the field. I still believe the only thing that saved me (other than God's protection) was the fact I'd stretched my sleeping bag out between some trees in our position area.

Sometime during the week, the Soviets moved their three extra divisions back. A day or so later, we completed our maneuvers and went home. All was back to normal.

Chapter 9
On a Sinking Ship...

Mama Mama can't you see,
what the Army's done to me.

They put me in a barber's chair,
spun me around I had no hair.
(Chorus)

They took away my favorite jeans,
now I'm wearing Army greens.
(Chorus)

I use to date a beauty queen,
now I love my M16.
(Chorus)
(Anonymous Army Marching Cadence)

1977 started out with my Judo classes at the Hanau Dependent Youth Association being closed down. I couldn't really blame the directors for closing the classes; I wasn't able to make it to teach the classes half the time because of duty commitments. It seemed like every time I turned around there was something coming up to keep me at work too late to teach my class. When I had returned to Germany in 1975 one of the first things I did was go back to the DYA and see if there was still some sort of Judo or Martial Arts program. What I found was about twenty kids showing up but none of the adult black belts in the area willing or able to make the commitment to take responsibility for the program. I didn't think I was ready to teach yet, but I stepped in to keep the program going. CPT Hendrikson, our new battery commander seemed to have no sympathy or support for my community service work with the kids as had CPT Kowalski. But that's the way it rolls in the Army, new commanders, new expectations.

But the battery was optimistic. We had another "Battery" Graf coming up in a few months. We would take our Battery (or company) level ARTEP. We would win our packs back.

From my pre-Army and Army experience and relationship

123

with CPT Kowalski as a supervisor and commander I always held and believe will always hold for him a special place of esteem and warmth. But the battery believed with Captain Hendrikson we had the man to lead us back to our former glory. After all, he'd been Executive Officer of Bravo when we'd been salute battery. He promised us this Graf we were going to get our pack howitzers back. We believed him. We were ready to do it. Our morale and *esprit de corps* were growing each day he commanded us. I believe the high point had come about a month before we left for Graf when we were called out on an alert early on a Saturday morning.

In Germany, every unit was subject to no-notice recall (alert). Within two hours of an alert being called we had to have seventy-five percent of our personnel back on post, ready to pull out of the kaserne to the field. This was the case three hundred - sixty-five and one-quarter days a year. In Germany, during the Cold War, we were the front line. Just a few miles down the *autobahn* (highway), traveling due east, was the enemy. Without trying to sound melodramatic, we were outnumbered by the Soviet and Warsaw Pact troops by over ten to one in just about every major area of military power. There were places where it would take less than two hours to drive the width of Germany. This meant we had to be ready to go fight quickly. In the 82nd, we emphasized readiness at a moment's notice. In Germany, if war broke out, we might have been denied the luxury of even that moment.

In my unit we used to have to hang our web gear (pistol belt etc.) and helmet from the ends of our bunks. It seemed to me a silly thing to do at the time. Looking back, I see the psychological point of it. It was a quiet way or reminding us we had to be ready at any time. I now see it as similar to the minuteman's musket and powder hanging by the door of his home.

If a callout involved going out into the countryside, the German people in the area, whose permission was needed to train on their land, would often warn soldiers they knew an alert was coming. This kind of defeated the idea of the thing. Married guys would stay close to home on evenings we were expecting a callout, single guys would stay by the barracks. Every now and then, though, security would be so tight we'd get caught off guard and really be put to the test.

The alert this Saturday morning was one of those times. We were awakened at six in the morning with news of the alert. The CQ came to get me because I had the keys to the orderly room and several other security areas. I was needed to get the battery moving before the BC and Top could make it in from their quarters. As I was the ranking guy in survey living in the barracks at the time, I got the guys up, got them moving (not that they needed me to tell them their jobs), and went down to the orderly room to see what was needed to be done down there.

As it was Saturday, the only NCO in the barracks was our CQ, a sergeant (E-5). All our officers were at home. As I made my way down to the orderly room to get the alert dispatches for our vehicles, so we could legally take them off post, the armorer already had the arms room open and was issuing weapons and protective masks to soldiers in the unit. Other men had dressed, drawn their weapons, and were rushing to the motor pool to load equipment and ready the guns to go to the field. Senior enlisted men had already worked out rotation schedules so the men in the section could take turns eating breakfast while progress continued in getting the unit to go out in the field.

Phones were expensive in Germany; most of the younger soldiers couldn't afford them. To notify soldiers living off post of alerts, several "alert routes" were drawn up. Messengers were sent out in all directions in jeeps. They were armed with maps to the homes of personnel living off post. Like modern day Paul Reveres, they ran their routes, running up to the doors and informing the soldiers of the alert.

One by one, our NCOs and officers began to filter in from their homes. They joined their troops in getting the battery ready for movement. It turned out that Saturday morning that CPT Hendrickson was the last man from the battery to come in. As he got out of his car the battery, completely loaded, was waiting for him at the "GO" line[63]. The XO had already been briefed as to our mission, he informed the BC. The BC's driver had already drawn his pistol from the arms room. He handed CPT Hendrickson his pistol. The BC got in his jeep and we drove off post. Our time, we were told later, one hour, thirty-seven minutes from first notification.

Out at our dispersal area, where in an actual war we would load ammunition, the BC called us together, and with tears in his eyes, said, "In all my years in the Army, I have never seen men get together and get the job done in such an outstanding manner without NCOs or officers. I have never been so proud of a bunch of men in

---

[63] Each unit on the Kaserne had an assembly point, or "GO" line where vehicles and guns would line up on any offpost movement as they got ready. Once every vehicle deploying was lined up the unit could leave the Kaserne. We were timed from the moment the alert was called until the unit was completely assembled at the "GO" line.

my life- you're the greatest." he paused for a moment, "We're going to kick tail in Graf next month!"

At that we all cheered. Whatever our personal differences might be with him, at that moment we would have followed him to hell. He was our commander. It's like that in the military.

Then we took our ARTEP.

That ARTEP in the spring of 1977 has to rank as one of the most painful memories in my military career. I knew from the start the evaluation team was out headhunting. I could tell by the attitude of the evaluators. I mean, unless you really messed up you're going to pass your ARTEP. By the same token, if the evaluators really don't want you to pass, there's no way you will. Maybe that was the magic of the new ARTEP system.

I had this awful feeling that our evaluation team was out for blood. We had been kept up with briefings most of the night before we were to go out. We only had about three hours' sleep before we had to roll out and hit the road. After that, we were hit with a new, "improved," stepped-up thirty-six hour test, in which we were expected to do everything we used to do during a three to five day test.

They ate our lunch. We got hit again and again, we were ambushed, we were gassed, and we were ambushed again - all in rapid succession. It seemed nothing we did was right. Murphy's Law was working overtime. Everything that could go wrong - did.

I remember pulling into one position and seeing an evaluator (I think he was a major) walk up to the Executive Officer and Chief of Firing Battery, whose job was to orient the battery to the Azimuth of Fire, "You're both dead!"

I and a fellow surveyor were measuring the distance between two points, one being where the M2 Aiming Circle (used to orient – or lay – the guns to their proper direction) stood, so we were close by. Hearing this, I ran over to the aiming circle. During my time as XO driver and in survey I'd learned to operate an M2 Aiming Circle. It could have been a time when my training and experience as a cannoneer, XO Driver, and surveyor could come in handy. I figured I knew enough from watching I could at least get the battery started in getting laid for Azimuth of Fire - we had just a few minutes. As I reached the circle, the guy kicked the circle over, "Mortar round!"

By the time CPT Hendrickson came running up and began laying the battery using a compass, it was too late, we'd busted time for getting the guns laid. All I wanted to do was wipe the grin off the major's face.

When the ARTEP ended early the second morning the men were exhausted. Top, on the other hand, was drinking out of his second canteen, which contained his favorite brand of whiskey, and was feeling no pain.

The BC told Top we were on Admin[64] status, "Put 'em all to bed, let 'em get some sleep."

Looking back, I think we all wish he would have chosen his words more carefully.

Again, Vinnie and I were close by and heard the conversation.[65] Top put everyone to bed without leaving a single guard up. He threatened to fire Vinnie and me when we tried to talk him into leaving someone up. When he got angry and cursed us we figured he was the boss and went to bed. I didn't like it but I was still just a SP4, who was I to argue?

The next morning the DivArty test team came in and found everyone asleep. They began picking up weapons left and right from sleeping soldiers. My M203 grenade launcher was snatched from my vehicle while I was underneath the truck in the mud, getting it ready for the vehicle inspection later that morning. I had placed it in what I thought was a safe place to keep it clean because they were supposed to be inspecting weapons.

It was humiliating. To have one's weapon stolen is the unforgivable sin in the Army. There is no excuse. I had an idea which of the evaluators had done it. I wanted to go over to his jeep and snatch him out of it. But that would have done no good, and I sensed our battery was in enough trouble already without me hospitalizing one of their evaluators. I didn't know they had grabbed some twenty other weapons that morning while the guys were sleeping. They couldn't have gotten mine from me when I slept, because I usually had mine tucked inside my sleeping bag with me to prevent such a thing. The only thing to do was to report my missing weapon to Top.

Top was still drunk and incoherent when I tried to report my weapon stolen. He kept asking me why I hadn't reported it to him. I

---

[64]ADMIN- in the field, this means a unit is in relaxed posture, as opposed to "tactical" in which a unit is kept at full combat readiness, with listening posts, and guards up at all times. However, it is common military sense that someone should be up at all times. Even in garrison, there is always someone up to make sure no one is murdering anyone, stealing anything, or just answer the phones. At the company level, these are called Charge of Quarters (CQ), at higher levels Staff Duty Officers (SDOs), or Staff Duty NCOs (SDNCOs).

[65] Yeah, it DOES seem like I had a knack for being in the right place at the right time – or the wrong place at the wrong time; something like that...

kept telling him it had just happened and I was reporting it now. I was already angry over the weapon and angry at Top because Vinnie and I had tried to warn him not to let everyone sleep the night before.

CPT Hendrickson was relieved of his command. It didn't seem fair to me at the time, but that's the Army way. Though it was Top's job to oversee battery security in the field, the commander was and is responsible for everything that happens and fails to happen in his battery. It was, for all intents and purposes, the end of his career. I ran into one of our former battery XOs years later at Ft. Bragg. He told me the BC had left the Army after over fifteen years of combined service as an enlisted man and officer. With a black mark like being relieved of command on his record he'd never be promoted, and in the Army it's move up or move out.

My battery suffered over his relief. Sure, there were things he did I didn't agree with. There were times he could lose his temper and take it out on a troop. I had born the brunt of that once or twice in my position with battery headquarters in garrison. But he was a leader - and basically a good man.

Perhaps that's what made the ARTEP so painful. We *knew* we were good. It seemed impossible for things to go so bad so quickly.

The battery night have survived that blow, as popular as the BC had been and as painful as had been his relief. Our new BC was CPT White, an experienced officer who had commanded three batteries before ours. He was one of the best commanders under whom I have served. He took us back out in the field a week after we flunked our ARTEP and we passed it.

CPT White had a way of building morale and reinstating our pride and Bravo seemed to be on the mend. We had lost a good commander. Many of us thought it was unfair, but we had received a good commander. We were healing as a unit.

Unfortunately for Bravo Battery, CPT White was due to be promoted to major. He stayed with us for only three months before moving on to become our battalion's S-3, planning and operations officer. That was right after the 5 Day War.

CPT Holloway, another experienced officer who might have helped us, replaced CPT White. Unfortunately, CPT Holloway had come down on one of the Army's post-Vietnam RIF (Reduction in Force) lists. He had been passed over for promotion the third time due to lack of education. They were kicking him out of the Army.

This was a pathetic time for Bravo. Guys would go home on leave and never come back. One guy signed in to an Army base near his hometown and requested compassionate re-assignment. Another kid lived up in North Dakota near the Canadian border. He decided to go to Canada instead of return to the battery. He wrote a buddy of his in the unit that he would walk across the border to visit his parents whenever he wished. In all, some six guys had gone AWOL the spring and summer of 1977. Top threatened to cancel my summer leave home when I teased him about not coming back.

If a soldier went to the BC with a personal problem, he was likely to hear CPT Holloway say, "I don't know what you're problem is. You ought to see what I've got on me..." Then he'd launch into a monologue of his problems. Indeed, he had many. He had a daughter who was suffering from either Cerebral Palsy or Muscular Dystrophy. I often remember seeing her when the BC's family stopped by the unit and wondering what would happen to her if her daddy couldn't get a job with decent medical benefits after he was out of the Army.

Sitting in the orderly room, I watched many poor soldiers leave his office shaking their heads, their problems no closer to being solved than when they walked in.

Top was no help. Top was of the school that said, "If the Army wanted you to have a wife, they'd have issued you one." He himself was doing a "separated" tour in Germany. He had left his wife in the States while he went overseas. He told me he liked it better that way, he could concentrate on soldiering.

"Sure Top!" I thought, "That's what I want to do when I get married, leave my wife at home while I go off for years at a time! 'Less arguing that way!"

It was like the powers that be couldn't do enough to poor Bravo. They had taken an excellent First Sergeant and replaced him with an alcoholic. Then, they relieved a great commander, replaced him with another great man to lift our spirits. This only made it hurt worse when they replaced him with a broken man so burdened by his own cares he couldn't bring us out of our valley.

In October 1977 we got hit by an "extra" Graf for 1977. We usually made two Graf trips a year – once in the spring for our Battalion ARTEP and another in the fall for our Battery ARTEPs. Somehow the powers that be had scraped up enough money to splurge on a third trip that year – maybe we hadn't spent all our training money that year.

I had thought I was done with Graf. I didn't really mind

going, there were good things about getting all the guys together in barracks for a period of time – and we were the FIELD Artillery. But I thought I'd done my part and was preparing to go home.

There was a barren flat section of the training area we nicknamed "the desert." Dominating this section was the ruins of a 9th or 10th Century church – Hofenoh Church. There was a survey control point (a known grid position we used to start our surveys from) near the church. We usually ended up at the church at least once during each field problem. I would go to the facility and write my name along with others listing the date and which Graf I had, such as "Woody – April 1976 – 2 Down 3 to Go!" Counting down the five Grafs (trips to Graf) a guy with 2 ½ years should have had to make. Not even two months before I had triumphantly marked "September 1977 – Last Graf – Eat Your Liver Crutes!!!"

Now our battalion was given a third Graf this year. I would get six. What was worse was I couldn't find a Flippy Rubber to mark this Graf on my Ear Plug holder.[66] As I was short and had requested to go back to a gun the month before and the BC needed a driver I got shanghaied into being the Commander's Driver my last Graf. In garrison it was easy duty; in the field it meant long hours and little sleep. But I managed to make a second final trip to the shrine on the hill outside the church and scribble one more message: "Woody – November 1977 – Sixth Graf! Screwed again!"

One night during that last Graf CPT Holloway and I were sitting in a position waiting for the guns to join us.[67] It was quiet. During these times we would talk. I enjoyed talking to him. In spite of his problems and shortcomings as a commander I believe he was a good man, an intelligent man. I couldn't help but think the Army was making a mistake in throwing him away.

I had met a fellow once who had served under him in

[66] Flippy Rubbers – Grafenwoehr, Germany was home to Lowenbrau Grafenwoehr, arguably the best beer brewed by that company. One of the reasons it was so good, many argued was the fact it was sold in re-usable bottles with a flip top cap ("Flippy") that were sealed with a rubber gasket. When I was in Germany Soldiers marked their time in Germany by stretching a "Flippy Rubber" around either their cigarette lighters or the round earplug holders we were required to attach to our uniforms, either by the left breast pocket button of our fatigue shirts or left epaulet of our field jackets in cold weather. On a previous Graf (I think Spring 77, the same Graf the BC got relieved) we discovered Lowenbrau had changed its bottle to a more modern vacuum seal cap. No more flippies. I'd had a few stowed, most guys did; flippy rubbers had numerous uses – particularly as gaskets in vehicle maintenance. I wouldn't be surprised if every vehicle in our motor pool had a flippy rubber on it somewhere. The maintenance inspectors used to go crazy over them during inspections – but they worked.

[67] In the Field Artillery, the BC (Battery Commander) leads the "Advance Party" to a new firing position to locate, scout out, and secure the new position for the "Main Body" – consisting of the guns and the rest of the battery. As a surveyor I was usually part of the Advance Party.

Vietnam. He told me how lucky we were to have a great commander like him. I didn't say anything to him, but at the time I couldn't help wondering if we were talking about the same guy. It was during this field problem, during lulls in activity when we talked, that I'd get a glimpse of the man he had been before his life fell apart. Then, one night he reminded me of how broken he was.

"You know, Wood," he told me that night, "the Army promotes mediocrity.

"You don't want to do something poorly," he continued, "that will ruin your career. By the same token, if you do something really well, they'll want you to do it again and again and again until you're completely burned out. The first time you falter, they'll chew you up and spit you out." he went on to talk about how his old battery used to do salutes really well. The next thing he knew they didn't have a single holiday off because they were always being called upon to fire the guns on the Fourth of July and so forth. It made them wish they had never been born.

"So what you want to do," he concluded, "is just enough to get by."

I had to admit that, from a certain perspective, he had a point. I thought back to when Bravo had been salute battery. Bravo held the guns proudly for three years. During those three years we always had to provide salute details to fly all over Europe to fire salutes on holidays. When I reported to Bravo some of our guys had just flown back from Washington, DC, where they had fired a salute on the Fourth of July.

I remembered how one man had cost us our packs during my first Graf.

I thought of how our previous battalion commander, LTC Walters, had used us in his climb up the career ladder by volunteering us for every special test or task that came along. We aced every test they threw at us. As I've said, in 1976 we were rated the best 8-inch battalion in Europe. For the eighteen months he commanded us, we never got a break. It was always something new to do, another evaluation.

We somehow got picked for a Department of Defense Nuclear Weapons Inspection right after we got back from the Graf we were named best in Europe. All leaves were cancelled while we spent the summer preparing for the test. We aced it. In the fall there was the AGI.[68] We were working sixteen to twenty hour days

---

[68]AGI - Acronym for the annual Adjutant General's Inspection or AGI. It was also called an "IG inspection," after the Inspector General, whose office had the responsibility for

getting everything cleaned up and ready for the annual "dog and pony show."

About a month before the AGI (about October 1976) we got pulled to go for two weeks to pull guard at Miesau Ammo Dump, the largest ammo dump in the world. Just about every troop in Bravo was pulled for the duty, along with large chunks of the rest of the battalion. We took that in stride, after all, units rotated that duty and it was just our turn. Then the First Sergeant we had at the time let it be known he had volunteered the battery to take the majority of the duty to get us all out of the barracks so he and his handpicked detail could get the barracks ready for inspection. I was kind of ticked over this because I had been Training NCO for over a year, though still only a PFC (the Army had frozen promotions to E-4 just as I became eligible – post Vietnam budget cuts) and I needed the time I'd be spending on guard duty getting the Training Room ready for inspection – not that I needed much time, I have always been a firm believer in keeping up to date on your work an never falling behind. I managed to have a "close out"[69] inspection but it was no thanks to Top.

A side note here, if I may. The guys got so ticked over that a bunch smuggled a footlocker full of booze on one of the five – ton trucks we were riding to Miesau. Bottle after bottle was passed around. By the time we got to Miesau there were several totally smashed. I guess I was fortunate I had a high tolerance for adult beverages because our Battery XO said anyone who was too drunk to pull duty that night would get an Article 15. Three guys took busts over that trip.

I was able to pull my duty, but believe me, I slept well the next morning when I was off my shift and had eaten a good breakfast.

Then right after that, during Christmas holidays when we were supposed to be standing down, we got plugged for a general alert and ammo upload. We were to go to our ammunition holding point at Friedberg and draw our entire basic load of ammunition to see how long it would take us to do it in time of war. We did it in less than twelve hours. LTC Walters told us we had broken a

---

conducting it. It was a general inspection, which was held yearly. Everything was inspected. All administrative files in a unit, supply records, barracks, equipment, vehicles, even in ranks personnel inspections were held. Everything was checked for accountability serviceability, accuracy, and cleanliness. In this way the Army made sure that at least once a year everything was up to standards. Failing an IG inspection was a major catastrophe that could get a unit's entire chain of command relieved.

[69] "Close out."

USAREUR record. We were in the Francois Kaserne Theater when he broke the news. He stood on the stage and ripped open his shirt in his trademark imitation of Superman. Underneath, there was a battalion T-shirt with our battalion emblem of a Jolly Roger type skull and cross cannons on the chest. The battalion went crazy cheering wildly with enthusiasm.

Then, word filtered down through the grapevine from LTC Walter's driver that we'd been used. LTC Walters had volunteered our battalion for the ammo upload, just as he had volunteered us for every other special test and mission we had been put through. He had taken the ammo mission from the commander of the 2-27th FA and bet the DivArty[70] Commander a bottle of scotch we'd break the old record. We did. I pulled a muscle in my back standing in the bed of a 5-ton truck catching 200 lb howitzer projectiles as they were pushed up the ammo racks and stacking them in the truck.

The next morning when we woke up we discovered about a foot of snow had fallen. Too tired to pitch tents, most of the guys just laid out their sleeping bags on the ground somewhere they hoped was being safe from being run over in the dark and went to sleep. I remember being wakened first and being barely able to move from the stiffness in my back and hollering at my buddies. All I could see was the freshly fallen snow; there were a few snowdrifts. I still smile at the memory of the sight of the snowdrifts beginning to move and my buddies crawling out of their sleeping bags. I remember heads popping out of the drifts and hearing the guys cuss wearily at the snow.

My back continued to act up during my time in the Division. It bothers me to this day.

The news we'd been used killed morale in the battalion. After that, we didn't cheer when the colonel gave his "death dealers" spiel. We were played out. But he didn't seem to care, his tenure as commander was ending. He was promoted to full colonel the day he changed command. We felt we had been used to get his promotion.

I felt sorry for his successor, LTC McCoy. There may be those who disagree, but I believe he inherited a unit whose spirit was broken. Many of the guys didn't even have enough spunk left in them to complain. When soldiers are too sorry to even complain you know you've a morale problem.

Sitting in the jeep on a Papa Alpha (Position Area) in Grafenwoehr on that cold October night, I could see CPT Holloway's point. At the same time, I felt sorry for my unit. That kind of mentality would not save my battery. What makes an Army unit (or any organization) a great unit is a desire for excellence on the part of every soldier in that unit. That attitude has to start from the top.

Poor CPT Holloway had had the desire for excellence beaten out of him. He was a defeated man, commanding a defeated battery.

There's one story that stands out in my mind from that last Graf that symbolizes the state of my battery – and maybe the Army at that time:

We were over off the main tank trail. If I remember correctly it was at the western edge of the training area between Main Post and the turn-off to Vilseck, where there was another kaserne and several US Army schools.

We were practicing a simulated nuke mission (the same one that had cost us the packs over two years before). The round had been loaded and we were ready to fire. I was sitting in my position in the BC's jeep monitoring our radios (the BC had two). As I recall, we were on the battalion command frequency and the battery fire control frequency.

Well, it's the last day of this particular field problem and this is supposed to be our last mission. I'm looking forward to getting back and getting a shower – even though we pulled Camp Kasserine (tent city) for the second time that year (we'd been there in March). Kasserine was next door to the post garbage dump and across the hill from the Graf Impact Area, where all the artillery rounds landed. Every now and again a round would fall short or overshoot and hit uncomfortably close to camp. I'd heard a story of an HE round hitting the camp one day years before. I know the previous March a German 175mm round fell short and landed about 100 yards from our motor pool while we were in the rear for a day of maintenance. When we crawled from under our jeep we found shell fragments scattered around the area. We had to turn in some of our tents for exchange (DX) because of the holes from the shrapnel of the round.

I'm just glad it wasn't closer.

We were just about to fire when the mission got called off. Now the crew had to "punch" the round and turn it in. The round wouldn't punch.

So I'm watching the show of this howitzer crew trying to punch that simulated nuclear round from the tube from my jeep when all of a sudden from my "command" radio I hear a snickering.

"Heh, heh, heh..."

By now the crew has given up trying to punch the round, the BC, XO, and Chief of Firing Battery are over there discussing what to do.

Over the radio, *"Heh, heh, heh..."*

What the heck is going on here? I ask myself.

"Look at that behind, heh, heh, heh..."

The battery command decides to try and punch the round out of the tube by pushing the rammer staff up against one of the many pine trees in the position area.

"I think I've been in the field too long... heh, heh, heh..."

By this time I've recognized the voice, it's the voice of SFC Brimley our Battalion Fire Direction Chief. I can hear the sound of tracked vehicle noises in the background. Evidently SFC Brimley is in the FDC track riding along a tank trail and talking on his CVC (Combat Vehicle Communication) helmet to his crew, unaware he is hooked into the command radio net and broadcasting to the battalion.

"Heh, heh, heh..." Brimley goes on to graphically depict his admiration for one of his FDC crew's bottom unaware anyone and everyone on the net can hear him. He's obviously joking – at least I hope so...

By this time a couple guys who are uninvolved in the simulated nuke round fiasco have gathered around the jeep and are enjoying the entertainment. I idly wonder if one of Brimley's guys has plugged him in to command on purpose...

Meanwhile, the gunners have driven their gun, the old M110 short-barreled 8 – inch self-propelled howitzer up to the tree with the barrel and the metal rammer staff pushed against the trunk of a thick pine. At the command the driver moves the gun forward.

Brimley is getting graphic by now. We are so close to the Czech border – and Soviet/Warsaw Pact troops we have often picked up their military signals. I wonder if anyone on the other side is hearing and understanding this – and what they are making of it.

Instead of pushing the round out of the tube, the gun has pushed the rammer staff through the trunk of the tree. Another idea is tried. While some guys try to recover the staff from the tree (and fail), someone comes up with the idea to raise the tube (gun barrel) as high as it will go and run the gun up and down the position area in the hope of jiggling the round loose.

While I'm watching the spectacle of the gun bouncing back and forth with and elevated tube (and wondering how long the hydraulics on the elevation mechanism will last) I hear the voice of the battalion commander on the command net demanding to know who the blankety – blank is violating radio procedures (I'm thinking he's violating a couple himself). At about that time the suspension on the howitzer breaks, leaving the gun in an elevated position.

Ultimately, someone gets the bright idea to call Emergency Ordinance Disposal (EOD), which in my humble opinion should have been done in the first place. A guy comes out, fills the tube with water, drops a small piece of C-4 plastic explosive down the tube, walks off a few paces, and ignites it. With a muffed "poof" the round is loosed and drops harmlessly into the well of the gun where the tube recoils when fired.

Simple.

That evening at chow, when the battalion is back in the rear, everyone busts out laughing when SFC Brimley enters the mess hall. I wonder if he ever lived that one down.

We never did get that rammer staff out of that tree. When I was at Bragg in 1980 we had a guy who'd just returned from Germany. He told me the staff was still in that tree.

Somehow, that crazy day in the field – maybe the last day of my last field problem of my last Graf (if I remember correctly) somehow illustrates for me what was going on in my unit – maybe the Army and military as a whole in that crazy post-Vietnam era.

Chapter 10
Just When I thought it couldn't get Any Worse...

Soldier, soldier don't feel blue, Frankenstein was ugly, too.
Soldier, soldier don't feel blue, my recruiter screwed me, too!
(Anonymous Army Marching Cadence)

It was about that time (late summer and fall of 1977) I found myself in the middle of a feud between my best friend and the First Sergeant. Vinnie Sarducci was, and remains, one of the closest friends I'd ever had. Elle, his girlfriend, who hailed from Essex, England, had to be one of the most patient women on the face of this earth to put up with the two of us. Particularly considering the clash of cultures between her, a refined, educated Englishwoman, and the American military environment in which she found herself.

"You two are dangerous together," she would say. "Vinnie gets a hair-brained idea and Woody figures out how to pull it off!"

It was true; we pulled some of the craziest stunts just for the thrill of it. One of our favorite pastimes was playing "base security check."

It all started one morning when Vinnie got in an argument with Top after pulling Charge of Quarters (CQ)[71] the night before. Top used to like to play games in letting the CQs off in the mornings when he came in. He'd give the CQ a list of things for the CQ's assistant, called a "runner" to accomplish at night when everyone was asleep. In the morning, nothing was ever done to his satisfaction and the poor CQ and his runner wouldn't get off until things passed his inspection.

On the morning in question, he berated Vinnie because he hadn't emptied a trashcan outside the barracks. When Vinnie tried to explain he let his runner go to breakfast and was going to have him do it when he got back, Top said he didn't want to hear any lousy excuses from a sorry NCO.

Vinnie had served six years in the Marine Corps; three and a half of those years had been spent in Vietnam in Marine Force

---

[71] Charge of Quarters (CQ)- In the Army you NEVER put everyone to sleep, even in garrison, someone stays up to answer the phones and stand watch over the rest of the company, usually a sergeant, called the Charge of Quarters, with an enlisted man. At higher levels such as battalion and above, a Staff Duty Officer (Lieutenant or Captain) stands watch with a Staff Sergeant or Sergeant First Class.

Recon. That's the Marine Corps' Special Forces. He had risen from the rank of PFC (in the Marine Corps that's E-2) to Gunnery Sergeant (E-7) in those years. He had a chest full of decorations, several of which carried the little brass Vs, which denote the medal was awarded for valor, a courageous act in the face of the enemy.

When Top questioned Vinnie's ability as a soldier over a lousy trashcan, he exploded, "Lousy NCO! Why I've got more medals for valor than you have on your entire stinking chest! Lousy NCO... I'm not the one who got drunk and pulled in the perimeter and got the BC relieved!"

"What do you mean I got the BC relieved?" Top demanded.

"You were drunk as a skunk that night and told everyone to go to bed, even when Woody and I tried to talk you out of it-"

"You didn't have no outpost set up-"

"We sure did, didn't we, Woody?" I had just come through the door from breakfast.

"What?" I wasn't quite sure of what I was getting myself into here.

"Didn't we have a perimeter set up?" Vinnie said, "We had a hasty perimeter set up!"

"What kind of junk is a hasty perimeter?" Top asked, "Where'd you get that from?"

"Look it up in the FM 100-5!" I think Vinnie was blowing smoke here, "Didn't we have a perimeter, Woody?"

Both men were looking at me, expecting an answer. I looked at Top sadly; I really didn't want to be drawn into this. I liked Top, but Vinnie was my friend, and the truth was the truth. I'd never heard of a "hasty perimeter" but I knew we'd been cursed and ordered to stand our positions down.

"It's true, Top, we had a machine gun post flanked by two rifle positions with a listening post further out."

Top looked at me, glared at Vinnie, and walked into the orderly room without a word. I had caught the tail end of the argument. I half expected Top to have Vinnie up on charges for insubordination. The only reason I can figure why he didn't is because Vinnie was telling the truth.

I dreaded going to work that day. As I said before, in garrison I worked in the orderly room. Top was in a bad mood for the rest of the day, but he didn't seem to hold it against me. Vinnie was another story. For the next year Top made Vinnie's life miserable. He brought him up on one bogus Article 15 charge after another.

Vinnie had spent his time between the Marines and the Army earning a masters degree in corporate law. I asked him what on earth he was doing in the Army as a cook. He told me that if he had taken the bar exam his father had almost demanded that he go with him into the family business. He didn't want any part of the family business, so he joined the Army to avoid being disrespectful to his father. He had worked his way through law school as a chef in fancy restaurants. At least the Army was taking advantage of some his peculiar abilities.

At the time, Vinnie wasn't working in the mess hall. With his training and education, CPT Hendrickson didn't want to "waste him as a 'spoon'." Vinnie was put in the Battery Survey Section, which needed an E-5 sergeant, since our previous E-5 had gone AWOL. There, Vinnie's intelligence would be put to good use as he OJT 'd (On the Job Trained) for a surveyor's MOS.

Vinnie waged a legal war of wits with the Battery chain of command. With his knowledge of law and the UCMJ, the Uniform Code of Military Justice, Vinnie would refuse to sign the Article 15. They were bogus and Vinnie knew no one would want to press an Article 32 hearing on them so the charges would be dropped.

In the meantime, though, Vinnie would be on post or barracks restriction until the matter could be resolved. This was Top's way of punishing him. Vinnie had no intention of letting Top get away with this; he wasn't about to stay away from Elle that long. So we would find ways to "break out" of the kaserne. As I wasn't in trouble I didn't have to break out, but I enjoyed the excitement of jumping the wall.

If we had gotten caught it would have been big trouble for the both of us. That's what made it fun.

Top knew Vinnie was breaking out. He just couldn't catch him. One night, he had the CQ check up on him. Almost the entire battery was in on what we did to the guy on duty.

Word had gotten out that the guy on CQ was the guy who had been narcing on guys in the battery for dope and making me look bad, not only with the BC, but with the rest of the guys. He was the reason the BC had begun nailing so many guys on urinalysis testing. He was seen going into the Battalion Commander's office on more than one occasion, for no particular reason. He was also awfully chummy with the BC. The only thing that kept him alive was the fact that he was married and lived off post.

I'd been asleep when he came in and asked me where Sarducci was, "That's Sergeant Sarducci, to you, Sergeant Jones!" I said.

"Well, where is he?"

"It's not my night to watch him!"

"Well, I'm writing him up for breaking restriction then!"

"Oh, all right," I said, having set the hook, "if you're going to be that way about it, he might be over in Holcombe's room." Then again, maybe not.

For the rest of the night, the guys in the battery sent him from one room to another looking for Sarducci. Unfortunately, he always missed him by a few minutes.

In the morning, Vinnie was called to the orderly room to explain where he'd been all night. Vinnie explained he'd fallen asleep in Baird's room. That was the one room SGT Jones hadn't checked.

After the Article 15 was inevitably dropped and Vinnie was free to come and go until the next time Top tried to burn him, he couldn't rest until he had told everyone how we'd done it. He would write up an official looking report on weaknesses in the security of the kaserne, explaining how terrorists could break in and cause havoc. Vinnie would go on to give advice as to how the deficiencies could be corrected.

The chain of command would be livid, but there was nothing they could do about it except close up the hole in security. The next time Vinnie found himself on restriction we'd have to find another way out. That was part of the fun.

In a way, Vinnie and I were doing the battalion a favor when we spotted breaches in their security. At least, that's what we told Elly with a wink of the eye. That was the way it was with Vinnie and me.

And security was a problem in Germany at the time. It seems most folks believe that terrorist acts against the United States began on September 11, 2001. Those of us who served in Europe during the Cold War know better.

Terrorism has been a real problem to USAREUR[72] dating back to the seventies. There were all sorts of anarchistic terrorist groups such as the Red Army Faction, also known as the Bader-Meinhof gang. One of their favorite pastimes was machine-gunning wealthy German businessmen.

In late 1976 there was a big concern over nerve gas the Red Army Faction stole from our ammo dump at Miesau. The training

---

[72] USAREUR- United States Army Europe

filters in our protective masks were replaced with actual filters in case we got hit.

When I visited the Bonn, the old West German capital in December 1977, it was like visiting a city under siege. Armored cars armed with machine guns patrolled Embassy Row. The embassies all had barbed wire and armed guards. The police in train stations and airports all over Germany- all over Europe, for that matter-carried sub-machine guns. This was because of the terrorist threat.

Another favorite pastime of the terrorists was calling in bomb threats to U.S. Army facilities to protest the American presence in Germany. For some reason, whenever there was a bomb threat I was always awakened to organize the search for the bomb in the battery area until the BC and First Sergeant arrived. I guess it was because I worked in the orderly room and most of the NCOs lived away.

Eventually, I was even sent to a class to learn how to search for bombs without setting them off. That's a convenient skill to have if you're going to be looking for bombs. I spent many an interesting night carefully opening doors and searching ledges and windowsills and combing the motor pool for bombs. We would sniff out every nook and cranny for a bomb that might or might not be there.

Usually, the bomb threats were hoaxes, but one couldn't take that for granted. Every now and then one would go off, killing and injuring people. My parents' apartment complex got hit with tear gas one time. I barely missed being caught by a bomb at V Corps' Headquarters in Frankfurt on June 1, 1976.

I had been sent on an errand to headquarters in my jeep. I finished my mission and left. As it was lunchtime, I decided to go visit my old high school, down the street from headquarters, and grab a bite at a *schnell-imbiss* on my way out. By the time I would have returned to Hanau, the mess hall would have stopped serving lunch, anyway. I heard the explosion as I pulled out of the parking lot, but associated it with some construction going on down the street.

When I got back, I discovered everyone had been worried about me. The office I had been in had gone up in smoke not five minutes after I left. Several people had been killed and injured. My unit, hearing the news and not being able to get a positive ID on any of the victims had been afraid I was among them.

When I explained what happened, everything was all right. The BC, CPT Kowalski, and Top Flick had been worried. "It's nice to know someone cares," I said at that. Their reply is unprintable here. It did feel good to know that your chain of command did care about you.

So, in our own perverse way we *were* doing the unit a favor when we found holes in base security. We just had so much fun doing it.

Through it all, Elle stayed true to Vinnie and loved me like a brother. She had the patience of a saint.

For a while she didn't understand why Vinnie and Top didn't get along. After all, when he came in to the place where she worked and talked to her about how he was trying to help Vinnie be a better soldier he seemed so concerned. Then Top asked her out on a date right after he'd written Vinnie up for another bogus Article 15. She understood what we'd been saying all the time.

During all of his feuding with Vinnie I had been torn between my respect for Top and my friendship with Vinnie. I liked Top, even though I felt he had been primarily responsible for CPT Hendrickson's relief. Top destroyed my respect for him when he asked Elle out. I felt it was taking undue advantage of his position. Still, I was a soldier, and I had to respect his rank and position and had a job to do.

Top didn't seem to hold my friendship with Vinnie against me, though he let me know he felt Vinnie was a bad influence on me. Perhaps it appeared that way to him, but I really don't think a person can blame anyone else for his or her actions. I never did anything I really didn't want to do at the time, right or wrong. I can only blame myself for my actions and their consequences.

Top and I got into it over a soldier's paycheck. In late 1976 the Army decided to streamline its administrative organization. All battery/company clerks and training rooms were to be consolidated at the battalion level. Until the system was completely worked out, I was moved into the orderly room and took over most administrative duties at the battery level. I was at one time the battery training NCO, the battery clerk, the battery mail clerk, the drug and alcohol abuse counselor/administrator, as well as working in the battery survey section out in the field.

One of my duties consisted of picking up the battery's paychecks on payday and making sure the troops got paid. The Army had stopped paying soldiers cash shortly before, and now issued paychecks.

We'd had a guy in the unit who had been transferred for his own safety. He had gotten beaten up over a redbelly[73] party that had

---

[73]It used to be a form of initiation to give new soldiers, "crutes," redbellies. All the "oldtimers," guys who'd been overseas awhile, would line up and slap the victim's bare belly

gotten out of hand when we were at my last Graf. He had come in while we were out in the field and was waiting to join us at Graf when some of the guys left behind, several of whom were short timers who didn't have enough time left in to go to Graf, or were "clearing post" to go home decided to give him a welcome to the unit. He pressed charges against a couple of old-timers, including Hokey the Wolf, who was clearing post getting ready to go home. There had been death threats. The command moved him out of Hanau. No one knew where he was.

Payday came and I found the kid's check in with the others. As no one had told me where he was or what to do with the check, I returned his check back to Battalion personnel, S-1. This was in accordance with Army Regulations. One can get in real trouble with other folks' paychecks in the Army.

When Top found out I had turned the kid's paycheck in he cussed me out and told me to go get it back. It turned out the kid was coming for his check that weekend. Had I known this, I would have hung on to his check. I had locked up a couple checks in the battery safe that belonged to men who were off at school. When they came back that weekend I'd give them their checks. As it was, I had followed regulations to the T and had been cussed out for it.

Things got worse when battalion wouldn't give the check back. They would get in trouble for returning it. Top fired me from all my duties in the orderly room, telling me to report back to survey.

That was it! I was being fired for following regulations? I had sat back the last year and watched violation after violation of Army regulations and procedure and held my peace, did my job, and tried to sweat it out until I could go home. In the meantime, I had watched my battery be run down the tubes, its morale be destroyed, and its combat readiness waste away to nothing. We had just failed our IG inspection. This was the final straw.

I reached into my desk drawer and brought out a notebook in which I had been keeping records of everything that had gone on over the last year (I was covering myself if things blew up). I took it over to see the Command Sergeant Major.

I told the Sergeant Major what was going on in the unit and what had just happened to me, "Sergeant Major, on a personal level, I really don't care about being relieved. I've got less than a month left in this Army-"

"Less than a month?" he said, surprised, "You're getting

---

one time for each month they'd been in Germany. When it was over, the guy was initiated and one of the guys. Eventually, he'd be allowed to give redbellies.

out?"

"Yes, Sergeant Major, I've had it. I can't stand to see what's happening to the Army."

The Sergeant Major looked sad at that. I thought I saw tears in his eyes, "I'm seeing a lot of good soldiers getting out of the Army, these days," he said, "If all the good soldiers get out, all we'll have left are the bad ones..."

"But, Sergeant Major," I said, "what's a man to do when the bad soldiers won't let the good soldiers soldier?"

I handed him the book. He looked at it, read a few pages. I saw sadness creep over him. He had served with the 40th Field Artillery in Vietnam during the 1969 siege at Khe Sanh and earned the Naval Unit Citation for its support of the Marines there; one of the few, if only Army units to carry that award. He wore the ribbon as a personal decoration. He had been First Sergeant of Bravo during its heyday, "What are you going to do with this?" he asked.

"I hope I've done all I need to do, Sergeant Major." I said, "I'm not out for vengeance, I'm just concerned about the battery, I'm just sorry I haven't done anything sooner."

After that, the Sergeant Major and I talked about my future. I mentioned some ideas Vinnie and I had been kicking around about putting our military skills to use overseas. He gave me the address of some companies in the Middle East.

I've had time to think of his words. They seemed so simple at the time. They were profound. It was true, it *is* true, when all the good soldiers leave the Army, all you'll have left are the bad.

It's the same with any organization. Any organization is only as good as its people.

At the time my feelings were too hurt to listen. I was young and wild, but no one could say I wasn't a good soldier. I had worked hard and done well in every area I'd been assigned. I had worked for and received a Secondary MOS of 82C, Field Artillery Surveyor.

I felt I had been treated badly by the battery. I'd had a conversation with the Personnel Sergeant a few days earlier; I had learned Top had gone along with Romanelli in passing me over for promotion to sergeant the previous summer because he said he needed me in the Orderly Room. This was insult to injury because I had requested more than once to be returned to the guns because I feared my chance for advancement was being hurt. I was told I was needed in Survey and the other positions and that it wouldn't hurt my advancement. So I stayed. Actually, it never occurred to me to not do the job. After all, I was a soldier.

To top it off, I discovered that a letter of appreciation I received shortly before leaving Germany had been downgraded from an Army Commendation Medal recommended by CPT White. By that time, the mediocre final performance evaluation I received from Top was expected in light of our falling out. MSG Clinton, our personnel sergeant, who had been our First Sergeant before Top, told me to rebut that. I should have. Later, I would regret not answering it. At the time, all I wanted to do was go home.

It may sound funny, but through it all, I never blamed the Army for what happened. I still believed in the system, even if individuals abused it. I also had to admit, in my honest moments that some of my problems were self-inflicted. I had yet to learn to choose my battleground wisely. As the pastor who discipled me later on was fond of saying, "You can be right in the wrong way and you might as well be wrong."

The Sergeant Major's words would stay with me. Was I running out on the Army when it needed me most? I couldn't say. I knew I couldn't change things where I was. Maybe if the re-up NCO hadn't told me that no matter what I re-enlisted for I'd have to spend another six months in Bravo and finish a three year tour before I could go anywhere I might have been more disposed to stay in. I still loved the Army. I still loved being a soldier – even if every day wasn't filled with giggles and joy.

If all the overseas opportunities fell through, I reasoned, maybe I could go to college. If that worked out, perhaps I could come back as an officer. Maybe then I could make a difference. I had always been told I'd be a good officer...

I remember looking at the lights of Frankfurt for the last time as my bird took off. I was leaving Germany, but a part of it would live on in me. After all, I had grown into manhood in the Fatherland. GI German, as GI Vietnamese, permeates my vocabulary, I still use expressions like *Mox Nix (Machts Nichts)* – "it doesn't matter"; or *was ist loss?* - "What's up?" in my daily vocabulary, though admittedly, carefully as most folks with whom I associate rarely know what I'm talking about.

Chapter 11
My Break in Service

Funky, funky boogalloo, marching down the avenue
Duffle bag in my hand, I'm gonna be an Army man
Ain't no sense in looking down, ain't no discharge on the ground,
Ain't no sense in going home, Jody's got your gal and gone
Ain't no since in feeling blue, Jody's got your sister too
Ain't no sense in lookin' back, Jody's drivin' your Cadillac
(Anonymous Army Marching Cadence)

My experiment with civilian life lasted just under three years. It was the first time since I was old enough to carry one that I didn't have a military ID card. The funny thing was, even then I wasn't really a true civilian. I had a three-year commitment in the Individual Ready Reserve. This meant I was still a reservist, subject to recall in case of a national emergency. Every so often, I would receive an individual data sheet to confirm I was still alive and available if needed. I could have done two weeks active duty stints in the summer had I chosen to.

Mom and Dad were in Alabama when I came home in 1978. It seemed as good a place to start over as any. So, after being delayed three days on the east coast by the largest blizzard to hit in twenty years, I made my way home to Montgomery.

I lazed around on unemployment benefits for a few weeks before boredom set in. I didn't know how long it would take for Vinnie's and my plans to get overseas work to pan out so I took a job surveying to kill time while waiting.

It was great work for a single guy, we travelled a lot – you have to go where the work was. I couldn't see myself making a career of it, though one could make pretty good money at it – particularly if you got your license. But living Monday through Friday (at the very least) on the road, coming home on the weekends didn't seem the life for a family man. Even the Army typically gave one more time with your family.

Meanwhile, back in Germany, Top finally managed to bust Vinnie. He lost a stripe. Without anyone to watch his back he'd been set up and couldn't get out of it. He told me later that, as he was signing his Article 15, he looked up at the BC and asked, "Does this mean I'm off the promotion list?"

I heard through Vinnie that my other roommate, Miller had also left Bravo. I haven't mentioned Miller before, but I believe he merits a passage before we move on.

Miller was another cook; an SP5/E5. Upon arrival in the Unit he volunteered for Night Baker in the consolidated *kaserne* mess hall. This meant he stayed up all night baking the pastries for the next day and was off during the day. This also meant our room (which had been christened "The Swamp" by the guys in the battery) rarely was inspected during the week. No one wanted to risk Miller's wrath by waking him up during the day. Not that any of us were worried about inspections. I believe anyone could have come in at any time and inspected and we would have passed – unless the inspector didn't want us to. I've learned from being on both ends of inspections one can always find something wrong with almost anything if one wants to.

Miller had been an infantry squad leader in Nam when his squad got ambushed going through a village. As I recall the story he told, he'd lost two guys and his RTO was shot up and bleeding out. The radio had caught a few rounds, too and was out of action..

He realized if his squad stayed in that position eventually his RTO would die and he'd lose several more troops so he ordered his troops, who were under orders not to fire, to respond. They killed several enemy troops and managed to drive the enemy (can't remember if they were NVA Regulars or Viet Cong) back.

When he returned from the patrol and filed his report he was informed he was up on charges for violating the Rules of Engagement (ROE) for that area. That village had been declared a "No Fire Zone" requiring Field Grade (or above) permission to return fire. He was facing an Article 15.

But his Company Commander considered the circumstances under which he had violated the ROE and decided to cut Miller some slack. Miller's orders for promotion to SSG/E6 were on his desk. The CO tore them up. Upon Miller's return to the States he was reclassified a cook. When I met him several years later he was still an E-5.

Miller had been watching our battalion mess sergeant, who was also NCOIC of the consolidated mess hall (our battalion being the largest separate unit on the *Kaserne*) selling food meant for the troops out the back door of the mess hall to the Black Market.

He was keeping a notebook with names, dates, and data on what was taken out on what day by whom. He had even taken pictures of German citizens hauling out sides of beef and loading them into their cars. I remember one series of pics where the German was actually smiling and waving at the camera.

No one really wanted to mess with Miller. They all knew he'd been on one patrol too many in Nam. Word got out that he, too, was a black belt – his art was Tae Quon Do.

Miller told us one night sitting in the mess hall drinking coffee one night while waiting for some cakes to bake that his uncle had left him a big ranch in Australia.

"What are you doing here?" Vinnie asked.

"I ask myself that myself," he said. "One of these days one of these [jokers] are going to do something and I'm gonna disappear."

Shortly, after I left, Miller went AWOL. No one thought much of it beyond the typical AWOL (remember, there had been a rash of AWOLs in the unit) until the investigations hit. It turned out Miller had sent copies of all his evidence to just about anyone he thought might be interested in the corruption in the mess hall before he left.

I figure he had some German friends in Ansbach, Germany, near where he'd been stationed before. He'd laid low with them before heading to Australia and his ranch. I never have discovered or heard what the trigger was for him to split like that.

As I said, Vinnie and I had been making our plans for after we got out of the Army in 1978. The war business wasn't so good in America, but it was great in other parts of the world.

The father of a high school friend, a retired first sergeant, who had taken a job working for a government in Africa trying to suppress a revolution. He had taken a liking to me. When I returned to Germany, I looked the family up to discover my friend had returned to America. His family became like a second family to me.

When my friend's dad came up for retirement in 1976 he told me of his plans. He told me if I was interested when my hitch was up to let him know. By then, he hoped to be in a position where he could help me land in a good spot wherever he was.

When I was getting short in 1977 I got a letter from him telling me the offer was still good and all I had to do was say the word. By that time, Vinnie and I were steadfast partners in whatever we did, so I consulted him. I wrote back about Vinnie, figuring he'd have no problem with his combat record. Poor Elle, when we sprang our idea on her she just rolled her eyes.

A few weeks before I got out I took a trip to Bonn, the capital of West Germany, to see about visas and the like. While there, I stopped off at a couple of other consulates to see about other opportunities in case this one fell through.

I was surprised when our Battalion Command Sergeant Major tried to help me. This was the same Sergeant Major who had testified for Phillips. It turned out he had a high opinion of me, in spite of our being on "opposite" sides of the case.

Shortly after I returned to Alabama, where my parents were now stationed, I got a nice letter. It was from the country's consulate informing me of the many opportunities to be had in their land for young men with my peculiar skills and abilities. It was all very proper. For some reason our government frowns upon foreign countries recruiting soldiers in the U.S.

I hadn't been home too long when the government of that country fell. I received a letter from my friend's dad telling me that it wasn't very safe to be a foreign soldier in that country right now. I never discovered if he got out safely. I haven't heard from him since.

I wasn't without other resources. As I said before, our Command Sergeant Major had given me the address of a company that supplied military experts to foreign countries to help train their armies. The advantage to this was that it was safer. And legal. These trainers were essentially civilian employees. One can lose one's citizenship for serving in a foreign army. I also had been in contact with several overseas corporations investigating work in pipeline security in the Persian Gulf.

Shortly after we had made tentative overtures to work training the Iranian Army, the Shah's government fell. We had another offer to work in Saudi Arabia. By this time I was getting the feeling that job security in this line of work was none too good.

Coincidentally, it was at about this time I gave up the idea of working overseas. I began looking into going to school. At first I didn't have any idea as to what would be my major. All I knew was I had my GI Bill now, so I wasn't going to have to ask anyone for help. I had figured out in the Army that if I was going to get a job with any kind of future in it, I needed all the education I could get. Ever in the back of my mind was the idea I could always go back on active duty – maybe this time as an officer.

The problem was: what did I want to do now that I'd grown up? I had always loved comic books as a kid. I taught myself to draw from my favorite comic books. For no good reason, though, I never took art in high school. Right after leaving the Army, while I was staying with my folks catching my breath, I had killed time completing a comic book. I had created my own characters, written the story, penciled, and inked it. I sent it off to my favorite comic book company just to see what would happen.

As I was trying to figure out what my major in college should be, I got a letter from the comic book company telling me I had a natural talent that merely needed a bit more honing. They encouraged me to get some formal training (I hadn't had any since grade school) and stay it touch, there was a future for me with the company. Maybe he was just trying to be encouraging but that settled it for me, what better way to spend a life than drawing and writing comic books? I started college as an art major.

The next two years were among the best in my adult life. I was spending time with my family and attending school. To make some extra money I started teaching Judo at the local YMCA. My three younger brothers got involved; the club became a family thing. We'd have a great time on the weekends because many of our tournaments were in places such as Panama City or Ft. Walton Beach, Florida. We'd have a tournament in the morning then go to the beach and soak our sore bodies that afternoon at the beach.

If one had looked at my life from the outside, it would have appeared my life was on track. By my second year in college, my Judo program at the YMCA was getting off the ground and I was scouting a location to open a second class. I was consistently making the "Dean's List" at school, and had been elected president of the student art guild. I was appearing as a frequent guest on a local TV show, singing my songs. I wasn't making any money doing that, but I hoped the exposure could open doors elsewhere. Even if the music didn't pan out I was looking forward to a lucrative career in illustration once I completed college. I was building a portfolio to submit to the company when the proper time came. And I was partying every chance I got with an old high school buddy I'd run into whose parents had retired in the Ft. Rucker area.

For the last ten years home had been wherever the Army sent my family or me. True, I had been born, and had spent the majority of my childhood in Illinois, but it was no longer home. I had been gone too long, my old friends and relatives were strangers now. There seemed to be nothing there for me anymore.

According to everything Dad had heard from DA,[74] he was likely to retire at Ft. Rucker. Alabama became home. At least the

---

[74]Department of the Army

family could be together here. A year and a half after I arrived in Alabama, Dad came down on orders for Ft. Richardson, Alaska.

Mom suggested I go to Alaska with them. I could change schools. I asked her what would I do in three years when Dad got orders to come back to the lower forty-eight? I couldn't move around with my family the rest of my life at the whim of the Army. I guess it was time to face the inevitable, as countless other military brats have done.

I stood in the parking lot of a roadside diner on a rainy late September morning and said goodbye to my family. It was just before dawn, the sky was still dark. In a few minutes, the first streaks of gray would appear. I watched them as they took off, headed north on Alabama Highway 231. I was thankful for the time we had shared this last eighteen months. Some of my happiest times were spent with my younger brothers, teaching them Judo, going to tournaments, and just being together. On some nights, if I didn't have a date, I would rather take my kid brothers to a movie or something than cruise the bars. That was over now.

Within a year I had married a girl with two kids from a previous marriage and after a stint drilling with a reserve Supply and Support detachment, and I was back on active duty, bound at last for Ft. Bragg.

I hadn't held out much hope for getting a good assignment as a prior serviceman. I don't know how it is now but back then the Army liked to "punish" guys who'd gotten out. My options were limited.

The fact I'd joined up with a reserve unit and was drilling didn't make the slightest difference to the Regular Army. Talking to the young men and women I've had the pleasure to teach who have entered the service the various branches of the military are practically seamless – at least compared to when I served. The reserve components have become a vital part of the defense structure. Not so in the 70s and 80s.

I was treated on the one hand as a soldier just PCSing (transferring into a new unit) but as a recruit on the other. After two years being out I began losing stripes, one for every six months or a year I stayed out (as I recall); they wouldn't reduce a prior serviceman below PV2 (E-2) and my college would keep me at PFC (E-3) – the same rank the Army gave a recruit with college. So even though I'd been a senior SP4 (E-4) in my reserve unit and had I stayed in the reserve a few months longer would have made SGT (E-

5), I was a PFC with almost six years active duty when I reported to Bragg.

I arrived at the Fayetteville airport late at night. I was surprised to find there was no post shuttle bus to the base. I had left every bit of money with Debbie and the kids, except for five dollars. I figured once I got to Bragg my basic needs would be taken care of – "three hots and a cot." My five dollars wouldn't pay for the cab to post. I was finally able to hitch a ride with an 82nd trooper who was returning to Bragg from TDY (Temporary Duty Assignment). He dropped me off at the 18th Airborne Corps Replacement Detachment. I signed in and was given a bunk.

The next morning I was awakened by the sound of *Reveille*. A few minutes later, I heard the sound of a formation singing cadence as they ran down the street. I smiled at that. I was home.

I had expected to be sent to some sort of in processing station before advancing to my unit. I was in for a surprise. As I had re-enlisted under my old MOS, my assignment was being treated as a regular transfer. When I reported into the 18th Replacement Detachment all they did was issue me my TA-50 (field gear) and update my shot records, giving me two shots in each arm before sending me to my unit.

It was with a mild temperature and sore arms I climbed the steps to the third floor of the barracks building where my battery was located. As I climbed the steps, loaded down with the two duffel bags of field gear, I was greeted by the First Sergeant.

"You need to get a haircut, soldier!" he barked at me before I even got to the top of the stairs.

Great, I didn't even have uniforms yet and he was screaming about a haircut. My hair met reserve standards. But this was Ft. Bragg. Welcome back to the Army.

Top went into the BC's office and asked him if he wanted to see welcome me to the battery.

"Not until he gets a haircut."

It was payday weekend. Welcome to Stateside duty; everyone was gone until Monday. Most of the soldiers in the unit, it turned out, lived within a couple hundred miles' radius of Ft. Bragg and went home at every opportunity. Top said he'd try to get me squared away Monday. In the meantime, I was assigned to a section and given a bunk. I had no blankets or sheets though. The supply room was locked up. A young soldier, who was getting ready to leave for the weekend, loaned me a blanket and pillow to use for the weekend.

It was a long, lonely weekend.

Monday morning rolled around and I still hadn't met my commander. I was quite the topic of conversation in the battery, as I had to fall out for first formation in civilian clothes. Eventually, I got squared away. I got most of my issue. I even got a few bucks in travel pay and per diem to get me by until I got paid. One of the first things I did was get a haircut.

The BC was at the PX barbershop getting his boots shined as I got my hair cut. He said nothing. Then, when the barber was finished and I stood up, he came to me, put his hand out and said, "My name is Captain Crowley, welcome to Bravo!"

I couldn't hide my grin. This guy was a piece of work. I liked him from the start.

My first impression was that my new unit had to be one of the sorriest outfits in the history of organized armies. It was history repeating itself. I remember wondering if I were some sort of jinx. When I arrived, they had just failed two major inspections, an IG and a Corps maintenance inspection in the same week. Poor CPT Crowley had taken over the battery just the week before the inspections. He later told me that the day he learned he was to take over command of Bravo he debated calling DA and asking them if it was a joke.

Though the powers that be didn't hold the failures against him because of his short tenure as commander prior to the inspections, he would be sunk if the battery failed re-inspection. With this in mind, he took drastic measures to ensure Bravo did not fail again.

First, he restricted every soldier in the battery to post. NCOs put up cots in the dayroom and hallways and lived in the barracks. Second, the battery worked in the motor pool up to eighteen hours a day. At eighteen hundred hours (6 PM), the battery would have a work call formation and march back down to the motor pool until ten or eleven o'clock at night. This went on for almost a month.

Though the battery passed their re-inspections, most of the trucks in the unit still weren't up to snuff. During my first trip out to the field we only had two trucks operating with which to tow our howitzers (M114A1 155mm howitzer; towed, affectionately called the "pig-iron") out to the field. The others were "deadlined," that is, out of action for mechanical problems that rendered them unsafe to drive. We ferried our guns out to the field and from position to position. What had been accomplished was that the maintenance problems had been identified, the proper parts had been ordered or work requested. We were covered on paper and the trucks would be fixed as soon as the needed parts came in. CPT Crowley made sure they were.

But until the parts came in – and there was a severe repair parts shortage due to drastic budget cuts in the Defense budget – those trucks would do us no good in moving our guns. And we were the XVIII Abn Corps – supposedly a Rapid Deployment Force unit – among the first to go if a war or conflict broke out anywhere in the world!

Morale was especially low in the unit. It was worse than even my unit in Germany. Situated between Ardennes Street and Gruber Road, we were sandwiched between the 82nd Airborne Division and the Special Forces areas. If we turned left on our morning runs we were subjected to the derision of the 82nd troopers who would call us "legs," a derogatory term for non-airborne personnel. If we turned right, we were in the middle of the green berets, who merely observed us with silent contempt. It was hard to feel much pride in your unit.

I asked myself, was this how bad the Army has gotten in the three years I had been gone? My unit was the supporting artillery for the 82nd, a first line outfit – *the* first line outfit in the Army. Jogging down Ardennes Street into the 82nd Airborne Division area, I was appalled at the sight of the Division barracks with chipped and peeling paint. Going down Gruber Road across Bragg Boulevard was 1st Corps Support Command (COSCOM) which did all the supply and logistical support for the XVIII Airborne Corps. They were still living in World War II barracks that had barely been "modernized" in the thirty-five years since the war. After I'd been at Bragg awhile visited one of the barracks with a neighbor, who was an NCO in one of the COSCOM units one night. I was appalled to see plywood room dividers separating living quarters. In some areas soldiers had hung curtains for privacy in their areas. I shuddered at the thought of what a stray lit match would do.[75] This was at Ft. Bragg, which was supposed to be one of the elite posts in the Army. If we were this messed up what was the rest of the Army like?

It was Jimmy Carter's Army – actually the entire military was in the same shape. Budget cuts, post Vietnam force reductions, the anti-military sentiment that pervaded the country had eroded the

---

[75] I got to see that a few years later when the barracks were destroyed to make way for new construction. We watched one of the barracks be totally consumed in less than two minutes, the wood was so dry.

force quality of the entire defense establishment. Jets were falling out of the sky because they were being forced to fly more hours and lacked spare parts. Mechanics were "cannibalizing"[76] equipment to keep their planes, trucks, and tanks running. Some air squadrons had almost half their aircraft grounded because they had been cannibalized to keep the other aircraft flying. Soldiers, sailors, airmen, and marines were getting killed in accidents caused by fatigue and equipment malfunctions.

The Army hadn't had a decent pay raise in almost four years. I couldn't even get a full issue of field gear from CIF (Central Issue Facility) because the soldiers were taking their gear downtown to the military surplus stores and either pawning or selling their equipment to get through to payday. Theft was rampant in my battery, you couldn't set anything down without it growing legs and "walking off."

My Command Sergeant Major's words in Germany often came back to me, "If all the good soldiers left the Army, all we'll have left are bad ones."

Well, for better or worse, I was back in the Army. I knew there were plenty of good soldiers left in the Army. I realized there were even some great guys in my unit, particularly my Chief, Sergeant Love.

With the election of Ronald Reagan a few days after I reported in to Bragg there was new leadership in Washington who promised to turn things around. I could only pray they would. There was hope.

As for me, I was back in the Army; I had decided I was in for the long haul. I hadn't realized how much I really loved the Army, how much I'd missed it until I woke up that morning at the replacement depot. I'd had three years to chew over what went wrong my first hitch; separate those things I could have done differently from those over which I had no control, and to learn from my mistakes. I would do better this time. I was in for the full twenty now, thirty if I really liked it. I had always tried to be the best soldier I could be. Now I was going to try to be a wiser soldier, too.

My first goal was to get my rank back. As I said, I had lost a stripe as a consequence of staying out too long. Once I got my E-4 back the Army would move my family to Ft Bragg. We could even get housing on base, if we wanted. Hopefully, I could make

---

[76] Cannibalizing equipment is where you take the parts off one broken vehicle and use them to repair other vehicles. Eventually, you hope new parts will be ordered to repair the cannibalized vehicle. If not, you haul the carcass to the junkyard.

Sergeant, E-5 before I implemented my next step, Officers Candidate School. If the Army were to be my career, I would go as far as I could.

I also wanted to go back to Jump School. It was the one thing I had set out to do that I had failed to finish. I also didn't want my failure being used as a rock in my rucksack to keep me out of OCS.

As I made my plans and set my goals I realized if there was one good thing about the situation in this new Bravo, it was that it would be easy to shine. It wouldn't take me long to come to the attention of my chain of command - hopefully in a positive way.

It didn't.

It came about when I had to bring my family up to Bragg earlier than anticipated. I had hoped to wait until I made Specialist (E-4) so I wouldn't be out as much money. I didn't have that luxury.

Mom and Dad had been letting us live in their house outside Rucker for some six months. But they needed to rent the house for more money and take some of the load off them. I was going to have to bring my family up immediately.

I took an advanced pay and an extended weekend pass coinciding with Christmas to get my family up to North Carolina. This put me further in debt, but at least we were together.

The trip back to Bragg was a nightmare. Our car, a 1977 AMC Hornet, wasn't built to haul a heavy load. It struggled along, pulling all we could bring of our family belongings behind. We had left so much behind in Alabama. I hadn't had time or money to store our furniture or do anything with it. The car was greatly underpowered for the job and drinking gas like it was going out of style. Our money was already low; we were coming in on a shoestring. I was depending on getting my next paycheck in the morning to pay the final deposit on the house trailer I had rented so we could move in.

We made it to Ft. Jackson, SC, some one hundred and fifty miles short of Bragg. I knew we weren't going to make it to Bragg. Our tank was near empty again and we were broke. It was late at night. I drove to the post headquarters and signed in with the Staff Duty Officer, explaining our dilemma. He signed me in on his register, arranged for us to be put up at the post guesthouse, and told me he would phone my unit and tell them where I was. This, normally, would cover me and keep me from being reported AWOL.

The folks at Ft. Jackson were great. They put us up in the guesthouse free of charge. The next morning the people at Army

Emergency Relief (AER) gave us some money to make it the rest of the way.

We still almost didn't make it. The Major at AER at Jackson had offered me more cash. I was reluctant to take it. I was grateful enough for the money they had given us. I didn't want to impose. I should have. It turned out we ran out of gas on the other side of Fayetteville from Ft Bragg.

I went over to a beauty shop and asked if I could use their phone to call my unit. When I called I discovered no one was there, they had all come in, been paid, and taken off for the New Years' holiday weekend. As Yogi Bera said, "Déjà vu, all over again." Worse yet, my check was locked up in the unit safe. I wouldn't be able to get it until Monday.

A lady in the beauty shop overheard my conversation and gave us five dollars to make it in to post. I later went back to repay her, but no one knew who she was or how to get up with her.

I discovered when I got to the unit the guy on duty the night before hadn't logged Ft. Jackson's call; otherwise, they would have saved my check for me. I might be in trouble after all.

I was told my Chief of Firing Battery was on duty over at Brigade Headquarters. I went over and explained to him what happened and to see if he could somehow get my check so we could move in to our trailer. He told me he couldn't get me my check, but asked me how much money I needed to get through the weekend. I told him. He reached into his pocket and handed me three one hundred dollar bills.

"You'd better pay me back Monday, Wood," he said with a grin, "or Mama'll come after you. You won't have to worry about me."

When I saw CPT Crowley in the hallway Monday morning, he crowed, "Wrong- as hell! 'Going to Jail!'"

"Maybe not, sir." I said.

"Oh no?" he asked, eyeing me with a raised brow, "Where were you Wednesday?"

"Sir, I signed into Ft. Jackson Tuesday night." I explained the trouble I was having with my car to him and what had happened.

"Pretty slick, eh?" he said, his face fell in mock disappointment. "Where'd you learn *that* trick?" he asked, with grudging admiration.

"Prior service, remember sir? Also, I'm an Army brat."

"Not a brat, too?" He gave me a long appraising look, "You're just full of surprises, aren't you?" He walked off, down the hall, shaking his head, muttering to himself, "Signed in at Ft. Jackson... I'll be... slick..."

A few weeks later I was selected to attend our Brigade's Basic Leadership Course (BLC). I graduated honor graduate, and was promoted to Sp4 shortly after. The plan was definitely coming together.

At the same time, I had to be sad at the irony. If I could have held off a month, the Army would have moved my family free and I'd have been saved the heartburn I endured getting my family up to North Carolina, not to mention the added financial burden of having to pay back the advance pay I had drawn to pay for the move. As it was I was further in debt. There seemed to be no end.

CPT Crowley never ceased to amuse me. He would promote a man in a heartbeat, but bust him back just as quick. We had several guys in the unit who'd been up and down the enlisted ranks several times. He gave one guy an Article 15 for slipping and calling him "Captain Tim" in the mess hall one day. As soon as the guy was eligible he turned around and recommended him for promotion. Everyone in the battery, including the First Sergeant, thought he was crazy. I could see the method to his madness; he was turning the battery around.

One morning, I doodled a cartoon of CPT Crowley on a napkin it the mess hall. The picture had a caricature of CPT Crowley, dressed in a double-breasted Civil War style officer's uniform jacket and boots. On his head was an Army fatigue hat with enlarged captain's bars. He was wearing Lone Ranger type gloves, on the epaulets were skulls and cross cannons. Instead of wire-rim glasses, I substituted super hero type goggles. His left fist was cocked on his hip; his right hand was pointed to the viewer. The caption read something like this, "If you idiots think I'm kidding, I'll have your WIVES in here on Saturday!"

Everybody at the table thought it was funny. One of the gun chiefs, SSG Gonzales asked if he could have it. I said, "Sure."

A few weeks later, I was in CPT Crowley's office. He wanted me to help him put together a battery Field Standard Operating Procedure (FSOP for short). It would be a sort of personal handbook for the soldiers of the battery to carry around in the field with them. He mentioned with my art background he also wanted me to design a cover with an illustration, which would become the battery emblem. It would be based on our nickname, "The Bravo Banshees."

While he was talking, I noticed my cartoon facing me. It was under the Plexiglas dust cover on his desk. He noticed me looking at the cartoon and grinned that grin of his.

"I see you like my artwork, eh?"

"Yes sir, it's quite interesting." I said nonchalantly. It was evident he knew I had done it.

"Yes, the fellow who drew that is obviously quite talented, I believe he caught the real me!"

"I'm sure he'd be quite pleased to hear that, sir."

After I graduated from BLC we spent two months in the field, preparing for our ARTEP. By this time, CPT Crowley's maintenance program was paying off. Every one of our trucks was in top running condition.

CPT Crowley was a ball of energy out in the field. It seemed he never slept. Our First Sergeant, who was about a year from retiring, would come down to the gun line to hide from the BC. He'd say he needed to take a break.

One night, the BC kept the entire battery entertained by giving the Fire Direction Officer (FDO) down the road over the battery intercom system. Our field phones were hooked to speakers so everyone could hear the fire commands as they came from FDC. We all cracked up as the BC questioned the FDO's manhood when he wouldn't call the forward observers to insist we use radar to fire night missions[77] in foggy weather.

That was the night I decided to try out for flight school. We had been scheduled to airmobile into our position that evening. We'd had everything rigged and ready to go; we were in the helicopters, ready to take off, when a bolt of lightening hit nearby and the mission was scrubbed.

The choppers went home, it not being safe to fly in lightening storms. We were left to move overland in the driving rain that came with the lightening.

If that wasn't bad enough, when we pulled into position, our howitzer slid into an old foxhole that hadn't been refilled properly. SSG Love and I were left holding the gun – all 12,488 pounds of it - as the guys all scattered to get out of the way. The trail of the howitzer was about to fall on my leg, which would have crushed it.

[77] In peacetime, for safety purposes, the artillery needs a spotter, a Forward Observer, to call rounds (in combat, we need someone to be our "eyes," too) and observe where they land. In foggy conditions, you normally can't shoot because your rounds can't be spotted. Modern technology has solved that problem by provided radar spotting systems which allow artillery rounds to be tracked electronically by radar. This allows us to shoot in all sorts of weather.

SSG Love hollered for me to jump, he had it. I did. When I was safe, he let go.

We both ended up with hurt backs. I had aggravated the old injury from Germany. SSG Love could barely move. He chiefed from a cot we'd set up for him that evening.

The rain lifted and we were left with a damp, cold, foggy night. We couldn't go to sleep because it was the last night of the field problem and CPT Crowley wanted to shoot all the rounds we had left before we went in so we wouldn't have to turn them in. The FDO was trying to explain that we couldn't shoot because of fog. CPT Crowley wanted to use radar to spot our rounds. The FDO didn't want to wake the radar people.

There's no way I could clean up CPT Crowley's end of the conversation. That was one of his idiosyncrasies; he had to be one of the most profane officers I had ever met. The Army stopped commissioning its officers as officers and gentlemen. CPT Crowley believed it was a good thing because, as he joked, he sure wasn't a gentleman.

Anyway, the conversation went on for about twenty minutes. Finally, CPT Crowley decided to go over to the FDC himself and raise some Cain with the Forward Observers (FOs) to get some radar-guided missions.

As I lay there under the ammo tarp we had set up as a shelter from the elements, wet, cold, tired, and in pain, I thought of those chopper pilots. They were probably home by now, in bed. I remember thinking, I was in the wrong Army, there had to be a better way to spend a life.

The Army was going through one of its periodic shortages of helicopter pilots. In the seventies, right after Nam, they had let go some ten thousand of them in a RIF (Reduction in Force) like the one that caught CPT Holloway. A few years later they realized they had shot themselves in the foot. Things were so bad they were being more lenient on some of the qualifications. One of which was eyesight. My eyes had greatly improved since childhood; I still had slight nearsightedness in my left eye that put my vision at 20/25. Normally, this would have disqualified me from Warrant Officer Flight School. With the pilot shortage, they were waiving the eyesight restriction if one's vision was correctable to 20/20.

That night, I decided to go for it. It wasn't OCS, but in many ways a Warrant Officer had it better than a Commissioned Officer. By the time I had my paperwork completed, though, there was a waiting list for flight school and they dropped the waiver of eyesight. Back to square one.

I was disappointed, but in the long run it turned out for the best I didn't go to flight school. A couple of years later they had another glut of pilots. A whole bunch of pilots who'd gotten their wings during that period were given their walking papers. A friend of mine received his. Who knows, I might have been one of the ones let go.

I did get the school I really wanted. Jump school. It took some time. My chain of command wasn't too thrilled at the thought of losing another soldier to the airborne. Usually, when a guy went to jump school and got his wings, it wasn't too long before he was volunteering for the 82nd. My request was denied at both battery and battalion level. But they had to pass it on and DA approved it to my relief and joy.

At the end of June, 1981 I loaded Debbie and the kids in the car and we headed to Ft. Benning. She would be staying at home with her parents in Alabama, only eighty miles from Benning. If I didn't have any duty on the weekends, she'd pick me up and I'd spend my weekends at home.

I remember driving up to the airborne student inprocessing office, which at that time was in the shadows of the 250 ft towers. Debbie dropped me off; I kissed her goodbye and watched them drive off. I looked up at the big towers looming overhead. "Well," I thought, "here I am. Don't blow it this time."

Chapter 12
Airborne at Last!

Two old legs were layin' in bed,
One rolled over to the other and said,
"I wanna be an airborne Ranger,
'livin' a life of constant danger."

Airborne, all the way! Airborne, everyday!
(Anonymous Airborne running cadence)

I'll never forget the first time my family saw me with my head shaved and mustache gone for jump school. They had dropped me off on the Friday afternoon before Ground Week (I missed "Zero Week" second time through), it was a week later, I had finished Ground Week and had gotten one of my room mates to pull my Saturday night fireguard so I could go home with my family that weekend. David, our oldest, summed it up, "Oh Mama, what have they done to my daddy?" He said it in such a somber way it was funny.

After I signed in at the in-processing center the previous Friday I was given my student company, the 45th. It was the same company to which I had been assigned my first time through. There seemed something portentous in this. I hoped it was good.

As I made my way to the barracks, the young privates hanging around snapped to attention and salute as I walked past. A bit confused, I did the militarily courteous thing and returned their salutes. It took me a few minutes to figure out why they were saluting me. It was my unit crests.

I was assigned to the 1st Bn, 6th Field Artillery. Its regimental crest was a golden winged Centaur shooting a bow and arrow. I was wearing the old summer khaki uniform. From a distance, I guess the Centaur crests on my shoulders and garrison cap looked like the eagles of a full colonel. The young troops, fresh out of basic training were taking no chances in not saluting a high-ranking officer, no matter how young he looked. When I figured it out, it was all I could do to keep a straight face, especially when the entire barracks snapped to attention when I walked in to report to my company. Couldn't they see the Specialist patch on my arms?

Oh well. I told them to be at ease and asked where the

162

Charge of Quarters was. He thought the whole thing was funny, too. Welcome back to Jump School.

I found jump school to be easier on me psychologically than the first time through, though the physical part was tougher (even with my problems the first time). After all, I was six years older.

Again, we washed out one-third of our class on the first day of Ground Week because they couldn't pass the PT test. We were using the new three-event PT test. It sounded simple at first. All one had to do was forty-five pushups in two minutes or less, forty-five sit-ups in two minutes or less, and run two miles in less than sixteen minutes. The catch was these had to be perfect pushups and sit-ups. The run was done in combat boots. The same standard applied to all male candidates, regardless of age. Females met a different standard.

When a soldier did a pushup or sit-up wrong the count would stop. The airborne instructor or "black hat" would repeat the count of the last perfect exercise performed, "Twenty-six, twenty-six, twenty-six..."until you corrected your error. Then the count would continue. You weren't told what you were doing wrong; you had to figure it out for yourself.

As one Marine who failed the test told me as we were doing the two-mile run, "The first forty-five pushups were easy - it was the second forty-five that got me!"

He failed the run by a few seconds. He almost caused me to fail when I tried to pace him to help him make it. As we were finishing the last lap they called the time left to pass. I apologized to the guy, but had to speed it up to make time. He nodded that he understood. I took off and, sprinting the last quarter of a mile or so, barely made it.

I saw the Marine later. They had separated the Marines from the other two hundred or so troops who failed the test. The Marine Corps liaison officer was dressing them down for disgracing the Corps. I felt sorry for him. I knew from experience that you feel bad enough when you wash out without someone coming along to make you feel worse; even when the reasons for failure are beyond your control.

The other guys who had failed would have the chance to go through another zero week, which would be dedicated to getting them in better shape for next week's class. They would get another chance to take the Airborne PT test. Most, I knew would be discouraged and withdraw, quit. There was a SP5 I'd made friends with the previous weekend who had failed. I remember trying with every bit of persuasion I had to get him to give it another try. But he terminated and was gone the next day.

I felt sorry for all the guys who had failed the test. At the same time, I didn't know for whom to feel the most sorrow - the failures, or those who had passed. Our ordeal was beginning, by the time we finished nineteen days later almost half our original class would be gone - washed out or quit. Others would replace them from previous classes who had failed in one way or another and were "recycled" to try again until they either passed (I believe recycles got three tries on a given week), or quit.

Having passed our PT test to become official airborne trainees our first lesson in Jump School was two hours of what they called "break area procedures." The Blackhats[78] were going to teach us how to properly fall out and fall in from the "break area." I think it was just another excuse to harass us. This instruction was augmented by hundreds of pushups, squat-thrusts, and grass drill, meted out as punishment by the Blackhats for offenses such as being too slow to fall out into the break area, not sounding off loud enough when told to fall out, or not being happy about being at Ft, Benning. No kidding.

The Blackhats paused a moment about half way through the lesson and asked the company if anyone wanted to quit. There were several, about five. They were fallen out of the formation and dogged on their way to the cadre shack – known as "the White House" (it *was* white) to sign their release papers.

Finally, they let us have a real break. We were put through showers. We had been taught how to roll through them in a modified pushup position so as not to get our boots wet. The whole purpose of this was to cool our bodies down and prevent heat exhaustion. As I said earlier, during my first time in jump school the wetness, acting with the straps of the parachute harnesses worn in training had rubbed me (and most my buddies) raw in places and had gotten infected. I warned some of my new buddies about this and told them to make sure they protected themselves and adjusted their straps carefully. I wished someone had told me that in 1975. I also warned them about unbuttoning the middle buttons on their fatigue blouses (shirts) when in the T-10 harness.

Ft. Benning is the one jump school for all the armed services, though occasionally other jump schools are held elsewhere.

---

[78] Blackhats- Airborne Instructors. They earn the name because the instructors wear black baseball caps with their rank and parachute badges on them. In the summer, a blackhat's duty uniform was a white T-shirt with his name and rank stenciled across the chest, white gym shorts, and jump boots. In the winter, a stenciled sweatshirt, duty trousers, and jump boots.

The green berets host a two-week "suicide school" at Ft. Bragg in the summer for ROTC cadets who want to earn their wings. I believe the 82nd has one occasionally for legs in airborne slots or anyone who wants their wings. Bragg soldiers can go to that if they have completed packets and have their unit's permission. But the real jump school is at Ft. Benning.

In a Student Airborne Company you'll see all four branches of service represented. At jump school, all inter-service rivalry is set aside, there's no time for it. Everyone has to pull together to make it through the school and earn their wings. Our officers go to school right beside us. When I went through we had a forty-three year old Colonel working for his wings. He endured everything we did with no regard for his rank. On the day we graduated he received his promotion to Brigadier General. He was pinned and promoted on the drop zone. The company carried him off the drop zone.

For almost fifty years the three weeks of Jump School were divided into three week-long cycles (not counting an unofficial fourth (or zero) week). The first two were spent teaching students the basics of static line parachute jumping, military style.

First there was Ground Week. The training in ground week consisted of learning the parachute landing fall, or PLF. Hours were spent practicing the roll required to ensure a paratrooper did not injure himself upon impact with the ground. We learned the five points of contact:

1) **Balls of Feet.**

2) **Calves**.

3) **Outer thigh.**

4) **Buttocks** (we were constantly told our heads were up our "fourth point of contact" when we messed up. The term became part of our dictionary).

5) **"Pushup Muscle"** on our back.

We started rolling on the ground, gradually moving to platforms off the ground before advancing to our "final exam in falling," which was riding a device on pulleys across the PLF practice pit. At a given point, the Blackhat conducting training would shout, "Land!" The soldier on the device would let go of the device; falling about five feet and executing a parachute landing fall. We were graded on the quality of our falls.

After this, we began to learn exit procedures from an aircraft by jumping out of mock doors at ground level. The final step in Ground Week was making proper exits out of the 34-foot towers.

The 34-foot tower was designed to simulate exiting the door

of an aircraft at a height. Soldiers rigged up in parachute harnesses (which was simultaneous training for proper donning of the parachute) and ascended the steps to a little room at the top, which was designed to resemble the inside of an aircraft.

The Blackhats hooked the troopers' harnesses to risers, which were in turn hooked up to pulleys running along cables stretched about forty feet in the air. The cables ran from telephone poles standing behind the tower, for about fifty to seventy-five yards, to another set of telephone poles, which stood behind a long earthen mound. A "mound detail" stood on the mound to catch jumpers at the end of their ride and unhook them.

At the signal, the jumper exited the tower as he would an aircraft in flight. He then proceeded with his four-second count as he rode the cables to the mounds. There, he was "caught" and unhooked by the mound detail. After being unhooked, the jumper then ran back to a Blackhat sitting at a station below the tower for evaluation of his exit. Usually, the critique was accompanied by a command to "Beat your boots" when there was a flaw in the jumper's technique – pushups were out of the question when in harness.

The 34-foot tower was the first obstacle one met in conquering one's fear of heights. We were told it was designed specifically for that purpose. The view from the mock door at thirty-four feet was supposed to bring out any hidden fear of heights one might have which would cause a jumper to freeze in the door, panic on the way down, and get himself or another jumper killed.

There was one case I personally witnessed while on mound detail. We had a Marine sergeant in my airborne training company. The cadre made him our student first sergeant. I'd had a few dealings with him during the week and found him a hard-charging - but fair NCO. I liked him. I watched as he jumped out of the 34-foot tower.

I heard him begin his four thousand count, "One thou-aaaaaaaah!" he screamed. I helped unhook him when he reached the mound.

He looked me in the eye. "This is the last one for me!" he said when he was loose. We watched as he ran down the path to the evaluation station and quit. I imagine he caught a hard time from the Marines, being an NCO and quitting like that.

Another guy came out the door and screamed in agony all the way down. When he got to us we could barely release him he was grabbing us in such agony, begging us to get him down. I took one look at his harness and realized what had happened. His leg straps, which fall from the bottom of the parachute harness in back

166

and are brought in between one's legs to be hooked on the harness in front, right on right, left on left, had slipped and caught him wrong in the crotch.

"You'd better see a medic, man," I told him when we finally got him down.

"You don't need to tell me, man," he said, his face still contorted in a grimace. "I've had it with this nonsense. I quit."

We watched him hobble down the path to quit.

Mound detail was a bear. The Blackhats were constantly dropping you for pushups if you didn't get a guy down fast enough or didn't hold your nose right. The hotspot on mound detail was the rope man. The rope man had a rope with a clasp on it. He stood at the base of the mound holding one end of the rope. The guys on the top of the mound had the other end, with the clasp. When they released a jumper from the risers, they hooked the risers to the rope. The rope man then had to pull the risers on the pulleys back from the mound to the Blackhat waiting in the tower. Thus, the rope man's entire shift on the mound consisted of running back and forth between the tower and the mound. If the Blackhat didn't believe the rope man was running fast enough he would drop the rope man for pushups. The rope man did a lot of pushups.

Those not actively involved in jumping or on rope detail were designated to sit on stone bleachers and observe the other jumpers coming out of the tower so as to learn from them what to do and what not to do. When you were observing, you were required to "sit at attention." Sitting at attention required one to sit with one's feet and knees together, hands on knees, looking up at the door. This is an extremely uncomfortable position to hold for any period of time. One had to keep one's eyes on the door of the tower. If you were caught looking anywhere else, it was pushups. During my first time through one Blackhat liked to play games with troops.

We called him the "Smiling Demon" – which, if I remember right, was the name he had stenciled across his chest: SFC Demons. He reminded me of the 1960s and 70s comedian Flip Wilson – on steroids.

He would walk by the towers on his way – about his business and suddenly stop and stand about fifty feet away from the bleachers, just in the trooper's peripheral vision. Then, he would pick his victim and stare at him. Now, when you're being stared at the impulse is to look back. No matter how hard you resist the temptation, if the staring continues, eventually you're going to look back. Someone always did. Maybe it was just a glance away from the tower. He'd get a big grin on his face and walk over to the victim.

"You know what you did wrong!" he'd say with a smile. "Now drop down and give me ten!"

This was just the beginning. He'd start messing with the troop, usually getting them to laugh with his cutting up; this would just get you more pushups. Before it was over you could have done a hundred pushups. One time he had about thirty guys down doing pushups, he'd managed to get them laughing at his messing with a victim and dropped the whole bunch. We were all down on the ground, doing pushups and laughing, and getting more pushups for laughing. That guy probably made me do more pushups than anyone in the Army, but I still have to smile when I think of him.

If you made it through Ground Week you were then passed to the Tower Committee for the second week of training, called, naturally enough, Tower Week. The training here consisted of even more PT. As the week progressed the students were put through more 34-foot tower drills. In Ground Week soldiers were put out of the towers one at a time. In Tower Week we were taught mass exits, four jumpers exiting at a time. After that students began to learn how to handle a parachute in the air. Hours were spent in the suspended harness (popularly known as the "suspended agony"), in which a troop was suspended a few feet above the ground in a parachute harness and drilled on steering a parachute. Emergency actions were learned and practiced. This was followed by even more training on PLFs. There was the swing-landing trainer, which gave fairly realistic practice in parachute landings (as I may have said, that might have been what got me my first time through). There was the wind machine that taught troopers how to collapse one's chute in a high wind (I later wished we'd spent more time on that!). And then there was the grand finale, the event every trooper waited for and dreaded from the moment we reported to jump school, the 250-foot tower.

The 250-ft. towers were originally carnival rides used at the World's Fair. The towers were moved to Ft. Benning when the Army started the jump school back in 1940 as it was realized they would be effective training devices in parachute training. The 250-ft towers were the closest things to an actual jump one could get without actually entering an aircraft.

The towers loomed ominously above the Ft. Benning skyline, dominating the post. I know I couldn't leave my barracks without a glance up at them. When I'd come back to the barracks at night I'd have to look up at their red aircraft warning lights. For me, the towers were second only to actually jumping in their intimidation.

There were three towers, two were used for training, and the other was used to give rides during open houses and special tours. Each tower had four arms at the top; rings were suspended from a cable running from each arm. Open parachutes were hooked to the rings with the apex (center loop) of the parachute attached to a hook from the cable from which the rings were suspended. A jumper's parachute harness was attached to the parachute by his canopy release devices.

Now attached to the chute and the ring, the jumper is pulled up to the top of the tower by the cable. Once at the top, once he has signaled he is ready, the student is released to ride his chute to the ground, receiving instructions from a Blackhat coaching him through a bullhorn. One must make at least one "successful" drop from the tower to pass the course. Sometimes, students get confused and steer their chutes into the tower. When that happens, a detail must climb the tower to get the student down. This, I was informed, was an automatic failure of the course.

The first time I ascended the tower, I was awestruck by the view. It seemed I could see everywhere from the height. After it was over, I was sold. I couldn't wait to jump.

This, in a way, was the final exam before we passed on to our third and final week of jump school - Jump Week. Jump Week would be the final test, when we would actually put "our knees to the breeze," and thumb our noses at death.

Each day of the first two weeks in jump school started out with a personal appearance inspection. Each student's boots had to be highly polished with a "spit" shine. At the PX near the student barracks "boot blacks" made a small fortune doing trainees' boots. I believe they used a mixture of liquid shoe polish with a particular brand of floor wax that gave our boots, beaten and battered after a day of training and the showers, a high glossy look. I didn't like the shine one got from the boot blacks – it looked fake to me, I preferred a real spit shine - but it was pretty well set in stone that if you tried shining your own boots you'd fail inspection and end up in the Gig Pit for PT. Too many trips to the Gig Pit might wash you from the course.[79] (There has been a persistent rumor among paratroopers the

---

[79] One could end up in the Gig Pit for a variety of infractions such as failing inspection or not completing the correct number of "perfect dead hang" chin-ups required for the honor of being allowed to do PT. In Ground Week that was six, Tower Week – seven.

Blackhats got a kickback from the boot blacks. My buddies who were Blackhats adamantly deny those rumors.) When I went through, before the Army introduced the camouflaged Battle Dress Uniform (BDU), our fatigues had to be highly starched, our hair had to meet airborne standards (meaning shaved off), mustaches were a no-no, we had to have our dogtags on, our parachutist's helmet had to be properly fitted and put together.

After inspection, we were told to prepare for PT. Men stripped down to their waists, the few females kept their T-shirts on. We usually did about forty-five minutes of heavy calisthenics, followed by at least a four-mile run. At the end of each week though, they would take us on a special run around post. This was much longer and we were told falling out meant to be recycled and have to go through the week's training again.

The worst one I remember was on the last day of zero week my first time through in 1975. They took us on a tour of the post. Years later, during a visit to Ft. Benning, I retraced the path in my car and checked the mileage. I found we had run over ten miles that morning. Guys were dropping out from the heat left and right. It was only six in the morning and already the temperature was above eighty degrees with humidity around seventy-five percent. I know and remember this because we passed the Ft. Benning National Bank at the beginning of our run and could read the time and temperature.

It got to the point I couldn't even think any more, except to pick one foot up and put the other one down. I stared at the sweat soaked back in front of me and just concentrated on staying in formation. Every so often, though, I'd look up and scan the horizon for the 250-foot towers. I used them as my compass; I knew when I could see them in front of us we were going home.

Men ached so from the strain they were crying. Some had lost control of their bodily functions and wet themselves; one could smell it mingled with the smell of sweat. On we ran, with the cadre detouring us so we had to run up every steep hill on post, it seemed. Then, we rounded the bend and saw the sight of the two hundred and fifty foot towers, which loomed over our barracks. We were almost home. All we had to do was hang on a little longer.

I remember fixing my eyes area on our barracks across the Tower Committee training area. As we turned on our final stretch, I looked for the sidewalk where every morning we would hear the

---

Troops in the Gig Pit had to do pushups, squat thrusts, or various other exercises while others were "catching their breaths" waiting for the NCO leading PT to announce the next exercise. In other words, folks in the Gig Pit got dogged.

command, "Quick Time, March!" which ended our runs.

A half a mile. Just hang in there, only a half a mile.
A quarter of a mile. Hang on, not far now.
A thousand feet. No problem we've got it made.
Pick 'em up put 'em down. Just keep going, 'not far now.
Five hundred feet. I can see the sidewalk now.
The lead man is at the side walk. Any second now.

We ran past the sidewalk. Down the street we went toward the Ground Committee. I think we lost half the company right there. I myself began to drop back, heartbroken. Then I saw the cadre come out from their hiding places behind the building. They reminded me of hungry wolves on a lost flock of sheep, yelling and screaming.

Maybe I can make it another few feet. I closed up with the guy in front of me.

The formation ran on for a half a block before turning around and returning at quick time. As the formation marched into the company area I saw all the guys who had fallen out of the run were being lined up by the company cadre for punishment PT. It had all been a head game.

The guys who had fallen out had set their sights on making it to the sidewalk. When the company ran past the sidewalk they fell out because they weren't prepared to go the extra mile, if need be. They hadn't girded themselves to finish the course, no matter how long it took. It almost got me. But I realized this was the key to being airborne. You don't have to be a superman to be a paratrooper; you just have to have the extra determination to go the extra mile, and to do whatever it takes to accomplish the mission. You had to be willing to go all the way.

Looking back, I've discovered there's a life lesson and a spiritual lesson to be learned there. Often our deliverance is just over the horizon, if we'll stay the course and trust in Him.

On Friday afternoon of Tower Week, after we had completed our last training, those of us who were still with the company were marched to bleachers, where we were given "malfunction class." Those who had flunked out of Tower Week had been pulled out of the class already and recycled.

During malfunction class dummies were raised to the tops of the 250-foot towers. They were hooked to parachutes that had been rigged to illustrate the different things that could go wrong with a parachute. The instructor would explain the causes of the various malfunctions and the action to take if we encountered it during a jump. After he finished the dummy would be released from the tower to show us what would happen in real life if this happened. Most of this was a review of what we had already gone over in the suspended agony trainer. However, watching a dummy "streamer in" from 250-feet had a sobering effect.

After the last dummy had been dropped, the instructor made official what all of us already knew. We had made it. All we had facing us was the supreme test Monday morning. He told us that of the six hundred and fifty students who had begun with our class twelve days before, there were only three hundred and seventy-five left. There were an additional hundred or so other students, who had been recycled from other classes, had joined the class on the way.

He began to recount the heritage of the American paratrooper, tracing it from the experimental platoon headed by LTC Billy Lee, through the near mythological exploits of the World War II airborne divisions, the 82nd, 101st, 11th, 13th, and 17th Airborne Divisions. He told of the roll of honor of the airborne trooper. He called the names of places where the American paratrooper earned the reputation as one of the most feared fighting men in the world, Salerno, Nijmegen, Eindhoven, St. Mere-Eglise, Corregidor, Tagaytay, Los Banos, Pyong Yang, Junction City... As he spoke, someone began playing SSG Barry Sadler's "Ballad of the Green Berets." As corny as it may sound now, all these years later, it worked. Tears began to fill my eyes. I had finally made it. Nothing was going to stop me from completing my five jumps and earning my wings!

Jump week was run a little differently than the other two weeks. Our whole purpose here was to make the five jumps necessary to qualify for the parachutist's badge. We didn't do as much PT here. I got the feeling the only reason they put us through any exercises at all was to see if anyone had been hurt on the previous day's jump(s). They would make us do some side straddle hops (jumping jacks), pushups, sit-ups, and squat-thrusts, and then run us once around the area; all the time watching to see if anyone was limping or favoring an arm.

Then, we'd go through our pre-jump training and briefing. Immediately after that we drew our parachutes and waited for our turn in the aircraft to jump.

We made one jump on Monday. On Tuesday we made two: one in the morning and one in the afternoon. On my third jump, in the afternoon, we were using the steerable parachute. A guy swept right under me in spite of my attempts to warn him and slip away from him. When I hollered, "Slip away!" he looked up with me like Bambi in the headlights. I slipped right; he slipped and came right under me. I ran across the top of his chute and hopped off before his chute stole my air and my chute collapsed. If that happened, I would fall through his chute, which would collapse under my weight. We would fall to the ground together and hope the burial people could separate the parts. I thank God we were jumping from twelve hundred feet instead of the eight hundred feet normally jumped by airborne units in daylight hours. Had that happened at eight hundred feet I probably wouldn't have had enough time to do anything.

As it was, as soon as I got off his chute and in the air I tried to get myself re-oriented. I got to facing the wind and after that I don't know what happened. The only thing I can figure is the wind was exactly the same speed as the forward drift of the steerable parachute, 9.5 knots, and therefore acted as a break to my drift. Maybe in escaping the other guy I got to oscillating – being swung back and forth by my chute. I've been body slammed like that. In any event, I'm under the impression I landed coming straight down, instead of moving at an angle, such as backward or forward. There was no angle from which I could do a PLF, I just kind of hit the ground and collapsed, folded up. In the process I banged up my shoulder pretty bad.

When I got up and took my parachute harness off, I discovered I couldn't move my left arm or hand. I was in intense pain. A couple of buddies saw me trying to roll up my chute single handedly and helped. One was a guy from another battalion in my brigade, Gordon Sims. The other was a young Marine who was going to join an ANGLICO (Aerial and Naval Gunnery Liaison Company) outfit, Roy Huang. Just about everyone in my stick (squad) knew this was my second time through the school. They all wanted to see me make it.

As we rode back to the airfield I wondered what to do. My arm was useless, but if I reported it, I knew I would be recycled and put on hold. My unit would be notified. They would probably want me back at Bragg. Remember, they didn't really want me to go to jump school in the first place. If I didn't finish jump school this week, I knew chances were I'd never get a chance to finish it. By the same token, if I jumped injured I would not only be risking my life, but possibly someone else's.

That evening I went down the hall to another buddy of mine. He was a Navy corpsman going to jump school after being assigned to a Marine Corps ANGLICO unit. I had him check me out. He told me it was probably just a bruised or pinched nerve. There was no bone damage that he could ascertain. I tended to agree with his diagnosis. I'd had plenty of experience with injuries such as this in Judo. I asked him if I should jump in the morning.

"Well, Woody," he said. "That's a tough call. There's a lot at stake here for you... If you were one of the guys at the unit, I'd say sit this one out..."

"Thanks." I went back to my room and rubbed some ointment on my shoulder. I'd see how it went in the morning.

The next morning my shoulder was worse. When the call went out for sick call I fought with myself over what to do. Then I decided I was going to go for it. I'd chute up and see how it felt then. The next problem was how I'd get past the Blackhats.

That morning I was helped a bit. They were running late and didn't have time to put us through too much. They ran us around the front parking lot to see if there were any leg injuries. That was no problem; I just stuck my left hand down the back of my pants with my right hand to keep my arm from flopping too much and hoped no one noticed. No one did.

Then, after we finished pre-jump, and I had bluffed my way through that (for the life of me I still can't remember how I managed the PLF platform – I can't imagine doing PLFs bummed up the way I was), we were run into the chute shed. It was here I almost got caught. The senior Blackhat came out and dropped the entire company for twenty pushups. As we dropped, I figured this was it for me. I decided to try and bluff it through again and did my pushups one-armed. In the middle of the pushups I glanced up to see if anyone was watching me.

I saw the senior Blackhat standing on a raised platform scanning the company. He saw me doing my pushups on one arm. His eyes flashed. I guess he thought I was being a smart aleck. I just knew he was going to mess with me. I expected any moment to hear my student number (marked in tape on my helmet) called. To my relief, he didn't, though I felt his glare follow me as we recovered and ran into the shed.

With a lot of help from my friends, I got chuted up. I discovered when I put my parachute harness on the shoulder straps somehow acted as a brace and I recovered full mobility in my arm with little or no pain. I wanted to shout for joy.

At about that time my stick leader, a second lieutenant, fresh out West Point, came up. He had just learned about my injury.

"Are you going to be able to jump, Wood?" he asked. I had to smile at his concern; he seemed like a nice kid.

"Yes sir!" I showed him my arm and explained how the harness helped. "No problem, sir."

"Are you sure you're okay, Wood?" he asked again, "You don't have to jump…"

"It's okay, Sir," I said, again, "Besides, it's a good day to die."

So I finished my last two jumps. I was okay once I was chuted up. I was great in the air and on landing. As soon as I would take my harness off on the drop zone, my arm went limp again. Sims and Huang would come over and help me get my chute together on the DZ. They even took turns carrying it off the drop zone until we got within sight of the Blackhats waiting for us at the assembly area. At that point, they'd place the kit bag with my chute in it over my head and we'd lope on in to the assembly area. Once there, we'd work together to shake out our chutes. I owed them a big one. I don't know how I could have gotten by without their help, though they told me I would have probably figured something out. As determined as I was to get my wings I probably would have.

It was one of the proudest days of my life when the Blackhat pinned my wings on my chest. When he came to me I whispered to him, "Blood wings, Sergeant Airborne!"

With that, he grinned. Then he took my wings and slammed the pins holding them to my uniform into my chest with his fist. I winced at the pain, and grunted.

He grinned, "Sissy!"

If only he knew.

But didn't care- I was airborne! To this day I still have two tiny pinhole-like scars on my chest today on my left breast. After all these years you have to look close to see them, but I know they're there.

Sporting my new wings, my family and I spent the weekend with her parents outside Ft. Rucker. Now that I was safely Airborne, I went to the Lyster Army Hospital Emergency Room. Of course, I wore my khakis, wings, and bloused jump boots with my garrison cap with parachute/glider patch. I remember the pride when one of the medics on duty reported to the doc they had a paratrooper in the waiting room. They x-rayed my shoulder and told me they could find nothing – it was probably just a pinched nerve. They advised I go to my TMC when I got back to Bragg.

Now I looked at my next goal: Officers Candidate School. One day, I would finish my college degree. I would have to. As I recall, the Army had a program that allowed guys like me to get a commission, but we had to get our degree within a certain amount of time to keep it. I had been making progress toward that end by taking CLEP tests at the Army Education Center next door to my barracks. As CLEP tests were free to active duty Army personnel, I would walk in during my lunch break and see what tests they had available. I would take any test I thought I would do well on. By doing this, I had earned over a year's credit in English and Social Studies, my strong subjects. I figured one day I'd walk into a college somewhere, throw my classroom transcripts down with the CLEP scores and anything else that would give me college credit and see if I could get some sort of degree.

I had given up my musical and artistic ambitions. I was able to get together with another judoka[80] and work out occasionally. That was difficult between my training schedule and family and the only formal classes on Bragg were for kids at the Youth Center. Now, my life revolved around my family and the Army. My only goal was to be a good soldier so I could advance in rank and provide a good life for my family.

Somewhere along this time I was hitchhiking my way into post one morning. This was still a common occurrence; it seemed the month had a way of lasting longer than the paycheck and I wasn't the only one who would get up a few hours early the last week before payday because there wasn't enough gas in the tank to make it in to post. After all, kids need their milk. I guess I could have qualified for Food Stamps back then. I know several of my fellow married enlisted men drew them, and we would have had it much easier, but it didn't seem right to me as long as I drew a check to get them. We made it through, never went hungry, and I always managed to find a ride into post. For that I am thankful.

One morning I caught a ride with a young guy and we hadn't been in the car long when he asked me a question, "If you died right now do you know where you'd go?"

The question set me back as it seemed to come out of the blue. "I hope I go to heaven."

"You don't know?"

"No," I responded. "Do you?"

"Yes."

"You've seen God's list? Am I on it?"

---

[80] Judoka- Judo practitioner.

I won't go into the conversation that followed. But I'd always been confused about such things and the guy's question picked at something that had been in the back of my mind. I thought it was time to find a church and take my wife and kids to Sunday school, but I didn't seem to have much time for that, with everything happening in my life. I always figured when I got married that would be part of my settling down. I was trying to be a Christian, but I was going it on my own and really didn't know how. It seemed every time we talked about going to church something would come up. Maybe one day...

Chapter 13
Jumping My Wings

Old Soldier, Airborne Soldier
Pick up your weapon follow me
I am Airborne Infantry

82ⁿᵈ, patch on my shoulder
Pack your chute and follow me
I am Airborne Infantry
(Anonymous Airborne marching cadence)

When I reported back to my unit, things had changed. I was no longer one of them. I don't know whose fault it was but it was as if the guys in the unit looked upon me as the enemy. I was a "wing dummy," the name non-airborne personnel had for paratroopers on Ft. Bragg. Even my NCOs seemed to change their attitude. One morning I got dropped for pushups during PT for doing an exercise, the "squat jumper," the *right* way! Everyone else was wrong; I knew that because it was a favorite exercise at jump school. I even went upstairs to the battery training room and looked it up in the FM 21-20, the manual for PT. When I pointed it out to my Chief of Firing Battery, he just grinned at me, "What did they feed you at Benning, Wood - gunpowder?"

Even though I liked so many of them, I began looking at my fellow soldiers as a bunch of "sorry legs." CPT Crowley had changed command while I was away at jump school. The new BC was a nice guy, too nice to be a successful commander of this unit. He just didn't seem to have the necessary toughness to command the respect of the soldiers. The battery was beginning to fall apart again. I could "feel" it.

Maybe this sounds like Prima Dona stuff, but I was getting tired of being punished all the time, even when I was straight. There were inspections where I would be one of the few guys in the battery to pass an inspection. But the section or the battery would fail and we'd all be working overtime at night getting ready for re-inspection. I'd been through this all in Germany. I was ready for a change.

I talked it over with Debbie. As much as she hated Ft. Bragg, she didn't want to move anymore. We discussed going on jump status.

"Where would you go?"

"There's always the 82nd or Group (Special Forces)."

"Well, you can forget Group." she said. "Unless you've got divorce papers you want me to sign."

"What about the 82nd?"

"That's not much better. Why can't you go to OCS?"

"Because the packet takes time to put together"

I was given another alternative out of the blue. The 18th Field Artillery Brigade Headquarters Battery (HHB) was on jump status. At the time, it was the only airborne unit in the brigade. They needed some vehicle drivers for their Brigade S-3 (Plans and Operations) Section. It turned out the slots called for my MOS (Military Occupational Specialty). As I had just completed jump school, my name came up. I was asked to interview to see if I'd be interested in transferring. After my experiences in Germany I had real misgivings about getting away from the guns but it was a jump slot and an opportunity to perhaps meet some field grade officers to sign my OCS packet and maybe give it more "oomph."

It turned out the time I spent with HHB was one of the best periods in my military career. We were the only element of the 18th Corps Artillery Brigade on jump status. This made us feel mighty proud compared to the rest of the brigade. We were sort of a "private army" within the brigade.

Our First Sergeant, Top Wilson, was like a big Daddy to his troops. If you were a good soldier and did your job, there wasn't anything he wouldn't do for you. If you somehow got on his bad side, and I had seen those who did, there was nothing he would not do *to* you. Having enlisted from Alabama and married an Alabama girl helped. Top Wilson was from Phenix City. We were "home boys."

In my own Section, the S-3 section we had a great bunch, from the LTC who was the Brigade S-3, to his two Assistants, who were majors. One of the majors had been Battery Commander of B 1/40th in Germany right before I signed in. I'd heard a lot about him – all good. It was turned out to be true.

One of our Operations Sergeants, MSG Clarke, had been a captain in Vietnam. Like so many others, he'd come down on the post-war RIF. Unlike CPT Holloway, he had stayed in, taking a reduction to Staff Sergeant, E-6. But, another thing he did was retain his commission in the Inactive Ready Reserve. Over the years he had risen through the ranks to reserve colonel. I was never there to see it myself, but the guys told me when he did his annual "drill" as an officer, he liked to do it at Bragg and would stop by the S-3 shop. For those two weeks his active duty boss – a lieutenant colonel – had to salute him.

I had never known duty could be so good. When we went out in the field the Headquarters took all the comforts of home. We slept in ARFABS, which were canvas tent-like shelters stretched over metal frames. We had electric lights for our living quarters and headquarters tents. We worked, with few exceptions, straight twelve-hour shifts, getting twelve hours off time during which we were pretty much free to do what we wanted. It was better than our trips to "sector" in Germany.

Having spent all my years in the Army in a Field Artillery firing battery this was the lap of luxury. In a firing battery, you are lucky to get four hours of sleep a night in the field. That is usually interrupted by a stint on perimeter guard or radio watch. Soldiers are issued shelter halves and one can theoretically pitch a tent, but artillerymen seldom do. When one has so little time to sleep, one is hardly likely to waste it pitching a tent.

Usually, you just roll out your sleeping bag wherever you can safely and pray that it doesn't rain, snow, or a tank doesn't run over your head (as almost happened to me one night in Germany). I have stretched out on my air mattress and found myself floating downstream in the middle of the night when rains flooded the hollow I was sleeping in. I've already described climbing out of snow one morning.

It wasn't until my last Graf in Germany when I was BC Driver that I gave our field living conditions much thought. I had gone back to the rear area to get a tracked vehicle mechanic from the 503rd Maintenance Battalion to work on one of our guns, which had broken down in the mud. The poor kid had never been out in the field before, having been assigned to a rear echelon unit. He was appalled at how we lived in the field. I remember him saying over and over again as I drove him back to the rear, "How do you do that? How do you guys live like that?"

I had always figured mud and rain and snow were part and parcel of a soldier's life. I guess a pig's happy with his slop until somebody tells him about corn. Maybe, I reflected philosophically, that's why we behaved like animals when we were in the rear.

I now laughed at the young soldiers in my section who complained about how tough their life was in HHB. I told them to try living in the field for weeks at a time with the air so cold if you touched bare metal your skin would stick to it.

Jumping at HHB was nothing like I would experience in the 82nd. While we did masstacs, we also did our share of "Hollywoods"[81]. One time we went to Ft. Pickett, Virginia on an Off Post Training Exercise (OPT) called an EDRE (Emergency Deployment Readiness Exercise). We conducted three that fall, one for each of the tube (gun) battalions in the brigade.

During an EDRE, the unit is alerted as if in an actual real world crisis and deployed. Sometimes, the unit would be deployed to another post across the country. In the 82nd we have deployed to foreign countries before. Once there the unit was put through its paces. Sometimes it was given a specific mission to accomplish. That year, we conducted the battalion level ARTEPS as part of the off-post EDREs. I thought this was a great idea. By conducting the ARTEPS in unfamiliar territory I believed we were getting a more realistic test of the unit's skills.

Often, when you're used to training at a place, you get to know the place so well there is no challenge to the training. We got to know Ft. Bragg like the back of our hands, this made moving from place to place simple. It was real hard to get lost. It was the same with going to Graf in Germany. I remember one time at Graf; we didn't even bother to conduct position area surveys. We had just been to Graf a month or so before and most of our survey markers were still in place. We just located our markers, looked up the data in our old logbooks, and were good to go. It was an easy field trip, but it wasn't good training.

By taking the soldiers out of a familiar environment and putting them through their paces they were being forced to use their land navigation and other individual skills to accomplish the mission. The 82nd conducted numerous off post operations for just this reason.

Top borrowed one of the CH47 Chinook cargo helicopters we'd brought for airmobiles one slack afternoon during the EDRE to Ft. Pickett. He had one hundred and fifty parachutes he had requisitioned in the back of a deuce and half (2 1/2 ton truck). Anyone who wanted or needed a jump and weren't needed at their post (or could get someone to stand in for them) was invited to hop

---

[81]A "Hollywood" jump is jumping without any equipment, save parachute and helmet. These are a luxury in the Army, where most jumping is done with full combat equipment, as described in Chapter 1. A masstac is a special type of jump that empties a plane as quickly as possible. Jumpers exit both doors of the aircraft at half-second intervals between each door. These can be risky if the jumpers get their interval messed up, this could have jumpers exiting both doors simultaneously, if that happens, the jumpers could collide beneath the aircraft with catastrophic results. A simple combat equipment jump is different from a masstac in that jumpers exit only one door at a time. It is slower, but safer than the masstac.

on another deuce-and-half and get some jumps in at Blackstone Army Airfield. These would be great jumps, Hollywoods at an altitude of between 3,000 to 5,000 feet. I got two jumps in that day and would have gotten more but darkness and rising winds interfered.

I had some interestingly hairy jumps, too. Jumping off post onto unfamiliar drop zones is always fraught with risk. The month before we EDRE'd to Ft. Pickett, we had conducted one at Camp LeJeune, Marine Base in North Carolina. We were airlanding[82] a leg battalion. Someone on Brigade Staff had discovered if we put out a few jumpers with each bird carrying the legs, the Air Force would help pick up the tab for the aircraft. It would be considered a training mission for their cargo pilots then. After we jumped, the Air Force would land our guns and crews. We'd save thousands of dollars we could use for other things.

So we loaded about five or six jumpers in each bird headed to LeJeune. I volunteered to be one. This was my second jump with the unit. My first had been a night jump and I had twisted my ankle when I landed on my rucksack, which I had lowered. I had caught a lot of ribbing from the guys in the unit for getting hurt on my cherry blast, or first jump out of jump school. But I didn't feel too bad; I had at least walked off the drop zone. A lot of jumpers had crashed and burned that night when we got dropped too late and half of us landed on the downward slope of Sicily drop zone or in the trees off the DZ. The jumpmaster on that blast had broken his leg. It was his qualifying jump for his "master blasters," or Master Parachutist Badge. He got his wings pinned on him still wearing a leg cast.

"Never try to do a PLF going uphill," he wisely told me.

When we dropped into Camp LeJeune the next month we were told we were jumping "Bluebird" DZ. It was called a combat DZ and was used by the Marine Recon and ANGLICO outfits at LeJeune. We were warned during our pre-jump briefing that about every obstacle one could expect could be found on the DZ. There was water because the DZ was located less than fifty meters from the Atlantic Ocean, and was separated from the surf by a small stand of trees and a narrow beach. High-tension electrical wires bordered the northern edge. Trees surrounded the DZ. The DZ proper was no picnic, either. There was a ravine running along one edge of the DZ, a ruined house in the middle, and a pad for Harrier jump jets. Oh, yes, there was concertina wire strewn here and there for good

---

[82] Airlanding- as it sounds is landing the aircraft and allowing passengers and equipment to unload in a traditional fashion.

measure around the DZ.

As we approached the DZ, I could see the eyes of the cannon crewmen widen as they watched us prepare for the jump. When the time came for us to jump, we had to climb over the big M198 155mm towed howitzers strapped down in the cargo hold. This was no easy task, considering we each were rigged for a combat equipment jump with some seventy-five pounds of equipment on us, not counting our chutes.

We were tailgating this one. That means jumping off the tailgate of the birds. We were making our final approach from the sea. As we stood on the tailgate of the C-130, the lure of the ocean was hypnotic. If I had been the first jumper I might have jumped. We were wearing water wings in case we got blown into the ocean. We had to be careful with them as the wings, packed beneath our harnesses, would crush our ribcages if we accidentally activated them prematurely with our harnesses fastened.

When the green light came on we went out, one after another. We didn't have time to waste, Bluebird was only about one hundred meters long, and we figured it to be a two and a half second drop zone. That means it only took the aircraft two and a half seconds to fly over the DZ. That's how long we had to get out of the bird before we missed the DZ and hit the trees behind it.

When I came out, my suspension lines were twisted all the way up to the skirt (edge) of my canopy. I began bicycling my legs to untwist them. Finally I got straightened out and could check my descent. I was much lower than I expected, under two hundred feet and running with the wind (we were jumping MC1-1Bs, the steerable chutes).[83] I remember thinking they must have dropped us at too low an altitude, I figured six hundred and fifty feet, as opposed to the eight hundred feet we were supposed to have jumped.

To make matters worse, there was a Marine on a tractor in the middle of the DZ, right in my path of descent, mowing the field. I was going to have to avoid him somehow.

---

[83]The MC1-1B is a steerable parachute. There are gaps in the rear panels of the canopy, which allow the jumper to steer the chute. The MC1-1B has a forward speed of 9.5 knots. This meant if there were no wind, a jumper would land moving forward at that speed. To slow a jumper down for a soft landing, a jumper would face the wind, by facing the wind; the WINDSPEED would act against the forward speed of the chute. Therefore, facing a 5-knot wind would have a jumper hit the ground at a forward speed of 4.5 knots - a soft landing. Jumping in a wind greater than 9.5 knots would have the jumper land using a rear PLF. A wind of 11 knots would have the jumper landing backwards at 1.5 knots, a great landing.
By the same token, if the wind is at the jumper's back, this is called "running with the wind." The wind speed is added to the 9.5-knot forward speed of the chute. You hit hard.

I was coming in fast. I was "running with the wind." There was no time to turn around and face the wind, the only thing I could do was keep my feet and knees together, relax, and prepare to hit hard.

The Marine on the tractor hit his brakes hard to keep from hitting the jumper in front of me, who had landed just a few feet in front of him. He turned and looked up to see me coming straight at him. His eyes widened and he hopped off the tractor, leaving it idling in my path. I came in, raising my legs just enough to barely miss it (skimming the hood of his tractor with my behind), and brought them down quickly to land. I hit hard.

I lay there, stunned for a moment. Then the wind caught my chute and began to drag me. I reached up, popped a capewell (proper name: canopy release assembly), which released one of my risers to allow my chute to deflate. Then, I began to do my post-jump body check, 'Toes wiggle? Yep, toes wiggle. Good. 'Fingers move? Yep, fingers move, great! I must be okay!

I stood up and smelled the air. It was so sweet. Off in the distance I heard a bird singing. I had never heard a bird sing so prettily. Nor had I ever seen the sky look so blue. Life was good!

At about that time Top and everyone came running up.

"Wood! Are you okay?"

"I think so! I thought I was going to break my airborne butt!"

One of the females in our unit, a medic, had been dragged and scraped up pretty badly. One of the other medics was checking her out. There was a great deal of concern over a tattoo of a dragon she had on her shoulder. She was greatly relieved to discover the tattoo intact.

One of the medics noticed my camouflaged fatigues had been torn at the elbow. It was stinging a bit. I removed my shirt and the sweatshirt I was wearing underneath to reveal my elbow had been torn open to the bone.

"I guess I broke my airborne elbow!" I said. I was taken to the Navy hospital where it took twelve stitches to close the wound. My airborne career was getting off to an auspicious start.

It was at HHB, 18th FA that I learned the refinements of military parachuting. Excursions like the one at Ft. Pickett allowed us to "play" with our chutes and learn what they would and wouldn't do. The two sweet jumps I made at Ft. Pickett seemed to break my "jinx." I made three more jumps with HHB without incident. When I left HHB I may not have been a "Master Blaster" but I felt fairly competent with a chute.

I think it was about this time I heard from Vinnie again. The last I'd heard from him he had moved to London with Elly. Not able to make anything work out for him in London, he hooked up with a bunch of guys who had been hired to overthrow a government in the southern part of Africa. He had managed to call me in early fall of 1980 to tell me if I could get a plane ticket to London he had a slot for me. The money was good. He told me it was around fifty thousand dollars for four week's work.

By that time I'd managed to get on active duty. The U.S. Army would have frowned on me hiring my expertise out to private concerns. They were funny like that. I couldn't have raised the price of a ticket anyway.

The operation went sour. Around fifty guys went in; they barely made it out alive.

Vinnie told me later he was on the aircraft escaping the country when he was hit with a revelation. It was an old transport plane; all shot to pieces; there was a guy seriously wounded near him. "I said to myself, 'a guy could get killed doing this sort of thing.'" This was after over three and a half years in Nam and at least three Purple Hearts!

After that, Vinnie was cured of his thrill seeking. By that time, unfortunately, Elly had enough. They split up shortly after that.

I really think that was another time the Lord was looking out for me.

One thing I enjoyed about HHB was the fact that, at a higher headquarters such as this, I got a look at how decisions are made at the top. We would participate in Command Post Exercises (CPXs) in which the headquarters of major units, individual brigades, such as ours, would get together to fight imaginary wars on paper with divisions and corps.

Back then, we traced troop movements manually on maps and umpires would determine casualties using complicated formulas and pocket calculators. Later on, as the age of high technology caught up with the Army (or vice versa) everything was done by computer. During CPXs we would test contingency plans for various scenarios. A simple way of saying this is we played, "What if?"

During one CPX in which I participated, we played, "What if the Soviet Union tried to grab the Persian Gulf oil fields?"

Remember, the Soviet Union had invaded Afghanistan a few years before and there was genuine concern over the safety of the world's oil supply.

XVIII Airborne Corps, as the Rapid Deployment headquarters for the Army, was tasked with getting the Corps' subordinate units, the 82nd Airborne Division, followed by the 101st Airborne Division (Air Assault), and, finally, backed by the 24th Infantry Division (Mechanized)[84], with the Corps supporting units, to Saudi Arabia and deploy them in such a way as to be able to slow a superior force until other, heavier units, could arrive from Europe and bases in the U.S.

During Operation Desert Shield, the U.S. military buildup in Saudi Arabia, prior to Operation Desert Storm, the actual Persian Gulf War, I watched with satisfaction as the plan we had used back in 1981 was played out. The only difference was, instead of defending against the Soviets, we were facing the Iraqis, a Soviet equipped and trained army. It made me feel good I had played a part, no matter how minuscule, in putting it together.

There was another "what if" scenario that made me think. One time we were given a scenario in which the Soviets were trying to invade the Middle East and seize the Suez Canal. We set up a defensive line in the Valley of Megiddo. As I looked at the map, it dawned on me that we were planning for the Battle of Armageddon.

I would have gladly spent the rest of my career at HHB, but DA had other plans. I came down on levy, or orders, for Chakmakli Turkey. Actually, Chakmakli was to be my headquarters, the base where I would actually be posted was further east at a nuclear weapons site on the Turkish-Russian border with a detachment of U.S. advisors to the Turkish Army.

Things such as this are part and parcel of military life. I was used to life overseas. As an Army brat I had lived in Belgium and graduated from high school in Germany. Actually, I preferred overseas duty to stateside duty, what I had seen of it. There was less unnecessary nonsense, fewer dog and pony shows. Unlike duty in the States, where we had to be prepared for any contingency in any part of the world, soldiers overseas during the Cold War knew what our mission was; we knew who the enemy was. We could prepare single-mindedly to oppose that enemy. I wasn't thrilled about going

---

[84] Since I left the Army, the Corps now controls four combat divisions: the 82nd and 101st which have been with the Corps off and on since World War II. When the 10th Mountain was re-activated in the late 80s it joined the Corps. After the end of the Cold War the 3rd Infantry Division colors were brought home from Germany and the 24th Infantry at Ft. Stewart, GA was deactivated and replaced by the "Third Herd."

to Turkey and leaving my family, but I could have lived with it. As a soldier, you do what you have to do.

After talking it over with Debbie, I discovered she was adamantly opposed to my going overseas, much less my going alone (the part of Turkey I was headed for was considered a "hardship" tour, families weren't allowed to go with soldiers stationed there). Weeping bitterly, she told me she didn't know if she could stand being away from me a year. I knew how rough military life could be on wives and children. I had seen what my mother had gone through with my stepfather's Army career. I tried to let my wife have input on as many career decisions as possible because I knew firsthand how much the family is affected by these things. I also knew it was inevitable that if I stayed in the Army twenty years as planned that we would eventually have to do at least one separate tour. I had warned her about this when I went back on active duty.

This levy could not have come at a worse time; the separation would strain an already stressed marriage. We had been through a lot in our two years of marriage and our financial situation wasn't too good. Perhaps I could delay it.

I went to see if I could get my orders changed. I had been guaranteed at least a year on jump status upon finishing jump school. I had finished jump school only the previous summer; this levy was a breach of contract. It took some doing. The fellow at our regional personnel center was dead set against even trying to get DA to change my orders because I had been handpicked by DA for this assignment. I figured it was because of my experience in the 1/40th FA in Germany.

I got a buddy of mine in the Brigade personnel section to bypass the regional office and call Washington direct. It turned out the people at the Pentagon had not been informed I was even airborne qualified, much less on jump status. They were highly upset. Had they known I was on jump status they would not even have considered me for this assignment. There was no sense sending a man with a "P" identifier on his MOS code (signifying Paratrooper) to nuke school as only the heavier guns could fire the nuclear rounds. Airborne units are issued lighter howitzers, which are air droppable. If they sent me to nuke school, the Army would never be able to get the maximum use out of my training. The Army liked to keep paratroopers in airborne units, the unique requirements of airborne operations requires experience.

DA dropped my orders immediately. Our personnel center was given a rebuke for not properly updating DA on my status. I don't imagine the personnel center was too happy about it. I've often wondered if all this had anything to do with what happened next.

Not a month after my overseas orders were dropped, I was told the slot I had occupied at HHB had been eliminated. I was going to be sent back to a leg line battalion. I was back to square one. That meant I'd be eligible for levy again.

I didn't want to go back to Legland.[85] I was told if I could get a letter of acceptance from the 82nd Airborne Division Artillery, my orders would be changed and I'd be spared going to Legland. I knew my old Chief of Firing Battery from Germany, SFC Jackson, was now a First Sergeant in the Division so I did what I had wanted to do for months, visit him. Now I had a "reason." My NCOIC, MSG Clarke, allowed me some time off to go.

It was good seeing him again, in my last year in Germany, he had been the only member of my chain of command I felt cared about the troops or knew what he was doing. It took about fifteen minutes to get my letter typed. For better or worse, I was on my way to the 82nd Airborne Division.

I signed into the Division on February 16, 1982. MSG Clarke had already made a phone call to the First Sergeant of HSB[86] 1/320th, an old friend of his, telling him I was on the way. told the Battalion Commander a guy with brigade level heaquarters' experience was on his way to the battalion. I didn't make it to the guns. The battalion was in the middle of its Intensified Training Cycle – I spent the next month and a half or so in the field.

On March 30, 1982 I jumped into Ft. Irwin, California for Gallant Eagle 82. The rest is, as they say, history.

---

[85] The nickname paratroopers give all non-Airborne soldiers is "leg," short for "straightleg." There are several stories as to where this name came from. One says it comes from the way paratroopers have to bend their knees when they prepare to land during a jump, non-airborne people are thus straight-legs. Another, more probable origin comes from the paratrooper's privilege of being allowed to wear bloused jump boots with their dress uniforms as opposed to regular low-quartered shoes. The bloused jump boots break the straight fall of the pant legs, therefore non-airborne personnel are called "straight-legs." I've always thought, after watching veteran troopers walk, with their limps from years of abuse on the knee joints, it might refer to posture, of course, that's my own personal take on the subject.

[86] HSB – In the 82nd DivArty, Battalion Headquarters and Headquarters Batteries (HHBs) were combined with Service Batteries into HSBs – Headquarters and Service Batteries, as far as I know this was unique to the Division.

Chapter 14
Coming Back from the Dead

The girl I marry has gotta be,
An Airborne Ranger, just like me!
Eight feet tall and six feet wide,
Tearing up the countryside.
I'll stay in shape for the rest of my life,
Just a'runnin' from my airborne wife!
(Anonymous Airborne running cadence)

Shortly after leaving the March AFB ICU the day finally came when all the inter-service bickering and fighting over my carcass came to an end and I was allowed to go home. It was decided I would be returned to Ft. Bragg where any further reconstructive surgery to be performed on me would be done by the Chief of Surgery of Womack Army Hospital.

Of course, I didn't know any of this yet. I was just the patient. I still hadn't been given a glance at my head.

Anyway, I was loaded on a medical bird with about a dozen other guys, among the last to go home, i.e., among the most seriously injured who couldn't have been moved prior to this time. Our first leg of the journey couldn't have lasted over forty-five minutes; we stopped at another Air Force Base in California. I want to say it was McNair AFB. We were to stay overnight before flying across country and home. The base had been a major clearing station for wounded returning home from Nam. One of the nurses, a civilian employee who had been with the hospital for years, told me Gallant Eagle had been keeping them busier than anytime since Nam.

The staff treated us like kings. The chow was some of the best I ever remember eating in the service. After chow, one of the orderlies brought in a case of beer he had bought for us. I didn't think I ought to be drinking beer with my head injury so I gave mine to another guy. I was touched by what, to the Air Force personnel, was an act of great consideration.

Our arrival the next evening at Bragg was accompanied by a flurry of activity. We were transported to Womack Army Hospital where a tall, elderly gentleman greeted me. I noticed his nametag, "Col. Luehrs." He smiled at Debbie, who was being held back by an orderly, "I assume you're Mrs. Wood?" he asked with kindly amusement.

Debbie nodded her head vigorously.

"It's okay," he said to the orderly. He turned to me, "I'm Dr. Luehrs, your doctor." His gentleness put me at ease. I realized I knew him. Just a few months ago he had removed a cyst from my arm. I felt greatly relieved; I was in good hands.

It didn't take me long to realize I was no longer with the Air Force. I was assigned a room and given sheets with which to make my own bed. Once I finished this one of the orderlies came in and gave me a sponge, a bottle of antiseptic with which to clean my head wound, and special scrubbing sponges with which to scrub the wounds on my arms. The Army has always gone by the axiom the more you can do for yourself, the faster your recovery.

"Welcome home," I said to myself as I headed into the latrine (bathroom). My room had a private latrine, so it wasn't much of a walk.

Dr. Luehrs had removed the big bandage the night before and replaced it with a gauze pad held in place with a type of net. This made the dressing a breeze to whip off.

I went into the latrine and turned the shower on. I snatched the dressing off and was about to get in the shower when I saw myself in the mirror. At first I just looked at my wounds curiously. It took a moment for what I was looking at to sink in. When it did, I could only stare in stupid disbelief.

My head looked as if someone had literally snatched off the left side of my scalp. The gaping wound started from the front of my head, extending like a stretched out half-moon to the back of my head. I could see numerous bald patches on the other side of my head where the hair had been scraped off by the drag, or shaved off my medical personnel trying to sew up the hundreds of tiny cuts and gashes across my scalp. I looked at the gash again, toward the front of my skull. Just above the hairline, I could see grayish patch, about the size of a half dollar. I leaned closer to the mirror for a better look. I tapped the gray area. It was hard. I realized it was my skull.

I sat down on the edge of the bathtub and began crying like a little baby. I thought of the dead men, three of whom I had known or met; I thought of all the troopers who'd never be the same again. I thought of myself, going through life maimed. I wept at the apparent uselessness of it all. An orderly came in and asked me what was wrong. All I could do was cry.

Finally, I got myself together, "I'll be all right." I said.

Five men were dead. A couple hundred were seriously

injured. I was permanently disfigured. Life goes on.

After I'd been at Bragg a few days and the Army folks had run their own tests on me (the same the Air Force had done on me in California), Dr. Luehrs decided he could send me home on an overnight pass. He taught Debbie how to clean and dress my wounds. She enjoyed playing nurse. I was sent home with the stern admonition to be back in the morning and not to overdo it.

This was my routine for the next few weeks. I would go into the hospital in the morning for a checkup and be released until the next day. I stopped by my unit to find things hopping - as usual.

The S-4 Officer[87], CPT Walton, was having his hands full getting inventories of all the personal equipment lost by and stolen from injured jumpers. As the stuff was lost due to no fault of the jumpers, and as the result of a military operation, the Army would replace or reimburse our losses.

At the same time, the Division was speeding up the issue of the new Kevlar helmet, dubbed the "Fritz" by the gurus at the Pentagon (though we troopers never called it that). The Kevlar had been in development since the mid-seventies. I had my first glimpse of it while stationed in Germany. The Army was supposed to go over to the new helmet gradually, with the Division being the first major unit to be equipped, sometime in 1983. The accident sped the whole process.

Investigating officers discovered that many of the helmet liners, though showing no problem upon a visual inspection, were actually unserviceable and unsafe because of their age. The inside webbing of many of the helmet liners, which were supposed to add support and protection to the wearers' heads, were, in truth dry rotted. The Army figured some of the helmets and liners had been around since World War II. Under normal conditions, there had been no problems. Subjected to the stress our helmets were subjected to in California, the helmets tore away, and actually causing injury in many cases, such as mine. The experts figured

---

[87]S-4 - the staff officer in charge of supply for the battalion. It might be advisable here to insert a note on the staff sections and their designation. The staffs at battalion and brigade levels are designated numerically, with an "S" in front of their numbers. S-1 is the staff officer and section designation of the battalion personnel section, in charge of personnel records, pay, and assignments. S-2 is the battalion intelligence section, charged with security and disseminating information about the enemy. S-3 is plans and operations, also in charge of co-coordinating and conducting training in peacetime. S-4 is the logistics section, in charge of supply. This also includes jurisdiction over the battalion motor pool and mess hall. At Division and higher headquarters levels the designating "S" is changed to a "G," hence, G-1, G-2, etc. There is also a fifth staff position at Division and higher level, G-5, public affairs; these are our public relations people.

when I hit the rock, the webbing in my helmet gave way. As my helmet was yanked off my head, the snaps and catches, which attached my headband to the inner webbing of the helmet liner, dug into my scalp snatching it away as the helmet pulled off my head.

Another item the Army was ditching was the old T-10 harness. This harness, with its pinch-type canopy release assemblies had contributed to many injuries (again, mine). I don't know how many times I've had people try to sharp shoot me and criticize me for not using my "capewells[88]." I did try to use my capewells, it's just they wouldn't work. I remember asking myself over and over while I was being dragged if I was doing it right.

The enormous pressure put on the T-10 canopy releases by the high winds pulling the chutes interfered with the proper functioning of the mechanisms. The Army had been in the process of gradually phasing out the T-10 harnesses, which had been in service for a couple of decades, and replacing them with the newer MC1-1B harnesses. This harness is equipped with a wire pull release. One slips one's thumb underneath the wire, pulls out violently and the canopy is separated from the harness. Troopers jumping with this harness had markedly fewer problems than those jumping the T-10. The Division Commander ordered all T-10 harnesses replaced immediately.

Other changes were instituted. The investigation determined the Air Safety Operational Procedure had been followed to the letter. However, there were holes in the procedure that allowed the accident to happen.

More safety officers were now required to take wind readings at various locations on the drop zone instead of just one at the leading edge. Wind readings had to be at safe levels for a longer period of time (ten minutes) prior to drop time before a jump could be declared a "Go." This would ensure wind conditions were stable at the time of the jump. Under the ASOP at the time of the accident, if the winds were safe at drop time, the jump could be declared a "Go," no matter how high they were a few seconds before. It was determined the winds had gusted as we were coming out of the birds in California.

The Division took steps to keep any adverse effects the disaster might have on morale at a minimum. Units hit hard by the jump were given extra jumps over the next few months. My

---

[88] Improper jargon for canopy release assembly, which as explained before, connected one's parachute harness to its risers. Disconnecting one canopy release assembly allowed the chute to collapse, preventing a drag.

battalion was jumped to death (no pun intended). Some of the guys were getting two or three blasts a week. It was a matter of getting back on the horse that threw you, so to speak.

Units were marched down to York Theater, in the 82nd area, and given a briefing on what went wrong on the jump. A film of the jump was shown. I was still in the hospital when all this was going on, but I had to watch it later. It was a tough experience. The hardest part was watching the trooper whose chute malfunctioned. This is a paratrooper's worst nightmare.

What had happened was a jumper exited carrying a Dragon Missile Jump Pack attached to his harness.[89] Somehow or another his equipment got tangled with his static line as he went out the door. He became a towed jumper, being dragged in the air behind the aircraft. The Safety[90] missed the towed jumper because his static line rode high on the door instead of at the bottom.[91] As a result, the jump wasn't stopped; six more jumpers left the aircraft, some of them bumped into the towed jumper, finally knocking him loose. His chute deployed normally and he landed safely on the ground. One of the men who bumped into him wasn't so fortunate. When he hit the towed jumper, twenty-three of the thirty nylon suspension lines which connected his canopy to his risers were seared, making it impossible for his chute to open.

The film showed him plummeting to the ground, his chute behind him in a "cigarette roll." Eight hundred feet doesn't give one much time to react. Evidently, the fellow was either unconscious or stunned, because it wasn't until he was about one hundred feet from the ground that the white of his reserve parachute appeared. By then, it was too late. There was not enough time for his reserve to open. He was killed instantly.

The CG discussed each death, analyzing its cause and effect. The motto of the 82nd Airborne Jumpmaster School is "The Sky, Even More than the Sea, is Unforgiving of the Slightest Mistake." It

---

[89] Dragon Missile Jump Pack- a canvas container for jumping in with the Dragon anti-tank missile launcher. A rather large canvas container, it attaches to a jumper's harness along his body from the ground to right under his armpit. It has to be lowered before landing by the jumper to avoid injury.

[90] Safety- Jump Safety NCO/Officer. A Jumpmaster qualified person who is responsible for ensuring static lines are not misrouted around a jumpers' limbs as well as helping the jumpmaster ensure all jumpers are safely exited from the aircraft.

[91] Static lines ride high when a jumper separates from his static line. The weight of the jumper no longer weighs it down. A towed jumper usually drags the static line down toward the rearward corner of the jump door. It is the safety's job to keep an eye on the static lines and spot a towed jumper. For some reason the towed jumper's static line rose like he had separated. The safety had no way of knowing SSG Moore was being towed and therefore allowed three more jumpers to exit. These all bumped into SSG Moore on their way out.

was the CG's stated purpose that if we could learn from each of these deaths then, even though tragic, these troopers would not have died in vain.   Many thought him cold hearted to objectively analyze these men's deaths the way he did. I remembered the tears in his eyes when he came to the hospital and saw us lying there. I've often reflected on what a heavy responsibility it must be to be a general, to order men to do things you know are going to cost them their lives, to live with their deaths afterwards. It takes a special something to do that. Call it courage, call it will, call it self-confidence or arrogance, whatever you will. Not many have it. I suppose that's why so few make it so far.

Two other men had died immediately from the same type of head injury I had suffered. A few weeks after my return to Bragg I was urgently called back to the hospital for further tests. The Major from the Engineers who had gone out the door a few jumpers ahead of me had suffered the same injuries as me. A blood clot, which had somehow gotten past all the tests, had moved. It killed him. The death toll was up to six. I was brought in and given a good going over to ensure I was okay.

They did my surgery toward the end of April. This consisted of stretching what was left of my scalp over the injured area. A skin graft was placed on the area where the scalp wouldn't stretch. I was left with a scarred area about the size of a silver dollar on the left side of the top of my head. Dr. Luehrs talked of a second surgery in a year or so, after the skin had a chance to stretch properly. But he retired that fall and the fellow who replaced him didn't see the sense in wasting time covering up my scar. After all, the hole was covered and, if I parted my hair on the right, it covered the hole.

If I ever go bald, as the men on my mother's side of the family are prone to do, I've considered having the Division Coin the CG gave me implanted where the scar is. It just about fits. The only problem there is I don't know which side to have facing out, the side with the paratrooper or the 82nd patch.

The night before my surgery they shaved my scalp, no easy task, considering all the other damage inflicted upon my noggin. After several failed attempts with a razor, it was decided to use a hair removing cream. I remember walking back out into the hall after they finished with my head and I had showered. I was looking for a nurse to re-bandage me. My wounds were exposed. I guess I wasn't really thinking about what I looked like.

There was a young boy about sixteen, a patient, standing out in the hall by the nurses' station with his girlfriend. When I came up

194

with my head all torn open I thought the girl was going to go into hysterics. I tried to joke it off.

"I'm sorry," I said. "I didn't mean to upset you, most people admire my open mind."

I apologized to the couple and told the nurse I'd be in my room. I was getting real good at scaring people. If it turned out I couldn't stay in the Army I could always get a job in a horror movie - or freak show.

After I was released from the hospital I was put on a thirty-day convalescent leave. We didn't have enough money to go anywhere, and I wasn't really up to it anyway, so we spent the time relaxing around the house and fishing.

Dr. Luehrs told me to try and increase my activity, so, aware of a growing waistline I assumed was caused by my inactivity, I began to exercise. I tried pushups the first week out and ended up rolling in agony on the floor. The moment I put any pressure on my right shoulder it gave out. A trip to the hospital revealed that I had another injury to add to my list, probably a dislocation. As it had already relocated, the only thing I could do was to take it easy a little while longer.

I began running after another week or so. I started out slow at first, short distances, around the block. Gradually, I built myself back up to two miles, praying "The Lord's Prayer" all the way. This was still not good enough. In the 82nd we ran a minimum of four miles a day.

I also took advantage of the time off to begin reading the pocket New Testament I had gotten years ago when I first entered the Army. I don't recall ever reading the Bible from front to back before. Now I determined to do it - at least the New Testament. The Old Testament would have to wait until I got a complete Bible. Ron, one of the maintenance men at the trailer park where we lived, helped my study.

He and Debbie had become friends while I was out in California. He had come over to do some repairs and found her in near hysterics after the accident. Ron prayed for her and gave her comfort with the Word. Debbie couldn't wait to introduce us. It turned out he had been heavy into drugs and on the verge of death from them when he found Jesus. After receiving Jesus, the Lord delivered him from drugs instantly. This fellow was a fireball for the Lord.

He'd come to the house in the evening and we'd talk about the Bible. I was hungry for knowledge of the Word and Ron was knowledgeable. Often, he'd stay for supper. One night I tried one of the off-the-wall theories that used to send Grandma into spasms. I got a reaction I had never gotten from Grandma. He rebuked me in the name of Jesus.

I had never been rebuked before. It blew my mind. I felt ashamed. I sure didn't want to be rebuked again. He broke this hound from sucking eggs.

I talked to Ron about getting baptized and getting into a church. He mentioned his church, a charismatic fellowship. I had been out of the church scene a long time. I didn't even know what a charismatic fellowship was and why it would be different from the Pentecostal churches I had attended growing up. Ron explained it to me.

Debbie and I talked about going to Ron's church. She had been raised a Baptist, but had attended a charismatic church at Ft. Campbell, Kentucky, with her first husband. She said she had loved it. We made plans to go that Sunday. The alarm didn't go off. By the time we got up it was too late.

The next Sunday it was something else. Ron soon stopped coming over except in the course of his job, though we remained friendly.

I went back to work for a week after my leave. It was an exhausting experience. I was still on a very limited profile[92] that restricted my activities to the lightest of duties. Each day still left me drained. I could barely drag myself out of bed in the morning to go to work. I hung on, though; all I had to do was last the week. After that, I'd have another month's leave to recuperate.

The most disturbing thing I discovered during my week back at work was my short-term memory had been affected by my injuries. I was still working in the S-3 shop. There were times when I would be sent down the street to DivArty[93] headquarters on an errand. To my frustration I found I often forgot my errand by the time I walked the block from my battalion headquarters to DivArty.

I would wander around the building, too embarrassed to tell anyone my problem. I would look at the nametags of individuals I saw in the building, hoping to jog my memory. Eventually, someone would recognize me and ask me if I wanted to call back to battalion and ask SFC Jones, the new Operations NCO what I was doing at

---

[92] Profile- a duty restriction, usually a medical limitation.
[93] DivArty- Division Artillery, the Administrative headquarters of the division's artillery battalions.

DivArty. By the end of the week it got to where SFC Jones had me timed. He'd be ready when I called.

"Hello, Woody," he'd answer before I even had a chance to identify myself, "You're supposed to see Lieutenant Dipstick about the Moxnix[94] letter."

"Thanks Chief." One time I was using Lieutenant Dipstick's phone while he was sitting across the desk from me.

I tried all sorts of memory aid tricks to help me remember, none of them worked. I wasn't about to start writing things down - at least not yet. That would be admitting defeat.

In the meantime, the battalion was hosting a group of troopers from the Canadian Parachute Regiment for the week as part of a unit exchange program. The 82nd used to do this quite regularly with allied nations. We'd send a company-sized unit of troopers to train with them and they'd send people in return. The high point of these exchanges was our men would get to jump with the host nation's equipment and earn a set of foreign parachutist's wings. By the same token, the foreign troopers hoped to earn a set of U.S. wings.

I was detailed to escort the Canadian troopers around for their orientation the first couple of days they were at Ft. Bragg. They had all heard about Gallant Eagle 82 and asked me about it. I admitted I had been on the jump and had almost been killed. They looked at me in awe, "'You going to jump again, hey?" a corporal asked me.

"As soon as they let me." I answered, trying to sound as hard core as I could.

I took them over to the DivArty classroom where they would be shown a videotape introducing them to the Division. It's a pretty good film. I stood at the door and watched with them. The opening really got to me. It was a complete jump sequence, from the ten-minute warning to the green light. I remember watching the film and feeling the tension as if I was in the aircraft. I fought the butterflies in my stomach as they showed the door of the aircraft open and the jumpmaster "hanging" out the door to do his last minute safety checks. I swallowed hard and tried to bring some moisture to my mouth. I looked at the others in the room and felt relieved to see that they, too, were experiencing the same emotions, were caught up by the video. A couple of them looked up at me apprehensively, noting the scars on my bare head. I wouldn't have blamed them for having second thoughts about jumping with the Yanks.

---

[94]Moxnix- GI German for "Machts Nichts," or "It doesn't matter."

When they finally did get to jump I was able to piece together an amusing story from two of the Americans involved in the jump, SSG Hawks, who had acted as jumpmaster on the bird the Canadians were on, and PFC Churchill, who had been at one of the parachute turn-in points on the DZ.

The Canadians did not use the C-141 Starlifter jet to drop their paratroopers, but only the C-130 Hercules, a propeller driven aircraft with a slower drop speed.[95] As I touched on earlier, one exited differently from a C-141 than a C-130.

On a C-130, a jumper had to take a proper door position and leap up and out of the aircraft forcefully to avoid being blown back into the skin (sides) of the aircraft by the prop blast of the plane's engines. On a C-141, the speed of the aircraft was much greater and the winds were, naturally enough, much higher. If one was caught by these winds he would be blown back against the aircraft. A windscreen was built into the doors of the aircraft to shield jumpers from the wind as they exit. As I explained earlier, jumpers exiting a C-141 did not really "jump" out of the aircraft, but step out the door at a forty-five degree angle so they did not get tossed back against the aircraft by the winds.

During the pre-jump safety briefings jumpmasters were careful to point out to the jumpers which aircraft was being used on a jump and to explain the method of exit required. Most Division troopers loved jumping out of a C-141. Our Canadian guests were jumping out of a C-141 for their first jump with the 82nd Airborne Division. Somehow, they didn't get the word on the difference in jumping the two aircraft.

I've yet to figure it out. SSG Hawks was usually a good jumpmaster. I always thought he was a prime example of an 82nd *Prima Dona* (we had plenty of them), one of those guys who think they are never wrong. Once they might have thought they were wrong, but that was a mistake on their part. Thinking they could be wrong, that is. They strutted around the Division area like roosters in the barnyard, chest puffed out, constantly crowing. These guys would get on my nerves more often than not. But I had to admit they were usually good – no excellent – at their jobs. It was their perfectionist attitude that made guys like Hawks a good jumpmaster. So I don't know how the Canadians missed the warnings about the C-141. They were good soldiers. I had watched them several days,

---

[95] Sadly, for this old trooper, the US Army no longer uses the C-141 or the C-141A; the last ones were retired in 2006. They were replaced with the C-17 Globemaster III, which has a larger cargo capacity.

during that time I was impressed with their professionalism.

Anyway, when they got up in the bird and the green jump light came on, SSG Hawks watched as the jumpers exited the aircraft. The Canadians were first. As each Canadian exited the bird, there was a "thud," as each jumper hit the skin of the aircraft. It puzzled him at first. As he watched the fourth jumper exit the aircraft, he realized what they were doing. They were taking up door positions as one would a C-130. As a result, they were jumping out past the windscreen and being blown back into the aircraft.

Before he was able to do anything the fifth jumper was in the door. Safety regulations forbade anyone touching a jumper in the door. He stopped the sixth man and told the Air Force loadmaster to make another "racetrack" (pass over the DZ to come in again). While the plane was circling around to make another approach he quickly explained to the Canadian troopers how to exit a C-141 so they wouldn't get hurt.

Meanwhile, down on the DZ, PFC Churchill was standing at the chute turn-in point when the first poor, dazed, Canadian, came staggering in. Church had been puzzled when only five jumpers exited, but didn't know what had happened.

"How'd you like the jump?" he asked as the trooper dumped his chute, stuffed away in their aviator's kit bags at his feet.

"Do you Yanks jump those planes often?" he asked, obviously still shaken from the bump his head had taken against the aircraft.

"Not enough for me!" Churchill said, innocently.

"You mean you *like* jumping those aircraft?" the Canadian asked incredulously.

"Yeah man, the C-141 is the Cadillac of aircraft!"

"You Yanks are crazy!" the Canadian said as he walked off, shaking his head. The rest of the Canadian contingent's jump was uneventful. I hope the five guys who came out first had a better blast next time.

Chapter 15
The Hard Road Back

When my granny was ninety-six, she did PT just for kicks
When my granny was ninety-seven, she up and died and went to
heaven
She met St. Peter at the pearly gates, 'said, "I hope I'm not too late"
Peter said with a big ol' grin, "Drop down granny and give me ten!"
(Anonymous airborne running cadence)

It happened that I returned to duty on the week before Memorial Day, which in the Division is also known as All American Week. This was an annual week of fun and games in which teams from the different units competed against one another in different events, such as tire throws, chariot races, push ball, and, my all time favorite game - the bear pit![96] There were other, more conventional contests, tug of war, foot races, military skills contests, etc...

These continued throughout the week, with playoffs for the Division Championship in each event culminating by Wednesday afternoon. Then, with Thursday, came the highlight of the week, the annual Division Review. The entire 82nd Airborne Division would march down to the end Ardennes Street in their finest set of duty uniforms (BDUs by this time), new berets, spit-shined boots, web gear,[97] and weapons with fixed bayonets. There we would stand in the sun, sweating in the ninety degree heat and seventy-five to eighty percent humidity listening to the guest speakers tell us how pretty we looked and how great we were (which fact most of us were already

---

[96] The tire throw was like the discus throw in the Olympics – only using a jeep tire. In the chariot races jeep trailers pulled down Ardennes Street by human horse teams. In push ball two teams of 20+ soldiers push a six-foot stuffed ball across a football field trying to get the pushball past the opponent's goal line or stop the other team from pushing the ball past your goal line any way they can. The only rule in pushball other than scoring is NO RULES! Do whatever it takes to win!

The Bear pit is a sort of "King of the hill" in reverse. It is a huge mud filled pit, in which two teams of equal number jump into the mud. The object of the game is to get every member of the opposing team out of the pit, using whatever means are necessary to do so (though outright punches and kicks are prohibited). The team with the last man in the pit wins the game. I loved this game. However, the Army began discouraging the Bear Pit and Pushball because of the numerous sprains and fractures incurred playing the games. Ah, our modern, volunteer Army in the sensitive post-Vietnam era!

[97] Web gear, pistol belt, shoulder straps, ammo pouches, canteens, etc. Also called variously, LCE (Load Carrying Equipment), or LBE (Load Bearing Equipment) according to which staff officer at the Pentagon needed to inflate is OER Support Form.

convinced of, anyway). Numerous soldiers would drop in the heat, endangering those near them with their bayonets as they fell. Some guys got hurt that way. I'd almost been skewered once or twice. Then, you'd dodge a bayonet and some First Sergeant behind the formation would yell at you for moving while you were at attention or parade rest. Only in the Army.

After an hour and a half or so of that, the long awaited moment would come when the Division Adjutant would step up to the mike and give the command, "Division!"

This would be echoed by the Brigade Commanders, "Brigade!"

This would be echoed by the Battalion Commanders, "Battalion!"

"Pass in Review!"

With colors and guidons flapping in whatever hot North Carolina breeze we had that day, the Division would begin moving, by battalion, from the right, to the left. The first battalion would execute a right turn and begin marching around the field to pass by the reviewing stand. The band would be playing and our legs, stiff from the lengthy time standing at attention and parade rest, would begin to limber up to the movement.

Sergeant Rob always said it was the Division's annual chance to show it couldn't march. After all, we rarely had the opportunity to practice parade style marching in the Division. We only used it for change of command ceremonies and the annual review. We would practice by battalion on Tuesday, with Division rehearsal on Wednesday before the actual event on Thursday. I thought the practices were worse than the real thing. During the actual review, we only had to do it once.

I once mentioned to Rob that we ought to double time past the review stand, considering we were much more used to running than marching.

"Shut your mouth, Woody!" he said in mock fear, "Someone might hear you and get an idea!"

I always got a kick out of the preparation for the review. On the morning of the review, as we stood on Carentan Street forming up to march, the First Sergeants would mingle through the soldiers, making last minute inspections of haircuts and boots. A dirty flash on a beret, a worn heel on your boot would get you out of the Review, but put on a dirty duty detail on Memorial Day weekend. I wondered at the fuss they would make over these tiny details. I got a picture of the Division Commander, standing about three hundred yards away from the nearest division trooper, looking out at over sixteen thousand paratroopers formed up in mass division formations by battalion. His eyes sweep the multitude of camouflaged BDUs and maroon berets. Then he stops, his eyes narrow, he motions over to the Division Command Sergeant Major.

"Sergeant Major!" he snaps, "That soldier over there, the five hundredth from the left in the fifty-sixth row... the heel on his left boot is worn a quarter of an inch!" or, "That soldier, one thousandth from the right, in the thirtieth row, his flash is dirty!"

I always thought if I had been the Division Commander I would stand on the reviewing stand and in my best Marlon Brando Godfather imitation, say, "I'ma da boss... and dese are my people..."

Maybe that's why I was never the Division Commander.

But I have to admit we looked good out there. I always felt pride to be a part of the 82nd. I would get especially choked up when the "Old Guard" would march past. These were the surviving original members of the 82nd Airborne, those who had jumped and fought through World War II. As I'd watch them limp or hobble past us, some using canes, some in a wheelchair, their bodies bent, but heads held high, I'd feel humble. I've read so many accounts of what these men experienced and accomplished during their war. I didn't feel fit to polish their jump boots.

Marching back was another special time to me and not just because the Review was over. When we'd be marching down Ardennes Street to our battalion area I'd feel it. Often Top Moore, a former drill sergeant, would lead the battalion in cadence. We'd be dead tired, our legs and feet tired and sore, but when we would pass DivArty headquarters at the end of our mile and a half march we would square our shoulders, lift our heads, and sing out with Top. To me, this was one of those magic moments that gave the term *esprit de corps* its meaning. I'd be overcome with a sense of pride in my unit, in my uniform, in my country. I would feel a sense of brotherhood with the soldiers around me, we were in this thing together; we would share whatever faced us as a team. We shared good times, bad times, comforts and hardships. We may not have particularly liked each other personally, but when the chips were down, we would pull together and accomplish the mission. These men were my buddies.

There were other times when I would get choked up with emotion at what it meant to be a soldier. Sometimes at "Reveille" or

"Retreat," or during "Taps." I used to get misty in Germany during a ceremony when the 3rd Armored Division Band would play the theme from the movie *Patton*, which was sort of the 3rd Armored's unofficial theme song. I'd feel close to all those who'd gone before. I'd feel a part of something bigger, more important than I. It's a feeling one seldom finds in civilian life.

I was too weak to stand the Division Review in 1982. I was on light duty, and had been all week. Top put me on Assistant Charge of Quarters. It turned out I was too weak to stay up all night as well. At about two in the morning I got terribly sick with stomach spasms and had to be rushed to the emergency room at the hospital. I didn't make much of it at the time, as I was to sign out on leave the next day anyway. I'd have a month to rest and restore. I was taking Debbie and the kids up to Illinois where we would meet up with my family, who were returning from Alaska to go to Ft. Lewis, Washington. I had been married two and a half years by this time and my family hadn't yet met my wife. Such is Army life.

I didn't get much rest on my vacation, though. First, we drove the eight hundred or so miles from Ft. Bragg, NC to the St. Louis area. We spent a little over a week there. After leaving Illinois we drove almost six hundred miles to visit Debbie's folks in Alabama. After that, we drove the five hundred miles or so back to Bragg. After a trip like that, one is ready to go back to work to get a break.

Dr. Luehrs was waiting for me when I got back from leave. He made a habit of checking the emergency room log sheets for any of his patients and saw my name. When I told him what happened he immediately wrote a profile exempting me from twenty-four hour duty. I was also forbidden to wear a helmet. It was thought this would keep me out of the field until I was completely well.

He meant well, but it didn't work. The people I worked for took me out anyway without a helmet. I was ordered to buy a BDU hat (in the field we called it patrol hat, but it was really a hated "leg" hat) after I got caught out in the field with my beret on, which was forbidden.

I was riding back to the rear in a jeep, trying to make a doctor's appointment when it happened. We passed the DivArty Command Sergeant Major. I had been riding bareheaded. When I saw him coming I believed it was better to put on my beret than be caught bareheaded in the field. I was wrong. The CSM stopped our jeep and asked me what I was doing wearing a beret out in the field.

I explained to him why I wasn't supposed to wear a helmet.
"Why not?"
I told him about Gallant Eagle and showed him my scars.
"You're Wood?"
"Yes, Sergeant Major."
"Who told you to come out to the field?"
"My boss."
"Who's your boss?"
I told him I worked for the battalion S-3 shop. He drove off saying he'd have a talk with someone. I ended up getting chewed out for that one. Why on earth did I put my beret on when we weren't supposed to wear berets "west of Gruber Road?" That is, out in the field.

I explained to my boss what happened. I was told it was better to be "uncovered" than to wear a beret in the field. I was learning that, in addition to the three ways I had learned of doing things- the right way, the wrong way, and the Army way- there was a fourth way, the 82nd way.

It never occurred to anyone what might have happened to me if I had hit my head out in the field, always a possibility, without the protection of my helmet. I didn't say anything about it, though I could have complained. After all, they were endangering my life and violating Army regulations. I figured it wasn't worth the flak I'd catch. I had too much at stake.

For one thing, I was trying to put together a packet to go to Officers Candidate School (OCS). I needed the support of my supervisors for that, letters of recommendation from officers, endorsements, etc. In order to do this I had to stay in the Army, prove that I could recover. I had to jump again. A person medically disqualified from jump status was hardly likely to be accepted to OCS. I was walking a tightrope, trying to convince everyone I was coming back, "able to hang." At the same time, I had to take care of myself. I had to make sure these guys didn't kill me. In another unit, on another post, it might not have been so hard. But this was Fort Bragg and the 82nd Airborne Division.

Very few people in my battalion really thought I was going to make it. After all, it was common knowledge I had been declared dead. The prognosis for recovery wasn't all that good. Even if I managed to stay in the Army no one ever expected me to be able to jump again. My speech was still slurred three months after my surgery, and my right leg still dragged when I walked. It still does, to a certain degree, but you really have to be looking to notice. And there was the shadow of SGT Ricardo hanging over me.

SGT Ricardo was a gun chief in our Bravo Battery. We had been on the same bird on the jump. I remember him joking and cutting up on the flight. He had suffered severe head injuries similar to mine. Our cases were similar in many ways, except I don't believe he was ever as close to death as was I. He had a harder time coming back, though.

We came back to duty about the same time. We were both on light duty, he in his battery, doing errands, me at battalion, doing whatever. I can still see him shuffling around the battalion area, with his crooked, friendly grin. He had been a hard charging NCO before the accident. Now, permanently brain damaged from his injuries, he was a shadow of his former self. His memory was so bad his wife would have to drive him to and from work. If he drove himself, he would get lost.

We would often talk to one another about what we were going through. I would tell him I was going to make it back and jump again. He would just smile and tell me it was over for him, he was just counting days until his medical retirement came through. After that, it was "live off Uncle Sugar!" He'd be smiling, but I could see the pain in his eyes.

One day I was over at Bravo Battery on business when I walked in on the First Sergeant getting on SGT Ricardo for forgetting to do something.

"What can I say, Top?" Ricardo shrugged, "I'm just 'dain-bramaged!"

Top looked over at me sadly and dropped his head.

I remember clearing him out of battalion when his papers finally came through. "Be careful, Woody," he said, "or you're next. 'Don't need no 'dain-bramaged' paratroopers in the 82nd!"

I began paying close attention to my walk. I made a conscious effort not to drag my leg. I watched my speech. I began to keep a notebook and write everything down. To me, it was a necessary compromise to convince my superiors I was getting better. I was getting better, but I sensed, my real progress was not fast enough for those in charge.

Of major concern was the twenty pounds or so I gained while on leave. This concerned my doctor for health reasons, my chain of command because of AR 600-9, the regulation governing the Army Weight Control Program. No one would bother me as long as I was on profile, during my recovery period. As soon as I was returned to duty I knew I would be expected to toe the line.

At the time, I wasn't too worried about losing the weight. I figured all I'd have to do to get back in shape was to get back into a good running program, cut back on some meals, and I'd be back down to size in no time flat.

I was on a profile to do PT on my own. I would make PT formation in the mornings for accountability purposes and break off as soon as the battery was marched off to the PT field for its calisthenics. Every now and then one of the NCOs would try to give me a hard time about leaving the formation and I would have to show them a copy of my profile. A couple of times I was even forced to do PT with the battery. Even though this was a violation of Army regulations, I would comply after informing the NCO of my profile. If you're going to survive in the Army you have to learn not to take an argument with a superior too far. If a superior gives you an order that is wrong, unless he or she is ordering you to commit a crime, you obey the order and complain later. If you refuse to obey the order, you become as wrong, if not more so, than the superior.

This is where many young soldiers mess up. They'll get into an argument with an NCO or refuse to obey the order and get busted because they have stepped over the invisible line and committed a punishable offense under the UCMJ. Sometimes, even if you are in the right, you learn it isn't worth the hassle of arguing. Sure, you can get the NCO a chewing out, but eventually, if the NCO holds a grudge, he can make you pay for it. You learn to choose your battlegrounds wisely.

I did have a run-in with one NCO over my profile. There was a Sergeant First Class in the unit who gave me some grief one time over the duty roster. He was acting First Sergeant while Top was on leave and had put me on Charge of Quarters (CQ). I went in with my profile to explain to him what happened when I tried to stay up all night. The guy seemed upset over having to change the roster. I apologized but explained to him again what happened when I tried to stay up. He thought about it for a moment, and then reread my profile.

"It says 'No twenty-four hour duty.'" he said, finally, "No problem, we let you off a half hour early. That way we don't violate your profile."

I couldn't believe my ears. "That's great, Chief." I said, trying to be as respectful as possible, "What'll we say to my doctor when I'm pulled in to the emergency room at two in the morning in convulsions?" I was trying hard not to sound like a smart aleck; after all it would be his behind if I got sick on duty and had to go to the hospital.

The guy got quiet, "Okay, okay, we'll change the roster."

A few years later the guy got promoted to First Sergeant. A bunch of us were thunderstruck by that. I looked on the bright side, if he could get promoted so quickly there was hope for us. Shortly after that I went up for promotion to Staff Sergeant (E-6). As one of the battalion First Sergeants, he was on the promotion board.[98] He was the only First Sergeant on the board to fail to recommend me for promotion. I've often wondered if he held a grudge over that stupid duty roster.

All in all I was pretty well left alone. On most mornings during PT, I'd leave the battery formation to go on my own private run. Sometimes I'd take off toward the "Old Division Area," across Longstreet and Butner Roads. On other days I'd head down the other way, through "Legland," to SOCOM (Special Operations Command (the Green Berets)) area and Smoke Bomb Hill. One of my favorite places to run was across Gruber Road in "Area J." A wooded area with numerous dirt trails that wound through it – I never did find the keys to Area J, but never failed to run into a deer or two whenever I ran there. There were days I'd jog up to eight or ten miles, just "airborne shuffling" at what I estimated was about an eight minute per mile pace.

When I got back from my run I'd go over to Towle Courts, across from our battalion area. There were racquetball and handball courts there. There was also a weight room and sauna. I'd pump some weights for a while and then hit the sauna for about ten minutes. After a shower, it'd be time to head for work.

One morning we were sitting in the sauna shooting the

---

[98] Promotion Board- During the time I was in the Army, promotions to E-5 and E-6 were handled by a "semi-centralized" system based on a 1000 point scale. A soldier received up to 750 "administrative points" time in grade and service, awards (medals, etc.), military and civilian education (college, service schools), etc. The soldier then appeared before a board composed of the senior NCOs in the battalion, usually First Sergeants and the Command Sergeant Major. That board could award up to 250 points and with a majority vote recommend promoting. Upon passing the Board the soldier's name was placed on a promotion list by MOS for at least 90 days. After that, if the soldier's points met the "cutoff score" (the amount of points needed to be promoted) for his MOS – which was set according to the needs of the Army, he was promoted. Troopers in elite units such as the 82nd, Rangers, or SF received bonus points as a reward and incentive to volunteer. With my prior service and college I actually had over the thousand points required for promotion both times I went before the board. As the highest cutoff score allowed was 999 points, I knew of at least one soldier who was getting promoted in ninety days no matter what the needs of the Army were. Yes, I was pretty smug at the time.

breeze. There was something about sitting in the heat with only a towel wrapped around your waist that made pretensions of rank seem ludicrous. When we left and put our uniforms on we would resume the roles necessary for military discipline and efficiency. In the sauna, we were just a bunch of guys, unwinding for a few minutes before a hard day's work. There were exceptions. On the morning in question there was an older man there, obviously with a lot of rank from the deference being shown him by the young officers there in spite of our informal surroundings.

He seemed like a nice enough guy though; he joked easily with the others in the sauna, and seemed kindly amused by their intimidation. Eventually, most everyone left the sauna; the older man and I were left alone. I was fixing to have to leave myself, as I had to be back at the office before nine o'clock. Somehow, the conversation came around to the scars on my head, still visible because my hair hadn't completely grown back yet.

I told him how I had gotten the scar. I saw it as a chance to tell someone what God had done for me. As I told him how I struggled with my chute, he sat there on the bench above me listening with a pained expression on his face. Once he reached out as if to touch my scars, but caught himself. He reminded me of my father when he first saw my scars in Illinois after the accident. Finally, I finished my story.

In a voice choked with emotion, he looked at me and said, "Son, I owe you an apology. I'm Colonel Dickenson. I command the Second Brigade. I planned Gallant Eagle 82. I'm the one who did that to your head.

"I don't know what I could have done differently," he said, almost to himself, "I followed the ASOP to the letter... but it wasn't enough. I should have spotted the problem, but there were so many details, the ASOP didn't count on anything like that...Sometimes you lose sight of the trees for the forest..."

I felt sorry for him sitting there. I knew he felt the responsibility for each soldier's death on that DZ. I knew he shouldered each life wrecked by that jump. I knew he'd carry it the rest of his life. I know I do. Even though Jesus has done so much to heal my wounds, physical, emotional, and spiritual, there isn't a day that goes by I don't see Morales hit that jeep.

We spoke some more. I told him about the medic who found me and refused medical help to help others. He told me to find out who the guy was and he'd make sure he got a medal for saving my life. He told me the 2/325th Infantry (Abn) was the only outfit with medics on that part of the drop zone. That told me the guys unit.

I went back to the office and received permission from my supervisors to find the guy. It turned out to be easy; there was only one black medic on the DZ that day, SP4 Joe Cress. I went to thank him. He was out in the field. That's life in the 82nd.

Armed with his full name, rank, and service number and unit I went back to my office and typed up a statement describing my accident and Cress' actions on my behalf, as I knew them at the time. I heard later he received an Army Achievement Medal for his actions. I never did get to thank him personally, every time I thought to go see him, he'd be in the field. Then we'd be out in the field, and so on...

It wasn't until a few years ago I was finally able to locate and contact Joe through the "miracle" of the internet and thank him personally. We remain in touch.

That summer I was recommended for promotion to sergeant (E-5). There had been a great deal of discussion whether or not to send me to the board. There were those in my chain of command against the idea. After all, the jury was still out on whether or not I would ever be able to be a fully fit soldier. If I was permanently disabled, the chances were slim to none of my staying in the Army. Even if I did manage to stay in the Army with a permanent profile, regulations fairly well closed promotions to soldiers on permanent profiles.

I was under a lot of stress. There was the responsibility of taking care of my family, trying to make ends meet on an E-4's pay, the struggle of proving to everyone I was going to be all right; and the internal problems, both physical and emotional, caused by the accident. I would dream I was jumping again and everything would go wrong, I'd be hurtling to the earth. The dreams were so real I could feel the sensation of falling through the sky toward the earth. I would often relive the jump; it was during this time I remembered watching Morales die. One of my greatest fears, somehow, was of having to jump at night again. This made no sense to me; Gallant Eagle had been a morning daylight jump. I had jumped at night before. It appeared rational thought had little or nothing to do with it. Considering the fact General Lindsay had the 82nd on a "No day jumping" policy, this would have to be overcome for me to ever be a fully fit paratrooper.

Debbie said she would often wake up in the middle of the night to find me out of bed. She would go into the living room to find me sitting on the sofa in the dark, staring straight ahead. She would call my name. I would just look at her blankly. She said she would take me by the hand and lead me back to bed.

I was having problems controlling my emotions. Debbie said one day I came home from the field and flung my helmet against the wall in a fit of rage. I don't remember doing this, but it is quite possible I did that. I know one day I flew off the handle and put my fist through the wall in the office when I learned they were thinking about taking me off the list for promotion.

SSG Rob came in, sat me down, and talked to me like a father to a naughty son. It wasn't really a reprimand; basically he was telling me I had better get a hold of myself. He looked at the hole in the wall, "This isn't you, Woody," he said, "You're better than this, you've got to overcome it."

I can still see him earnestly talking to me with all that concern in his eyes. I don't know what I would have done without SSG Rob keeping me straight when I needed it. After scolding me Rob walked over to CSM Carlson's office and got him involved. The Sergeant Major knew me, when he took a look at my records; he walked in to the Battalion Commander's office. According to Rob, this is what he said, "Take a look at this man's records. Sir, he's not an average Sp4. He's got prior service, college, overseas service, and numerous decorations. He deserves promotion."

"But Sergeant Major," the Commander replied. "We're probably going to have to medically discharge him."

"Then, sir," the Sergeant Major said. "The least we can do after we've messed him up this badly is give him enough rank so he can live off any pension he gets!"

With that, the matter was settled. I went before the board. I passed and was recommended for promotion. With all the promotion points I had accumulated it was a sure thing that I'd be promoted after the mandatory ninety-day waiting period. I knew that sympathy for my situation had a lot to do with the perfect promotion board recommendation. It galled my pride a bit. After all, I felt that I had proven myself and earned my promotion. But, sympathy aside, once I got the stripes I knew I'd be on my own. NCOs in the Division aren't allowed many mistakes.

Dr. Luehrs retired that summer. When he left I felt as if I had lost not only a doctor, but also a good friend. As the summer drew to a close and my profile was running out I still wasn't quite sure I was going to be able to handle full duty in the Division. I was still having problems. One of the last things Dr. Luehrs did before he retired was to refer me to Mental Hygiene for counseling for post-traumatic stress disorder.

When Division G-2 (Intelligence) found out I was undergoing counseling I lost my security clearance. Without a security clearance I couldn't do my job, nor would I be accepted to OCS. As an officer I could have no lingering doubts over my emotional stability. So I persuaded the shrinks that I was doing okay and got my clearance back. But I still had nightmares.

I was struggling physically, too. I would come home after a day at work both physically and mentally exhausted. I was fractious around the house, and was losing patience with the kids. Debbie had always been protective of the kids and we were fighting more and more. All I needed was some peace and quiet.

I was having doubts about being able to hang on regular PT. I was actually running farther in the mornings than the battery was, but I was running at a slower pace than the unit. I clocked myself every morning and figured I was running at an average of a nine-minute mile on a six-mile run. The Division standard was four miles in thirty-two minutes, an average of an eight-minute mile. Division units usually ran faster than that in the morning. To fall out of a unit run in the morning was shameful.

Unless I showed some marked improvement I would not be able to hang in the Division. Months before, Dr. Luehrs had offered me a permanent profile against jumping. I had refused. As I said before, profiles were a curse on advancement. By the same token I had to jump again. At least once. After that...

My newfound relationship with the Lord was helping me through this, somehow. Though I wasn't in church, I was reading my Bible and praying regularly.

As I said earlier, there had always been a nagging doubt about my relationship with the Lord. My experience on the Drop Zone had removed all doubts. I knew I needed to be in church, though I was having problems deciding which church to attend. Still, I knew He had reached down and saved me and He never does anything without a purpose. Somehow or another, He would work everything out. I remembered somewhere from a childhood where the Bible said, "Everything works out for the best for people who love the Lord."

Even though I wasn't completely back on the right track yet (I still had a foul mouth, in spite of my best efforts to clean it up), I knew I belonged to Him. This was something I had never been completely sure of before. This time even the most hardened skeptic couldn't shake my faith in my salvation.

The important thing as far as I was concerned was to try and do the right thing and leave the rest to Him. I had learned a new scripture in my Bible studies that gave me great comfort, Phillipians 1:21: "To live is Christ, to die is gain." I could understand that, after all, I could say, "'been there, 'done that."

Chapter 16
Rolling Thunder

Beautiful Streamer
(to the tune of "Beautiful Dreamer")

Beautiful streamer open for me
Blue Skies above and no canopy
Counted nine thousand - waited too long
Reached for my ripcord - the darn thing was gone.

Beautiful streamer, why must it be
White silk above me is what I should see
Just like my mother looks over me
To hell with the ripcord, twas not made for me.

Beautiful streamer, follow me down
The time is elapsing and here is the ground
600 feet and then I can tell
If I'll go to heaven or end down in hell.

Beautiful streamer, this is the end
Gabriel is blowing "My Body Won't Mend"
All you jump happy son's of a gun
Take this last warning - Jumping's no fun
TAKE THIS LAST WARNING - JUMPING'S NO FUN
(Anonymous Airborne Song)[99]

As the end of the summer approached word came down that the battalion OPT (Off-Post Training Exercise) to Ft. Pickett had been approved. We would be spending about three weeks training and conducting battery-level ARTEPs in a fairly unknown environment. As I have previously stated, OPTs were good training as they put its soldiers' skills to the maximum test.

We were surprised the commander at Ft. Pickett had approved the 1/320th to go back there after what had happened the previous Fall when the battalion had trained there. I had first heard

---

[99] This song – and other Airborne favorites – sung by the 82nd Airborne Divison Chorus was played over loudspeakers placed along Ardennes Street throughout the Division Area during PT every weekday morning.

about it when I was still with the 18th FA Bde (Abn) S-3. When our boss had approached Ft. Pickett for permission to conduct one of our battalion OPTs there in the Fall of 1981 we were told they were reluctant to host another Ft. Bragg unit – particularly an Airborne outfit after a battalion of paratroopers from the 82nd had taken on a Marine Amphibous Unit (MAU) a month or so before our visit was scheduled.

On that visit to Pickett I remember that even though we weren't a Division unit we were allowed to train on Pickett but I don't recall us getting too much time on main post. During the one visit I remember making to Main Post on official business with a couple of our sections NCOs we visited the EM/NCO club for a cold soft drink (honest!). While we were there the bartender noticed our berets and talked about the problems the previous month.

According to him, both units had been in the rear for some down-time between field problems at the same time. Things had been going pretty well between the Marines and the paratroopers. As I've said, in my time there was always a mutual respect between the Marines ("jarheads") and paratroopers ("wind dummies"). The trouble started – this is what I was told – when some Marines wanted to trade their dungaree hats (or covers) for some of our guys' maroon paratrooper berets. Normally, our guys would have been willing to trade. The problem was, most of our guys packed only one beret for the trip, not figuring they needed a spare (most paratroopers only owned one beret at a time and if they had an extra they didn't take it to the field). So the troopers had to regretfully refuse to trade.

The story goes that one of our guys left the club alone – always a mistake – and was heading to our cantonment (or rear barracks) area when a couple Marines jumped him and stole his beret. War was on.

A paratrooper's beret is sacred. We had only had our berets restored to us a few months before after having them taken from us by the Chief of Staff of the Army in 1979. That came about as a reaction to an epidemic of crazy headgear being worn by the US Army in the 1970s at the tail end of Nam. Commanders begin the practice of getting their troops to wear special headgear in hopes of instilling some sort of unit pride in their troops.

I think (but can't say for sure) the paratroopers started the practice first by adopting the maroon beret, which has been the almost universal headgear of paratroopers around the world (Soviet and Warsaw Pact troopers in sky blue berets being an exception). When the 101st Abn Division was taken off jump status their troops started wearing navy blue "air assault" berets; tankers started wearing black "tankers" berets. When my dad was at Ft Carson different colored baseball caps representing various units replaced the old green fatigue hat (which was an improvement – in my humble opinion – as most of the old standard issue fatigue hats lost their shape after a washing or two). Those are just some examples. The ultimate (again, in my opinion) was the 1ˢᵗ Cavalry Division who had its soldiers wearing Stetson style cavalry hats.

The thing was, except for the black berets of the Rangers (before another Chief of Staff of the Army allowed EVERYONE to wear a black beret to feel good about themselves) and the green berets of the Special Forces, all this special headgear was unauthorized and had to be paid for out of the troops' pockets. Most guys didn't mind – and if they did, they didn't make a big deal about it because it was considered just the cost of doing business. It was like the special company-level t-shirts we used to buy to wear for PT. I have a drawer full of old t-shirts from every battery I served in I bought with my own money. I will probably never be able to wear them again and wouldn't if I could, but I keep each one as a precious memento of my days in those batteries.

But, as in everything, all it takes is one guy to complain. As I understand it, with the headgear two guys complained about having to shell out what was then a large chunk of their paycheck for a Stetson cavalry hat. So the Chief of Staff responded by forbidding any and all unauthorized headgear the troops had to pay for out of their own pocket. That included the maroon beret of the paratroops.

To add insult to injury, in his statement accompanying the order he said, berets were reserved for "elite units" such as the Rangers and Special Forces. With all due respect to those superb units, his remarks were like spitting in paratroopers' faces. So getting our berets back became a matter of pride to those of in airborne units. The 82ⁿᵈ Airborne Division Association lobbied Congress and anyone else who listened to get the beret restored to US Army airborne units. Finally our beret was officially restored effective November 28, 1980.[100]

---

[100] Troopers from the 504ᵗʰ PIR, which made up 2/3s of the Division's 1ˢᵗ Brigade at that time performed a "military funeral" for the beret in which a beret was buried behind one of the barracks. When the beret was restored to the paratroops, several 504ᵗʰ paratroopers "resurrected it. There was a ceremony where the troopers dug the beret up and found it in pretty good condition in spite of having been buried almost two years as the troopers who had buried it had put it in a sealed container. Local papers

I insert this at this point of the story to make it clear to the reader and even current paratroopers, how precious our berets were to us at that time. For someone to steal a beret from a trooper was an unpardonable crime. Perhaps the crime was compounded by the fact it was a Marine who did it – mutual respect notwithstanding. For with that respect came rivalry.

As I said before – war was on.

We were told by the bartender that day at the Ft Pickett EM/NCO Club – and this was confirmed by some of the guys I talked to who were with the battalion at the time, including some NCOs – that the guys from the 1-320th literally attacked the cantonment area of the MAU; someone told me some of the guys had their E-tools (entrenching tools, or personal shovels) and used them as clubs. Our battalions compliment was between 400 – 450 officers and men; and MAU could have had over 2000. I don't know how many were at Pickett at the time.

We were told it took every MP on Ft Pickett with the assistance of the battalion NCOs and officers to stop the brawl. Our battalion was permanently banned from training at Ft. Pickett.

But our Battalion Commander, LTC Henderson, had managed to talk the powers-that-be at Pickett into changing their mind; with the caveat that we absolutely HAD to be on our best behavior. I know in the S-3 shop as plans were laid for the conduct of the OPT time and time again the battery level commanders and staff were told one disciplinary problem would get us tossed – a black-eye for the Division. Not good.

So we were going back to Pickett. The trip was to be given the code name "Rolling Thunder 82."

Oh yeah, the same MAU the battalion had brawled with in 81 was going to be there at the same time.

As planning proceeded the pieces began to come together. First, my wife's hopes that somehow I'd be left behind because of my profile against wearing a helmet were dashed. Perhaps my doctor should have more carefully worded it. Once more I would don my "patrol cap," drive the section gamma goat, and man the radio and situation maps at the TOC. It could have been worse.

Looking back, there may have been a part of me hoping I would "get over" on this one and be left behind on rear detachment; but I knew also, if I hadn't gone along I would have regretted it. I'd hate to miss something.

and I believe even *The Army Times* ran stories on the ceremony.

I learned the firing batteries would be jumping in on Blackstone Army Air Field – where I'd made two chopper blasts the year before. This year I wouldn't be making a jump at Pickett. I'd be watching from the ground with the DZSO team.

There was some eye rolling when we learned the unit dropping us was an Air Guard unit from out West. Just the last summer they had dropped us on a jump I was driving the DZSO on. As I recall the battalion was jumping in on Holland DZ and I was parked in the parking area just off the road leading off the DZ, not too far from the tree line. I could tell when the guys came out that the birds had dropped them too soon. They were over the trees and the winds were too light to carry them safely to the DZ. Roughly half the jumpers on the drop hit the trees.

As I've said before, tree landings can be nasty.

I saw that the first jumper out of the bird was going to hit near me. Figuring he might need help I started running in his direction. I heard the guy hit the brush, heard him crash through the branches as I ran toward the sound. I came to a small clearing just in time to see him come crashing through the branches. At least he wasn't going to be hung up dozens of feet in the air but I just knew he was going to hit the ground hard as he'd been braced for a tree landing and might not have been prepared for the ground. To my amazement – and his – I saw his toes barely touch the ground before the branches above him, which had caught his chute, pulled him up. He was left bouncing lightly, his feet a bare inches off the ground.

"Wow!" It was LTC Henderson, our Battalion Commander. He had broken his collar bone on Gallant Eagle 82 and this was his first jump since being cleared to jump again. I'll never forget the joyful, almost boyish surprise on his face as he hung there in his chute unharmed. He looked at me, recognized me, "Hello Wood! I thought I'd bought it that time!"

I ran to him, checking him all right, "Are you all right, sir?"

"Yes," he answered looking around at the ground, a few inches below his feet. "I couldn't have managed this better if I'd tried…"

I had just helped him to the ground and we had managed to get his chute out of the branches when his driver came up and took him back to the rear. Whenever I think of LTC Henderson I remember that warm North Carolina night in the pines. And I smile.

Jumping off post onto strange DZs is challenging enough without having trust issues with the outfit dropping you. Crazy things happen jumping on OPTs. Some of the old-timers in the battalion recalled jumping into "Gopher DZ" at Ft Hood Texas and discovering to their dismay how the place got its name. There were dozens of breaks and sprains from guys hitting gopher holes on their landings. Some guys even told of a few jumpers who got rattlesnake bit when the holes weren't empty. Ask any Division trooper who's been to Panama about the "elephant grass" down there. Are they all old soldier tales? I can't say for sure; I do know I have more than a few of my own. And I have the scars to prove them.

There's a lot of teasing that goes on between the branches of service. Most of it is good natured. I like to tell my former Air Force buddies that the Air Force is for folks who wanted to wear a uniform but can't handle military life. I know most Air Force folks refer to us Army guys as "grunts." Marines are "jarheads," sailors are "squids," and of course, the Army is composed of "dogfaces." But I have and I think most of my fellow paratroopers share a great respect for the guys that put the "air" in airborne. I have nothing but gratitude for the treatment I received at that Air Force hospital in California and by all those "Flyboy" corpsman and medical personnel. And most of those squadrons that flew us to our targets and dropped us there did magnificent jobs.

But this one outfit was beginning to get a pretty bad reputation – at least in our battalion.

I was part of the DZSO detail at Blackstone Army Airfield on the day the battalion dropped in. I believe most of the troopers from HSB had driven up the day before along with some advanced party personnel from the firing batteries to take control of and set up the rear cantonment area where our batteries' personnel would stay when they weren't in the field. The firing batteries would do airborne assaults onto the post one – by – one, conducting heavy drops of their M102 howitzers and vehicles (gamma goats and jeeps, trailers, etc), followed by personnel drops. As usual, the jumpers would follow the equipment by about ten minutes, take off their chutes, turn them in, and then go de-rig their guns and vehicles. If this had been a test, such as an ARTEP, the event would have been timed. The clock would be stopped at some point to allow the jumpers time to turn in their chutes (which would not have happened in an actual combat drop – the chutes would be left where they were). At some point the evaluators would start their watches again and we would have a given time to de-rig our guns and equipment and put the first round downrange in a Heavy Drop Mission. This was a graded event on an Airborne Artillery Firing Battery's ARTEP. I don't think this drop was graded.

It was a good thing.

The drop was a near-disaster. First off, the heavy drop was a disaster. We lost at least one gun and one gamma goat that streamered in. I remember a sickening feeling in the pit of my stomach as I watched the platforms come out of the aircraft, tip over in the air and land upside-down in the dirt between the lanes of the airstrip. The gun was almost completely buried with only the platform visible. The goat was barely recognizable for what it was as it appeared to almost shatter under its platform. I seem to recall another gun burning in but can't say for sure.   Another battery lost a gun somewhere. We watched the birds drop the loads and counted the guns as they dropped: "One, Two, Three, Four, Five – where's the sixth one?"

"One of those birds didn't drop a load!"

Something went wrong in the bird?

The personnel drops were just as bad. I don't believe any of the drops landed the troops directly on the DZ. One of the batteries overshot the DZ completely, its troops landing amid the airfield buildings, the control tower, hangers, and headquarters building. I remember seeing one troop barely miss getting caught on the control tower while another hit a hangar. The poor guy tried to do a PLF and rolled down its rounded roof onto the ground. I think the only thing that saved him was the fact his chute hadn't completely deflated. I think that battery caught the worst of it. The miracle in my mind was that we didn't have that many serious injuries – at least none I know of – and in my position with S-3 I would have heard about it.

I remember after the second heavy drop crash and burn (I think this was after the missing gun), I looked over to LTC Henderson, who was anxiously watching the proceedings – after all there were several million dollars worth of equipment that was now basically scrap out in that field. And he was responsible for it.

"Well, Sir," I said as optimistically as I could. "The 320th Light Infantry[101] does have a nice ring to it."

I was standing a little behind the colonel to his left rear. He looked over at me and rolled his eyes, then gave a little laugh, "Wood..." he said, shaking his head and smiling sadly. I really thought the world of that man. 'Still do.

Someone high in the battalion contacted the Air Force brass

---

[101] Which is what we basically would be without our guns – though we'd need a LOT of squad tactics training to truly fill that bill.

to find out what happened to our missing gun. The guys at Pope AFB contacted the squadron who dropped us and learned they reported all heavy drop packages had been delivered.

The firing batteries gathered themselves together and carried on with their airborne missions in the wilds of Ft Pickett while the S-3 Section went into the field as well. Someone had decided the S-3 would operate a "permanent" Field TOC during the entire OPT. A nice clearing in the Virginia woods had been selected and we had spent the previous day before the drop setting up our battalion's field headquarters. We were still using what we called the "Mobile TOC" – which was a GP (General Purpose) Small Tent, designed to sleep four to six troops in the field that was attached to the rear of our section gamma goat. Operations maps were set up along the walls of the tent, in the middle were a couple of field tables with some folding chairs.

In the back of the gamma goat, which had bench type seats built into the frame we had a Battalion situation board toward the front, radio mounts and brackets set into the bench on the right side. We put a folding chair and table there in the center between the bench seats. The RTO sat there with the battalion log, monitoring transmissions and recording important messages that came though the radios. Incidents, unit movements, fire missions and other pertinent events were recorded there as the official record of the operation.

We also had a set of field lights which were strung strategically and sparingly throughout the TOC. These were powered by a gasoline generator. I don't know if I've mentioned this before but light discipline is vitally important in military operations. A white light can be seen for miles in the wild. So the US military uses colored lenses, preferably red, as it has been proven red lights cannot be seen as well or as far as other colors. This is the reason if one looks at a military map one won't find any red lines or markers on them. One could not see red lines at night with a red flashlight lens.

In our TOC we had red lights but most often used bare white bulbs. Therefore we had to take great care there were no "leaks" in our tent or vehicle – particularly where the tent met the back of our vehicle. We placed large sheets of OD canvas over potential gaps to block out light. There was a double cover over the two entrances to the tent, troops entering and leaving made sure they closed the opening behind them before they went through the next. Every so often we'd send someone out to ensure our light shields were holding.

I knew with batteries out in the field and with us being away from "home" it was important we monitor the activities of our units as they trained. This wasn't made any easier by the fact the general consensus was our hosts at Ft. Pickett didn't want us there and might use any excuse to kick us off post. Still, I couldn't see what more we could accomplish out in the stix that we could do from a nice warm building in the cantonment area.

But it wasn't too bad really. As I recall, the weather was pretty good most, if not all the time we were there. Typical Fall weather in that part of the country, cool to cold in the morning, warming up a bit by mid-afternoon, then cooling down again as the sun set. I don't remember too much rain. It was one of the few times in all my years in service I actually used my shelter-half. I had bought extra pegs, pole and half so I could pitch a tent by myself (typically a troop is issued the parts for half a tent and two guys share a tent). I made myself quite comfortable in my new hooch. It was great because I knew we were staying in this position for the entire trip.

We would have our chow brought in from the mess hall back in the cantonment area; typical field rations for the Field Artillery in the woods A-rations (hot chow) – C-rations from a can – A-rations. We'd get a hot breakfast; eat C-rations for lunch, and a hot dinner. I think every two or three days we were allowed to go back to the cantonment area for a shower. Again, it wasn't bad if we had to be out there. I had plenty of chance to save "John Wayne" bars to bring home to Debbie and the kids.[102] I knew better than to come home from a field problem without at least one for each of them.

As things got underway there was an investigation to be run as to what went wrong with the heavy drops. And our S-4 Section had to scramble to get our sections replacement guns and goat quickly to our batteries. I knew there was at least one spare or

---

[102] "John Wayne Bars" – Our nickname for C-ration chocolate bars. There was more than one kind of bar in C-rations, depending on the type of meal we had: B-1, B-2, B-3 each had different configurations of entres (if you could call them that) cakes or canned fruits for desert, or candy bars. There were actually two different kinds of bars – a smaller bar chocolate or chocolate with nuts – we'd get two with a meal. These were also called "Audie Murphy Bars" after the most decorated soldier in World War II who was nicknamed "Little Texas" by his buddies. The other kind was larger – like John Wayne – with chocolate covering coconut or mint filling. My kids preferred the Audie Murphy Bars.

"Float" howitzer in the DivArty motor pool. Firing batteries took turns pulling routine maintenance on it. I also knew no one really wanted to use it unless they had to.

There was also an investigation to be conducted to determine what went wrong and to fix responsibility – blame – if there was any to fix. If we, the Army had done something wrong in rigging the platforms or the chute then whomever along the chain of responsibility was found at fault would pay for the damage; be it parachute rigger who rigged the chute wrong, or someone in the chain of command of the men who rigged the platforms and readied the "packages" for drop if it was discovered the equipment had been improperly placed on the platforms and that had caused the malfunctions.

And we still had to find the lost howitzer.

SFC Gamer managed to arrange for a chopper (I think we had a couple laid on for one and two-gun raids and airmobiles) to fly him back along the flight path to Bragg, retracing the route the birds flew to see if he could find what was now considered to be the misdropped gun. He found it about fifty miles toward Bragg – hung up about fifty to sixty feet in the air in the branches of several Virginia Pines!

It wasn't even in a field!

We had to get a CH-54 Skycrane to extract it.

We had to laugh about that when he got back and told us; after all, it might have been understandable had someone mistaken a farmer's field for the DZ and dropped it, but the thing was up a tree in thick forest! How incompetent can one be?

I think the damage was minimal and the crew was able to use it but I don't know that for sure. Talking to some of the guys from the battalion recently some have said it was a gamma goat in the trees. I don't remember that. I do remember a goat burning in, but I don't think I'll ever forget SFC talking about that gun.

The investigation didn't take long to finish. The investigators took one look at the chutes and saw immediately the loadmasters had pushed at least one of our guns and goats out the back door of the C-130s without hooking them up! Some Air Force loadmasters were going to have to pay a chunk of change for those goofs. But our battalion commander, at least was off the hook.

There are very few in the US Army Airborne who do not hold the pilots and crews of the Air Force Military Airlift Command (MAC) in the highest regard. After all, they put the "Air" in airborne. Oh yes, we "grunts" may tease and make fun of the flyboys and their "soft" lives. I had a buddy who was in the Air Force whom I used to always tease by saying, "The Air Force is for folks who want to wear a uniform but cannot handle military life." Sometimes I think we're just jealous – a bit – even as we have grudging pride that we can "take it" – the tough life we live in the Army. I do know I will always feel a warm spot in my heart, a debt of gratitude for the care Air Force medical personnel rendered me after Gallant Eagle 82. And I daresay, we admire the competence of those Air Force pilots, both active and even Reserve and Guard (who often have decades of flight experience under their belts).

However, after Rolling Thunder (which some wag – I won't confess – nicknamed "Rolling Blunder") 82, whenever we learned we had drawn this particular air squadron to drop us, the guys at the "Three Shop" (as we nicknamed the S-3) would roll our eyes. I remember a few months later we were planning another drop – this time on Bragg. We got the Air Letter, informing us of the details. SFC Gamer rolled his eyes, "THOSE guys again. Maybe we'd better station a DZSO Team at Fuquay Varina..." which is some fifty miles or so away from Ft. Bragg.

The batteries got down to business gearing up for their ARTEPs, we at the Field TOC settled in to our own routine of monitoring the radios and keeping up with the movements of the batteries around post and making sure we didn't have any problems with conflicts of interest with the Marines, who were out there. Fortunately we were able to stay out of their way and they were able to stay out of ours for the most part they used one part of the post's training area while we used another.

One day the entire range was shut down when a high explosive round went off close to Main Post. As we were the only Field Artillery unit in the field firing at that time Range Control [103]

---

[103] Range Control – The office on an Army base that has administrative control over that post's training areas. If a unit needs to run a weapons qualification range the S-3 has to request that range for the day in question. If a unit wants to go out on a field problem the commander has to submit requests to use the position areas (PAs or Papa Alphas) he will require – usually through the S-3 – to get approval to use them from Range Control, who compares and coordinates requests to ensure there is no conflict in scheduling or training between units in the field. Range Control is also responsible for safety downrange. Any safety violation, such as a round missing the Impact Area (or target zone) is immediately reported to and investigated by Range Control. Until that investigation is complete Range

immediately blamed us.

We may have been the only Field Artillery unit in the field at that time but we knew the Marines were also firing 81mm mortars, too. I know we were a bit offended that Range Control was so fast to blame us before doing a Shell Report (Shell Rep) an investigation of the site of the crater for shell fragments to determine the weapon that caused it. But, Range Control held the cards and whether we did it or not our training was shut down until we could be cleared to fire again and continue with our training. This was called a "checkfire."

So LTC Henderson hopped in his jeep and drove to the location where the rounds hit and did his own Shell Rep. He found fragments of a mortar shell at the site and immediately drove over to Range Control with his evidence to get the checkfire lifted off our batteries so they could continue training. We were spending a ton of money out there and we sure couldn't afford to be sitting on our thumbs.

It didn't take long for the colonel to present his evidence and get Range Control to lift the checkfire. We got word over the radio directly from Range Control on their dedicated frequency – which all units in the field were required to monitor.

LTC Henderson was driving back to the field having won his battle. I was manning the radio, sitting in the back of the gamma goat with the radios on my folding chair with the field desk logging traffic. I think SSG Rob was up there with me, we had been shooting the breeze. SFC Gamer was in the tent section of the TOC when the colonel broke over the command frequency, "Hotel Three-One, this is Hotel Zero-Six, over."[104]

"This is Hotel Three-One, over."

"This is Hotel Zero-Six, be advised Range Control has lifted the checkfire and I'm heading back to your – oh sh-" I heard what sounded like an explosion come over the loudspeaker, or "bitch box" set up so everyone in the tent could hear the radio conversations. I didn't think it would be a good idea for me, a SP4, to advise a Lieutenant Colonel to observe proper radio etiquette. If what we all in the TOC suspected had happened even his sense of humor had

---

Control can shut the entire range down.

[104] Not the real call signs. I'd be doing good if I remembered them. Notice, though, the military never uses "Oh" for "zero." There is no such thing in the Army as "Oh-six-hundred" – it is "Zero-six-hundred." And one rarely uses numbers past ten – particularly in radio communications. Twenty-one is "spelled out" "two-one."

reached its limit. "Hotel Three-One, this is Hotel Zero-Six, over," the colonel's exasperated voice came back over the radio.

"This is Hotel Three-One, over," I answered.

"This is Hotel Zero-Six, call a checkfire over the battalion; I'm going back to Range Control – out."

What had happened was as soon as Range Control lifted the checkfire one of our batteries, who had been in the middle of a fire mission when the checkfire was called, fired a "Battery One"[105] that landed about 100 yards from the cantonment area back at Main Post. It was a miracle no one was hurt.

We went under immediate checkfire – again. As I recall, it took some time for LTC Henderson to talk Range Control into lifting the checkfire, someone said at the time we were close to being tossed off post. I don't know if that was true, but every Field Artilleryman knows how serious a thing it was to miss the target – lives were (and are) at stake. I remembered the SNAFU at Graf years ago.

From what I learned about what happened at Ft. Pickett it was fairly much the same circumstances; a change in the Azimuth of Fire (direction) that wasn't properly calculated by the Fire Direction Center (FDC). The battery Fire Direction Officer (FDO) in charge of FDC was relieved (as had ours in Germany). I don't know the details of what happened – it seems to me I heard later someone had tried to warn the lieutenant about the problem but he had ignored him; like Germany. Whether that was true or not, the lieutenant was responsible, just as in Germany. He was relieved of his job. That mission had been halted before it fired. This mission had fired and as I said, it was only a miracle no one was killed. Maybe that was what saved the battery commander his job. Remember, in the Army (or military in general) the commander or person in charge is responsible for everything that happens – or fails to happen in his or her area of responsibility or command.

Eventually, the checkfire was lifted and training continued without further incident, as far as I know.

A few weeks later, after the batteries had completed their ARTEPs and the entire battalion, the S-3 Section finally struck camp and had the opportunity to sleep in the barracks that had been requisitioned for us. I don't remember much about that, personally. Maybe we didn't spend enough time for the impression to stick. If

---

[105] "Battery One" – Battery One Round. All guns in a battery (in a 105mm battery six guns) firing at once at the target.

you've seen one World War II era wooden barracks you've seen them all anyway. I do know we spent at least a day back in the cantonment area doing maintenance and cleaning up our equipment prior to the two hundred or so mile trip back to Bragg.

I do have a vivid memory of what I think was our last night at Pickett. As I said, the entire battalion was in the rear now. Each battery had passed its ARTEP, we'd been at Pickett about three weeks most of which had been spent in the field – even during weekends. As we used to say in Germany when we'd go to Graf, "Sundays are only on the calendar." We had been away from wives, families, girlfriends, or whatever, had worked hard, and were about to go home. It was the closest thing to our trips to Graf I'd experienced since coming back on active duty.

Oh yeah, the Marines were in the rear, too.

A large group of our battalion troopers were at the snack bar imbibing in adult beverages of the brewed variety. I was staying with soft drinks as I still didn't think it too smart to be drinking alcohol while recovering from a severe head injury. Remember, I was still having some short-term memory problems and headaches. The last thing I needed was to kill some brain cells. It seemed like the entire battalion's enlisted men were crammed into that place, but I know that wasn't true because there were just as many Marines in the place, too and I know we couldn't all have fit in there.

I think the NCO/EM club was closed that night. Maybe that was coincidental.

I was sitting at the table with a group of NCOs from HSB. Remember, I was really the only enlisted man (holding a rank under the grade of SGT/E-5 or CPL/E-4), but I was only a day or two from getting promoted as my ninety day waiting period after passing the board was up and I knew I had enough points to make the cutoff score for promotion. SSG Rob was there, as well as SSG Hawkins from Battalion FDC and a few others, whom I can't remember now after all these years.

Our guys, a rowdy bunch already, had been letting off a lot of steam all evening. The presence of the Marines had not gone unnoticed, nor uncommented upon. There's always that element of interservice rivalry. Heck, when I was in Germany we had fights between battalions. At Graf in particular these types of fights were common. But I remember hearing stories of when the 567th Engineers Company moved in to Francois Kaserne in Germany and went to "Frenchy's", the EM club on the Kaserne. There had been a riot then. I missed that one but was there for when the 2/6th FA moved in to Hutier Kaserne across Lamboystrasse from Francois Kaserne (ours) in 1976 or 77. Many major brawls broke out when the 2/6th came in to "our" clubs. Eventually it died down though and peace was restored. I always appreciated the irony when I found myself in the 1/6th FA, the 2/6th's sister battalion when I first reported to Bragg.

But I'm rambling here, back to the night at Ft. Pickett. Our guys are getting rowdy. I have (hate?) to say it but the Marines looked like they were being on particularly good behavior that evening. Maybe they had received orders similar to ours (I'm sure they did) and were adhering to their orders a bit better than ours. Maybe they were more subtle than our paratroopers, and I missed it. I do know the consensus of the sergeants at the table was that if someone didn't do something quick we'd have a repeat of 1981 and that would be bad – not only for the guys involved, but for the battalion for giving the 82nd a black eye. So, while the sergeants were mulling over their limited options – after all, they didn't have the authority to close the snack bar and in the shape the guys were in trying to get them back to the barracks before the snack bar closed might cause a worse problem than it solved.

About that time the manager of the snack bar came up to our table. She, too was concerned at how rowdy the guys were getting and didn't want a riot breaking out. I reckoned she remembered 1981. So she told the sergeants she was planning to shut the snack bar down and asked them – as the highest ranking Army guys in the place – if they could get the 82nd troopers out of the bar first, ahead of the Marines so as to avoid trouble.

Our sergeants all nodded their heads; after all, they had been thinking the same thing. The lady had just given them an "out."

I don't remember who came up with the scheme to get our "happy" troopers out of the snack bar in a peaceful and orderly fashion but I know it was SSG Hawkins to seemed to take the lead. SSG Hawkins stationed himself in the middle of the large room while the other sergeants posted themselves at strategic places around the room, near the main entrance/exit to the place and a couple quietly placed themselves in the street outside. With everyone in position, SSG Hawkins looked around and began going through jump commands a if he was a jumpmaster in an aircraft on a jump.

"TEN MINUTES!!!" The command was echoed by the NCOs stationed around the room, getting the troops' attention.

Immediately our guys got quiet. Training and conditioning kicked in. I'll never forget the look on the Marines' face when, as one, every paratrooper in the place shifted in their seats, stomped their boots on the floor, and in unison, like in an aircraft, responded, "TEN MINUTES!!!"

And so there, in front of our amazed and stupefied Marine Corps brethren in arms, SSG Hawkins, SSG Rob, and the other sergeants led our guys through the jump commands.

"OUTBOARD PERSONNEL, STAND UP!"

"OUTBOARD PERSONNEL, STAND UP!" Troopers sitting at tables lining the walls stomped their feet and stood up.

"INBOARD PERSONNEL, STAND UP!"

"INBOARD PERSONNEL, STAND UP!" All the troopers sitting at tables in the middle of the room stood up. The sergeants ensured they were put in line with the others, forming a single line of "jumpers" around the room with the first guy in the line facing the door, where the "jumpmaster" stood.

"HOOK UP!"

"HOOK UP!" Everyone simulated hooking up their static lines snap hooks to the imaginary static line anchor cable around the outer edge of the room – just like in pre-jump training.

"CHECK STATIC LINES!"

"CHECK STATIC LINES!" Everyone simulated ensuring there were no cuts or weak spots on their static line and then inspecting the static line of the "jumper" in front of him tracing the route the static line made as it criss-crossed the back of the parachute pack tray, making sure the rubber bands holding the static line in place were properly placed, ensuring the ¾" cotton webbing (string) was properly tied off holding the chute together and nothing else.

"CHECK EQUIPMENT!"

"CHECK EQUIPMENT!" Everyone simulated ensuring their helmet was properly fastened with chinstraps in place, etc,; then they simulated inspecting their parachute harness, reserve, combat equipment that was attached to their parachute harness to ensure everything was properly attached and there were no twists or tangles or loose buckles that might cause injury to the jumper in the prop blast or on the way down.

"SOUND OFF FOR EQUIPMENT CHECK!"

"SOUND OFF FOR EQUIPMENT CHECK!" Beginning with the "last" jumper, who was near the snack bar door, with his back to the door, the jumpers slapped the outer thigh of the jumper and said, "OKAY!" That jumper then repeated the action with the jumper in front of him and so on around the room until the "first" jumper, with the "door position," stomped his left foot and gestured with his left hand (the door being on his right) with a knifelike motion, "ALL OKAY JUMPMASTER!"

I don't remember them giving a six minute warning. It was kind of pointless anyhow. But SSG Hawkins, being a stickler for detail might have included it. That was what made him an outstanding FDC Chief and jumpmaster.

I do remember the sergeant playing jumpmaster at the door doing a simulated door check as if he was in a C-130. I don't think there was a peep from the Marines; they were so intent watching the guys going through their motions. Probably confused about what was going on, but also curious. I know in my dealing with Marines they've exhibited curiosity about jumping – well these were getting a close up view of pretty much what happened in the bird on a jump.

Well, with our guys all under control and prepped, there was only one thing left – well, two. "STAND IN THE DOOR!"

The first trooper in line took up a door position, just like a C-130 as every other trooper sounded off with loud "HUUAHs!"[106]

The Marines had and have their "Ooorah!" but I wonder whether they had ever heard the barking sounds that were our "Huuahs!"

"GO!"

The first jumper launched himself out the door with an exit that, in spite of his inebriated condition, would have made a jumpmaster proud. He cleared the small porch outside the door (it

---

[106] You have to understand, the "HUAH" (said "HOOOOO – AH!") we used doesn't sound much like the "HUAHs" you hear today. The word was originally "HUYAH!" or "HOOOOOOYAAAAAH!" meaning "Heard, Understood, and Yes, I will comply." Today it is spoken, or maybe shouted, using the lips and mouth mainly. Back then, it was as much a barking sound as it was a word – originating in the chest more than the throat. And if I'm not mistaken in the Army it was originally used in the airborne units; probably picked up at Jump School from the Navy SEALs – at least that's the first time I heard anything like it. But again, this (where it came from – not its original meaning) is my opinion based on observation.

I'll never forget the first time I heard someone use the "new" all-Army HUAH; it was on a documentary about Basic Training on TV. I'd been out about ten years at the time. I heard this Ft Jackson Drill Sergeant explaining a task to his students and finish his spiel with what I considered to be a weak "Huah?"

The trainees answered, just as weakly, "Huah." I remember thinking had we answered so lamely we'd have been doing pushups for a week. In my humble opinion the Army had castrated the HUAH! Just my opinion. But I guess old soldiers are always skeptical of change.

was a good thing the step onto the porch came from alongside the building and not the street) and landed with a PLF in the street. There he was policed up by one of our NCOs waiting in the street.

One by one every 1/320th enlisted man in the snack bar made their jump out the door. As they recovered from their landing, sergeants policed them up and formed them into a formation with a four man front. Even some of the sergeants made the "jump." When all the guys were formed up and the last sergeant out had ensured there were no paratroopers left in the snack bar one of the sergeants brought the formation to attention.

"DOUBLE TIME –"

There was an answering roaring growl from the troops.

"-MARCH!"

With another growl the formation began airborne-shuffling down the street to our cantonment area a couple blocks or so away. One of the sergeants began calling cadence.

"C-130 rolling down the strip..." sang the sergeant.

"C-130 rolling down the strip..." the troopers echoed.

"Airborne Daddy on a one way trip!"

"Airborne Daddy on a one way trip!"

I was at the rear of the formation. I remember looking back and seeing the Marines, now filing out of the snack bar on their own, watching us as we ran off down the road, some shaking their heads as if they couldn't believe what they had just seen.

But a second "Battle of Fort Pickett" had been avoided through the ingenuity, leadership, and professionalism of a group of the battalion's NCOs. And we left the next day.

By the time I got back to Bragg my profile had expired. I knew my unit would have me on the next available jump. Before I jumped with the unit I wanted to make sure I would be okay.

There was a Saturday Proficiency Jump the weekend after I got back. We called them "Fun Jumps." They were sponsored at least one Saturday a month so paratroopers could get in practice; accumulate jumps needed for advanced parachutist ratings, or keep from losing jump pay. Airborne units took turns sponsoring the month's jump. Any parachute qualified trooper with hazardous duty orders (officially designating him as being on jump status) could participate.

I got up early that morning and drove out to Sicily DZ with my neighbor, Jerry. They usually didn't start jumping until nine or ten o'clock in the morning. In order to make sure you got a chute, though, you'd best get there early; some guys actually camped out at the DZ the night before. There was already a crowd when we arrived, just before dawn. We took our place and waited.

Finally, after a three-hour wait for registration, another hour of pre-jump training, and another hour or so wait for our turn on the bird, we were loaded on a C-7A Caribou, flown to an altitude of about five thousand feet and let go.

I remember lying on the drop zone after I activated my canopy release assembly. I wiggled my toes and fingers, sniffed the air, enjoying the aroma. The sky was so blue. It was good to be alive. For better or worse, I was officially back on jump status.

Chapter 17
AIRBORNE Artillery – the Fourth Way

When I get to heaven, St. Peter's gonna say,
"How'd you make your livin'? How' d you earn your pay?"
I'll reply with a little bit of anger,
"Blood, guts, sweat, and danger,
I made my livin' as an airborne Ranger!"
(Airborne Running Cadence)

With my promotion to sergeant, I knew my days in S-3 were coming to a close. I had been out of my MOS almost a year and a half; it was time to go home to the guns where I belonged. Remember, I had originally been headed for the battalion's B Battery when I reported to the 82nd when Battalion S-3 snatched me.

Not that I'm complaining, I had made some good friends at battalion. There were Rob, and the other NCOs in the shop. And, surprisingly, there was CPT Herbert.

CPT Herbert was the Assistant S-3 (A/S-3). He was definitely a Type A, workaholic, driven personality. At one time we teased him that he was the most hated man in DivArty. This was sad to me, because deep down inside I really believed he was a nice guy who wanted to be liked, but didn't know how. It seemed he was always angering one of us NCOs with his incessant demands.

We'd work all day long to get all our assigned tasks done so we could get home after Top's afternoon chiefs' meeting at 1630 (4:30 PM), just to be told that everything we had done that day had to be changed. The S-3 would come back from DivArty headquarters, where the afternoon staff and commander's call was held, and everything – all the paperwork, letters, training plans, and whatever other work we had done that day – was changed and had to be redone. And it had to be redone before COB (Close of Business). Often we would find ourselves not going home until late in the evening.

This made us real popular with our wives at home, who might have gone to all sorts of trouble cooking a nice dinner just to have it go cold. I finally told Debbie not to wait dinner on me, go ahead and feed the kids and I'd eat whenever I got home. I quipped one time that we ought not to come to work until four in the afternoon. That was when we did all our real work anyway.

One day I was rewriting a letter of instruction for the third time. I looked outside at the setting sun and reflected on the fact that I had been at work since around five o'clock that morning, before dawn. "You know, sir," I said, "I'm sure glad we don't work in a coal mine."

Why's that, Woody?" CPT Herbert asked, without even looking up from his paperwork.

I looked over at Rob, who was watching me expectantly, "If we worked in a coal mine we'd never see the light of day."

At that, CPT Herbert looked up at the clock, then out the window at the darkness outside, he grinned sheepishly, "You've got a point, Woody," he said, "Everyone call it a day."

The guys in the section wanted to treat me to a beer at the bowling alley that night. That was the section's home away from home. Sometimes, I'd go over and tilt a brew with the guys after work, just enough to let them know that I wasn't too good to associate with them. I'd always call Debbie and let her know where I was so she wouldn't worry. But it was getting to the point where the guys were going over there every night and going home wasted. I knew it was having an adverse effect on their marriages. I wasn't about to get on that merry-go-round. My marriage was too important. I had gotten married to stop all that horsing around.

But I could sympathize with the guys. The pressure in the office seemed unbearable sometimes. Often, there didn't seem to be any sense in what we were doing. One night CPT Herbert had my replacement working after hours on some piece of correspondence that had to be done before we went home. I had just been promoted to sergeant, and by the rules of Army etiquette and leadership an NCO does not go home before his troops. By the same token, a leader does not eat until he is sure all his troops have eaten.

So here we were: four NCOs and a captain, sitting around waiting for a private to finish this letter. I went back to the cubicle where the guy was working to check on his progress. You can imagine my dismay when I discovered that the all-important letter was a Letter of Instruction (LOI) concerning the Officer's "prop-blast" party to be held that Saturday. CPT Herbert had been named the Officer in Charge of conducting that month's prop-blast and, true to form; he was going to make sure that this was the best organized prop-blast the battalion had ever held.

The "prop-blast" is a sort of hazing or initiation ceremony, which all new officers to an airborne unit must survive. Without going into too much detail it consists of an afternoon and evening of quizzing new officers on Airborne trivia, a lot of drinking, and various physical exercises inflicted as punishment for wrong answers to questions asked of the "blastees." Upon being "prop-blasted" officers are issued prop-blast cards and certificates they are supposed to keep for the rest of their career. An officer reporting to an airborne unit who has lost his or her prop-blast card must endure the ritual again. New lieutenants to the battalion had been pestering everyone in battalion all week getting the answers to various airborne trivia questions they might be asked Saturday.

All of it is meant in the spirit of good-natured fun, but to have an enlisted man working to all hours of the night preparing a letter, which basically lay out, which officers were to bring the booze and who was to bring the chips and dip? I was fit to be tied. When I showed SFC Garner, the Operations NCO, what the trooper was working on, he hit the ceiling. He went in and told CPT Herbert respectfully, but firmly, that he was not holding his section any longer for such trash. He could do that because he was in the right. The letter was finished the next morning.

I don't want to sound noble or anything, but I figured I had to like CPT Herbert because no one else did. There were the times when he'd get me to the point where I felt I was about ready to kill him. Then, he'd pucker his lips, blow me a kiss and say, "I love ya Woody."

I'd just shake my head and have to grin. Every now and then, I'd get back at him. I was able to have fun with my head injury until I got a clean bill of health from the shrinks. Like the time he'd started pushing too hard and all of a sudden I got this glazed look in my eyes. My buddy Vinnie used to call it the 'Fisheye" look. I'd used the look more than once in Germany to get out of a fight. A guy would get hostile and want to step outside. I'd look at him all crazy eyed and smile like I'd like nothing better than to rip his head off his shoulders so I could spit down his neck. The next thing you know the guy is not so hostile,

So, I looked at CPT Herbert with this wild look in my eyes and said, "You know, sir, I was thinking. With this head injury I've got a license to kill... You got anyone you don't like?"

Poor CPT Herbert looked at me to see if I was kidding or not. The problem was, he was never quite sure. I turned around to wink at SFC Garner and Rob, who were struggling to keep a straight face.

One develops a close relationship with your co-workers in the military that you'll never find in civilian life. Take my first jump with the unit after I was back on jump status. No one knew yet that I had been out on the fun jump that Saturday. As soon as I was off profile Top Englund had me manifested on the first available bird. He evidently took great pains to ensure I was taken care of.

All the jumpmasters and safeties were from S-3 except, Major Peterson, who had been S-3 when I was injured and was now the Battalion XO. The others were CPT Herbert, who was assistant Jumpmaster; SFC Garner and Rob, who had finally just completed jumpmaster school, were the safety personnel, or "safeties." Everyone was paying special attention to me. I must have been JMPIed eight times that day.

When we boarded the aircraft I discovered I was manifested to jump right behind Father Watson, the battalion chaplain. It may have just been a coincidence, but I really got a kick out of that. I really liked Father Watson. There seemed to be a sort of aura around him, a holiness I found missing in many preachers. It wasn't a religious thing, either; there was just something about him. If I had seen him out on the street in blue jeans and an old T-shirt I would have said, "There goes a man of God." Sometimes, looking into his eyes, I felt I was actually looking into the eyes of Jesus. It was eerie. When he came around everybody's language automatically cleaned up, but no one felt uncomfortable around him. We all called him "Father," even those of us who weren't Catholic, even though it went against our Protestant upbringing.

I remember that jump with fondness. It felt as if every eye in the aircraft was on me that day. We were jumping a C-141 again, and I remember giving CPT Herbert and Rob a thumbs up as I exited the aircraft. The CG had relented on his total darkness policy and we were jumping in the late afternoon. It was a beautiful day and I floated smoothly and safely to the ground. Again, I lay on the DZ for a few seconds after landing and pulling my canopy release assembly, doing my physical function check, just smelling the air, listening to the birds sing, and admiring how blue the sky was.

A few days later I was promoted to Sergeant. Top told me to check the duty roster before I went home. He winked.

Major Petersen, who had been the S-3 when I first came to Battalion and was now the Executive Officer (XO), came up to me to offer his congratulations a bit later. He took me aside in a fatherly fashion.

"Now that you're a sergeant, Sergeant Wood," he began and

smiled at the sound. "It's time to start thinking about the future." He paused. "You've your extra pay from your promotion now, take half and spend it on yourself, you deserve it. The other half put back in bonds - or better yet - open up a mutual fund. You'll never miss it and you'll build up a nest egg for later on in life; college for the kids, a home, retirement..."

I don't think I've felt such warm feelings for a man since my "stepfather"[107] came up the night I graduated from high school and offered to take out a loan to send me through college. Back then I didn't think it was fair for him to go into debt when he had three other kids to think about raising, even though I knew he would and I loved him for it.

I looked at Major Petersen and knew he was giving me advice he would give his son. It was good advice, too. I listened intently and nodded, recognizing his wisdom. I didn't have the heart to tell him I wouldn't be able to take him up on his advice, as much as I would have loved to have been able to.

Since I had gotten married three years before, life had seemed to be one crisis after another. As a result, we were up to our necks in debt and seemed unable to escape.

My promotion to SP4 (E-4) helped relieve the pressure a little bit, and Jump Pay helped more. Still, times were tight. We often lived on macaroni and cheese mixed with canned tuna or chicken, I called it "Macaroni tunie-weenie-beenie" off of the old "Sanford and Son" show. Our big treat was taking the kids to a burger place on payday.

As much as I appreciated the Major's advice, it would do me no good at the moment. For me, my promotion and extra pay meant that I wouldn't have to hitchhike in to work at the end of the month because I didn't have money for gas. It meant we would be able to eat meat every night of the week.

CSM Carlson was forced to retire around that time. He'd crushed two vertebrae in California and didn't even realize it until a medic noticed him limping around in the field two days later and "ordered" him to submit to an examination. I was told there were two huge bruises along his spinal column and X-rays confirmed the suspicions.

CSM Carlson had been in the Army twenty-eight years, served six years in Nam, where he'd earned three purple hearts, spent twelve years in the Special Forces, made over twelve hundred static

---

[107] I've always hated that term.

line jumps and almost eight hundred HALO[108] jumps. He'd lost part of his left lung in Nam, had so many injuries garnered over the years, he didn't think anything of the agony caused by two crushed vertebrae.

He was medically retired, though he was already eligible with twenty-eight years. I wondered what he would do now, without the Army. One of the things not reflected on his "201 File" (Military Personnel Records File) was the three divorces incurred over all those years of running through the jungle with a knife in his teeth. Without the Army, he was alone.

The new CSM, CSM Diamond, figured that with my promotion I had better get back to working my MOS. This was okay by me; one can only go so far working out of MOS. It had been my intention when I enlisted two years before to stay in my MOS. I had learned a bitter lesson during my first enlistment about wandering too far from my specialty. I was ready to get back to the guns. I was promoted in October 1982. In February, almost a year to the day of my reporting to the battalion, I reported to Bravo Battery.

The next eight months were quite a ride. I had to learn, or rather relearn, all about a new gun, the M1O2, 1O5mm towed howitzer. I had trained on the M1O2 during AIT.[109] That had been eight years before. I hadn't seen the gun since. In the meantime, I had served on the M110, 8 inch self-propelled howitzer and the M 114, 155mm towed howitzer, as well as having done various stints in other jobs on the administrative and operational side of the fence. And remember, as a soldier, I'd learned the three ways of doing things: the right way, the wrong way, and the Army Way. Now I was learning the *fourth way*- The 82nd Way.

I was greeted with some skepticism by the cannoneers in Bravo Battery. Soldiers in front line companies tend to view all personnel in support and headquarters units as having an easy life. We had a name for support personnel – REMFs (roughly translated Rear Echelon Individuals). I remember sitting in my office watching the line batteries getting the afternoon off or playing games as part of "organized athletics" while I worked on and thinking they had it made. I suppose it's true, the other man's grass is always greener.

Coming from the S-3 shop probably made things worse. I had been the enemy. As a matter of fact, my first XO in Bravo rode

---

[108] HALO- High Altitude, Low Opening Jumps- Military skydiving. Normally reserved for special operations units.
[109] AIT- Advanced Individual Training. The school where you learn your job (MOS- Military Occupational Specialty).

my back fairly hard. It wasn't until he left that I understood why. He gave his replacement his "S - Stick," on which he had printed the names of folks whom he felt had done him wrong during his tenure as XO of the battery. These were enemies of Bravo Battery for the new XO to watch for. I wasn't surprised to see the names of every member of the S-3 Section, including mine, on the stick. I guess he held a grudge for every time I had to return his training schedule for corrections. Having me in his "power" he had taken his revenge at every opportunity. I couldn't even recommend a troop for a commendation without him tagging some snide remark to his required endorsement.

There were a couple of SP4s in the section I was assigned to who were up for promotion. They looked upon my arrival with a great deal of resentment. I was seen as a barrier to their advancement. This wasn't true, but perception is often more relevant to an individual than are the facts. It was awkward because while I had much more experience and was expert on several different weapons systems - as well as having a great understanding of general Field Artillery tactics and techniques from my varied experience - when it came down to it these men knew more about the M102 howitzer than I.

As if things weren't awkward enough, I had a personality conflict with my section chief. He was another young E-5; actually I outranked him in both time in service and time in grade. But, he was chief when I came into the section. I wasn't really ready to take over a section. He knew the M102. I didn't grumble at first. He was an outstanding soldier, one of the best artillerymen I have ever served with. He knew it.

I was still trying to overcome my injuries. To all outward appearances I had made an astounding recovery. Indeed, with God's help, I had been brought a back from the brink of death. It could only have been God who had brought me back and healed me physically, much less given me the nerve to jump again. But there were residual complications haunting me.

I still had problems with my short-term memory. I didn't trust my memory any longer. I had less stamina than before. Memories of the jump still haunted me. And there were still the blinding, gut-wrenching headaches.

My fears about keeping up with unit PT were realized. I kept falling out of the morning runs. When I first came back to full duty I was proud of the fact that I as able to keep up with the battery on the morning runs. Top Englund liked to run us over long distances, sometimes up to eight or ten miles in the morning, but he would run us at a steady pace, eight or nine minute miles. I found I was able to keep up with this, after all, this was about the pace I was running and it met the Division standards.

Shortly after my return to duty, though, Top Englund was promoted to Sergeant Major and transferred to DivArty Headquarters. His replacement was Top Thompson, nicknamed "Marathon Tom." Top Thompson said he hated running, he often told us NCOs that when he retired he was going to burn his running shoes and ride a go-cart to the bathroom. But the Army wanted everyone to run and by thunder we were going to run. Boy could that guy run!

I remember the first morning he ran us for PT; I managed to hang with his pace for about three miles before I hit the wall. When I fell out of the run I felt angry and humiliated. I hated falling out of anything. I was also puzzled. My legs were in great condition and didn't seem too tired. I wasn't out of breath. All of a sudden I just ran out of gas. I would slow down; unable to keep up the pace they were keeping, before finally halting, almost too weak to stand.

I always made high scores on my PT tests. I always did the maximum number of pushups and sit-ups and completed the two-mile run in plenty of time to make a passing score. My new section chief in Bravo Battery had gotten a bit upset when, during a section competition I had actually scored some twenty points higher than he, making the maximum possible score on both pushups and sit-ups. It was only on the two mile run that he beat my score. That wasn't by much.

I therefore concluded it wasn't a matter of conditioning. When the battery ran at a slower pace I was able to complete the run. When they tested us to see if we could run four miles in thirty-two minutes according to Division standards I always crossed the line, with at least a little time to spare. I hoped the problem would work itself out in time. Inside, though, I had the feeling that, for all God had done to bring me back, there was a part of me left on that drop zone in California. Though I tried to convince myself differently, it appeared I had progressed to a certain point and stopped.

Gallant Eagle 82 was a thing of the past for most of the troopers. Few who had been seriously injured were left in the unit to tell about it. Dr. Luehrs had remarked to me one day I was the most seriously injured survivor of Gallant Eagle. I suppose he was talking about nearness to death. It never ceased to amaze me that I had come back to jump again.

There were so many others who had been banged up badly. They were reclassified and medically removed from jump status. Several were medically retired or discharged. Then, there were the two from our battalion who had not come back. The mess hall put up a plaque in their memory for a while. I thought it a nice gesture. It stayed up a year or two before it was replaced by some other memento. Life goes on. The Division moved at too fast a pace to spend much time brooding over the past.

Life in a line unit in the 82nd was, as we used to say, a "fast train." Division units were always flying away somewhere to conduct training in all sorts of geographic environments and climates. In any given week the Division could have had a battalion down in Panama for Jungle Warfare Training, another battalion up in Alaska attending the Northern Warfare School, and yet another battalion off in Egypt as part of the U.S. Peace Keeping Force in the Sinai Peninsula.

The Division theoretically conducted this training on a three part training cycle. There were three training cycles lasting from six to eight weeks on the average. At any given time of the year each of the Division's three infantry brigades and their supporting elements were on one of these cycles.

The first cycle we'll look at was the intensified Training Cycle (ITC). During this cycle the unit is usually out in the field conducting unit training in preparation for either their company/battery or battalion ARTEPs, which, as I've explained before, is an evaluation of the unit's ability to perform certain tasks and missions which might be required of it in a combat situation.

There was so much more to artillery in the 82nd than in the other units with which I'd served. Being airborne and airmobile put a whole new meaning to the phrase, "Shoot, Move, and Communicate." We did the RSOPs (Reconnaissance Setting Of Position), hip shoots and standard Field Artillery missions the leg units did. One difference I noted was that in the 82nd, the Chief of Section (SSG in charge) would hop out of the truck and run ahead of the truck as well, guiding the gun into position personally at the direction of his advance party man and check out the position chosen for his gun. It has occurred to me more than once that if that had been SOP back in the 1/6th, my previous FA unit, my chief might have seen that big foxhole and moved the gun before unhooking it, night or not. That might have saved both our backs. I know that when I became chief of section of my own gun I moved my gun once or twice for different reasons. But I didn't have to do it much – I had great Advance Party men who were conscientious to pick good terrain to emplace our gun.

In so many ways it was good old fashioned Field Artillery, but in the 82nd, with the M102 howitzer, which was so light and versatile there was a whole new realm of things one could do. We did airmobiles (which I'd had experience with in my previous "leg" artillery unit at Corps), but there were one and two gun "raids," where a single howitzer section might be taken off by a Huey or Blackhawk helicopter, dropped in a field and required to direct fire at a target not a thousand meters (or less) away.

Then there was the ultimate specialty of Airborne Artillery – the heavy drop mission. We had to be able to rig our guns for parachute drop behind enemy lines, jump in behind our equipment, rally on our guns and trucks, de-rig them, and begin shooting from the drop zone. It was all great stuff and a new challenge to be overcome. And the "One-oh-Deuce" was such a pleasure to work on after the heavy guns I'd been on. The 105mm round it fired only weighed 35 pounds compared to the 205 pounds a fused 8-inch round weighed or even the 95 pounds the 155mm round weighed. The "One-oh-Deuce" was a toy I fell in love with.

But, as this stuff was new to me I had to learn it. I would learn it. But, as a sergeant I was expected to already know it. In one way it was good I was assigned going into the ITC, because I had plenty of opportunity to be in the field and learn what I needed to know. On the other hand, there was a problem because at the end of ITC came our ARTEP, and I had to learn fast to help my battery pass it.

To add to the stress that training cycle had to be one of the most intense I have ever gone through. It got so bad that one night the entire battery fired a mission in its sleep.

We'd been out in the field about three days going on about two to three hours of sleep a night, interrupted by time on guard. The weather was intensely cold.

I remember sitting by the gunner's sight, waiting for the next fire mission, I was looking at the luminous numbers on the sight that gave deflection (direction). The next thing I remember was being startled by a loud blast.

While I was getting my head cleared, FDC was coming

across the speaker phone, "Attention on the gun line, we need the last data fired by piece."

We all looked at each other stupefied; the last mission we'd fired had been over an hour before. The chief looked at Coronado, our Radio Telephone Operator (RTO), "Coronado, what data do you have?"

Coronado looked down at his fire mission data record sheet, "Gee, chief, I don't have no mission…"

"Sergeant Wood, what data do you have on you sight?"

At about that time guns one through three had reported and FDC wanted our data. I looked at my sight, "Three-two-seven-five."

"Deflection three-two-seven-five." Coronado repeated into the phone.

"Walker, what's your quadrant?"

Our Assistant Gunner read "Three-niner-five" off his quadrant sight.

Coronado repeated that data then gave them the standard powder charge for that position.

"Good data, Gun Four."

We all heaved a sigh of relief.

Shortly thereafter, Smoke Franco ("Big Frank") called for a chief/NCO meeting behind the gun line. As we gathered together, I could tell by the sheepish looks on everyone's face, they'd all done the same thing.

"Listen, guys." Smoke began, "It's late, it's cold, we're running low on sleep. Try to keep the guys alert 'cause I don't know how long the XO's gonna want to play, okay? We don't want to take out Cross Creek Mall or the Rod and Gun Club with a 'battery one', okay? I've got the mess hall brewing some coffee and making soup. Rotate your guys down when it's ready, okay?"

We finally passed the ARTEP and the unit was pronounced "combat ready." A story sticks out in my mind from that test.

My gun was situated in an area with rough terrain by a crossroads. The ground was so uneven and covered with trees and bushes we really couldn't see anything past fifty meters away.

Now, as gunner for the howitzer one of my jobs was to draw up a range card for the piece. Range cards were required for all crew served weapons to pinpoint possible avenues of enemy approach, obstacles behind which an enemy force could hide, and even friendly positions so if someone else was to take over your piece (or even you) they could rapidly ID these points and coordinate the weapon into the position defense.

All I could really see from where I was – other than trees and small hills, was that danged intersection. It was only about 25 – 50 meters from the gun – really too close to engage – but it was there and the most likely avenue of approach of "enemy" armor. So I marked the crossroads down and then had to mark the road to our front and everything behind it as "Dead Space." It was all I could see.

Now, there was an Assistant DivArty S-3, whom I'll call Major Balls. He may have been loved at the "O" club and at DivArty, but the opinion among the NCOs and troops I'd served with both at Battalion HQs and Battery level was if the guy was to buy a round at the local bar we'd pay for it ourselves. His Ops Sgt, MSG Clinton, was another former captain who'd gotten RIFed after Nam (or so I was told). He'd been Maj Balls battery commander in Nam when Maj Balls was a lieutenant.

Well, we're sitting in our position at the crossroads waiting for a mission and along comes Maj. Balls and MSG Clinton. The Major strutting his stuff like the only rooster in the henhouse and the sergeant coming along behind with an ever present smile on his face.

The Major starts inspecting our position, grilling the troops on basic military knowledge, maximum effective range of the M16, the antidote for a nerve agent,[110] how many 2LTs can you fit on the head of a pin... Our guys were doing pretty well.

Then he came to me, the brand new gunner. He took one look at my range card and made a face, "Tell me, Sergeant Wood. How far away is that road junction?"

Well, here we go, I remember thinking. I knew where he was going with this, the road, being too close to really engage with the howitzer, shouldn't have been on the range card. But it was the only thing I could see. I thought I had an answer prepared, though.

"About fifty meters, sir." I answered.

"How far does an HE round have to travel to arm?"

Well, I started doing the calculations out loud for his benefit. After all this was show and tell on how much we knew or didn't know. One thing I'd learned doing all those special weapons inspections in Germany was how to put on the dog during an inspection or test. I explained how the PD (Point Detonating) fuse had to spin at least 25 times to arm, calculated how fast the shell would exit the tube if we fired full charge 7 (which we would), how

---

[110] Which it seemed like they changed every six months...

fast the fuse spun and how long it would take the fuse to spin 25 times and how far the round would travel in that time (I could do all that back then, wow.). I came up with an answer of about 200 – 250 meters, can't remember which.

Now, the major smiled, "So are you going to shoot a target that close knowing it won't do any good? And if you're not going to shoot it why put it on there?"

"Well, sir," politely. "First, it's the only point of reference I can see and it's the most likely avenue of approach of any enemy force. Second, if a T-72 pokes its nose around that corner I'm going to shoot it – I don't care if the round explodes or not I'm doing something! Maybe the concussion will daze the crew long enough for us to get out of here."

Major Balls just stared at me a moment, then turned and left our position for other game. I remember MSG Clinton grinning and winking at me before he left our net.

ITC ended and the unit then entered the next cycle, Mission Cycle.

Chapter 18
Mission Cycle

C130 rolling down the strip
Airborne Daddy on a one-way trip
Mission uncertain, destination unknown
Don't even know if we'll make it home
(Anonymous Airborne Running Cadence)

During Mission cycle, the infantry brigade and its supporting units acted as the DRF (Division Ready Force). The primary element of the DRF was the infantry battalion with its direct support elements, called a battalion task force. This was what one Division Commander I served under used to call the Division slice concept. Under this concept picture the Division as a pie cut into nine slices, each representing an infantry battalion task force.

In each slice was an infantry battalion, an artillery firing battery, an armored, engineer, and commo platoon from respective battalions in the Division. Each "slice" of the Division was given a DRF designation numbered one through nine. In case of an emergency the DRF1 slice will be the first to go, with DRF9 the last. A slice's status would depend on which cycle the unit was in.

When a unit was on DRF1, the personnel were on two-hour recall. This meant that in case of an alert everyone in the unit must be able to report back into the base within two hours of the original callout. The telephone became all-important in this situation. No one was allowed to live off post unless they had one or could supply a number at which they could be reached. If a trooper went anywhere he had to report back to his unit CQ and let them know where he was. He'd better leave a number where he could be reached. I imagine now that cell-phones and pagers are quite popular in the Division.

It was quite a common occurrence to be sitting in a movie or at a restaurant, or any public place in Fayetteville and have an 82nd trooper's name announced. Nothing was said, but everyone knew the guy's unit had been called out.

More than once I've gone in to work in the morning and not come home for a few days or even a week. We'd gotten called out and flew away somewhere on an EDRE (Emergency Deployment

Readiness Exercise, a fancy name for an alert). A few years back, I was talking to David. We were reminiscing about life in the 82nd. He told me the first thing he'd ask when he came home from school each afternoon was, "Mama, is Daddy coming home tonight?"

Debbie would have to answer she didn't know.

The other two battalions in the infantry brigade acted as DRF2 and DRF3. When the DRF1 battalion was called out the DRF2 battalion immediately assumed DRF1, and so on. There was always a battalion of the 82d Airborne Division standing by on two-hour recall, ready to be in flight to any destination in the world in eighteen hours or less.

The third cycle in the Division's calendar was Support Cycle. This was where the units in the Division not on Training or Mission cycles took all the menial support details around post. Before the Division went on a "block leave" policy in which an entire company or battalion was given the chance to go on leave (take a vacation) this was about the only time a trooper could take his leave. As a unit was only allowed to let a certain percentage of its personnel go on leave at a given time you can see there might be a great deal of jockeying by the troopers to go on leave. The Army gives you thirty days leave a year. They just don't guarantee you'll be able to take it when you want to.

The administrative dilemma for the battery and company level first sergeants to meet all the demands for personnel to fulfill various commitments was enormous. I don't know how the infantry battalions handled the details but in the artillery we always had a "duty battery," which alternated weekly to take care of each detail the battalion was tasked for. Requests for personnel to do each detail was handed down to the battalion S-3 from higher headquarters, in turn, the tasking NCO, usually the Battalion Operations Sergeant, would pass the tasking letters down to the duty battery first sergeant, who would try to juggle his troops to meet the commitments. I remember one day Top Moore was having a fit in the S-3 office over the commitments he had received for the day. He had about eighty men present for duty that day and was tasked to provide one hundred and fifty men for various details. I thought he was going to climb over SFC Garner's desk before they finally got it straightened out.

In the summer this schedule slightly altered as the entire post of Ft. Bragg was given over to support the annual ROTC summer camp. The various units of the Division not on mission cycle worked with the other units on Ft. Bragg to provide training cadre and logistical support for ROTC cadets entering their second year of training. Certain units were chosen to give the CAPEX (Capabilities Exercise) showing off their branch to prospective officers who were about to choose their career fields in the Army. The basic idea of these shows was to convince the cadets that whichever branch is being shown off is the most exciting, most fun, and most important branch of the Army. In other words, it was one big snow job.

For instance, in 1983 my battalion was given the responsibility for the artillery CAPEX held at OP (Observation Post) 5 on the edge of the MacRidge Impact Area on post. The title of the show was "Artillery, King of Battle!"[111] I think they used the same skit every year, with the same script. At least it was the same every time we did it.

It began with an infantry squad being overwhelmed by enemy fire (actually, it's a bunch of cannon cockers masquerading as infantrymen) when an artillery forward observer stepped in and said, "Don't worry, the artillery's on the way!"

At about that time a battery of artillery came on the scene to the theme of the "Lone Ranger." Some years, the script called for the battery to be airmobiled in on Huey or Blackhawk helicopters with the howitzers slung beneath the choppers. In 1983 budget problems forced us to come in towing the howitzers behind our trucks. It wasn't as impressive as riding in on the choppers, but you do what you can with what you have. We came barreling over a protective berm[112] to the left front of the bleachers, swung the guns around, unhooked them, set them up, and began firing different types of missions at various targets set up in the impact area.

Of course, we scored direct hits on every target. After all, we had been practicing every day for a month before the actual demonstrations began and had every target zeroed in. There was no chance we'd miss. The cadets sitting in the bleachers didn't know this; they just ate up the show.

Our battery spent every day during the summer of 1983 doing the routine. We'd be in to work every morning between three and four in the morning for first formation and be out at the OP by 0800 (8:00 A.M.). The demonstration would begin at 0930 (9:30), our part would be done by 1100 or 1130. We'd clean our guns, perform daily maintenance checks on our vehicles, and be off by

---

[111] Napoleon is quoted as saying, "Infantry may be the 'Queen of Battle' – but artillery is the Queen!"

[112] These protective berms were earthen mounds, which ran from each side of the bleachers out at an angle toward the impact area. They were placed as protective walls against explosions in the impact area.

1400 (2:00 PM.). This schedule ran seven days a week throughout ROTC Support Cycle. Sunday's often just another day on the calendar in the Army.

After the cadets were finished watching our show, they would be marched over to static displays of equipment set up by the other firing batteries in our battalion. At one position they would actually be allowed to fire the howitzers. Thrill, thrill.

We had one battery commander who told me it was the CAPEX at Ft. Bragg that had convinced him to choose the artillery as his branch. He was a real nut about the artillery and was always experimenting with different artillery techniques, which were seldom used in the real world. In the field, he drove us NCOs crazy keeping us up all night doing "starshots" and hasty surveys[113] after we'd been going all day moving and shooting.

It was during this ROTC Support Cycle that my Grandpa Phelps died. I remember the last time I saw my Grandpa alive. It was in the summer of 1982, when we were home on leave after Gallant Eagle 82. I walked into the living room of their house. He was sitting in his chair watching the St. Louis Cardinals play baseball. I remember kissing him on his bald head as all his children and grandchildren had done for years. He'd always grin when we kissed his head like that. He had gone bald by the age of twenty-three. His explanation for baldness was that it was a sign of his intelligence; after all, grass doesn't grow on a busy street.

He had suffered a stroke in 1974 and had been partially paralyzed since. It was sad to see my Grandpa, who had always been a pillar of strength to the whole family, laid low. But he seemed to be enjoying himself. He had worked hard all his life, now he could sit back and even watch a baseball game without interruption. Grandpa was a diehard St. Louis Cardinals fan. The Cards won the World Series in 1982. I was really thankful Grandpa got to see them go all the way one more time before he went home.

I had been trying to get home for some time to see him. He was failing again and the doctors didn't give him long. Leave after leave request had been cancelled because of duty requirements.

By the end of June he had been hospitalized with little hope of recovery. I was calling Illinois every day or so to check on him.

---

[113] These are alternative methods of improving the accuracy of your artillery fire by pinpointing your grid location on a map. The "starshot" uses Polaris or Kolchab to establish location, hasty surveys, use landmarks, and directional measurements to achieve the same end during the day time when one can't see the stars. It was all boring to me, because I'd learned it all in Germany during my first hitch as a surveyor.

248

Each day the news got worse.

Then, one evening, I called my grandparents' house and Grandpa answered. It took me a minute to realize who was talking; he hadn't spoken so clearly in years.

"Grandpa?" I asked surprised.

"Yep."

"How're you doing?"

"Just fine, never better."

"I'm surprised to hear you home. I guess you're doing okay." Everything's great, it'll be okay, don't worry."

"Well, I guess they can't keep a good man down, can they?"

"Nope."

"Well, Grandpa, I've got to go now, you take care. I'll call back in a few days, okay?"

"Okay."

"Well, so long, now. I love you, Grandpa."

"I Love you too, you be good. Don't worry, everything'll be okay."

Two days later, I got the news he was dead. We had just finished firing the demonstration for the day. I looked up and saw my old section chief, the one I didn't get along with, standing by the bleachers. He only had a few days left in the Army and had signed over the section to his replacement, a new staff sergeant returned from Italy.

Somehow I knew what he was there for. He sadly nodded his head when I asked him if it was my grandfather. I appreciated his compassion that day.

When I got back to the rear, Top Boss'e was waiting with an emergency leave form, it was already filled out, and awaiting my signature and how many days I would need. As I walked over to battalion headquarters to sign out on leave, he said, "Don't look so sad, Sergeant Wood, your Grandpa's in a better place."

I thought about it and smiled, "You're right, Top. He sure is." Grandpa had worked from his tenth birthday up to the time of his stroke at age sixty-two. The last ten years of his life he had been plagued with all sorts of health problems. But he died knowing his Savior. Now he is in a place where there is no pain, no sorrow, and no hardship. He's looking Jesus face to face. I knew this to be a fact; I'd visited there myself a couple times. Many is the time I've had a homesickness to go back to heaven. My grief was selfish. I was going to miss him, just knowing he was in Illinois, a phone call or visit away.

I had called my dad up before we left to let him know we were going to be in town. He offered to let us stay with him. As we really couldn't afford a motel room and with all the relatives pouring in from across the country staying with those few souls in the family who still lived in the St. Louis area, his offer was a blessing. After the dust cleared from the funeral, we had a week or so to spend together and get reacquainted.

I saw cousins I hadn't seen in years. Many of them I had to be introduced to, they had been born or grown up from infants since the last time our family had gotten together. It seems these days the only time family gets together is when someone either gets married or buried.

By the time I got back to Bragg ROTC Support was over and the battalion was back in ITC getting ready for another ARTEP prior to going back on Mission Cycle. Life goes on in the Division. After a couple of months of field training we passed our ARTEP, were declared combat ready, and entered Mission Cycle.

My battery started the cycle in October 1983 as DRF1. That meant we had to load our equipment in our gamma goats (trucks) and break down our howitzers and trucks for air transport. After doing that, the trucks and guns were stored in a holding area and kept under guard so that in the event of an emergency all that needed to be done for us to deploy was to drive them down to the heavy drop rigging site for final preparation for heavy drop.

Life during Mission Cycle tends to be a mixture of boredom and tension. The boredom comes from the fact that with our equipment loaded up and prepared to fly away at a moment's notice it doesn't leave us much to do with our time. Oh, we would march down to the motor pool where the holding area is and perform general maintenance on the equipment, i.e., checking the oil on the trucks, keeping the rust off the guns, etc. But there is only so much you can do of that.

Mission Cycle is supposed to be the time when individual training is accomplished, as a matter of fact, the personnel in the unit are supposed to have completed the individual training mandated by Army Regulations such as weapons familiarization and qualification, site zeroing, NBC (Nuclear, Biological, and Chemical) training, and PT tests before the unit enters Mission Cycle. Thus, administratively speaking at least, each trooper and the unit as a whole are ready to go to war,

Unit field training is supposed to be a no-no, as a unit out in the field is not immediately available in the event of a callout. However, I have seen battalion commanders send out their units, gambling there wouldn't be a callout. I remember one time in 1984 when our battalion commander had us out on a battalion FTX (Field Training Exercise). My battery was DRF2 and A Battery was DRF1.

This was a direct violation of the Division RSOP (Readiness Standard Operating Procedures). I remember standing around with the other gun chiefs (I was a gun chief when this happened) wishing we'd have a callout so the battalion commander would get caught.

It wasn't that we didn't want to be out in the field. No one likes the thought of field duty, but once you're out there it isn't so bad. Besides, we were used to it. Field duty is a fact of life in the artillery. We were just upset at what we perceived as an unprofessional breach of regulations, which, if it came down to it, we would have to pay for somehow.

As the DRF, our battalion and the infantry brigade we supported provided the mainstay of any force that would be sent to a trouble spot anywhere on the globe. In an actual situation time is of the essence. The time it would take us to get in from the field, clean up our equipment, and rig it for airdrop could make the difference between the success and failure of a mission.

It so happened we did get called out during the time I am talking about. We had just occupied our first position and were preparing to fire a mission when word came down through our FDC (Fire Direction Center) that A Battery had been alerted. As DRF2 we had to go in, clean up our guns and trucks, break them down as described before, and assume the role of DRF1 until A Battery got back from wherever they were being sent. This wouldn't have been too much of a problem except we were given a specified time in which to accomplish this. That time was shortened by the fact we had to drive almost twenty miles back to main post at convoy speeds before we could even begin the process.

Somehow, the NCOs and troops managed this, and even passed the inspection, which the people from Division HQ give a unit assuming DRF1. They even boasted about how "squared away" the artillery always was. Yeah, we did it. After all, it was our job. But I couldn't help but remember something Rob told me after another stupid stunt the brass put us through.

"You know, Woody," he said. "As long as we keep pulling their fat out of the fire, they'll keep falling in. The more we give 'em, the more they ask."

He was right.

As Mission Cycle in October 1983 began, nothing out of the way happened. We fairly well stayed close to home and conducted classes in individual soldier skills around the battery area.

A warrant officer recruiting team came down from the Pentagon to interview qualified personnel to determine whether or not they were interested in attending the new Warrant Officer Candidate School. My name was on their list and I was interviewed and, of course, I was interested.

I saw the board on a Monday. I was told they were going back to Washington Friday. If I could get my "abbreviated packet"[114] back to them before they left I would be able to appear before the next board in January. I could be at Ft. Rucker attending the new Warrant Officer Candidate School by summer. I went home that night and began filling out the forms and getting the needed documents together.

We got called out at about 0300 (3:00 AM) Tuesday morning. It was just an EDRE (Emergency deployment Readiness Exercise). We flew out to Camp McKall (where they conducted the Special Forces Qualification Course) and practiced an extraction exercise. The scenario was that American civilians and diplomatic personnel were being held hostage by terrorists in a Central American country and the 82nd had been called in to rescue them.

Originally, the infantry commander had chosen not to take along his artillery. This was his call, based on the situation. Our battalion commander had gone over the infantry battalion commander's head to the brigade commander and demanded his troops be taken along in the name of good old inter-branch cooperation. So, off we went.

We were airmobiled to the site on some of the Army's new light cargo helicopters, UH-60 Blackhawks. We rode inside while our guns were sling loaded and hanging loose beneath the choppers. We spent a day or so at Camp McKall sitting out in a field, with our guns emplaced, doing nothing. All dressed up with no place to go. Then all the fun was over and helicopters came and extracted us. We hadn't done a thing. The infantry commander might have been forced to take us along but he didn't have to use us.

By the time we got to the rear and got everything cleaned up and back in the holding area it was Thursday evening and I wasn't

---

[114] Normally, it takes an extensive amount of paperwork to complete a packet to attend Warrant Officer Candidate School, or Officers Candidate School. During this initial recruiting period, the board was accepting "abbreviated packets," to ease the process until they got enough candidates to fill out the first class. These required a lot less paperwork than was usual.

able to complete my packet and get it back to the team from the Pentagon before they went home. There was no point in getting upset about it. I decided I'd finish it off and send it off through channels the next week. As things turned out, it would take me much longer to complete the packet than I had expected.

Monday, October 24, 1983, began like any other day in the Division. We ran PT in the morning; we went through our daily routine. One of our brigades was preparing to fly to Europe to participate in the annual REFORGER[115]exercises in Germany, one of the infantry battalions in the brigade we supported was preparing to relieve a battalion of the 101st Abn Division (Air Assault) from duty as part of the Multi-National Force and Observers in the Sinai Peninsula. Everyone was talking about the two hundred and thirty-nine U.S. Marines who had been killed in Beirut by a truck bomber. We wondered if we would be sent in to relieve the Marines left there. The guys who had been killed had been about go home. The Marines who had been on their way to relieve them had been diverted enroute, however, to provide a presence down in the Caribbean. There had been unrest on a tiny island off the coast of South America and there were supposed to be a couple of hundred American college students down there. When you're on DRF you pay attention to the newspapers, today's headline may be where you pitch your tent tomorrow.

I got off work late that evening. This upset me. I had wanted to get home early because it was Debbie's birthday and some friends were coming over for dinner and cake.

By the time I got home dinner was ready. We had just finished the main meal and were eating birthday cake when the phone call came in.

"SGT Wood?"

"Yes?"

"This is SGT Jones, come in and bring in everything you've got. Bring your POW[116] if you've got one, you might need it."

"No problem." I said as I hung up. I tried to act calm.

"What is it?" Debbie asked as I hung up the phone.

"'Crazy Division's playing games again!" I said, with mock irritation to hide the adrenalin rush I was feeling. I was trying not to

---

[115] REFORGER- REturn of FORces to GERmany exercise we used to run every two years during the Cold War. Stateside units were sent to Germany for two to three weeks to train in Europe and familiarize themselves with the countryside if war broke out.

[116] In this case POW meant Privately Owned Weapon.

worry her, "I guess we didn't have enough fun last week they've got to fly us off again. I swear I'm going to terminate. I've had it with this nonsense!" I stormed back into the bedroom to pack my shaving kit and other essential items I'd need. Most of my stuff was in a locker at the barracks, but there were things I'd need on this trip I didn't normally pack.

"Look," I said, trying to be nonchalant about it. "I'll probably be back tomorrow sometime. If not, you know the drill, come in and get the car." I gave my wife a kiss. I remember studying the faces of my family, trying to memorize them. I didn't know when - or if- I'd be seeing them again. "Germany's looking better all the time." I said as I got into my car.

I hoped I sounded a lot more cheerful than I felt, because this one was for real. Eddie, the sergeant who had called me had tipped me off when he told me to bring my own weapon if I had one. You didn't take your own private weapons on practice alerts. This was not a drill. I couldn't say anything to my wife about it as much as I wanted to. It was a matter of national security and her own good.

For now I turned to matters at hand. I didn't know where exactly we were going, but wherever it was it was going to be an interesting time.

My mind was working overtime as I drove the thirteen miles from my house to my barracks. I ran over the newspaper headlines in my mind, attempting to figure out to which trouble spot we were being sent. One by one I eliminated each, citing the reasons we wouldn't go there. The only possible answer kept coming up over and over again - Beirut.

Chapter 19
Not Just Another Callout: Urgent Fury - I

Trooper, oh trooper where do you roam?
Far 'cross the ocean, far, far from home.
Trooper, oh trooper what do you do?
I fight very proudly for the red, white, and blue.
Trooper, oh trooper where do you fight?
I fight where they send me, both day and night.
Trooper, oh trooper where have you been?
I've been 'cross the water and back again.
Trooper, oh trooper what did you see?
I saw the 82nd Airborne[117] fighting for me.
(Anonymous Vietnam era Marching Cadence)

When I got to the unit SGT Jones was sitting at the CQ desk in the entrance, "Grenada," he said as I walked in.

"Lovely." I replied. I was surprised, the situation there must have been worse than we'd heard.

"Where the heck is Grenada, anyway?"

"Off the coast of South America," I said. "They produce some of the loveliest stamps you ever want to see. For collectors."

"Stamps?"

"Yeah, I used to collect stamps when I was a kid. Some small countries like Grenada have made an industry out of producing pretty postage stamps for young kids to buy. You ought to see some of the stamps I have from Grenada, all sorts of butterflies, tropical fish, flowers and stuff."

Jonesy shook his head, "Stamps..."

"Of course, Grenada is also noted for its spices..."

"You're a walking geography book!"

"The benefits of being well read, Jonesy!" I retorted and went upstairs to the off-post locker room to pack for the tropics.

"Stamps..." I heard Jonesy mutter to himself, still shaking his head.

The next few hours were chaotic. We began having muster formations to ensure accountability of all the battery personnel. The time an alert is called is called N-hour. At N + 2 (two hours after N

---

[117] You can insert your unit of choice here.

hour) one hundred per cent of an alerted unit's personnel must be present or accounted for. At this formation we received the first official report on our status. At this time the grunts (infantry) didn't feel they needed artillery support as resistance was expected to be light. It was a replay of last week's trip to Camp McKall.

"Sure," I remember thinking wryly to myself. "Take the hill with bayonets and die like heroes."

We experienced both relief and disappointment at this news. At least I did. I could see it on the other trooper's faces. I mean, no one in his or her right mind really wants to go into combat. At the same time, this is what we had been training and preparing for all this time. Now, when the balloon finally went up for real we were being told we weren't needed.

Perhaps CPT Herbert, who was at this time commanding our A (Alpha) Battery, summed it up best. Their (Alpha's) infantry battalion was preparing to go to the Sinai so they stayed at Bragg, providing personnel to make up for vacancies and acting as support for the two batteries from our battalion which were finally deployed) He told me, "When I found out we were being left behind I felt like a kid who had helped prepare for a birthday party, and then wasn't invited."

That's about how we felt - let down. It's like on a jump, there's a bit of fear involved, but once you get manifested, chuted up, and are on that bird you're pumped up to go out that door. If the jump is cancelled for whatever reason, you are disappointed. Civilians (and some soldiers) find this attitude hard to understand. I guess you have to go through it.

We were released from formation to go back into the barracks and wait further word from higher headquarters. The XO called me into his office and told me he wanted me, with my headquarters' experience and security clearance, to act as the battery's runner to the infantry battalion's headquarters. Telephone communications weren't to be trusted. It was a bit of a mundane task, but important. I didn't mind. It beat sitting upstairs not knowing what was going on. I was sent to pick up a sealed dispatch from the infantry battalion commander.[118]

It turned out the infantry had changed their minds and decided to take three guns. I learned later the Rangers who spearheaded the operation with a jump onto Point Salines airstrip had

---

[118]Once an infantry battalion is called out, the supporting units fall under the tactical control of the infantry battalion commander unless, or until the artillery battalion headquarters is deployed. Even then, the artillery battalion headquarters may only exercise administrative control over the batteries, depending on the situation.

run into more resistance than expected.

The Battery Commander would go ahead with the First, Second, and Third howitzer sections and an element from our FDC. Fourth, Fifth, and Sixth sections would remain behind with the Executive Officer and the remaining personnel from the battery. Our Forward Observers (called FIST, Forward Infantry Support Teams) had already gone to join the infantry. If the guns didn't go they'd be used as an extra squad or fire teams by their infantry units.

I was in the Fourth section at the time. We watched as our buddies were marched to waiting "cattle trucks" to be transported to the staging area where they would be issued ammunition and whatever else they needed for the operation.

I was standing beside SSG Svenson, my section chief, as we watched the trucks depart, "There'll be a rift in the battery between those who went and those who got left behind." I told him.

"You're just mad because you're not going with them, Sergeant Wood," Svenson said with a grin.

"Maybe so, chief, but it'll be bad on morale,"

We got word sometime in the early morning that Battalion Task Force 2-325 Infantry was "wheels up" (that is, taking off) at approximately N + 9 hours. We had beat the Division standard (18 hours) by half.

Eventually we were told to "stand down" and get some sleep until further notice. As we were not released to go home, those of us who lived off-post had to catch a nap wherever we could. One of the men in my section's roommate had been deployed with the first bunch to go. I slept on top of his bunk that evening, using my own blanket.

We were wakened early in the morning. I went downstairs to the dayroom where a bunch of the guys were gathered around the television watching the first reports of an "invasion by a foreign force" on the tiny Caribbean island of Grenada. The network showed a map of the island on the screen while the reporter told of heavy fighting around Point Salines Airport after paratroopers (the Rangers) from an unknown foreign country landed on the island during the night. Fighting was reported to be heavy, but it appeared as if the invader had just about secured the airfield. There were cheers and "Hooooaaahs!" at that, for we all thought at the time it had been our boys who had made the jump. The early reports were sketchy,

One of the guys said something about how we had better get called out soon or there wasn't going to be any war left for us to

257

fight. I thought about Debbie and the kids. If she was up and had heard the news she'd be in a panic because she'd know that we had been in on it. I wished I could call her and let her know I was okay and had been left behind. It would ease her mind. But I couldn't call her; it would be a violation of security. The mouthpieces to all the pay phones and off post lines in the barracks had been removed, anyway.

We were marched over to the mess hall for breakfast. Shortly after we returned I was sent after another dispatch.

I brought it back to the XO. He opened it. His eyes widened. "We're going!"

After that it was, as we used to say, "asses and elbows" as the troops were notified, we grabbed our gear and hustled down to the formation area to await transportation.

We were loaded up on cattle trucks and hauled down to Green Ramp. There, we were issued ammunition, C-rations, tropical gear, and numerous other items we'd need for the operation. Things were done in such a hurry that it fostered a great deal of confusion – of which thanks to the tutelage of my Drill Sergeants at Ft. Leonard Wood I took advantage. Whenever someone came around asking if anyone needed food or ammo, I always raised a hand. I was able to get two to three days extra food and ammo for the section. In all, I was able to scrounge an extra thousand or so rounds for the section's M-60 machine gun. I also managed to get four hundred rounds of .45 ammunition. Top Franco had a .45, so I gave two hundred to him. I figured he'd find a use for them on the island. I kept the other two hundred, perhaps I'd be able to find a .45 no one needed any more. The ammo would come in handy.

One of the guys protested when I gave him the extra food, "Gee, Sergeant Wood, I don't have room for anything else in my ruck[119] with everything that's in here..."

"Then you'd better make room, son," I said. "We don't know what's waiting for us on the other end, or when we'll get resupplied. You'd better take everything you can with you because it might have to do you for awhile."

"I guess I don't need all this junk anyway." he said, pulling out some winter clothing items.

I could see the other NCOs moving through the troops checking to make sure they were taken care of, giving words of encouragement here and there. I looked over at one trooper, recently married, who had only been in the unit a month or so, "How long

---

[119] "ruck"- short for "rucksack" slang for field pack.

'you been in the army, Supertroop?"

"About six months, Sergeant Wood."

"You lucky dog! You're going to get to do in six months what I've been waiting almost nine years to do - go somewhere and kill somebody!"

He looked at me for a moment sheepishly, and then grinned, "Airborne!" he said.

In a way, I did envy him. As a private, he only had to look out for himself. I was a sergeant, a leader. As gunner of a howitzer section I was the assistant section chief. As such, I had to set an example for my men. There might come a time when men's lives would be depending on me. I hoped I would be up to it when and if the time came. At the moment, all I could think of was all the things I wished I could do better.

After cooling out for a couple of hours at the holding area we were marched over to the loading area at Green Ramp for departure.

We spent several agonizing hours in suspense waiting for a bird. During this time we heard several conflicting reports on what was going to happen next. First, we were told we were going to chute up at Green Ramp and jump in at Point Salines Airport. This brought a round of "HOOAAHs!" a sound of approval, from the troops. After all, this was what we trained for. The guys immediately began talking about a combat star for their parachutist's badge.[120]

At one point some of us actually drew our chutes and were preparing to put them on when we were told to wait. A little later we were told to hand them back in.

Then, we were told we were going to fly to the island at Barbados, where the rest of the battery was waiting, link up there with the rest of the battery, and jump in. A little later, we were told the airstrip was too hot for a jump. There was a squadron of helicopters, UH-60 Blackhawks waiting for us at Barbados. We would load up on the choppers with our howitzers sling loaded beneath them and airmobile from Barbados to Grenada, a distance of some ninety miles. I didn't figure where an airmobile was any safer than a jump onto a hot DZ/LZ[121]

Okay, whatever, let's just get the show on the road if we're

---

[120] Traditionally US paratroopers have adorned their parachutist's badges with a gold star (or "mustard stain) for each combat jump they have performed. Prior to Grenada/Urgent Fury this was not regulation, just a tradition started by WW2 troopers. After Grenada it was finally written into the regs.

[121]DZ/LZ: Drop Zone/Landing Zone. A Drop Zone, or DZ, as already explained, is used for a parachute jump. A Landing Zone is for airmobile/airland operations.

going, okay?

Then, we were told to stand down again. We weren't going to be needed after all. We had to turn in all our ammo. I was disgusted. All that hard work I did scrounging went down the drain. We had no sooner turned in our stuff than we got word we were going; talk about a roller coaster ride! I was able to get my goodies back because I had stacked my stuff all neatly to the side of the big pile of ammo the guys had dumped.

Shortly after that, we began loading on our aircraft, five or six men at a time, riding with our guns and trucks. The last word I got before boarding the aircraft was we were going to Barbados before we did whatever it was we were going to do. This was in the early morning hours of D+1, October 26, 1983.

The bird I got on was carrying my section's truck and gun. On board with me were five or six young privates, none of them in the Army a year yet, and another E-5, SGT Frank Rousseau, chief of 5th Howitzer Section.

The plane was extremely cold from the air-conditioning so I dug out my poncho liner, a light nylon blanket-like sheet used in tropical regions I had been issued at Green Ramp. Rousseau and I each took an end and curled up in the poncho liner and went to sleep on the outboard personnel seats of the aircraft. Who knew when we'd get our next sleep and what else was there to do?

When I woke, I didn't know how long we'd been in the air but it was daylight outside. I now have learned the ride took between four and five hours. The aircraft seemed to be circling. I looked outside the window and could see the ocean below. The aircraft banked and I got a glimpse of dozens of warships of all types and sizes in the water below. I looked over at SGT Rousseau, who was also up, "Man, it looks like D-Day!"

Rousseau was looking out his window and shaking his head in disbelief.

"By the way, I don't even know your first name, SGT Rousseau. My name's Wayne, my friends call me Woody. "

"Woody, my name's Frank."

The aircrew was shuffling around the aircraft. They seemed nervous. A female crew chief came over to me, "We'll be landing in a few minutes, Sergeant, we can't stay long, the runway's busy, so if you can get your men hot unlashing the tie downs it'll help."

"Sure." Frank and I looked at each other. What was she so nervous about? I didn't like the answer to that question which came to mind. We began waking up the troopers who were still asleep, getting them ready for what had to be done.

The plane made the final approach and we touched the ground. As the plane taxied in we heard this "pinging" off the skin of the aircraft. I remember thinking if I didn't know better I'd swear someone was shooting at us.[122] We looked at each other in consternation. The bird hadn't even stopped yet and the crew was already undoing lashings and tie downs. Then the Plane reached the end of the runway and swung around. The tailgate was lowered. Frank and I were at the rear of the aircraft. When the tailgate lowered we were hit by a blast of humid tropical air and the sound of gunfire.

We put the troops to work undoing the guns and stood there for a moment on the tailgate, trying to figure out what on earth was going on. We could see soldiers running to and fro in combat crouches. Off in the distance, we could hear the sounds of small arms fire, followed by an occasional burst from a heavy machine gun. Clouds of dust kicked up not fifty feet from where we were standing.[123] Someone was shooting in our direction with automatic small arms fire. Then, there was a ripping sound which shook the island and sent chills down my spine. I later learned the sound was the Gatling guns of the AC-l30 gunship, known as SPECTRE. In Vietnam they called the C-47 version of it "Puff, the Magic Dragon."

Frank and I looked at each other again. As I said, everything we had been told back at Bragg said we were to land in Barbados. I know this seems dumb, but remember, we had been briefed. We trusted our briefing, if they had changed plans, you'd think they'd have notified us.

"Are you thinking what I'm thinking, Frank?"

"What are you thinking, Woody?"

"I don't think this is Barbados, I mean, from everything I've heard, Barbados is supposed to be a tourist paradise."

"Do you think the war could have spread?"

"Maybe..." I looked over to the left of the aircraft and saw Top Moore standing on the edge of the airstrip, feet spread about shoulder length apart, his M-l6A1 slung over his shoulder, thumbs

---

[122] To this day I can't figure who might have been shooting at us or from where. I am recording my impressions at the time. This is something I will try to note throughout these chapters on Grenada.

[123] A buddy of mine who was there a few minutes before me, has said he and another guy didn't receive fire while they were there. The impression I received at the time was that we were receiving at least light small-arms fire. Again, I don't know now from where the fire might have come. By the same token, if there was no fire, why were the guys ducking and dodging?

hooked in his pistol belt, looking for all intents and purposes as if he was having the time of his life while all mayhem was breaking loose around him.

He was the only guy standing up straight on this section of the airstrip. He looked like the war god without a care in the world. Top, with at least a couple tours in Vietnam was one of our most experienced combat soldiers. The joke was you could tell when Top Moore changed his shirt by the different airborne combat patch on his sleeve.

What on earth was he doing here? He was Alpha Battery's First Sergeant and Alpha had been left behind. This whole situation didn't make any sense.[124] "There's Top Moore," I said, "Let me go over and ask him what's going on, 'you want to help the troops?"

"Sure." Frank said.

Let me state here there was a surreal aspect to everything. It seemed to me as if I had stepped out of my body and become an observer of everything happening all around me. I was aware of the danger, but it seemed like I was watching myself in a dream.

At the same time, I knew that I had to at least put on the appearance of confidence for the sake of the young soldiers for whose lives I was responsible. I don't claim to be a hero or anything like that; it was just a matter of doing what needed to be done. I wasn't going to do myself or anyone else any good by falling apart.

I walked over to where Top was standing. I was trying to be casual. He was briefing one of Charlie Battery's officers, who apparently had also just landed. I waited for him to finish. Top turned his attention to me.

"Good morning, First Sergeant." I said. I was reminded of an Army recruiting commercial out at that time. It was all I could do to keep from snickering.

"Good morning, Sergeant Wood." he said with a little twinkle in his eye. I wondered if he was thinking of the commercial, too.

"This may seem like a stupid question, but am I correct in assuming that this is not Barbados?"

He looked meaningfully up at a little house situated about

---

[124] I later learned that Charlie (C) Battery had been deployed along with the 3-325 Infantry. Their First Sergeant (who had the nickname of "Screwy Louie" and was the same guy who'd given me a hard time over my profile the previous year) had suffered a stress fracture while running a marathon that weekend and couldn't come along. He had thus traded places with Top Moore. It was probably the best thing in the world to happen to Charlie Battery. Top Moore was one of the best, with three tours in Vietnam and six months in the Dominican Republic.

halfway up the mountain, which was billowing with thick black smoke. I heard the Grenadian PRA (People's Republican Army) had been using it as a sniper's nest since the landing. They had been having a great time harassing our troops on the airstrip below. Then our guys blasted it.

Top and I examined the scene for a few seconds, "No, Sergeant Wood, you are on the island of Grenada."

"Thanks Top," I said, reaching for a thirty round magazine and loading it in my M16A1. "It's nice to know these things."

"It sure is."

"I think I ought to tell my troops."

"They'd probably appreciate it. When you're ready I'll show you where the batteries are."

"Thanks, Top."

I walked nonchalantly back to where the truck and others. I could see the apprehension on the young troopers faces. It was important to appear calm, "Gentlemen, you're in a combat zone, act accordingly."

Our first position on the island was on a strip of land between the airstrip and the sea, directly across from the air terminal. Our guns were just arriving, one at a time. As they arrived, they were identified by their waiting crews and emplaced. I was proud of the young soldiers as they went about their business just as if we were back at Bragg, almost ignoring the sounds of gunfire.

I was told the first contingent from our battery had laid over at Barbados. They had actually chuted up to jump in on the island, in spite of the fact their guns had not caught up with them yet. As a matter of fact, at the time, all our guns were still back on Bragg waiting for birds. Before they could load on the aircraft, word came in the Rangers had finally secured the northern end of the airstrip and cleared it of debris so aircraft could land. Two engineers from the Division had jumped in with them for this purpose.

General Trobough, the Division Commander during the invasion then made a decision which, though tactically sound, was debated then and has been debated by Grenada veterans since. He decided to call off the Division jump onto the island and have us airland[125] instead,

He had good reasons for doing this. For one thing, the very nature of a night combat jump at four hundred and fifty to five hundred feet onto an unknown drop zone raises the probability and percentage of casualties. There was also the problem of the

---

[125] That is to land the aircraft on an airstrip and have us walk off, rather than jump.

Caribbean Sea, which was only a couple hundred meters away from the airstrip we would have used for the drop zone. For another, one could argue the jump was unnecessary. The airstrip had been secured; there was no point in risking needless casualties showing off.

On the down side of his decision, we were upset because jumping into combat is what the 82nd is supposed to do. It is what we were trained to do. It is what the 82nd has always done. We were disappointed. This was our big opportunity - the first since World War II - and it was lost. On the tactical side of the argument an airborne operation would have put a large number of troops on the ground immediately instead of taking hours, even days. Some accounts of the battle I've read revealed this to be a major concern, as it was took so long to get troops on the island in the first hours of the operation. Remember there was only one narrow airstrip so only one bird could come in at a time and offload while other birds had to circle the island, as mine had done. While the artillery was positioned in our initial location across from the incomplete air terminal, landings had to be postponed when we were firing missions, further delaying deployment of our troops. Personally, I think a masstac[126] would have had an enormous psychological impact on both our enemies and the world at large.

Of course, the General had a handicap going into the operation in that many of the Division old-timers didn't consider him to be one of "us." He had completed Jump School way back in 1956 but, looking over his record, published when he assumed command, he had served most of his time in "leg" units. He hadn't even completed the jumpmaster school when he assumed command of the Division (a requirement for any command position in the Division). I've heard it said more than once that if General Lindsay, his predecessor, had been in command we would have jumped. General Lindsay was considered to be "Airborne" – hence his nicknames "Jumping Jim" or "Jungle Jim."[127]

It may have been a defendable tactical decision, but it just wasn't popular with most of the troops with whom I've spoken. There are some, who touched down with our first group (who landed without their howitzers) who have since admitted some relief. After all, if the Division had been forced to jump in it meant something

---

[126] As previously noted, a masstac is the method of dropping large numbers of fully combat-rigged troops on a target in a short time through use of both sides of an aircraft at ½ second intervals.

[127] In the tradition of our great WWII commander, "Jumping Jim" Gavin.

had gone terribly wrong with the Ranger drop – what good would cannon cockers have been without their guns? This was a valid concern, at the time, considering what we, or anyone else knew about the tactical situation on the island.

As for me, after we turned in our chutes, every scenario I had heard about deployment described us going to Barbados and organizing before proceeding to the island. I think I would have preferred jumping – at least I would have known where I was jumping instead of wondering where the heck I was.

The first gun to arrive on the island belonged to our 3rd Section whose chief was SSG Jimmy Jaeger. The grunts had been trying to take the Cuban barracks and were meeting stiffer resistance than anticipated. Third Section got the mission and dropped nine or ten rounds on the compound. Then Naval Air Support, in the form of A-7s, and AC-130 gunships, who had been previously unable to properly identify the enemy positions, honed in on the smoke of the 105 rounds and hit the compound hard, neutralizing the enemy and allowing the infantry to take the objective. It was the first artillery mission against a hostile force since Vietnam.

Shortly after we got our gun emplaced our FDC Chief came on over our field telephones. We had hooked out phones up to remote speakers so everyone in the section could hear fire commands, "Congratulations, Sergeant Jaeger, you got 12 hostiles in the house. Be advised that yours is the first artillery round fired against a hostile force by the 82nd Airborne Division since Vietnam."

A loud cheer went up from the troops on the different guns. While we were all patting ourselves on the back and cheering Jimmy's crew, we suddenly got quiet, as if on cue. One of the guys spoke our minds, "Those were human beings in that house." We weren't just firing at targets anymore.

All of our guns had yet to arrive on the island so we divided up our crews among those guns available. On my gun, for instance we had five NCOs from the various sections; SSG Johns of Sixth Section was short handed so I went over to give him a hand. He was a good friend of mine and we got along. He intimidated many of the gunners in the battery because he was a hard NCO from the old school.

One story I'd heard about him said he had been a professional football player back in the sixties. He somehow got drafted and sent to Vietnam. When he got back from Nam a knee wound ended his football career. He decided to stay in the Army and make it a career. He was a tough man to work for, demanding. His nickname around DivArty was the "Big Black Bear." I always called him "Big J," or just "J". He had been in the Division for years, it was said Jaeger had written the "Dash Ten," or Operator's manual, for the M102 howitzer and Johns had made the corrections. He could be intimidating, especially when he lost his temper.

One summer, when the battery was assigned to support National Guard training he had been assigned to evaluate a howitzer section during a field exercise. He had been getting onto one of the NCOs for smoking under the gun's camouflage net, which is not only a safety violation, but also stupid, considering there was ammunition[128] under the net.

After telling the guy twice to put his cigarette out, Johns picked the guy up bodily and literally threw him out from under the net. "I told you not to smoke under my net, turkey!" he bellowed.

The guy flew ten or fifteen feet, hit the dust and rolled several feet.

"He'll know the next time he smokes under my net!" he said to no one in particular. He went back under the net and said to the rest of the crew, who were staring at him in total astonishment and intimidation, "Anyone else want to smoke under my net?"

I didn't have any problem with J. Whenever he'd start going off I'd look him dead in the eye and invite him to meet me around the back of the truck. He'd have to grin at that. "You're about crazy, Woody." he'd say or something to that effect.

There was no doubt that in spite of the fact I knew Judo, Karate, and twelve other Japanese words, he'd bend me over his knee and break me like a twig. That is, if he could catch me, or I was stupid enough to hang around and let him.

---

[128] We're not talking about the artillery rounds here. It would take more than a cigarette to explode an artillery round without a fuse in it. But the propellant powder charges used to fire the rounds are another matter. Highly volatile, the powder burns at 4000+ degrees Fahrenheit and would probably ignite the shells.

Chapter 20
The King Roars - Urgent Fury 2

I'm not the preacher I'm the preacher man's son
But I'll do the preaching 'til the preacher man comes
Stand Up, Hook Up, Shuffle to the Door
Step Right out and Count to Four

I'm not the killer I'm the killer man's son
But I'll do the killing 'til the killer man comes
Stand up...
Anonymous Running Cadence

"If infantry is the Queen of Battle, artillery is the King!"
Napoleon Bonaparte

After Jaeger's mission, the next few hours passed as if we were spectators to a grand show. From our position, we could see a great deal of what was going on. We watched a Navy A-7 zoom over the airstrip and past a mountain in the distance. We watched as tracers from an antiaircraft gun placed on the side of the mountain arced up toward the aircraft. The fighter swung around and flew past again as if to confirm it had been fired at from that position. On the third pass, it was joined by another A-7 and they let loose on the gun position with everything they had, as we cheered them on. A few hours later, we saw a truck roll across the airstrip pulling a wrecked Soviet built antiaircraft gun. We assumed it was the gun knocked out by the A-7s.

In the meantime, we had a scare when two unidentified cargo ships rounded the southern tip of the island and headed straight toward our position. We didn't know who they were, could they be reinforcements sent by Castro to help repel the invasion? As of yet we only had the elements of the two Ranger battalions and a couple of battalions of infantry from the 82nd on the island with some of their supporting elements. We didn't yet know about the different special operations units on the island. In any event, according to my learned estimation, and even more limited knowledge at the time, though the operation seemed to be going well, we still weren't on the island in force enough get too cocky. We still didn't know exactly what we were up against. The intelligence estimates we heard through the day kept changing the size of the enemy strength opposing us.

We knew there were a couple hundred Cuban military advisors on the island, professionals. In addition there were between six to eight hundred Cuban "engineers," who were on the island to build the airstrip. As we discovered, they were capable of other things. They had evidently taken up arms and joined in the defense of the island and had been fighting rather well in close combat. But, of course, in Cuba, military service is mandatory and all these men had received some sort of military training. The big unknown was the Grenadian PRA (People's Republican Army) and the PRM (People's Republican Militia). Intelligence estimates at the beginning of the campaign were varied, stating that they numbered anywhere from between fifteen hundred and two thousand troops of unknown quality. And we didn't know how many of them would remain loyal to the government and fight. In addition, there was always the question of how the civilians would react to us.

The big concern in my mind, if not the brass' was that Castro would make an attempt to relieve the island and repel the invasion force before we could get a strong enough hold to resist.[129] It appeared this is what might be happening. Orders came down for a couple of our guns to swing around, face the ships, and to be prepared to fire upon them if they didn't halt. I guess FDC was hot on the radio with higher headquarters trying to get an ID on who these ships were.

We were just about to get truly nervous when an American destroyer came around the bend. The two unknown ships veered away from the destroyer and again we cheered as the destroyer chased them out of sight. It was beginning to seem to us as if our purpose on this island was to root for the visiting team. We were developing into a great cheering section.

This may have been because no one on the front line knew we were on the island yet. Or at least, they didn't know we had at least half of our guns in place and could provide fire support for them. I know the guys who had arrived on the island hadn't been resupplied since they left Bragg. They had eaten just about all the rations they had been issued on Monday night. My scrounging had paid off. I was able to share some of my booty with a couple of the guys who were really hungry.

---

[129] We didn't know Castro had refused to reinforce his people on the island while ordering them to fight to the death. The commander on the island was court-martialed for surrendering rather than dying. That Fidel- what a guy!

I had seen a stockpile of what looked to be C-rations at the far end of the airstrip when we landed. I told Top about them. He pulled off in his jeep and came back with several cases, enough to feed the battery. I have since learned that some of the grunts, deeper into the island didn't get resupplied for a couple days. The food was there sitting on the tarmac, it just needed someone to get it to the guys who needed it.

Our position was about one hundred yards from the airstrip, between the tarmac and the sea. Part of one of the Ranger battalions had set up a makeshift CP (Command Post) at the southern edge of the airstrip. We had been observing the flurry of activity for some time. We watched as several helicopters landed. The Rangers loaded up in the birds and flew off to destination unknown.

They came back about thirty minutes later to disgorge their passengers. It was at about this time I noticed a conversation at what I had assumed to be the command jeep. One of the guys talking pointed back in our direction.

"Hey," I thought, "someone's finally noticing we're here!"

A couple of guys walked back to our position and were led to our BC. Shortly thereafter, we began receiving data for an H-hour sequence.

An H-hour sequence is designed to drop rounds on chosen targets at precisely determined and coordinated times so that they explode just before our advancing troops reach each point. This "neutralizes" the enemy by either killing him or dazing him and rendering him unable to resist our attack saving friendly lives. If a round falls short, or long, is a split-second to soon or late and the best case scenario is an enemy still able to fight. The worst-case scenario is our rounds hit friendly troops. An H-hour sequence, like a Time-on-Target mission, is one of the ultimate tests of gunnery for an artillery battery.

As we waited for the mission to begin, we NCOs were called to a chief's meeting where the particulars of the mission were explained. There were a couple hundred American students being held hostage at the medical school across the island. The Rangers had done a reconnaissance in force and found the place to be heavily fortified. An open all-out assault would be expensive in both friendly and enemy lives.

The Ranger commander had asked us to fire a prep to "soften up the position." We were familiar with the H-hour sequence. We had fired many of them back at Ft. Bragg during live fire exercises. The 82nd had the reputation of conducting more live fire exercises than any other unit in the U.S. Army. Once more, we were told of the importance of exact timing in this operation. If we fired a second too soon, any surviving enemy soldiers might have time to recover from the shock of the explosion and offer resistance. A second too late, and we would land our rounds on our own troops.

It was going to be a tricky deal, as we lacked adequate military maps of Grenada. The Army has literally hundreds of thousands of maps of places all over the world in all different scales on file for contingency. The 82nd with its worldwide deployment mission has an extensive library. When we got the call to go to Grenada though, there wasn't a single military map of the island to be found. Someone was sent to a travel agency in Fayetteville to pick up some tourist maps of the island to use in a pinch. These were photocopied and gotten out to the units deploying. I always joke that we couldn't tell you the grid coordinates or elevation of our position (items vital in military operations, particularly the artillery), but we knew where the best restaurants and historical markers were on the island. This isn't entirely true, though. Someone at Division HQ had imposed a fairly decent grid pattern on the maps so troops within the Division, at least could coordinate locations. The problem came in dealing with other units and branches who had devised their own systems. Later someone did find military style maps of the island, which may have further added to the confusion. I think this confusion of maps (or lack thereof) contributed greatly to some tragic incidents in the campaign.

The mission went off smoothly. We might have been following a script. We watched the Rangers take off from the airfield in their choppers, CH-46s courtesy of our brothers in the USMC. A few minutes later we were at battle stations and began firing our rounds. About fifteen minutes after the last round went downrange the Rangers returned with the students.

I saw one of the Rangers point toward us, it looked as though he said something. The students began shouting and waving at us, I guess they were thanking us. After being called a baby-killer in the post Vietnam seventies, it felt good to be appreciated.

The Rangers were grateful as well. They had penetrated a heavily defended position, rescued the students being detained in their dorms, and suffered only one serious casualty. We were told one Ranger had broken his ankle jumping from the chopper when they touched down. There were, I've since been told, several other minor wounds and injuries. Still, not bad considering they were going against we fairly well defended position. Though he didn't mention us in a later interview to the press, the Ranger commander at the time told us he'd never seen a prettier H-hour sequence during his entire career. Interestingly, there is not a single book I've found on the battle that mentions the Field Artillery's part in the rescue, even though I've had communications with Rangers who remember our rounds going off right before they landed on the target. I've since learned that there was also close air support involved and most accounts mention that, neglecting our participation.

I think it was about that time we heard about the Navy SEALs who had been dropped too far offshore in high seas; several of them drowned before they got to land. What a waste of superior troops. There was another outhouse rumor about Delta Force personnel that circulated but I've since learned that was bogus.[130]

I think we spent one night at that position on the Southeast corner of Point Salines across from the terminal. Then we received orders to move to a new position just north of the airfield. It wasn't really far, but it was closer in where we could fire deeper into the island.

Our CG, MG Trobaugh, by deciding to take the cautious route of airlanding us instead of dropping us by parachute hadn't taken into account the fact that due to the single airstrip and its limitations only one bird could come in at a time. His decision was greatly slowing down the buildup of the troops he was calling for – not to mention the vital food, fresh water, and in some cases, even ammo the grunts up ahead needed to carry on the battle. Tales from the grunts abound with suffering from the heat (which we shared on the guns) and hunger as well as a resistance from the enemy that was stiffer than anyone expected. Those tales are also filled with acts of kindness of gifts of food and water from a grateful population.

Our first position made a difficult situation worse as our line of fire crossed the airstrip. Our fire missions interfered with the takeoff and landing of the birds, slowing the flow even more. This

---

[130] Thanks again are due to to USMC Gunnery Sergeant (Retired) Joe Muccia. It was a great story – as most are – but not true; all about mistaken identities and shoot-outs between Rangers and the Delta guys. These things abound. There was one rumor about one of our chopper pilots being butchered by PRA guys after his bird crashed. Again, that turned out to be untrue. Joe and I agreed these should not be in the main text lest someone confuse them with fact. But I felt they were important as illustrations of how rumors fly and infect the judgment of troops on the ground during battle.

Joe's exhaustive research on Grenada for his book has not only served to re-unite many of us Grenada vets but also answer a lot of our questions on the operation. I am looking forward to its completion as it looks to be the definitive work on the subject – long over due in my humble opinion

has been mentioned in the after-action reports and in several accounts of the battle. The common sense solution was to move us north – where with Charlie Battery from our battalion, we were joined by Alpha and Bravo Batteries of the 1-319th AFAR, a sister battalion in the Division.

It was an impressive – if tactically incorrect – sight, all our M102 105mm howitzers (I've been told one gun from one of the other batteries was absent) lined up in battery order almost hub to hub. But I believe the message that sight sent to the world was worth the risk.

I began to get the idea this operation was becoming a show of strength to let the bad guys in the region know what we were capable of. Ronnie (Ronald Reagan) was putting the world on notice he wasn't playing around.

The Alpha 1/319th first sergeant had brought an American flag with him from Bragg. After we were back at Bragg, I had a troop who had been with the 1/319th who told that he had been keeping it in his desk in case the balloon really went up. When the call came for his battery to be deployed he tucked the flag in his jacket and brought it. One of the first things he did when the battery set up was to attach the flag to some camouflage net poles and raise it on a piece of high ground behind the gun line. I remember cheering at the sight of old Glory flying over Grenada.

Some photographers came by and saw the flag as a great photo opportunity. They got some of the guys from the 1/319th to pose for a shot in front of the flag, which they gladly did. The picture appeared in all the papers and magazines. The guys looked good and Hollywood combat hardened, decked out in camouflage paint, flack jackets, and drive-on rags on their heads, holding their weapons menacingly or above their heads. The irony is my guy told me they had only been on the island about two hours when the picture was taken.

Later in the day (D+2, October 27) we got word we were going to fire another H-hour sequence. We began receiving data on the gun line. It was something big. I learned from the DivArty Chaplains what was going on. Chaplain Watson, the Catholic Chaplain and Chaplain Ross, the Protestant Chaplain, were making a visit of the gun line. Chaplain Ross was former Marine Recon and a Vietnam veteran. He seemed to be having the time of his life. I looked into Chaplain Watson's eyes and saw only sadness at everything that was going on.

Chaplain Ross explained the mission to us, "The grunts (infantry) have about a battalion of Grenadians and Cubans holed up in a place called Calivigny Barracks. They've given them a time limit to surrender. After the time expires we begin shelling them, one round every forty-five seconds. Either they surrender or we level the place. After it's over we go in, count up arms and legs, divide by two and get a body count."

This time it was what is called a "Zone and Sweep Mission" where the guns pound preset targets adjusting to move the rounds so that by the time the firing stops an entire area has been pounded. I later learned the Fire Support Officer (FSO) had distributed Fire Support Plans to each firing battery giving us each our own areas to pound to prevent overlapping. Each gun was given a list of targets, we would fire one, set the data for the next target on our list, and wait for our next turn as each gun fired its target. In artillery that is called "Right-by-Piece."

The genius of this particular mission from my worm's-eye point of view was that the targets were organized so that the rounds would land randomly around the target area. It might look sloppy to the casual observer but it deprived the folks in the target area the luxury of anticipating where the next round would hit.

After it started I felt sorry for the guys at the other end of our bombardment. We were giving them one awful pounding with all twenty – plus guns. It's a terrible thing to endure an artillery bombardment. It is one of the ultimate tests of an army's discipline and morale.

I figured out how far we were from the target. Calculating the charge we were using and how fast the projectile traveled, I could estimate how long it took for our rounds to hit the target. We could hear our rounds bursting. I counted off one round, we heard the burst, it was followed by a dark cloud of smoke billowing up from over the horizon.

"Whew boy!" I shouted, "We hit something, look at that fireball!"

I didn't realize it, I was so busy working, but there were TV cameras behind us as we worked. They picked me up when I shouted. I was broadcast across the country. Everyone told me when I got home that they saw me. The phone lines burned up as everyone in my family, spread from Washington State, to North Carolina and points in between, called one another to tell each other they had seen me. My brothers argued over whether or not the guy who looked a lot like me from the back was really me until I shouted. There was no mistaking my voice.

Gee, I thought, I had been a celebrity for my fifteen seconds and didn't even know it. What a shame.

I later read somewhere the bombardment hadn't been effective. That wouldn't be surprising considering we were working with such ineffective maps. One book, reputed to be the best on the subject, stated the bombardment was ineffective because we left our M-2 Aiming Circles back at Bragg. That's a crock! I know that at least my battery had ours because as a gunner we used them to lay the batteries.[131] I think I would remember something like that. Even had we left our Aiming Circles at Bragg we could have still "laid" the batteries using compasses and would have been quite accurate in our fire. The book dramatically depicts a colonel flying over the scene helplessly watching our rounds falling harmlessly into the sea, unable to do anything about it because of the incompatibility of our communications system (which was a real problem on the island between the services). The question that popped into my mind was – where were our FIST doggies? (Forward Observers) They could have observed the fire and corrected it. That's what they're paid for.[132]

I always thought the "fireball" was from one of my section's rounds. It was timed perfectly. It has been contended it was a Navy A-7 hit that caused it. My question might be, "What was a Navy A-7 doing flying over the target when we were firing a mission?" except for a particularly tragic incident.

As we were shooting our mission a Navy A-7 Corsair flew overhead and buzzed a building about a half a mile away from our position. It was sitting on the opposite slope of a slight valley, inland from the airport. The pilot flew right in our path of fire, causing Big Sven to call a checkfire (that is, a halt in fire for safety reasons).

We had just resumed firing when the bird flew over again. This time, it opened up with everything it had on the building, sending dust and smoke flying from everywhere.

We watched as men jumped out of windows, doors, any

---

[131] This became a topic of discussion among 1/320th veterans of the battle during observance of the 30th Anniversary of the battle. One of our officers produced a photo of our firing position; the M2 Aiming Circle used to "lay" the battery is in plain sight.

[132] My troop from the 1-319th always contended the story of the rounds landing in the sea came from the fact that the 319th, who had stayed after the 320th went home (first in-first out), had the job of getting rid of all the ammunition we had left after the battle. There were literally thousands of rounds. My gun alone had to hand in over 150 rounds of various types. Much of it was unsafe to transport because it had been broken into and rain had soaked the fibers, so the 319th had the pleasure of firing thousands of artillery rounds into the sea off the coast of the island before coming home.

opening they could find to escape the death within. Several of our troops laughed, thinking they were enemy soldiers.

"Gee," Svenson said, "I didn't realize the enemy was this close."

I wondered at that as well. I could see the burned out hulks of two BTR-60s, Soviet Armored personnel carriers sitting at the bend in the road. A little before, I watched some infantrymen shoot them with Light Antitank Weapons, LAWs. Later on, I discovered those vehicles had been knocked out on the first evening. At the time, though, I was under the belief that we had been in danger. Svenson almost called our gun out of the mission to direct fire against them.

I tried to get a better look at the men fleeing the building, "Hey, Chief," I said, "those guys are ours!'

"Oh, man," Svenson said, "I think you're right. Somebody's going to fry! "

It turned out the building was part of the 82nd's 2nd Brigade Headquarters. Two men were killed and fifteen wounded, including a guy from our battalion who was working as part of our Field Artillery Fire Support Team liaison. He lost both his legs in the strafing.

We heard several stories about how it happened. One said a Marine ANGLICO (Air, Naval Gun Liaison Company) team got lost and inadvertently called in fire on the headquarters, thinking it was a Cuban position. Another account says the pilot inexcusably fired on the wrong target, in spite of ANGLICO's frantic efforts to correct him. Another story said that the ANGLICO team called in fire on itself. I found this hard to believe. I had worked with ANGLICO before and found them to be pros. They are among the best of an already fine outfit.

The best explanation at the time seemed to be there was confusion over the differences in maps.

It took me years and the Internet to find – if not satisfactory (I don't think the term can apply here) – at least plausible explanations for the FUBARS that happened that day.[133]

In keeping with my respect for privacy of individuals (for

[133] Again, many thanks to Joe Muccia, who acted as referee as several of the Field Artillerymen involved in this mission – as officers, NCOs and enlisted men – debated and ironed out the most plausible explanation we could find for what happened that day. Joe's interviews with commanders and troops from every involved unit over the years – along with the input of the Field Artillerymen who represented about every level in the chain of command as well as chain of fire control were invaluable in getting to the heart of what happened at Calivigny – AND the 2nd Bde TOC.

the most part) I am going to refrain from naming names. I've been in contact with some of the folks involved, I have been unable to contact others, I believe discretion is in order.

The Field Artillery officer assigned to the Ranger battalion as Fire Support Officer (FSO) tried to co-ordinate the fires between the four batteries. He had worked out zones of fire for each battery with the idea that we would drop rounds in random pattern in our respective areas at the prescribed intervals. So far so good.

Each battery (at least in the 320th – I've been able to confirm that) knew their targets and were aware of the different grid systems being used by the Rangers and the 82nd so there shouldn't have been a problem there. Bravo and Charlie $1/320^{th}$ FA had a fairly easy task as our target zones were almost directly due east from us. So what went wrong?

Again, it is neither my place nor purpose to point fingers here but it appears that someone higher up came along and altered the fire plan. At least that is the best consensus we can come up with.

It is still baffling to me because I am familiar with and have served with or under every officer whose name was involved in the FUBAR and know them *all* to have been superior officers, leaders, and artillerymen. The whole thing still baffles those of us who have rehashed the thing over and over again.

Even that explanation brings up more questions: Why wasn't a correction made when the observers realized the rounds were missing the target? For some reason the Rangers and other infantry elements on the scene say they were unable to contact us and call for corrections. This is another baffling situation as we were all Army units. There was much made about the incompatibility of equipment – particularly commo between services after Vietnam that was revealed at Grenada. But we were units in the same branch. How much trouble could it have been to have switched frequencies or to find the right frequencies? But these things are all above my pay grade. All I can do is wonder and fume. The mission on Calivigny had been the big one, and I know there were many of us who took great pride in that job. We were commended at the time on the great job we had done. To find out later only a few rounds (many accounts say only ONE) hit the target – well, for once words escape me.

I can at least take some satisfaction in the fact the screw-up wasn't at our end of the situation. We did our job on the gunline and even FDC. We appear to have been given bad data.

The artillery can't see its target; it can only shoot from the information given to it by the folks on the front line. Though the gunners sometimes make mistakes, most Field Artillery friendly fire incidents are caused by guys calling rounds on their own position or not being able to read a map. That's why the Army began training guys to do nothing else but work with the infantry and call in fire missions for them. They've always had forward observers. Now, it's arranged that every infantry company has a Fire Support Team (FIST) to be the "eyes of the artillery." That's what ANGLICO does for the Marine Corps. As I said, they're pros. But pros can make mistakes too.

But at least Calivigny doesn't seem to have caused any casualties – on either side. I wish I could say the same for the strafing on the 2nd Bde TOC (HQs).

The best explanation for the tragedy at the 2nd Brigade TOC turned out to be a combination of poor target identification on the part of ANGLICO and the pilot failing to ensure he was hitting the right house. An element of 3rd Brigade, 82nd Abn got hit with sniper fire from a house. The call for fire from the ANGLICO team assigned to the 82nd's 3rd Brigade Headquarters was answered with Navy A-7s. In a classic case of using a sledgehammer to swat a fly the Navy bird answered the call nailing the wrong house. The cost – well, I've already talked about that.

There isn't a day goes by I don't remember seeing that house get hit. I've spoken with others who were there and they tell me the same thing. And then there are the guys who were in the building.

It's rare for me to criticize fighter jocks flying around at speeds in excess of 300mph misidentifying targets. I imagine how difficult it is to properly ID and decide whether or not to engage a target at that speed. I don't know that I could do it. But one has to wonder who called in the A-7s for a sniper in a house? Using the term overkill is putting it nicely.[134] At brigade level command or higher – the level of command according to my understanding of the Rules of Engagement we (the Artillery) were operating under – that would have the authority to authorize the strike – we're not talking about raw untested leaders here; all the higher ranking authorities involved had combat experience in Vietnam. They weren't rookies.

Friendly fire incidents abounded in Vietnam. Friendly fire accounted for most of our casualties in the Persian Gulf. Many could be attributed to untrained observers calling in fire on the wrong

---

[134] In communicating with Joe Muccia who, as previously stated, has interviewed hundreds of veterans and many – if not all – of the major unit commanders involved in the Op I have learned no one could give him a satisfactory answer either.

position in the heat of combat. My first battalion commander in Germany used to like to tell the story of the time he got a call for fire from a guy out in the field, "Bravo-zero-six, this is Lima-niner-one, call for fire. There are Charlies around me, over."

"This is Bravo-zero-six, what is your location? Over,"

"This is Lima-niner-one; I'm up a tree, over."

Again, in indirect fire Field Artillery we can only fire where we're told. We're only as good as our data. For fighter jocks life and death ride a split-second time hack to make a decision.

As they say, "stuff" happens. And there is nowhere where stuff happens like combat. Stuff definitely happened that day in Grenada. Geez, what a clustered SNAFU/FUBAR all rolled into one.

Chapter 21
The Stench of War: Urgent Fury III

Emmy, Emmy, Emmy Lou,
'love my rifle more than you.
You were once my Cajun queen,
Now I love my M-16.
(Marching Cadence)

The day after Calivigny Barracks (D+3 October 28) I had my first close encounter with a Grenadian civilian. Behind our position was a barracks area. I believe it was close to the old True Blue Campus where our Rangers had rescued the first American medical students. Evidently, prior to the invasion, it had been used as a military school. Some of the men from the battery found papers and notes taken by the military students in some of the rooms. We found materials on spreading the Communist revolution to other countries. Some of the notes detailed how to defend against an American invasion.

It was a freaky thing reading the notes (they were in English, which is the official language of Grenada, though they speak the Caribbean dialect). The Cubans had fairly well outlined the invasion plan we used. Of course, certain details were omitted, but one notebook detailed the probable American attack as being spearheaded by airborne forces and followed up by amphibious landings. This, of course, didn't take a genius to figure out. After all, there are only so many ways you can attack an island. They knew where we would probably land, and what our primary objectives would be once we were on the island.

After finding all the deadly goodies they had stored on that island; thousands of assault rifles, many mortars, anti-aircraft guns, and other toys of modern warfare, much of it still in the crates, I heaved a sigh of relief that if we were going to attack them we had attacked when we did. From our position to the north of the airport we could see where engineers had been digging emplacements for mortars and antiaircraft guns. If we had attacked a couple of weeks, or even days, later those emplacements would have been armed and would have completely covered the drop zones. Our Rangers would have probably suffered heavy casualties, if not annihilated. Forrest's alleged axiom for winning at the game of warfare, "gittin' there firstest with the mostest," had certainly held true.

I shudder to think of it now when I see the rigmarole and hoops current Presidents go through to get permission to use military force. Sure, let's go to the U.N. and give our enemies plenty of warning we're coming.

We also found pictures in one room, which showed a black man, obviously a Grenadian soldier, in a fur coat and fur hat standing in front of a building. There was at least a foot of snow on the ground around him. I figured the pictures were taken at a school of which I knew outside Moscow that was run by the KGB. My suspicions were at least partially confirmed by another picture with the same man, the same coat and hat, standing in front of a wall. There was a poster on the wall lettered in Cyrillic (Russian) alphabet. Four letters stood out from the rest, CCCP, the Russian abbreviation for the Union of Soviet Socialist Republics. I sometimes wonder if the guy survived the invasion.

After the area had been secured the barracks was converted to a refugee holding area. A prisoner holding area was also back there. In order for the POWs[135] and refugees to get to the area they had to pass through the battery position. Even though they were escorted by MPs, we had to provide an armed guard to get them through our position without a mishap. I can still see the haunted look in many of the prisoners' eyes as they were marched through our area, particularly the ones captured after we had bombarded them, such as the guys they brought in after we hit Calivigny barracks. I couldn't help but pity them.

The civilians were even more pathetic, they would stagger wearily through our position carrying everything they could bundle up in bags or rolled up in blankets. I was in charge of seeing one bunch through our perimeter and back to the holding area. One poor woman was trying to carry two large suitcases and a little boy who looked to be about two or three. I gave her a hand with one of the bags while keeping my M-16A1 at the ready. We hadn't really been briefed on what kind of attitude to expect from the local populace. I expected them to be hostile. I wouldn't have blamed them. If I was living peacefully on a little island in the Caribbean and suddenly from out of nowhere a bunch of soldiers dropped in and began blowing my home to pieces, I believe I might have harbored at least a little resentment.

As we walked, I found the silence embarrassing. I suppose I

---

[135] POW- in this case, Prisoner of War.

was just a little bit more than curious to see how the people felt about us. I tried to make some conversation.

"It's a nice island you have here." This was true. In spite of all the wreckage we had caused over the last few days, the natural beauty of the island stood out.

"Denk you," she said in a thick, melodious accent. "We lak it ver' mooch. "

"'Sorry we have to blow it up on you."

"Dat's all rat, you do what you haf to do, dan mabbee you gif it back to us an' ever't'ing be lak it was."

I was surprised there was no malice in her tone. She actually sounded glad we were there. A couple of years later I told this story to a group of college students. They were amazed I could fight in a conflict that I knew so little about. I was asked how I could go and kill people when I didn't know why I was fighting or, for that matter, really even whom. My reply was simple. In the United States the military does not decide who to fight, sometimes we have no say in how to fight, as in Vietnam. We just go where our civilian leaders send us. The U.S. military does not make policy; it enforces it. I told that group of college students they had better be thankful our system was that way.

When we got to the compound the mother gratefully dropped her bundle and set her little boy down. He looked up at me with big brown eyes. Somehow, he reminded me of the little four year-old I had waiting for me at home. I remember feeling so sorry for the poor baby, so little to be going through so much.

"Do you want some candy, Babe?" I asked him.

He nodded, as if he was almost afraid to speak.

"Well let me see..." I dug around in all my pockets; surely I had a C-ration candy bar somewhere in all these pockets. But all I could find was some gum. I had left everything else in my field pack. I was disappointed, but offered him the gum nonetheless, "Here you go, Sugar.'Sorry, but it's all I can find."

"What 'you say?" his mother asked.

"Danks."

"You're welcome." I picked him up and hugged him, missing my own little boy at home.

A guy came up to me who'd been in the crowd. There was something about him I didn't like from the start; I don't know what it was exactly. For one thing, he didn't fit in. He wasn't Grenadian. Grenadians are of African descent. This guy appeared to be more Indian or middle eastern. I wondered if he could be Cuban.

"Sergeant," he started, in excellent English. The guy definitely didn't have a Grenadian accent. I was reminded of guys in the city offering to sell you hot watches. "Could you see about getting these people some food? Some of them have been without food for over a week."

I eyed him up and down for a moment, looked at the pathetic folks standing around, "I'll see what I can do." I don't know, maybe the guy was just nervous about approaching a soldier; after all, not every army is as friendly as ours.

On the way out, I spoke with an MP and asked about getting some food for the people. The MP assured me they were going to be well taken care of. The Army was bringing fresh meat and produce in from the States for refugees. They'd be eating better than we were! That seemed fair to me, after all, they hadn't asked for this.

They brought some more students in. This time they escorted them through our position. There were a couple of hundred of them. As they walked through our area, the male students shook our hands and hugged our necks. One guy threw a football to one of our troopers, the younger guys made use of that later, when things settled down. The females hugged our necks and kissed us on the cheeks. We really hated that.

One of the things that did irritate us was the students kept asking us if we were Marines. Each time, we responded to their questions with an emphatic "No! We're U.S. paratroopers!"

We were beginning to get a few newspapers in from the States. There were pictures on the front pages of anti-war protesters already screaming bloody murder about "No More Vietnams!" This bugged some of us. There was also talk of Congress invoking the War Powers Act. This would have forced President Reagan to ask Congress for a formal declaration of war or pull our troops out. It could have given the enemy a great boost in morale and incentive to fight.

Another thing that burned us was seeing pictures of 82nd troopers in action, you could tell by the patches and the Kevlar helmets, being identified as Marines. The Marines did a great job up north, don't get me wrong, but according to the pictures and articles, they practically did the job single-handed.

I figured the press' mistakes were caused by the fact the Marines who landed on Grenada had reporters with them, while we didn't. After all, their first destination had been Beirut, not Grenada. Maybe some of the pictures coming back were from reporters with them. The editors in the States, not knowing any better, figured the reporters were with the Marines and mislabeled the pictures. Since reconnecting with Marines who were there I've learned this wasn't true.

I remember watching Clint Eastwood in *Heartbreak Ridge*. I've always been a Clint Eastwood fan. I was enjoying the movie, until the Grenada sequence. When the movie depicted Marines, wearing Kevlars, rescuing the students at the medical college I became upset – as did the troopers in the theater with me. There were numerous hoots and catcalls throughout the Grenada sequence. For me it was more personal. After all, I had participated in some small way in that rescue. It's bad enough when you read books about the battle and they forget to mention the artillery bombardment which took place prior to the rescue that made it possible. I've yet to read a book or article about the battle which got the order of battle right as far as the artillery was concerned. They always had us as "B" Battery, 2-325th Infantry.[136] But now, Hollywood had even given the credit to another branch of service! Sadly, for many people, that movie will be their understanding of the Battle of Grenada as it will probably be the only movie ever made about it.

I talked to a Ranger who made the jump into Grenada. He told me that originally the producers of the movie had wanted to make a movie about the Rangers but some of the brass were offended by the language and refused to cooperate so the swapped services instead. Unfortunately for history, they didn't do much to change the action sequences and had Marine recon doing what the Rangers did (with our help – I have to put that in there, with all due respect to the Rangers).

As far as the mislabeled photos I've been assured by my Marine brother vets they had no assigned photographers with them and were prohibited taking cameras. So we chalk it up to media ignorance of the military. For me there is no excuse, after all, how long would a sportscaster keep his/her job if every time a football team scored he/she screamed, "HOME RUN!"?

On about Day Three or Four (I'm thinking it was the evening of the 28th) our platoon (guns four through six) was given marching orders. Our battery was being split, with half staying at the airstrip with the rest of the artillery; the other half being sent farther into the island to support the movement of our infantry north, into the hinterland of Grenada. We were now in a "mopping up phase,"

---

[136] They put us in with the infantry battalion we supported, the 2nd Bn (Abn) 325th Infantry.

routing out pockets of resistance and making sure there weren't any large forces hiding in the jungle out there waiting to surprise us.

We waited till just about dark so our movements would be concealed. We weren't too far down the road when we passed the two BTR-60 Soviet-made armored cars the Rangers and SPECTRE had taken out on D-Day. A couple of our officers took pix of them; later our FDO had copies of the pix he took made for those of us who didn't have cameras – which we weren't really supposed to have in the first place. Those are the only pictures I have of Grenada.

Next we passed a foxhole with a dead Grenadian or Cuban soldier lying inside. He had been there for days in the heat and was quite ripe by this time. I was told later he had blown up a jeep with four Rangers with a Soviet made RPG-7 (Rocket Propelled Grenade Launcher) on the first night, killing two and injuring another. The fourth Ranger, unhurt, got revenge. We were warned there was a fear that bodies might be booby-trapped so they were left in place for EOD (Emergency Ordinance Disposal) to clear before graves registration would touch them. We smelled this one before we saw him. That smell would become familiar to us before we left the island. It is my strongest memory from the battle.

You know, no matter how realistic Hollywood or anyone else can do to try and make a realistic war movie they all fail in one important aspect. They can't capture the smell. War stinks – the stench of rotting corpses, human and animal; the smell of gunpowder; of uncontrolled body functions by both the dead and the terrified; even the acrid tinge to your own sweat that comes from the adrenalin release. War stinks. I've never seen a movie capture that. If they did, who would go to see it?

Not too much farther down the road our convoy came to a sharp curve. I think it was right before we turned on to the road where the Drive-in was. There was a cinder block house on the inside of the curve. As the BC's jeep rounded the curve, an enemy soldier popped out of a window with a rifle and began shooting at us. The BC sped the jeep up and signaled for us to follow in accordance with the SOP.[137]

I had seen the guy appear in the window. When he fired, I raised my M-16A1 to deal with him. I had him in my sights and was about to squeeze when an infantryman came out of nowhere. He was in between the enemy and me, in my line of fire. He flashed us an

---

[137] Standard Operating Procedure for a convoy when it is ambushed is not to stop and fight it out, as tempting as it may seem, but to speed up and try to plow through it, rather than get trapped and suffer more casualties.

"OK" and tossed a grenade in the window. I watched as the Cuban was blown to pieces.

It happened so fast I wonder if any of the other men on the truck even realized what happened. No one spoke of the incident later; we were too busy with other things as we pulled into our new position.[138]

We later learned the rest of our battery left in the position north of the airfield had been subjected to sniper fire while we were being shot at on the road. I couldn't say whether the attacks were coordinated or not. The rounds came quite close to our battery position back near the airfield. One poor fellow lost control of his bodily functions during the attack when the rounds came too close. Some laughed at him. They shouldn't have, he wasn't the first man to have reacted like that in combat.

Our destination was a cow pasture located across from a brewery. We would spend the next few days there. It was a full time job keeping our troops from the brewery and the grateful watchmen who were only too willing to give free beer to their liberators. Booze and combat do not mix. What made it tougher for the troopers to resist was the fact the beer was ice cold. After several days in the tropic environment, a cold drink was a terrible temptation. We did take advantage of the soft drinks the guard offered us.

Because it was dark when we pulled in to the position and set up, we couldn't really get a good look at the lay of the land. Top and the BC were with us, the XO and Chief of Firing Battery had been left behind to supervise the other three guns. As we were in a relatively unsecured area and were subject to a fire mission at any time, we kept a fifty percent watch. This meant half of the battery personnel are up on watch at all times. In my section, the chief and I agreed to pull two-hour shifts.

I spent a fairly restless night in the hooch I'd set up beside the gamma goat with my shelter half. I'd just get to sleep good after pulling my shift and it would be time to get up again. Sporadic gunfire kept waking me up. Just a shot or two, or a noise that sounded like a shot and I'd grab my weapon. I'd hold it at ready for a few minutes till I decided it was safe, then I'd roll over and doze till the next time, or it was time to pull my shift.

There was a terrible odor in the area. A couple of us made mention that we needed a bath real bad. You know you're beginning to stink when you can't stand your own smell. I'd been on the island

---

[138]I've since talked with one of the troops in the goat with me and he remembered it happening, too – I guess there was too much going on to dwell on it at the time.

five days at that time, I believe, without a bath. I had been able to change underwear but was wearing the same uniform I had worn on the night of the callout. My rucksack had fallen off the truck when I first arrived on the island. When I found it, someone had taken my extra uniform out of it. Our duffle bags, or "A bags" with changes of uniform and extra gear not practical to carry had been unloaded from the trucks at Green Ramp for weight purposes; they didn't catch up with us until December. By that time we were back at Bragg.

Top had made arrangements for the men in the battery to take a trip to the beach for a bath. A bath in salt water might have been worse than staying dirty. Some of the guys got to go. We got orders to move to the cow pasture before I got my chance. All through the night we suffered through the smell.

By the next morning the stench in the air had gotten worse.

We discovered the cause when our driver, PFC Herrera went to the front of the goat to pull his daily maintenance checks, "Sergeant Wood, look! We don't have to worry about taking a bath, it's not us stinking."

We all came around to see what Herrera had found. It turned out there was a dead cow lying in a ditch, not a foot from our right front tire. Maybe it had gotten caught in crossfire when the infantry pulled through there. Maybe an infantryman killed it so he could say he had fired his rifle in combat. Who knows? It had been there a few days and was quite ripe. This wasn't going to do, there was no telling how long we'd be here and the thing wasn't going to smell any better. I ambled up the slope to where our FDC and the BC's jeep were located. I asked Top if we could get his driver to haul the thing out of the area.

"Don't worry about it, Sergeant Wood, we're not going to be here that long." was his answer.

As the day wore on the smell got worse. Attempts to bury the poor thing were unsuccessful. The soil there was thick and claylike, it fell in clumps on the corpse. The only solution was to haul it out of the area. DePaul and I went into the village surrounding us and found a rope. We finally got it hauled away from the guns and our position by tying the rope around the cow's legs and dragging it off by hand. The thing burst open after a few feet, its entrails spilling on the ground and making the stench even more unbearable; but through perseverance we finally got the thing far enough away from us we couldn't smell it. It was a good thing, too, we stayed in the position another two days or so.

That was when the boredom set in. Prior to this, there had

always been plenty to keep us busy while we were on the island. Now, with the organized resistance broken and the infantry fanning out across the island in mopping up operations, there was little for those of us in the artillery to do but sit around and wait for calls for fire.

FDC would call a fire mission and give us data with orders not to load until told. We lay the guns on the data, with the round ready. Then we'd wait for the command to fire, which never came. After awhile, FDC would call back over the phone, "End of mission."

We'd stand down and wait for the next mission. It was a letdown after the excitement of first few days of the operation.

There were warehouses next to the pasture we were in. Some of the guys visited them and got some recreational items such as baseballs, bats, and gloves made in Cuba from the troops – if any - guarding the warehouses. There was tons of the stuff stashed away in the warehouses and it was there that I got a squint at some of the weapons caches.

Some of the guys were following the new guidance down from higher headquarters to get to know the Grenadian people and win their friendship; particularly with the female population. From morning till dusk young girls from the surrounding town would come to the fence surrounding our position. They would talk to our young soldiers who were only too happy to improve our international relations. Young kids would lead us to where Cubans and Grenadians had stashed weapons, uniforms, and even tell us where the enemy soldiers were hiding.

We found one uniform and weapon beneath a Grenadian lady's clothesline. She was standing there cussing up a storm because, "That dorty Cooban stole my hoosban' clot's!" The guy had done a quick change when he found out the American soldiers were on his trail.

It was about this time Top told some of us about a weird thing that happened to him on a ration run. He was returning from the supply point at Point Salines Airstrip with our daily supply of C-rations and the new MREs[139] when he passed a vacant lot. In the

---

[139] It was in Grenada we had our first taste of the Army's new combat rations, Meals, Ready to Eat (MRE) which would replace the old Class C Rations (C-Rations or C-Rats). MREs came in plastic pouches which made them more light weight for the trooper to carry as opposed to the old C-rats which came in cans. There were uses for the cans and they would be missed. We were issued one MRE and two C-rats per man per day. The guys would fight for any spare MREs. Six months after Grenada, after all the old C-rats had been eaten, the guys were moaning about how they missed the old C-rats. You can't please a soldier.

middle of the lot was a package, wrapped in brown paper like it was ready to mail. He told his driver to stop the jeep and got out to take a look.

"I came up on the thing careful, you know? No telling who'd put it there or why. Who knows, they might still be there, you know? So I get up on it and it's addressed to some guy in New York City. Weird.

"Well, I decide to take a closer look. I got my Ka-Bar[140] out and felt around careful under the package looking for a trip wire. Well, I figured it wasn't rigged from the outside, so I poked a bit at the package. Then, I accidentally stuck the tip of my knife in the package and - Whew! - the awfulest stink came out of that thing!"

"So what'd you do?"

"Well, I cut the string tying it together (holding my breath, don't you know) and carefully undid the paper, pulled it back with my knife, I cut open the box. Inside there was a human head, wrapped in a plastic bag."

"Was it American?" one of the guys asked.

"I don't know, it was hard to tell, it had been dead some time."

"So what did you do, Top?"

"Well, I reported it to G-2."

We never did find out what happened to that head or to whom it belonged.

After the curfew was lifted and the Grenadians were able to come out at night we could hear them singing songs praising the Americans and thanking God for sending us. I remember sitting up against the gun hearing the folks laughing and singing one night.

"That sounds familiar," one of the guys remarked.

We listened carefully, trying to make out the tune beneath the Caribbean beat or at least understand the words, which was difficult between the accent and the distance. I think it hit us all at the same time.

"They're singing 'God Bless America!'" Talk about making a guy want to choke up.

Our Battalion Commander came down to visit us on our second day in the cow pasture. The Command Sergeant Major was with him. The new CSM stood at least six foot six, but looked like he weighed less than ninety pounds. He had scared the devil out of a

---

[140] **Ka-Bar-** A survival knife issued by the Marines but popular with all branches of service.

section in the field one night with his appearance and deep voice. He had been "nosing around" the firing battery area. He came under a gun section's net, surprising and about scaring the daylights out of the crew when he spoke with his deep voice. It was raining that night and he was wearing his poncho. With the poncho and his Kevlar helmet he was quite a sight.

"He looked like Darth Vader!" one of the troops said. The name stuck.

So, the Battalion Commander and Darth Vader paid us a visit. We were the forward most element of his command at that time. We were still hearing occasional sniper fire, particularly at night; some of it was real close. We were running low on water; we hadn't been resupplied since our move forward. We needed to conserve every bit of water we had for drinking. We were, therefore, a grungy looking lot.

I pardoned myself for not saluting as the colonel approached. I'd had a lieutenant say something to me about it a few days before back at Point Salines Airport.

"Well, gee, sir," I had told him, "I didn't think you wanted to find out if there were any snipers nearby. But, I can always salute you if you want me to."

The lieutenant thought a moment, "No, Sergeant Wood, I see your point."

"Airborne, sir."

"Thank you, Sergeant Wood."

"No problem, sir." He us a good kid, it was just this crazy peacetime Army where they had you saluting in the field, and running dog and pony shows when you should have been playing tactical. It was like the brass was always saying, "You fight like you train."

We had brought a whole generation of soldiers up to salute officers and report formally in the field. In the Army I was brought up in, where most of the NCOs and officers were Vietnam veterans, we learned quickly not to salute in the field unless you didn't like the guy. Charlie's snipers had been quick to pick off officers.

So, I excused myself to the Colonel, "Pardon me for not saluting sir, but I don't think you want to find out whether there are any snipers watching, do you?"

He grinned at that. Lieutenant Colonel Weller was a nice guy, actually. He just didn't seem too popular with the troops in my battery (couldn't speak for the battalion). This wasn't entirely his fault. It was the fact that his previous assignment had been at the

Pentagon, where he had spent five years in various duties. The word I'd heard from battalion HQ, where I still had some buddies, that when he came up for a command he had been given his choice of five battalions that were due a change of command. He had picked ours because it was in the 82d, which to career minded officers is an A-number-one hole to punch in one's ticket. The troopers didn't consider him one of us, as our previous commander had been. He was considered a political officer, a "perfumed prince." This was in spite of the fact he had served in several airborne assignments through his career, and even commanded a firing battery in the 101st in Vietnam. The Division troopers can be unforgiving of those who don't fit in or live up to their demanding standards.

That day, he and the CSM showed up at our position in starched camouflaged-fatigues, clean-shaven and smelling of aftershave lotion.[141] Big Sven sat in the background and let me do most of the talking. This told me he didn't like the Commander.

I have to admit, I could sympathize with the colonel. There were those in the battery who still felt the same about me because I had come to Bravo from S-3. Oh well.

The CSM asked me why I hadn't shaved that morning. I showed him a five-gallon water can, which was only half full.

'This and the water in our canteens is all the water we have, Sergeant Major." I said, "We haven't been resupplied with water in two days. We didn't think it wise to waste water shaving under the circumstances."

LTC Weller took note of the water cans.

"I see what you mean, Sergeant Wood," he said. "We're all getting kind of grimy; I'm down to my last clean set of BDUs myself."

Remember, I was still wearing the same uniform I'd deployed in. Several of us were.

He spent a few more minutes at our position showing us the strange properties of the grasses on the island. They had one type of grass, which was carnivorous, eating small flies and bugs. When you touched the blades they closed up trying to trap whatever it was which had set it off. So we had a new pastime between laying for fire missions - messing with the grass,

A couple of the troops complained of the boredom. The Colonel commiserated with them, "Yeah, that's the one drawbacks of combat that you never see in the movies- the boredom and the

---

[141] I have since looked at a picture of him taken at our position that day and he doesn't look so clean now – maybe he just seemed clean compared to our grungy behinds that day?

tension of waiting for something to happen. Even in Nam there were long periods between the actual fighting. It drives you crazy waiting for something to happen, then, just when you let your guard down, all hell breaks loose.

"There's nothing to do about it. What we're doing right now is covering the infantry's advance. You're laying on targets which are potentially dangerous until the infantry can clear them. And according to the rules of engagement as they stand right now, an artillery mission has got to be cleared all the way up to Division level before it can be shot. The orders now are for us to avoid damaging civilian property as much as possible so as to curry the friendship of the Grenadian people."

Well, at least we had a reason for our boredom. Our battalion commander left our position. We received fresh water later on that afternoon. It was the last visit he paid to our gun line.

After a couple of days at the cow pasture we got word we were moving out that evening (about October 30?). I was working with SSG Johns again; his regular gunner had gone back the day before with a bird taking non-essential personnel and guys who needed to be back to the States. His wife was pregnant, due any day, he and Jimmy Jaeger, who'd been in school when the callout came, were allowed to go home. My section was told to send someone over.

There were two qualified gunners in the section, Guerrera, a SP4 we were trying to get boarded for sergeant, and myself. I didn't like leaving my section, but Guerrera didn't want to go. I volunteered. I worked well with J. Besides, my section would be better off, as Guerrera was actually a better gunner than I. It was a good decision for me as J taught me a great deal about gunnery in the short time I was with him.

That we were beginning to send folks home was a sign the thing was winding down. Word was that the first people in would be the first people out. The Rangers had already gone home a few days before.

We were ordered to prepare to move again. We took our trucks to pick up ammo and equipment left back at the airport. We would return to the cow pasture, march order the guns, and link up with the rest of the battery as they passed us on the way to the new position. We were told to be on our guard, as there had been enemy activity in the area we were to pass through. Snipers.

Chapter 22
Golflands: Urgent Fury IV

Running through the jungle with my rifle in my hand
I'm a mean motor scooter I'm a fighting man!
(Anonymous Running Cadence)

It was much later that evening and those of us dispatched back to the old position were now waiting in the cow pasture with our guns hitched to our goats. We were waiting.

Then we saw the rest of the battery move down the road toward us. Actually we heard their struggling engines and then saw the pin point glow of their "blackout drive" headlamps.

In gunline order we exited the cow pasture and joined the convoy. The axles on our goats creaked under the weight. We were overloaded with equipment and ammo. It was only under the urging of a couple of us NCOs that we weren't loaded any more. When I first returned to Salines the order had been to load all the ammo and any section equipment left behind when we moved to the pasture. It didn't take too long to realize if we did the vehicles couldn't take the stress – especially with what we had facing us. Big J had put me in charge of loading 6th Section's Goat with a couple of guys, I went to talk to Top and saw a couple other sergeants already with him. Top heard us out, nodded, and said, "I'll go talk to the BC."

Word came back we would send a truck back in the morning to pick up the rest of the ammo. I know I heaved a sigh of relief, but my section's goat was still overflowing with about one hundred rounds of 105mm, section and personnel equipment. Where were my troops going to fit? I could see them hanging on for dear life on top of the load – particularly if we were hit.

Now we were passing through a built-up area. It looked as if we were going into St. Georges. Finally, we stopped at the foot of a steep hill. It looked to be about a forty-five degree angle. We were told to get off the vehicles. The hill was too steep for the goats, burdened with all the equipment and ammunition, to pull the howitzers with us on them. We were going to have to walk the rest of the way. I wondered how the powers-that-be had expected our trucks to make it to the top overloaded with the ammo we'd left at the airstrip.

It was quite a walk, the street was narrow and dark, and the beams of the moon didn't seem to penetrate where we were. Every so often the hairs on the back of my neck would stand on end as someone in the houses lining the street would open up a door or window shutter to check out what all the noise was about. Under the new rules of engagement we had to be certain a target was an enemy before we fired. Under the circumstances, the only way we could be sure of that was to let ourselves be fired upon.

So, I'd hear a door or window creak open and freeze, and wait for any tell-tale sound which might indicate the individual was going to shoot. I don't know if the other guys thought about this or not. I can only speak for myself as we were spread out tactically. Occasionally, we would smell a dead body as we walked up the hill (we had gotten well acquainted to the odor by then). Sometimes we would see its vague, still outline in the road; often we couldn't. One of our young troopers stumbled over one of the bodies in the road and fell, putting his hand in the corpse's face. He almost freaked when the thing fell apart under his hand. A couple of us sergeants rushed over to him and got him calmed.

Occasionally, one of our trucks would wheeze past as on its way up the hill. The weight of its load taxed its powerful engine to the maximum. We were sending the guns up one at a time in case one of them didn't make it to the top. Once at the top, personnel waiting there would radio personnel at the bottom to send the next truck up.

I, for one was glad we had left some of the ammo back at the airstrip. I don't believe our trucks would have made the climb otherwise.

Finally, I reached the top of the hill; it was as if someone had turned the lights on. I looked up at the sky and saw a full moon and a beautiful star filled sky. We were on a golf course. After the dark road I had just trudged up, it seemed like paradise.

There was no rest yet, though. We still had to set up our guns. Now we were told we had to put up our camouflage nets, which we had heretofore left stowed in our trucks. We had quite a time putting ours up – I should say *trying* to put ours up, it was twisted and tangled from being stowed, buried under a ton of equipment and ammo. It was hopeless in the dark. Finally, we just gave up. Big J said we'd mess with it when it got light. I didn't argue. I didn't see much point in messing with the thing now, after most of the fighting was over anyway.

We tried to rest as well as we could. We were told there would be an airmobile from this golf course the first thing in the morning. Three of our guns would lift off in support of the 2/505 Infantry, which was going to check out a small island just off the coast of Grenada. Word had it there were up to one hundred PRA and Cubans holed up there. We would land our guns on the island and set them up in direct fire mode and demand their surrender. It sounded like a tactical masterpiece in the tradition of the Little Bighorn to me. But, ours was not to reason why...

I was too tired to think much about it anyway. I felt as if all the air had been let out of me. I sat next to the gun in a semi-conscious state. We only had two or three hours before they'd be waking us so I didn't see the sense in setting up a guard roster. I let the troops sleep and held the field phone in my hand where I could hear if anything came over the line. I lay against the trail of the gun facing out so I could scan the hedge that lined our perimeter.

"Guns," came the voice over the field phone a few minutes later. It was FDC.

There was no answer, either everyone was asleep or they were ignoring the call, as I was trying to do.

"Guns."

Still no answer.

"Attention on the gun line."

"Gun six." I finally answered. He wasn't going to shut up until someone answered him anyway.

"We need someone to come check out our rear area. We've heard noises back there."

"Don't you have anyone to check it out?'

"We're busy right now preparing for the mission."

"Roger..." I made a face. I'll be down in a minute." I handed the phone to Rolands, the A/G, "If you hear shooting or anything, come running, okay?"

"Sure, Sergeant Wood, do you want me to come along?"

"Naw, it's probably the Oh-five[142] moving in."

I stumbled down to where the FDC vehicle should have been. I saw the entire section in the back of the truck.

"What's the problem?"

"We've been hearing noises back there," one of the men said.

---

[142] I was referring to the 2nd Bn (Abn) 505th Infantry; I've since discovered the guys were from B Co. 2/505th Infantry, which was filling in for C Co. 2/325th Infantry. C Co. had been left behind because it was a new experimental company trained under the Army's Cohesion Operational Readiness and Training (COHORT) Program, where all its troopers had gone through training together and were serving together. It was hoped such a program would instill cohesivemness in the unit and make it more effective in combat.. C Company had lately arrived at Bragg and had not had time to be properly evaluated under the ARTEP system and therefore wasn't considered combat-ready. They stayed home.

"It's probably the Oh-five."

"It needs to be checked out."

"I reckon so. If I'm not back in a few minutes or you hear shooting, get someone from the guns to come running." I grinned.

I left them in the truck and went to where they said they'd heard the noises. It could be the Oh-five. Then again, it might not. I couldn't see why they couldn't have checked it out themselves. Then I realized I was just ambling down the fairway, out in the open. I was a good target in the light of the full moon. I moved quickly to the shadows of a hedgerow, thanking the Lord I had come to my senses before someone named Miguel picked me off from the shadows.

The section of the golf course I was at was bordered by a high row of hedges. Over the top of the hedges, on the other side, I could see some rich looking houses.

I followed the hedge line cautiously till I came to a break in the row. It was an entrance to the golf course from the wealthy houses on the other side of the hedge.

I heard some movement and someone talking in low voices come from the other side. They were speaking too quietly for me to make out what they were saying so I couldn't tell which language they were using.

I crouched down by the corner of the hedge, in the shadows and waited. I had made sure I was still locked and loaded when I left FDC. Now I slipped my M-16A1 from "safe" to full "automatic." I know the prescribed setting is "semi-automatic," but I didn't know how many men were on the other side of the bush or how they would come through the entrance. I figured I'd spray the area; I might not have time for a second shot if I had the weapon on semi. Sometimes you just need "Rock-n-roll."[143]

The men on the other side of the hedge got quiet. I could sense they somehow knew I was there. I tried to figure out how, as I had been very quiet – or thought I'd been. I guess I hadn't been quiet enough. I began kicking myself. I should have brought someone with me. I had violated the primary rule of combat- always have a buddy to cover you. There was no time for that now, however. I hunched down and prayed the guys on the other side were friendly.

Suddenly, the men on the other side broke through the entrance. I was just about to cut loose when something stopped me. Maybe it was the outline of the troopers in the moonlight, perhaps it was instinct, maybe it was the fact I knew the 2/505 was in the area

---

[143] "Rock-n-roll"- is the GI nickname for full automatic fire.

that caused me to hesitate, who knows? Anyway, it turned out to be a good thing. The two soldiers standing before me were infantrymen from the 2/505th. We froze there a few seconds facing each other, then broke out laughing.

"Man, I thought you were -" we all said simultaneously.

"I almost tossed a grenade over here-" one of the infantrymen said.

"Well, I'm glad I didn't spray the hedge..." was my retort.

We identified our units and ourselves and promised to put the word out there were friendlies on the other side of hedges. It had been a close call.

I went back to the FDC truck and told them it was safe.

The next morning they cancelled our part of the airmobile operation. We watched as the Infantry, "our" battalion, 2/325 (with B 2/505 Infantry, I suppose) took off in Blackhawks. For all I knew they were taking off for Caracao without us.

I heard the infantry landed and discovered the island was deserted – at least no bad guys. It is only recently that I discovered the Marines had been sent to Caracao after leaving Grenada and rounded up the PRA there. They then went on their way to the hell that was Beirut. Again, the fog of war is really thick the lower you are. In either event, the artillery was stood down again.

We spent the next few days doing basically the same thing we had done at the cow pasture, getting ready for fire missions and then standing down. We had been issued Rocket Assisted Projectiles (RAP Rounds) which greatly increased the range of our guns so that we could hit any target on the island.

Both B and C Batteries were set up next to one another with our battalion headquarters comfortably ensconced in a country club that overlooked the golf course. It became known as The Palace.

We were told we could rotate our troops up to the Palace to make use of the locker rooms' showers. I figured I'd finally get to clean up. When the first batch of troops came back and reported they hadn't seen a shower, but had only been allowed to use some washbasins, I spat on that idea and decided to improvise.

I took a metal fuse box, filled it with water and used it to scrub myself and wash my uniform. The good thing about the camouflage nets other than the shade they provided is that they did afford us some degree of privacy from the prying eyes of the local population. I would wrap my poncho liner around my waist while waiting for my clothes to dry in the sun. It didn't take too long, never more than twenty minutes. In the meantime I made quite a sight in my poncho liner, flak vest, and helmet, as I went about my business under the net.

We made a point to keep our helmets and flak vests on. My first sergeant, when I first got to Germany, had once told me he had spent three tours in Nam and never had a man killed. He attributed this to the fact he had always made his troopers keep their vests and helmets on, no matter how hot it was. They could strip their shirts off, but had to keep their armor. It had saved many lives.

When we first hit the island we'd had problems with the troopers taking off their helmets and wearing boonie hats and the like. They were trying to be Rambos. And face it – coming from the late fall climate of North Carolina – it was hot down there. That had stopped when they brought us a Kevlar helmet with a Soviet AK bullet hole in it. The guy wearing it had been knocked flat, but had gotten up unscathed, except for a sore neck and powerful headache. After that, we became believers in the Kevlar. The guys needed no more prodding to keep their pots on.

As I said before, the local population had been really pathetic when we first arrived on the island. Many of the kids we spoke to told us horror stories of the atrocities committed by the PRA and the Cubans. They also told us of being locked in their houses, afraid to go out to even get food lest they be executed for violating the curfew imposed by the Coard government.[144] Many of them were hungry. In the tradition of every American soldier since we began venturing across the oceans to fight our wars, we gave the kids whatever food we had.

By the time we got up to the golf course the kids in the area had it down to an art. You'd see them roaming through the battery area from net to net with large sacks like trick-or-treaters.   One kid in particular stands out in the crowd in my memory. He came under our net like he owned the place.

"Gimme sum't'ing." he said, holding his bag open, revealing a load of booty that would have put Captain Kidd to shame.

"You mean, 'trick or treat." I said, as I tossed some MRE cheese spread into his bag. It had dawned on me earlier it was Halloween.

"Huh?"

[144]Deputy Prime Minister of Grenada Bernard Coard. It was his ouster of Prime Minister Maurice Bishop on October 13, 1983 and his subsequent "reign of terror" which destabilized the political situation in Grenada and caused enough concern for Grenada's neighbors to ask the U.S. to step in.

"Never mind, kid." I said. I thought of my own two kids who would be going out trick or treating that night. I always got a big kick out of going out with them.

The kids had a racket going. Mom was getting food at the distribution center while Junior was panhandling MREs and C-rations from the GIs. They were eating better than we were. By this time the rear echelon jerks had arrived and were earning their pay making the fighters' lives miserable. We had to account for every meal issued. Any food we gave the kids came out of our mouths. We didn't mind it so much when we thought the kids were hungry, but now we felt as if we were being played for suckers.

The bureaucratic nonsense increased. The XO began coming around the sections and inspecting our position areas to ensure they were laid out according to the DivArty SOP. He wanted me to put my M16A1 on the weapons rack each section was supposed to have set up, a camouflage net pole pounded into the ground with a spreader. The weapons were to hang from the arms of the spreader by their shoulder straps. It looked good at Bragg, but it went against everything I'd been taught as a young soldier about combat. And the nightmare of that ARTEP in Germany stayed with me throughout my career. I respectfully declined. Even though we hadn't drawn fire in a day or so, the island still hadn't been declared safe. My weapon was going to be no farther than an arm's length away from me. My troopers were ordered to sleep with theirs, as did I. J nodded agreement when I said it.

FDC was asking for ammo counts every hour or so. I couldn't figure it out. Even though we were laying for missions off and on, we weren't shooting anything so the ammo count remained the same. But someone somewhere couldn't get the numbers to add up so we'd have to go through the same drill over and over again. We had about one hundred and fifty rounds of different types of 105mm howitzer ammunition on our gun alone. Most of the fibers had gotten wet laying out in the open at Point Salines and were unreadable, so every time FDC came down the line asking for an ammo count we'd have to tear open the fibers and inspect each round to ensure type, weight, and lot number. This put the already deteriorating fibers in even worse condition. After the third time going through this and coming out with the same count I told my troopers not to worry about it and gave the same report.

In the meantime, DePaul and another trooper had a minor adventure with some East German citizens who invited them over to their house for a drink and a shower. Of course, DePaul didn't know at the time the couple were East German. He discovered that after he got back all nice and clean and was immediately called to report up to Division G-2 with his buddy.

When he got back he told the story. It turned out they were agents from the East German government. They had tried to pump information from the two soldiers. They gave the two some drinks and tried to casually ask questions about morale, unit strength, etc. Of all the troopers in the Division they had to pick DePaul.

Division G-2 had been watching the couple for days when they saw DePaul and friend come out of the house they pulled them in for debriefing,

"I had the guys at G-2 cracking up." DePaul said later, "I told them all the garbage I told those two. I figured something was funny the way they kept asking these offhanded questions. I told them we had so many submarines patrolling the waters around here I was surprised they didn't bump into each other. I told them it was true what the Russians say about us that we have to kill our parents to become a member of the 82d. I told them I killed my sister too, just to make sure I'd get in. They asked me how we felt about being here. I told them we were having a ball, that this was a great break from what they put us through back at Bragg. I told them we got up and ran ten miles each morning before breakfast and that the food we were eating here was a lot better than the garbage we got back at Bragg. I told them when we're out in the field we have to find, kill, and eat our own food. I told them I hated the thought of going back..."

Anyone else would have been court-martialed or at least given an Article 15. For a while there I was afraid the BC was seriously considering it. Only DePaul could get away with a stunt like that. I recalled the time DePaul had blessed out the Chief of Firing Battery and gotten away with it.

We'd been out in the field for three days straight on a battalion run field exercise. According to the scenario, we were supposed to go admin every night at 2200 hours (10 PM) and go back to tactical at 0500 (5 AM). This meant that except for guard duty, we'd get a pretty good night's sleep for a change.

Our battery XO had other ideas. He was the same guy who'd had it in for me. This was his last field problem in the battery; he was on orders for Korea. The battery had never liked him much and he knew it. So he decided to get even with us.

When battalion set us free for the night, he ordered us to tear down our guns, drive them out from under our nets, and practice emergency occupations, called "hip-shoots," all night. We'd pull back into the position we had left at daylight, just in time for the battalion to assume control and begin the day's training.

By the third day all our nerves were stretched.

To make matters even more fun, we had a new Chief of Firing Battery (Chief of Smoke, or "Smoke" for short). He was letting us know he was there. It appeared his idea of leadership was to stand in the middle of the battery area and scream at everyone while we worked. We were setting up our guns and our new Smoke was screaming at the top of his lungs.

We were being led.

I was gunning; DePaul was acting as my Assistant Gunner, or A/G. I was busy getting the gun ready to fire. DePaul was elevating or depressing the tube as I told him. He was muttering to himself about the situation, as was his habit, thinking out loud, asking himself questions about why we were doing the foolish things we were doing. Then he'd offer himself an explanation. I was listening to him and chuckling, as I usually did. DePaul sometimes made it worth going to work in the morning. My chuckling woke him out of his reverie; he often didn't realize he was talking out loud.

At about that time Smoke looked over at DePaul, "Hey you!" he yelled, "Come here!"

I saw a cloud cross DePaul's countenance; he'd had less than three hours' sleep in the last three days. The last thing he needed was someone messing with him while he was doing his job. He got up and angrily stormed his way over to Smoke. Smoke was a little guy. DePaul stood 6'5" and weighed in at two hundred and fifty pounds, solid. He got up at four-thirty in the morning and worked out on a weight bench he had in his room for two hours before running PT with the unit.

"What seem to be the problem here, soldier?" Smoke asked.

"I'll tell you what the problem is," DePaul answered angrily, and launched into about a diatribe on how messed up the field problem had been, with us playing games all night and not getting any sleep, and how everyone in command seemed to have their heads in a dark place and on and on.

Smoke listened calmly to DePaul's explosion. He waited for DePaul to pause to take a breath.

"Not that," he said, "what are you doing sitting around while everyone else is working?"

"Oh," DePaul said, the anger gone, "I'm A/Ging for Sergeant Wood."

"Oh. Okay, carry on."

With that, DePaul returned to the gun and Smoke went on as if nothing had happened. After Smoke had been in the battery awhile and calmed down, he turned out to be one of the best Smokes I'd ever worked for, besides Big Frank.

DePaul was a good soldier. He was one of the few soldiers I have ever had under me I felt I could totally depend on. If you gave him a job to do, he did it, and did it right. Of course, he was older than your typical soldier, being in his thirties. Several of the NCOs felt intimidated by him because they didn't intimidate him.

"I'm not some snotty-nosed kid just out of high school." he'd say, "I've been around the block, it takes more than a few stripes on the collar to intimidate me."

Top used him once in Grenada to get rid of a car he had commandeered.

When we first got to the island it took a while for all our vehicles to catch up with us. We had one truck that didn't get to the island until the day before we flew back. The poor driver stayed with that truck at Green Ramp for almost two weeks waiting for a bird south.[145] He finally joined us just in time to load his goat back on the bird to go home.

Anyway, some soldiers commandeered civilian vehicles, hotwiring them and using them for military purposes. Some of the cars got shot up pretty bad. Top had a Mercedes he used for running rations and water.

On about D + 4, when all the brass finally got set up on the island, an order came down from on high: any and all commandeered vehicles were to be taken to a holding area just north of the airport and dropped off by a certain time. Any soldier found driving a civilian vehicle after the deadline was subject to courts-martial.

Well, Top missed the deadline. He sure didn't want to get busted for having a civilian car. So he called DePaul over to the side and asked him if he thought he could get the car down to the holding area, which was just below our position, without getting caught.

DePaul waited till after dark. He drove the car down to the lot like he owned it. No one stopped him. He began to calmly walk back to our position up the hill when he saw someone light a cigarette off to his right. To his horror, he realized he had forgotten

---

[145] Ironically, he was the only trooper from our battery to have his picture appear in any of the Grenada memorials or literature. The last time I was at the Division Museum, his picture was still in the Grenada exhibit. He was behind the wheel of his gamma goat asleep, waiting for a bird to take him to Grenada

the password.

"Oh man, he thought, "I'm out this time." The sentries were understandably jumpy, tending to shoot first and ask questions later. Then he had an idea.

"Hey you, soldier!" he barked, "What are you doing smoking an unshielded cigarette on guard duty? Don't you know you'll give your position away to the enemy?"

"Oh, sorry sir," came the reply. "It won't happen again!"

"It had better not!'

"Airborne, sir!"

DePaul walked past the sentry without a problem.

DePaul was sketchy about what he did for a living before he joined the Army. Every now and again he'd tell a story or two, but he didn't go into detail so I didn't ask.

I do know he had been to college. He said once he'd had to have some sort of special paperwork to get in because of his age. Someone recently told me he was prior service and a Vietnam vet – a fact he kept well hidden in the time I knew him; but then again though he was in my section and I held him in great regard, I couldn't really be his buddy back then. His reason for enlisting was simple. His wife was dying from kidney failure and needed a transplant. He needed the Army's medical benefits.

Once through basic, AIT, and jump school, he had brought his wife down from the DC area where they had been living and got her hooked up with kidney specialists at Walter Reed Army Hospital and Womack Army Hospital at Bragg. The only possible donor was his sister-in-law and she was reluctant to give up a kidney as the family had a history of bad health and kidney disease.

Finally, with her sister on death's door, the sister-in-law agreed to donate her kidney. They ran the compatibility tests. Time was of the essence; DePaul's wife only had a few days before her system shut completely down. She was already suffering from the residual effects of kidney disease, eye problems, heart problems, etc.

In order to speed up the process the doctors began blood transfusions to reduce the chance of rejection. They were working with bare hours. When the test results came back they discovered they had made a fatal mistake in attempting to save her life. She and her sister had been perfect matches to begin with. The blood transfusions, which had been given prematurely to save time, had messed up the match. Now, they would have to find another donor. Until then she would have to go on dialysis.

She refused to go on dialysis, preferring to die rather than spend her life hooked up to a machine waiting for a donor. She was already in permanent ill health from the kidney disease. She was tired.

The unit had been pretty good about supporting DePaul during this period. He had been given a job in headquarters where he didn't have to be in the field and had given him plenty of time off to be with his wife during the crisis.

He was with her when she died. He told me about it one night in the field. He had held her in his arms as she drifted off to sleep. He said he felt her light breath against his chest. And then she stopped breathing. He told me he held her like that for at least an hour, not wanting to let her go, knowing when he did she'd be gone forever. The hospital staff was nice, he said. They waited until he left the room to come in. They had to know she was dead; after all, they had her hooked up to the machines. But they gave him time to say goodbye to her.

Now he said he prayed for death. Every time he jumped he said he hoped for a malfunction. He couldn't kill himself. He was a Catholic and that was a mortal sin. No, it would have to happen naturally.

"If there's a heaven," he said, "I figure she's got everything squared away, waiting for me. She's probably got a good job, a nice apartment... She's just waiting for me to join her."

Most of the guys in the section didn't take him seriously when he spoke like this. They figured DePaul was just being DePaul. I could look in his eyes, though, and see the grief, and the wistfulness there. I knew he was serious; a large part of him had died with his wife. Up to that time, I don't think I had ever seen a man have so much love for a woman. I was awed by it. I'd try to share Jesus, as much as I could. At the time I was still learning about Him myself. And I wasn't a very good witness.

He had a curiosity about God and the afterlife which, considering his state of mind was understandable. Often, when he'd see me reading the Bible out in the field he'd ask me questions about things. I'd answer him as best as I could.

One time in Grenada DePaul saw me reading my little pocket New Testament. That little Book got a lot of use on that island, just about everyone in the section asked to borrow it at one time or another. As they say, "There are no atheists in foxholes." Anyway, I had been reading the Bible and DePaul asked me if I could explain the book of Revelation.

I had just finished reading a couple of books on the subject

303

of endtime prophecy and felt like I was up on it. I tried to explain it. I told him about the signs of the times, the rebirth of Israel, and the Rapture.

He stopped me on the Rapture and asked me to explain it. I took him to 1 & 2 Thessalonians and the 24th - 26th chapters of Matthew and explained the catching away.

"Do you really believe that one day millions of people are just going to disappear," he snapped his fingers, "like that?"

"DePaul," I said, "I believe in a God who created the heavens and earth in six days, flooded the earth, destroyed two great cities with a word from His mouth, turned a woman into a pillar of salt, brought His people out of Egypt through ten miraculous plagues, parted the Red Sea. Then He came to earth as a man, healed the sick, raised the dead, gave sight to the blind, walked on water, and resurrected from the dead on the third day. Now, if I can believe all that, I can believe in the Rapture."

He thought about it a moment. I can still see his face; he was literally chewing on it mentally.

"You've got a point," was his final verdict.

Chapter 23
Homecoming

Around her neck she wore a yellow ribbon
She wore it in the springtime and the merry month of May.
If you asked her exactly why she wore it.
She wore it for her trooper who was far, far away.

Far away, far away.
She wore it for her trooper who was far, far away.
(Anonymous Marching Song)

Ben Franklin once said idle hands are the devil's workshop. It certainly held true in Grenada. The fighting for all intents and purposes was over, it was apparent there was little left for us to do and we were doing it. I knew things were getting bad when battalion headquarters put word down through channels that, starting the next day, we were going to start going by a "hip pocket" training schedule.[146] In a combat zone!

But the guys were getting restless. Some of our guys were caught by our Battalion Commander in a Grenadian Store not too far from our position trying to buy some Cokes. He was steamed. Maybe a hip pocket training schedule was a way to keep the guys occupied. I knew it would only serve to tick them off. It was time to go home.

We'd been on the Golf Course two or three days when we were put on fifty percent alert one night, the first time since the cow pasture. When we moved up to the golf course, Top had set up a roving guard made up of troops from each section. Of course, each section was still to run its own guard roster, keeping at least one man up to man the field phone and keep an ear out for anything unusual.

We were told word had come down from Division that Castro was going to try an air evacuation of the remaining Cuban

---

[146] Hip Pocket Training Schedules- These were probably the bright idea of someone with an MBA to "maximize" our time spent in the field training. Section Chiefs were instructed to make out and carry lesson plans for short classes to be held during down times in the field. Usually, these were lessons in basic soldiering skills, such as reading a compass, or detecting the presence of a toxic chemical weapon. It looked good on paper, but trying to teach a class to a group of men who've been in the field for days, going on a few hours sleep a night, in temperatures far below those considered comfortable, lost something in the translation from the drawing board to practice.

soldiers and engineers on the island. The golf course was one of the few suitable places on the island for an LZ (Landing Zone) they could reach. We knew he had given up any plans he might have had for reinforcing the men he had on the island at least a week before, ordering those in place to "defend to the death." Now that the battle was lost, rescuing his stranded troops might be a way for him to save at least a little face.

So we sat up that night and waited for an attack that never came. However, at about midnight something did come. It was an old beat up dump truck the battalion S-4 was using to haul supplies. The truck pulled up to our net, "Good evening, Sergeant Wood," CPT Newton said, "We've come to pick up your ammo."

I watched as he and his Assistant S-4, 2LT Hunter began grabbing our rounds and loading them.

I went around my gun waking my troops. Many of them grumbled as they drug themselves out of their hooches and set to work. One man was really angry.

"Listen, man, I said to him, "Don't you know what this means?"

"Yeah, they're messing with us again."

"No man, we're turning in our ammo- we're going home!"

My bird finally touched down at Pope AFB sometime after midnight before. I had to drive B-16, sixth section's gamma goat, towing sixth section's howitzer. I had watched as the battery personnel loaded on a homeward bound C-141. I was waiting for my turn on a bird home. Fourth section's gun and goat, my "home" section, were on the bird with me.

There was one major from an infantry brigade whose leg was in a cast. He told me he had broken it running through a house on the island in pursuit of a Cuban soldier. The floor had given under his weight (he was a big man) and his leg had snapped in two. There were two Soviet assault rifles slung over his shoulders. I imagined rank had its privileges. We had been searched thoroughly before we even left our position on the golf course that morning to ensure we had no contraband. I had to leave a baseball bat and gloves that had been given to me by some warehouse guards. I had saved them, thinking they would make good souvenirs for my kids with the "made in Cuba" stamp on them.

But, I had managed to carry home a few tokens of my adventures on the island. Some Soviet style rank epaulets had been given to the troops to take home. I had managed to scrounge several sets, a pair each for my kids, and three sets for my little brothers. They'd get a kick out of that. I regretted having to leave the baseball gear behind. I had a couple of leaflets we had dropped on the island for the benefit of the Grenadian citizens, and an enemy uniform shirt for which the previous owner had no further use. And I had gotten a pair of large seashells for Debbie while waiting for a bird at Point Salines. I wish I could have taken my kids the gear.

We had an hour layover in Puerto Rico while the bird refueled. I called Debbie to let her know I was safe and coming home. I figured she'd relay the information to the rest of the family.

When we finally touched down at Pope AFB the first thing that hit me was the cold. After spending the last ten days in a tropical ninety degree heat, the chilling forty-five degrees of North Carolina in November was quite a shock to the system.

The second thing I noticed was there was an armed escort waiting for us. Our new S-2[147] Officer, a lieutenant, was waiting for me. What on earth was going on? I watched the other passengers on the plane disembark and go their merry ways, including the major with his AK-47s.

We were told to follow the S-2's jeep from Green Ramp to Towle Stadium, across from our battalion area. The lieutenant was polite enough. It just didn't smell right to me.

The other driver about gave the lieutenant a heart attack when he went straight down Ardennes Street, instead of turning at the Division Chapel. He had given a couple infantrymen a ride to their unit area. I told the lieutenant this, but he didn't seem comforted. His relief was visible when the other goat came roaring into the stadium just moments after us.

Towle Stadium was quite a sight, every floodlight was on in the place and all our vehicles and guns were lined up on the football field. Troopers from Alpha Battery, which had been left behind, were standing guard. I was watched as I unloaded my personal gear from the truck and was escorted to the B Battery dayroom so my gear could be inspected. I discovered we were the last troopers in; the rest of the battery had been released hours ago.

The S-2 NCO, MSG Reese, observed me as I unpacked my gear. I had no sooner started than Debbie came running into the room with a squeal. She had been sitting in the battalion headquarters for four hours, arriving shortly after I called from Puerto Rico. The Battalion XO had been trying to get her to go back home as there as no telling when I'd get in, much less be released. I

---

[147]S-2- Intelligence

myself had told her to wait until I called her from the barracks.

Finally, it was determined I hadn't packed away a cannon or an atom bomb in my rucksack and was allowed to go home.

Now, the idea of my having an atom bomb in a rucksack wasn't as crazy as it might sound. We had a guy in the unit who was a fanatic about explosives. He had lost digits on a couple of his fingers when his homemade bombs exploded prematurely. I think there was something wrong with the guy mentally (of course, I'd hate to rush to judgment). He got transferred to the battalion mess hall on temporary duty (Top wanted to get the guy out of his hair). There was no room in HSB (Headquarters and Service Battery), where the cooks lived, so the guy had to stay in our barracks.

On his days off he used to stand in his window with a crossbow, loaded and aimed at the back of Top's head during formation. With his back to the barracks, Top couldn't see him. One of the NCOs would get Top's attention and point to the window.

We'd rush up to the second floor and break into his room to find no trace of the crossbow. We tore that place up several times looking for the hiding place, we checked for loose bricks in the walls, we looked in the space between the ceiling tiles, you name it. No sign of the crossbow.

Finally, the guy got busted in downtown Fayetteville trying to buy some plutonium isotope so he could activate a nuclear device he had constructed in his room in the barracks – so we were told. Sure enough, when the CID searched his wall locker they found the device. No telling how long it had been there. As he wasn't assigned to our battery and hadn't pulled his crossbow routine in some time, none of the NCOs in our battery checked his wall locker. Evidently, neither did any of the NCOs from the mess hall. He was busted. The last I heard of him he was doing time at Leavenworth.

We never did find that crossbow.

But I digress. Eventually, we got home. The kids were already in bed. A neighbor had stayed with them. All I wanted was a hot shower and a soft bed. It was after one o'clock in the morning and I had to be at work at eight thirty.

The next morning the battery marched over to Towle Stadium. We were told to strip our vehicles down. We were to take every piece of equipment out of the back of the trucks and lay it out on the grass. We even had to take certain access panels off the bodies of the gamma goats so our officers could peek around inside the wells of the trucks.

It didn't take a genius to figure out they were looking for

something specific, particularly after my greeting last night. I figured it was weapons. I later learned that I was right.

When the main body of the battery personnel arrived back at Bragg the night before, someone slipped a note on the BC's desk informing him there were Soviet assault rifles, AK-47s, stowed away on two of the gun section's vehicles, B-14 and B-16[148]. I could see my career go up in smoke – if I could stay out of Leavenworth. B-14 was Fourth Section's assigned vehicle and B-16 was Sixth Section's vehicle, SSG John's section. It was the vehicle I drove back and escorted on the aircraft. No wonder they had treated us like public enemies last night.

It didn't look good. I had worked with two different gun sections on the island and illegal weapons had been stashed on both section's vehicles. Would they believe I didn't know about the weapons? After all, I hadn't worked with my regular section that much during the battle. But how on earth did someone sneak a weapon in under Sixth Section's net and put it in the body of the vehicle?

Big Sven, the section chief, had stashed the weapon on B14. Our battery maintenance sergeant had stashed the weapon on Big J's truck. When I learned this months later, after everything died down, the whole thing made sense. I even remembered when the guy did it.

We were on the golf course. I had just washed my uniform and was kicking back with a poncho liner wrapped around my waist for propriety's sake. I was lying in my hooch (basically my shelter half pitched against the side of the truck as a lean-to) reading a book and trying to stay inconspicuous, as there were dozens of Grenadian children running through the battery area begging food.

Sergeant Dubois and one of his mechanics came under the net. "'Got to do some work on your goat, Chief." he said to me. Big J was out of the net at the time.

"No problem." I said. After all, that was his job.

They climbed up in the back of the goat and were busy there for about twenty minutes. I was wondering what on earth they could be doing there, but there are a lot of wires running through the body of a gamma goat (as in any vehicle). It all seemed innocent enough

---

[148] For purposes of identification military vehicles were assigned bumper numbers, which were stenciled on vehicle bumpers. In the artillery, gun section vehicles were labeled with the battery's label (A, B, C, etc.) followed by the section's designated number, 11 for 1st section, 12 for 2nd section, etc. The first ten numbers, 1 through 10, were reserved for the battery headquarters' vehicles, numbers twenty and up were reserved for support vehicles. Each number on a vehicle would tell you to whom the vehicle belonged, B-6, for instance, was the commander's jeep.

at the time.

Things went bad for Big J. Of course, he didn't know about the weapon either. One can imagine his thoughts when his troopers opened up the cover on the goat's body and found the pieces of an AK-47 stashed away in between the inner and outer wall of the truck. When he saw the weapon he didn't believe the BC would take his word he didn't know anything about it, or how it got there. He told one of his men to take the weapon and lay it by a tree, out in the open where the right people would be sure to see it. J wasn't trying to destroy the evidence; he just didn't want to get caught with it. It turned out to be a stupid thing to do. Maybe he just panicked for the first time in his life.

J didn't know the BC knew exactly where the weapons were hid. When the captain reached inside the body and didn't find the weapon he knew Big J had gotten rid of the weapon.

Top had already figured out how to cover his troops. He called the Division Museum the first thing in the morning and told them he had two weapons, war prizes from Grenada, to donate. The idea was to take the two weapons over to the museum and that would be the end of it. Big J, in panicking, had almost ruined those plans. The BC now wanted to press charges against him for tampering with evidence and obstructing justice. The "weapons thing" was far from over.

Before going down to Towle Stadium that morning we were told that we weren't officially back in the States yet. For security reasons, also, we were told there would be an official welcome home ceremony Friday, the next day. We weren't to wash the uniforms we wore home and put them on one last time tomorrow before we burned them or otherwise sanitized them. We were also told not to shave so we would have a true battle weary look.

The next day, we dressed up in our grimy best and were marched over to the Tucker Field House (the Division area gym). Let me tell you, it was no easy thing to put those duds back on. One of the privates got the chain of command irritated when he showed up in a clean uniform saying his wife took one look at his Grenada uniform and threw it out. A parade, in which we would march down Ardennes Street with our respective infantry battalions in combat gear, had been cancelled. The arrival schedule of the birds they were flying in on got messed up. As a result, aircraft bringing home troopers were flying in at two-hour intervals. All day long, truckloads and formations of troopers paraded down Ardennes Street beneath banners with all sorts of welcome messages. They were cheered by small scattered crowds of well-wishers. So much for our victory parade. It was a nice thought, though.

We were treated to "Welcome home, job well done," speeches by various brass. Then they unleashed the press on us. After that was over, we were given the rest of the day off. The bloodhounds in the press saw our one clean soldier and honed in on him asking him why he looked so clean. His lame excuse that he'd had time to run into the barracks and change only seemed to give them a greater scent of blood. After all, why was he the only one who had time to change? Some of us NCOs tried to run interference for the guy but there was no way they were going to let him go; I guess someone smelled a Pulitzer Prize. I think Top finally saved him by sending him on an errand.

Debbie had saved all the newspaper articles on the invasion, as well as several national news magazines, which devoted much of their issues to the battle. It was interesting reading the overall view of the operation. Some of the things that happened on the island began to make sense. As I said before many of the pictures accompanying the articles identifying soldiers as Marines were irritating.

There was an MP and CID investigation over the weapons, but it was hard to prove anything. Top told me to act dumb when I went over to talk to the CID investigator. I didn't have to do much acting; at that time I hadn't been told who had stashed the weapon in J's goat. I told the investigator it would be hard to pin stashing the weapon on anyone. After all, the aircraft we flew in on had stopped at Puerto Rico. We stayed over an hour. Anyone could have gotten to the goats during that time. I remembered some of the guys on the bird had acted mighty nervous when we were told there would be a customs inspection when we touched down in the States. Particularly that infantry major with a broken leg and two AKs slung over his shoulders. I didn't mention him. I'd liked the guy, he had us all laughing with the story of how he'd broken his leg. I wondered if anyone investigated him?

Big Sven got off free. He used to joke about going down to the museum's Grenada display to see his AK-47. Big J was another story. After a couple of months of investigations they finally managed to pin an Article 15 on him and he was busted a grade back to E-5. I believe he appealed the Article 15. Somehow he got his rank restored.

For me, it was a lousy finale to what otherwise had been one of what for me, was one of the most worthwhile jobs I've ever done as a soldier. There has been some controversy over the operation, but I felt good about what we accomplished down there. We did the job.

Personally, I was embarrassed by all the "Welcome Home Heroes!" signs posted along Ardennes Street and in Fayetteville when we came home. It was nice, particularly after the way folks treated us in the Vietnam era (and remember, I'd gotten a piece of the tail-end of that, though I was too young to go myself). But I never considered myself a hero.

Most soldiers I've known were embarrassed by the word. It's usually an insult to be called a hero in the Army. It means you're a hot-dog who'll get someone killed. We didn't really need it. But, then again, maybe folks felt guilty about how they treated the guys coming home from Nam and have tried to make up for it since then.

By the same token, after the operation was over and everything turned out right, I didn't think all the snide comments about what a joke the operation was were fair either. I remember when one of my high school students snickered and commented about how Grenada only lasted twelve minutes. He'd heard it in a popular movie.

My comment, "It lasted forever for the Americans, Cubans, and Grenadians who were killed there."

I get tired of hearing what a picnic Grenada was, usually by people who weren't there. I won't tell you that I went through the terrible experiences that the guys in the Second World War, the Korean Conflict, or Vietnam went through, but even in these wars each soldier or sailor's experiences vary depending on the assignment. I surely didn't go through what our grunts did on the island.

When we received our initial briefing on the operation we were told to expect to be gone at least six months if everything went well. Our battalion task force spent ten days on the island. I believe the longest any combat troops spent there was three months (we had MPs and other civil affairs units on the island longer). I think that's pretty good. Yet, veterans of Grenada (and Panama and now there is even a little sniping at the veterans of Desert Storm) are criticized because our "wars" were so short. In my mind, that means we did something right. Would people have preferred we spent years and lost thousands of lives on the island?

Much has been made of the mistakes made in Grenada. It's true, there were many. Most of them were command and control problems made by the higher ups. However, when one considers the

Army hadn't been officially engaged in combat since Vietnam, I thought we were doing fairly well. Consider that in my battery of some one hundred and ten men, there were only two combat veterans, Jimmy Jaeger and Big J. The rest of us guys had missed Nam. Even Top Franco, Big Frank, never went; he'd been assigned to the 1/509th Airborne in Italy and never came down on levy for Nam. Mistakes were going to be made, I've mentioned a few I made and I'm sure if I think hard about it I can think of at least a couple more. But stupid mistakes have been made at the beginning of every war we've fought, from the Revolution right up to Vietnam.

I try to put what happened to Grenada in proper perspective. It definitely wasn't Omaha Beach or Pork Chop Hill but we had been yanked out of a peacetime environment and put into combat with little or no notice. In other wars where this happened, the survivors had time to learn from their mistakes and improve. I am thankful I didn't have to pay full price for my goofs. I am even more thankful none of my troops did. In Grenada, we went with what we had. We had to learn our lessons quickly.

I remember watching one infantry company land on the island after we had moved to a position right above the airstrip. From there, we could see the aircraft unload their cargoes. It was maybe the second or third day on the island, there was a lull in our activity.

A C-141 taxied in and whipped around and the tailgate dropped. Within seconds troopers came marching out in full combat gear, cammied up, ready to go. I watched as they headed out the aircraft, up the hill, and past our position into the bush. I thought of how young some of them were. Yesterday, they had been probably swaggering up and down Ardennes Street in beret and spit-shined jump boots. I was proud of them. No telling what was waiting for them out there. At that time, many of us on the ground still suspected major concentrations of enemy soldiers hiding somewhere on the island. Some of the younger guys, with dreams of John Wayne and Audie Murphy dancing in their heads, may have actually hoped it.

I thought of the troopers in my own battery. We'd had about half a dozen kids report into the unit from jump school the Thursday before we deployed. What a welcome to the Division. Here we were, setting up the guns, unloading ammo, under occasional sniper fire, and these boys, no - men, were doing it just like back at Bragg.

One particular conversation comes to mind. I was put in charge of a detail unloading ammo to the guns. There were several new troopers I had never seen before helping me. I looked at one, "What's your name, troop?"

"Webb, Sergeant," he said, quietly, not missing a beat with his work.

"I've never seen you before, how long 'you been with the unit?"

"I signed in Thursday."

"Welcome to the Division."

He smiled, "Airborne, Sergeant."

I looked over at another troop who looked a bit older than our typical recruit, "What's your name troop?"

"Gearing, Sergeant."

"This is a heckuva welcome, ain't it?"

"I always heard field duty in the 82nd was realistic."

I had to laugh at that one, "You can always say your first field problem in the Division was Grenada.'"

"It was nice of the folks in charge to break me in right, Sergeant."

"We in the Division like to treat our folks right!"

"Airborne, Sergeant!" he said, with a grin.

In light of that, the operation turned out okay all-in-all. After all, we had been sent down there with no notice and plunged into a combat situation where many of us had little or no idea of the nature of our enemy or his strength. But we took the island in record time; I don't care what the armchair experts have to say about it.

I had been fired upon by hostile forces during the battle. Some of those rounds came uncomfortably close. Nineteen Americans died on the island, another 118 were wounded. The combined enemy losses, depending on who you listen to, run from between twenty to one hundred killed and one to three hundred wounded.[149] The actual fighting lasted only a few days, but as I told that young man - those dead are just as dead as the dead from longer wars.

Another jab I hear is how it took seven thousand troops to take the island. This is pure misunderstanding of how the modern U.S. military operates. For every soldier on the line, there are about ten support personnel backing him up. When one recognizes this, he realizes many of the personnel involved in the operation were not front-line soldiers, but support personnel who made sure we in the combat arms units had everything we needed to fight the battle. As

---

[149] I quote the best official estimates I can find. In the past I have suspected these as I had seen piles of bodies on the island. Perhaps they occurred prior to our landing when Coard's government went crazy doing executions.

far as actual combat troops involved, the number was much less. And of those combat troops, many were sent not to "take" the island, but to make sure we were on the island with enough force to discourage anyone such as Cuba from trying to retake the island.

Grenada gave us a chance to show the world how fast we could deploy a large number of troops to an objective in a short time. The lesson was learned. If one will think back, there was quite a bit of chest pounding coming from Cuba and Nicaragua until Grenada. Central America was literally on fire with revolutions and insurrections. Most of the trouble could be traced to, either directly or indirectly, Cuba and Nicaragua. After Grenada things got relatively quiet.

There was criticism in the press about the number of medals given. It's true, to the person on the outside it seemed as if there were a great many medals given, considering the number of actual personnel involved in the operation. This is only if one doesn't understand the nature of different types of awards and decorations given by the U.S. military.

Not all medals are given for heroism. Most medals are what we call "Been There Badges." There are medals or ribbons given for service and those given for achievement. For instance, every soldier in the theater of operations received the Armed Forces Expeditionary Medal (AFEM) for their participation in the operation. Prior to this, the Expeditionary Medal had been given to soldiers who participated in the Dominican Republic Operation. I believe it was also given later to participants in the invasion of Panama.

Soldiers have received campaign medals in previous wars. There was a Victory Medal given to soldiers in World War I. In World War II, service members received medals for each theater they served in. In Korea and Vietnam, soldiers not only received a campaign medal for serving in a combat zone (Vietnam vets actually received two, the Vietnam Service Medal and the Vietnam Campaign Medal) but every service member on active duty during the time of the conflicts was awarded the National Defense Service Medal for being on active duty in time of war (this has since been extended to those on duty during the Persian Gulf War through today). Awarding veterans of Grenada a campaign medal was not out of line.

As far as the other awards are concerned, many received Army Commendation Medals (ARCOMS) or Navy Commendation Medals, etc., for service on the island. These were not awarded for any singular act of heroism, but more as a pat on the back for a job well done. ARCOMS are often awarded in peacetime upon transfer or for a particularly outstanding individual achievement[150]. A few Bronze Stars were awarded, mostly to higher ranking personnel. Our Battalion Commander received a Silver Star for the operation. But even these higher awards were not given, for the most part, for acts of heroism, but for excellent service rendered. These medals mentioned (up to Bronze Star) can be awarded for heroism. If this is the case, as I've noted previously, a little "V" device is attached to the ribbon of the medal to denote it as awarded for valor.

Then, there were service awards of "peacetime" decorations such as the Army Achievement Medal (AAM), ARCOMS (which can be awarded for either peacetime or wartime service), or Meritorious Service Medals (MSMs) to the troops who stayed behind and supported us. Even though they didn't come under enemy fire, they still made important contributions to the success of the operation by making sure we had all the ammunition, food, gasoline, and other supplies we needed to fight. We could not have done the job without them. They, too, deserved recognition.

Many of the veterans of previous wars objected to the awarding of the Combat Infantryman's Badge (CIB) to every infantryman on the island. I can understand that, after all, veterans of WWII, Korea, and Vietnam spent months, even years on the front to earn that badge. Grenada lasted only a few days. The Army lightened the requirement for award of the badge to Grenada veterans, and has since given the award to veterans of Panama and Desert Storm. I personally didn't feel that every infantryman on the island should have received the award; after all, many didn't even arrive on the island until after all organized resistance had ceased and never heard a shot fired in anger. And to tell you the truth I don't know if everyone did. At the same time I don't know of a fair way the Army could have given the award. The rationale for the change in policy was it was doubtful we'd ever been in an extended campaign again – this was before 9/11.

Of course, there were abuses of the system. There were a lot of younger officers from units not deployed who hopped a flight to the island so they could get in on the party. Things got crazy. Rob, who was still with our battalion S-3, told me they had so many extra officers looking for something to do during the operation, that

---

[150] When I was in service, ARCOMS used to be awarded to the distinguished (top) graduate of each class at the NCO Academies. I believe this was stopped in the mid-eighties by some general who believed the automatic award of a medal for an achievement such as that was devaluing the medal. I doubt he turned down his Legion of Merit for changing command.

captains were manning the radio in the TOC[151]. The only thing he and the other NCOs had to do was kick back and laugh at all the nonsense going on in the TOC as the lower ranking officers tried to impress the brass. CPT Herbert, who was by this time commander of our Alpha Battery (which, remember, didn't get deployed) left the supervision of his battery's support activities to his Executive Officer and hopped a flight to the island. While his battery worked details to load aircraft with supplies for Bravo and Charlie Batteries, he was used to run messages for the Battalion Commander.

From my neighbor, I heard the story of two lieutenants from his company, one of the Division quartermaster companies. They hopped a flight down to the island after everything had cooled down, and spent the day spear fishing in the warm Caribbean waters. They caught a flight back that evening. They put in for and received their AFEMs for their "participation" in the campaign. I suppose there are characters like these in every war. We had a clerk typist in Germany who had been forced to award himself two Bronze Stars while in Nam so his unit could make its quota for medals. In my mind, they are a slap in the face of every soldier, sailor, airman, or Marine who has faced death in combat.

But that's the way the system works, for better or worse. In Nam, many units had specific criteria for soldiers' awards after their year was up. If a guy was an enlisted man (E1 - E4) he was awarded an ARCOM; NCOs were awarded Bronze Stars (without the valor device), and so on. Officers were given somewhat higher awards, as befitting their ranks. This type of criteria lives on. In 1986, the XVIII Airborne and Ft. Bragg commander issued an order that no one under the rank of Sergeant First Class (E-7) would receive any award higher than an ARCOM. It was his opinion no one of such low rank deserved better, except in extraordinary circumstances. Doesn't that stink?

There will probably never be a "Grenada Memorial" to the nineteen casualties of the battle in Washington. Nor will there be one to the Gallant Eagle Six. Maybe they'll set one up at Bragg one day, alongside the memorial to the fallen of the Dominican Republic, another "forgotten" war.

No matter what anyone says, I feel good about what we did down there. Sometimes, I can still close my eyes and hear the people singing "God Bless America." If you've got to fight, it should be for a worthy cause. Giving those people their island back seems worthy to me.

---

[151] TOC – Tactical Operations Center: A fancy name for headquarters in the field.

In the last couple years, thanks to the internet, Grenada vets have begun to reconnect on various web pages. It's been great to shoot the breeze with others who understand and re-establish contact with folks you haven't seen in almost thirty years.

One of the side benefits of our Grenada sites has been that a number of the students and faculty members from the medical school have contacted us. Their thanks for what we did re-affirms the worthiness of the action. Ask them if it was a joke.

A few years after the battle, I was attending a college sponsored by one of the major Protestant denominations. A minister from the denomination was invited as a guest speaker in one of my history courses. He talked about his work in South and Central America, having traveled to Nicaragua to speak with the Sandinista government and El Salvador to report on the communist insurgents there. During the course of the class discussion (which became a bit heated, as there were several retired servicemen in the class who viewed these people he was treating with as enemies) the subject of Grenada came up.

After class he and I continued the discussion of Grenada in the hallway.

"Of course, you know," he told me with a smug grin, "the invasion was totally illegal from the point of international law."

"I don't know about that exactly," I said, "the people wanted us there. And we won this one."

To me, this was the final word on the subject.

It didn't take long for life in the Division to get back to "normal" after Grenada. We had hoped to get a break after the campaign; after all, most of the Third Brigade was still on the island doing occupation duties. They wouldn't be back until the end of the year. We had a battalion from the Second Brigade in the Sinai on peacekeeping duties, and the 101st had assumed the 82nd's duties as the DRF during the campaign. It looked as if the Second Brigade would get some time to kick back.

We should have known better. We were given a couple of three day weekends as a reward for our service on the island, but less than a month after our return were put back DRF1.

Rumor control had it that we'd be in Nicaragua by Christmas. Reagan was tired of playing with the Sandinista's and was going to send the Division in. Because we had done such a great job in Grenada, the story continued, the brass wanted Second Brigade to spearhead again. As November passed, things did indeed look an awful lot like we were going somewhere.[152]

In my opinion, Reagan was trying to undo the damage inflicted upon U.S. prestige and interests in the years between Vietnam and his inauguration. He had inherited a mess from the previous administration. The U.S. government had turned its back on some of our closest allies in some very sensitive regions.

President Carter had withdrawn support from a pro-Western government in Nicaragua and allowed the Sandinistas to take control of the government. Don't get me wrong, Anastasio Somoza, the "Presidente" of Nicaragua was a crook, but as JFK said about the man, "He may be a [dirty dog] but he's our [dirty dog]. As it turned out no sooner had Manuel Ortega, the head of the Sandinistas taken charge than he revealed himself to be a Communist, made alliances with the Soviets and Cuba, and just about every neighboring country in Central America began catching grief from revolutionaries.

Then there was the Middle East, which is still causing us grief. For over thirty years our one true friend in that region (other than Israel) was Iran and the Shah of Iran. As I mentioned in an earlier chapter, Carter withdrew support from the Shah's government believing the Shi'ite Muslim religious leaders would set up a benign theocratic socialist government. They would thank the U.S. for helping them come to power (believe me; I've seen this in actual intelligence bulletins I had access to in the early 80s). What they got was a bunch of rabid dogs who hated everything about the U.S. They declared us to be the Great Satan and threatened to spread their "Islamic Revolution" throughout the Middle East and the world.

The instability brought about by the collapse of the Shah sent us scurrying for friends in the region. Particularly after the Soviets, sensing our weakness (and it didn't take a whole lot of savvy to do so), invaded Afghanistan. We needed friends in the region. Enter Saddam Hussein. Formerly a buddy with the Soviets, he hinted he might be someone we could do business with. After all, he wasn't a radical Islamic fundamentalist; seemed to embrace western culture, much as the Shah had done; furthermore, he was involved in a war with Iran. As the Middle Eastern saying goes (and any American doing business in the Middle East needs to remember this) "The enemy of my enemy is my friend." The flip side to this is "The friend of my enemy is my enemy." You can see the trouble we have

---

[152] Rummaging through my old trunk full of mementos from my time in service recently I found several of my "Memo Books" we used to take notes at meetings and I used to replace my short-term memory until it began to return. In several places in my "Chief's Meetings" notes taken at our daily briefings from the First Sergeant I found notations to warn the troops not to say anything about our jumping into Nicaragua or Managua off post.

trying to be everyone's friend in the Middle East.

So Reagan and later Bush were trying to stick their thumbs in a leaky dike and win the Cold War. He was not only fighting the creeping (or rampant) spread of communism in the Third World, but Congressional opposition at home. Because of our unique missions, the 82nd and other Bragg units figured prominently in the overall picture.

As a member of the 82nd, it was causing friction at home. After Gallant Eagle, every jump became a death drop. Debbie would worry until she knew I was safe and sound. Now she had another terror to deal with. Prior to Urgent Fury, alerts had merely been one of those nuisances one had to put up with as part and parcel of life in the Division. After Grenada, she now suspected that all our "flyaways" hadn't necessarily been "fun and games." I would try to tell her if you listened to every rumor that spread through the community you would worry yourself into nervous exhaustion. The best way to survive was to take each day as it came.

I couldn't really tell her much about what was actually going down for security reasons. At the same time, I had discovered after Grenada I couldn't tell her much about what I could talk about. I tried to answer Debbie's questions about what happened and what I'd seen, but every time I'd tell her about something that happened, like the night on the golf course, she'd get upset and accuse me of taking stupid chances trying to be a hero. I had just figured I was doing my job. I learned to keep my mouth shut.

I grew up listening to my parents' generation (the World War II and Korean folks) talk about how you could tell the guys who'd really seen combat because they were the ones who didn't talk about what they'd been through. After coming home from Grenada, I discovered I wanted to talk about what I'd seen and done, I needed to talk to someone about it just like I had needed to talk about what happened at Gallant Eagle.

That summer, while on leave, I was at a family gathering at my father's house in Illinois, several of my cousins (who'd never served) came over and asked me what Grenada was like. As I began to tell them about the smell of rotted bodies and what it was like to hear a bullet pop past your ear and watch a guy get blown up by a hand grenade, I noticed the glazed look come over their eyes and changed the subject. I understood why the World War II vets never spoke. No one really wanted to hear their stories. No one except another vet would have understood.

I remembered how the Vietnam vets would get together

during my first hitch and swap stories of "The Nam." As previously stated Vietnam had cast a long shadow on the early Volunteer (VOLAR) Army. It lived on in the hearts and minds of the veterans who had served there. It hung over those of us who hadn't gone.

Those of us who missed going were often filled with mixed emotions over the war's end. All of us probably heaved a sigh of relief that we had been spared. But I believe there was a part of us hidden inside which envied the "real" vets who had been tried by fire and come through. We, who came in too late to fight, were left with a question mark over our heads. Could we have passed the test? Would we pass the test if it came? We sensed the combat vets felt a bit superior to us, the untried, "virgin" soldiers. With the erosion of military and veterans' benefits after the Viet Nam era we felt society agreed. Oh, the vets would tell us we hadn't missed a thing. Then they would launch into another series of stories about "the Nam."

One night we were sitting in the mess hall after it closed. Vinnie, Miller, my other roommate, and a couple other guys were swapping tales. They were telling some horrible stories of the things they'd been through. A guy would finish a story and we'd all bust out laughing as if he'd told a great joke. Unfortunately, Elley was sitting there with us listening to the stories in horror. Finally, after one particularly gruesome story she stood up and ran out of the mess hall.

Vinnie gave me this helpless look and took off after her.

"I guess we forgot we had a civilized person here." Miller muttered sheepishly.

After a few minutes and neither had returned, I decided to get up and see if I could help mediate. I found them standing just outside the door.

"-those were human beings, Vinnie, and all of you were just laughing about them as if it were all a joke! I don't understand you…"

"Aw, Elly," Vinnie pleaded. I could see his heart was breaking. He looked over at me.

"And you, Woody!" she said accusingly, "You were with them! I expected better of you, how could you?"

"Elly," I said as gently as I could, "You've got to understand. Those *were* real human beings we were talking about. A lot of times, soldiers have to laugh to keep from crying."

Drill Sergeant Godwin in Basic once warned me about sharing too much with my wife (when I got married): "After I came home from my second tour in Nam, my wife kept nagging me to tell her about what was eating me. So one night I broke down and told her what I'd been doing as a LRRPs.[153] She never looked at me the same way again. She left me."

Several years back, my Uncle Earl, who (as I've previously stated) was one of the original Navy frogmen,[154] was visiting my mother. One night, after everyone else had gone to bed, we stayed up and talked. For years the family shared stories of his exploits we'd learned second-hand from a tractor salesman who'd served with him in the Pacific. That night, he told me his version of his experiences in World War II. After forty years he was finally able to get all the horrors off his chest. I was honored he picked me.

As a schoolteacher, the kids loves to hear my "war stories." Every now and then I'd get asked if I've ever killed somebody. I try to laugh it off, "I certainly hope so, if I didn't I was wasting my time and the Army's money."

One time I had a particularly persistent student, a young girl, who refused to be deterred, "How many men have you killed?"

Now, for an artilleryman, that's often a difficult question to answer, even if you wanted to, considering the fact we seldom see our targets. Then, firing a cannon round is a group effort, does one claim each kill personally or divide them up? So I answered, trying to end the conversation, "Let's just say more than one and less than a hundred."

"How do you live with yourself knowing you've killed someone?" She asked. Did this kid never give up?

"Well," I said, after a pause. "It sure seemed to beat the alternative at the time."

My students always talked about the "war stories" I told in class." But I never told a lot of real war stories (not that I had that many to tell). I tell them about my accident (I owe that to God); I tell them funny stories from Basic Training and so on. I occasionally tell them told them about how I arrived in Grenada; it's kind of funny now. I always tried to tell a story that illustrated the lesson (which wasn't hard considering I taught Government and History) or had a life lesson. But I didn't tell real "war stories." I learned.

Back in 1984 I finally told Debbie there was no point in going crazy over every rumor that flew around the 82nd Airborne Division. She was going to have to live with the Division and its

---

[153] LRRPs- Long Range Reconnaissance Patrol- the forerunners to the modern Rangers, they conducted "search and destroy" missions deep into hostile territory among other functions.
[154] Frogmen were the nicknames of the Navy UDT- Underwater Demolition Teams, the forerunners of the Navy SEALs.

stresses if she didn't want to go overseas. The only thing keeping me in the States and at Ft. Bragg was the fact that I was in the 82nd. Any attempt to leave the 82nd would get me on a fast track to Germany, Korea, or worse.

Though a transfer to a less demanding duty station might be what the doctor ordered, I figured I'd hang in there somehow; I was managing okay so far. Shortly after our return from Grenada I was put up for promotion to Staff Sergeant, E-6. I had been back in the Army less than four years. That was pretty good for back then.

To be perfectly honest, I couldn't see myself serving in anything but an airborne unit any more. For all its hassles and demands, I realized I loved being a paratrooper.

I still tried to get into Warrant Officer Candidate School. There was no law saying I couldn't be an airborne warrant officer. I finished a packet as soon as I got back to the States. Because I had gotten sent to Grenada, I had missed the deadline for the next class. When I finally got my packet in my name had gotten lost in the administrative shuffle. My packet was kicked back because they had no record of my appearing before the recruiting committee. By the time I got that straightened out, the whole procedure had changed and I would have to start all over again. Disgusted, I figured I'd just stay an NCO; the way I was progressing through the ranks I might be a Sergeant Major long before I retired anyway.

Chapter 24
Windshifts

My recruiter told me a lie,
'Said, "Join the Airborne, and learn to fly."
So, I left my woman way out west,
'thought this jumping life was best.
Now she's somebody else's wife,
And I'll be jumping for the rest of my life!
All the way! Every day!
Two miles, no sweat! Three miles, better yet!
Four miles, all the way! Five miles, green beret!
Airborne! Airborne
(Anonymous running cadence)

Shortly after Grenada there was a big levy in the Division. A lot of guys came down on orders for overseas, others got sent down to Legland. Big J and another NCO got caught on the Army's "Fat Man Program" under AR 600-9, the height and weight control regulation. I don't think J ever recovered from the flak over the AK. He had seventeen years in service and was barred from re-enlisting because he was overweight by Army standards. He may have been heavy, but the guy was built like a tank! I'd seen him pick up the trails of a M102 and move it by himself when his advance party man put the gun in a location he didn't like. But I think he got a "bullseye" on his back over the AK deal. It happens – one incident and suddenly you're in the sights – "Tag – you're it!"

I had always considered the Army my home. There was a saying, "The Army takes care of its own." I had always found that to be true. We were like a large family. We didn't get along sometimes, you may not like everyone in the group, but you stuck together when the chips were down. When a soldier messed up, unless it was extremely serious, he was punished, but the Army tried to stand by him. The system was designed to get the job done and take care of the troop. A good soldier could be forgiven a mistake.

Big J was my friend; but I figure whatever you thought of a guy personally, a soldier who had given seventeen years of his life in honorable service to his country deserved better than that. I'm not saying J was a saint. But he was a soldier, and a good one. I believed that should have counted for something.

I thought of SSG Phillips in Germany not ten years before, who had been a criminal, and how he had been allowed to draw his pension. His entire chain of command, taking into account his years of service and excellent job performance, had gone to bat for him. And I thought of Big J, whose sin had been to weigh too much. Was it just a matter of individual circumstances, or was the Army changing?

I heard the other NCO in the battery had gotten disgusted and just gotten out after struggling with his weight problem. He was another just naturally big guy in an Army that wanted "lean, mean, fighting machines."

I watched this with some interest because I knew there were those in power who had their eye on me, even though I always scored high on my PT tests and met the body fat standards laid out by AR 600-9, but I was always "borderline." And I had to fight to maintain that. On my performance evaluations, I always lost points on appearance and physical fitness because I "looked heavy." Eventually, I knew that no matter how well I performed, these might eventually come back to bite me; somewhere down the line a similar fate awaited me. AR 600-9 was touted as being the Army's way of ensuring a physically fit combat force. They didn't want to send out of shape soldiers to war. On the one hand I can understand and agree with that. On the other, I saw – and still see irony in that. No one had been sitting at Green Ramp on October 24, 1983 with a scale to see if we were "fit to fight." No one said my two buddies couldn't go to Grenada because they were overweight.

As 1983 ended, we found ourselves on DRF once more. The rumors were flying about spending Christmas in Nicaragua. I didn't really believe them, but one couldn't totally ignore them either. For one thing they were so persistent. For another, at our "Threat Briefing" prior to going on DRF we had received a particularly detailed analysis of the Nicaraguan Army's capabilities. We were treated to the knowledge that since Grenada the Nicaraguan Armed Forces had been beefed up with armored cars, Soviet made Hind helicopters and new anti-aircraft weapons. We were shown aerial photographs of fields strung with wire to hinder airborne drops. I don't know about anyone else, but as for me, I was of the opinion if we were going, let's go ahead and get it over with. The more we stalled and put off the drop, the more prepared the enemy were. If we didn't go soon, any operation would be a bloodbath.

Back at the home front I was boarded for promotion shortly

after returning from Grenada. I'd had a talk with my superiors; they appeared to think I was ready. I had more than enough time and grade and service and more than enough points. Once again, despite the fact I hadn't done as well on the board as previously, once all the points were counted up, I had more than a thousand points. Once more I knew there would be at least one artillery sergeant in the Army getting another stripe (really a rocker) once the required 90 day wait was up.

I took over our fifth howitzer section shortly after being boarded. Top told me I had my work cut out for me the evening he gave me the section, "Good luck, Sergeant Wood," he said, "You're going to need it." At the time I had no idea of what he was speaking, but I was about to find out.

The next few months were a nightmare as I grew into my new stripes and tried to mold the section together to work as a team under my leadership. Had this not been my first section, it would have been an easier job. Over the next few months, I believe I learned the true meaning of responsibility. I had run sections before for my chiefs, but I had always had the chief to fall back on. When you're a chief of section you are responsible for everything that happens - and fails to happen - in that section. You've got to get the job done (accomplish the mission) while looking after the welfare of your troops. Often the two tasks appear to be at odds with one another.

Finally, it began to come together. By the summer of 1984 I had grown into my stripes and had a good section I would put up against any. By that time, "No Slack" had come and it was a whole new war.

I had just signed in from leave when I heard Top Franco had swapped jobs with our Battalion S-2 NCO, whom I'll just call "No Slack."[155] This was the second time in my career one of my First Sergeants I'd seen this happen. Both times, it spelled trouble for the troops.

I knew we were going to have fun with this guy when Jimmy Jaeger told me not to call him "Top." He had made that mistake on the new First Sergeant's first day in the battery.

"Don't call me Top!" the new First Sergeant had barked, "What do I look like, a top that spins around? My rank and title is

---

[155]Master Sergeant and First Sergeant are the same grade. The difference is in the position the sergeant holds. A Master Sergeant usually holds an administrative or staff job, while the First Sergeant is the senior NCO in a company and is designated by a diamond in the space between his/her three stripes on top and three "rockers" on the bottom. A Master Sergeant's space is blank.

First Sergeant!"

Oh boy, I thought, one of those.

The name "Top," to be sure, is an unofficial nickname or title. It hails back to the old brown boot army when the First Sergeant was known as the "Top kicker" who usually could - and would, when necessary - whip any man in the unit. It was a term of respect and honor. Now that I had fairly well decided against going for a commission, I looked forward to being called "Top" by my troops.

Our new First Sergeant had just completed jump school the year before; prior to that he had done a two-year stint as a drill sergeant. Before that he had spent two years as an instructor at an NCO Academy. This told me that he was full of Army regulations and brand new ideas from the wonderful Land of Oz, which had nothing to do with life in the trenches – much less the 82nd Airborne Division – which had its own way of doing things. He once made the comment he had gone airborne when he learned all his buddies he'd come up through the ranks with who had wings had made E-8.

One night he caused half our battery to land in the trees during a jump when he appeared to freeze in the door. As First Sergeant he was expected, along with the Battery Commander, to be the first out the doors of the aircraft.

We were jumping Holland DZ, which has a nasty slope on the far side. If you miss the DZ you land and roll, and roll, and roll… which is what I did while trying to avoid the scrub pine which grew profusely on the slope. I couldn't help but remember the words of my jumpmaster on my cherry blast, "Never try to do a PLF going uphill!"

I figured I was blessed that night because a lot of our guys wound up hitting the trees, getting caught in branches and such. We were still fortunate (if you'll pardon my choice of words) no one was hurt seriously. I've seen guys impaled by tree branches if they hit them just right.

Well, I'd banged myself up pretty good and twisted a knee, but not quite serious enough to call for real medical attention. So I rolled up my chute and limped to the assembly area in time to hear the First Sergeant talk about his jump.

"When that green light came on, I looked down and saw nothing but trees. I'll tell you right now, I don't jump unless I see drop zone…"

Jimmy Jaeger was standing next to me, our eyes met and I could tell he was thinking what I was thinking. Of course, being me,

I had to say it, "Hasn't he ever heard of a CARP?"[156]

Jimmy rolled his eyes and said, "Cheeerrreeeee!"

We might have gone easier on him had he been easier to live with himself.

I now see his arrival as an example of a growing trend. After General Lindsay left the Division in early 1983, DA (Department of the Army) began transferring a lot of experienced officers and NCOs out of the Division. We got a lot of company commanders and first sergeants that had never served in jump units before, or had not served in an airborne unit in years.

1LT Goodson, our XO at the time, told me that DA was trying to break up the so-called "Airborne Mafia" and give everyone a chance to serve in the 82nd.[157] This sounded all nice and democratic, but I wondered at the military wisdom of it all. My own opinion was this move hurt the Division because we lost a lot of good men who knew and understood airborne warfare, which is unique. I remembered my own adjustment to the 82nd way of doing things, and I had come in as a SP4. It took me some time to learn the ropes.

One time during the summer when the battery was typically on some sort of support cycle I, a gun chief, had to plan a heavy drop airborne operation for the firing battery. None of the top leadership left (we had several folks gone on extended TDYs and details), who were all new to the Division, had ever conducted a heavy drop. Several of our gun chiefs were off on some sort of detail that day and I was the only one left in the area who knew how to plan and conduct the mission. So I sat in the Orderly Room and taught our new BC and First Sergeant how to conduct an airborne artillery heavy drop assault.

I was glad this was training and not the real thing, otherwise we would have been in a mess on a "hot" DZ with folks shooting at us and a chain of command not sure of what to do.

I am not belittling these men; a few years before I had been in the same boat as they. Once I explained what they needed to do and how to situate the guns and mark them, and load the personnel so they would land near their equipment, they did a great job. It's

---

[156] CARP - Computed Air Release Point. The Air Force calculates the windspeed and direction and determines the point at which, if they release jumpers, the wind will carry them on to the drop zone. Any trooper who has made more than a few jumps knows about the CARP and knows even if they jump out over trees, the wind is likely to carry them to the DZ.

[157] I guess this mentality was infecting all the elite units. In the late eighties I began seeing Special Forces units running in company formation instead of team formations during morning PT.

just that the mission of a parachute division requires special skills not required of regular units, just as the mission of an armored division requires skills a career paratrooper lacks. The difference is the 82nd, with its rapid deployment mission, must be ready to go anywhere in the world within eighteen hours at a moment's notice. As General Lindsay often said, "In eighteen hours there's no time to get any smarter, any faster, or any better, you go with what you've got."

I remembered my flight to Grenada, thinking of all the things I wished I could do better. It turned out all right in Grenada, but what about the next time? Leaders in combat don't have time to learn, they have to *know*, their soldiers' lives depend on it.

Okay, off the soapbox, back to "No Slack."

If we had any lingering doubts about life under the new regime, they were soon dispelled. He announced at formation he expected us to be waiting for him when he stepped out into the formation area. At formation time he would blow his whistle (a souvenir from his time as a drill sergeant, I guessed) and begin counting backwards from ten. Anyone who wasn't in place in formation by the time he reached zero was dropped for pushups.

One day he dropped our Chief of Firing Battery. Well, equal opportunity, I guess. But I was embarrassed to see an E-7 pushing gravel.

As if this wasn't embarrassing enough, he expected us to sound off with a loud and thunderous, "No slack!" when we snapped to attention. This became Bravo Battery's slogan. Failure to sound off loud enough caused the entire battery, NCOs and all, to be dropped for pushups. We were back in basic training!

Soon, he had the words "No slack!" stenciled on every door in the battery area. We soon became the joke of the entire battalion, word soon spread throughout DivArty. It was humiliating.

Then the guys started laughing when he blew the whistle. I knew something was up. Being an NCO, it took me about a week to find out the gag.

A couple guys who'd received Article 15s got their revenge one night while on extra duty. While cleaning the Orderly Room and Commander's Office one of them found the First Sergeant's whistle. The guys rinsed it out in the commander's toilet.

There was a part of me that wanted to tell the First Sergeant about his whistle. Then I thought about it. It was really too late to do him any good, wasn't it?

Me being me and him being him, I guess it was just a matter

of time before we locked horns over a troop he wanted to bust. I'll call the kid Cooper.

Cooper's problems started even before he signed into Bravo.

One Monday morning in the summer of '83 our BC decided we should take the Army's new urinalysis test for THC instead of doing PT. So we were marched into the latrine and told to pee in the bottle. The brass were shocked when some 33 of our 110 or so troopers came back positive. It must have been some weekend.

They were immediately put on the drug control program (something I knew about from my days in Germany). About twenty of those guys failed the program and were facing discharge when Cooper signed in from Jump School. Top Dubois, our First Sergeant at the time,   had pulled these guys out of their sections and really out of the battery, using them for various details while waiting for their discharges to come through. He even moved them into rooms in their own section of the barracks away from the rest of the battery to prevent their bad attitudes from spreading through the battery.

Enter Cooper. When Cooper came to the battery, Top had run out of bunks everywhere except in the "quarantined" area. He had no choice but to put him in with the druggies. A few days after he signed in, Top busted a bunch of guys in Cooper's room smoking pot. Cooper went down with the rest. He was given an Article 15 and sent to Charlie's Chicken Farm[158] for a couple of weeks.

When he came back, he had a bad reputation and an attitude.

I found him to be a pretty good troop, as far as performance was concerned. I knew when I told him to do something it was done right. He'd had a problem for a while getting up in the mornings, but I had been able to square that away. Unfortunately, I hadn't been able to rectify the problem before "No Slack" got him in his sights.

Cooper got screwed when he agreed to take a buddy to visit his folks in Tennessee one weekend on the condition that the buddy pay for the gas. It was really too far to go on a weekend, but they left Friday night – it was doable, provided they started back first thing Sunday morning. The problem was the "buddy" told Cooper once he was home that he was going AWOL and refused to pay Cooper for gas to get back to Bragg.

I found Cooper and his girlfriend in their car on the road outside Laurenburg, NC Monday morning after arriving at work and learning he'd called the night before asking for help and no one had gone to help him. Worst, no one had called me so I could go get him.

---

[158] Charlie's Chicken Farm- Nickname for CCF or Central Confinement Facility: the modern version of the Guardhouse.

I chewed some butts over that.

When I asked him why he hadn't called me, he told me he'd lost my number. We poured some gas I'd brought into his car. I gave him some money, with orders to get some food (they hadn't eaten since Sunday morning), get his girlfriend home, and report to work immediately. I followed them to the nearest gas station and, made sure they had enough gas to get home, took off to get myself back to work.

I couldn't let him get away with missing a formation. By the same token, there were extenuating circumstances behind it all. When I got him back to post I was going to make him work for me that weekend in the motor pool to make up for the time he owed the Army. In addition, Cooper was to meet me at the CQ desk, ready for PT, every morning for the next two weeks. I'd write him a counseling statement to that effect with the warning if he was late one morning I would recommend he get an Article 15.

But I wasn't going to get the chance to discipline my troop. I got back to the battery to find the First Sergeant waiting with instructions for me to write the guy a counseling statement so No Slack could give him an Article 15.

We debated this for a while. I explained what happened and how Cooper had tried to do the right thing. In return, I heard everything Cooper should and shouldn't have done to have prevented all these things. The First Sergeant was the kind of guy who always knew what should be done AFTER it's all over with. I knew Cooper had done a stupid thing, but how many of us had done stupid things when we were nineteen? I argued as forcefully as I could for my troop. I believed he had the potential to be a good soldier, if given a chance. Finally, the First Sergeant agreed to reduce the punishment he wanted to give Cooper.

"Thank you, First Sergeant," I said, "I appreciate your willingness to compromise." I knew it was a waste of time to argue any longer, but the matter wasn't settled, as far as I was concerned. As I recall, I wrote Cooper the counseling statement I had intended to write but I never recommended for the Article 15.

When it came time for Cooper to face the BC, I had to be there when they read him the charges. The BC asked Cooper what he had to say for himself and dismissed him to hear what I had to say.

"Well, Sergeant Wood, what are your recommendations?"

"Sir, I recommend that these charges be dropped."

I thought the BC and First Sergeant's chins were going to hit the floor.

"But didn't you recommend this Article 15?"

"No, sir, I didn't." I replied, "I was called in and told that I was to write him up so he could be given an Article 15. I told the First Sergeant that I was taking measures to correct my troop. I wanted to handle it myself. I protested then, and I protest now."

The BC didn't know what to say. So he called Cooper in and busted him in spite of my recommendation. He did tell Cooper the only reason he was getting off as lightly as he did was because I had stood up for him. I bit my tongue. I had done my best, but I knew the conclusion to this farce had been foreordained.

I really didn't blame the BC and still don't. He was a good guy and doing what most good officers do – listen to their NCOs; in this case, his First Sergeant. That's why the Army pairs an officer with an experienced NCO at every level of his or her career.

The First Sergeant was fit to be tied. When we went back to the orderly room he started, "Sergeant Wood, I thought we had agreed on what we were going to do..."

"No First Sergeant, I never agreed with you on this. My exact words, if you'll remember, were, 'I appreciate your willingness to compromise.' And I do. But, I'm going to fight for my troop."

He didn't know what to say. He dismissed me. From that moment, I knew he was really out for my blood. I remember thinking I may have just blown my career. Had this been Cooper's first strike I might not have fought so hard, but this was his second "strike," his third, he was out.

In the end, No Slack got enough on Cooper to throw him out. I don't know that Cooper just didn't get fed up and give him the ammo to get him. Maybe he was a lost cause from the start. 'Can't say. After he finished with Cooper, No Slack set his sights on me. He looked for fault in me until he found my Achille's tendon- my weight problem.

If I had it to do over again, even knowing what I know now, I still believe I would have done the same thing. Cooper was my troop. I fought for my troop. In my mind it was the right thing to do. If I didn't take care of him, who would? I may bust him, but no one else had better mess with him.

I had to think, where would I have been if it hadn't been for all the NCOs and officers who had looked out for me when I was coming up? I wouldn't have made it through my first hitch if I'd been Article Fifteened every time I goofed up.

As for No Slack, well, I'd been in Bravo over two years at that time. Since then, we'd been through two BCs, three first sergeants, three XOs, and three chiefs of smoke. They had come and gone. I had gotten along with most of them. I tried to if I could; I had tangled with a couple. I was still here. All I had to do was continue to soldier well, watch my back, and wait it out. This, too, would pass. Either he would leave or I would, and life would go on. That was one of the neat things about the Army.

Shortly after that I came up for re-enlistment. It was the beginning of 1985. As an E-6 there weren't really many options open for me. The higher in rank one rises, the harder it was to change specialties. But there were some hard to fill specialties that even offered bonuses for which I was qualified. I talked some of the alternatives over with Debbie, as any change in specialty probably would require a transfer. I finally re-enlisted for Present Duty Assignment (PDA) with the option of attending a local college during duty hours for a semester. That semester would give me a two-year degree, which at that time would have set me civilian education-wise for the rest of my career (though I still harbored hopes of eventually getting my BA).

One of the good things about the Division at that time was the fact one could "homestead." After all, by this time I'd been at Ft. Bragg for over five years with no sign of leaving unless I chose to. Every time I had come down on orders since the Turkey scare they had been "deleted." I'd missed the big levy. Someone at Division Headquarters considered me a valuable asset to the functioning of the 82nd. At least it made me feel good to think so.

I knew guys who'd been in the Division for over a decade and met one who'd spent his entire career at Bragg, going overseas only when the Division deployed. And the guy wasn't even jump qualified. He had one of those jobs.

I knew what it was like to have to move every couple years or so. We had a joke in our family that when we'd been in a place so long we couldn't go anywhere without running into someone we knew it was time for Dad to come down on orders. Sure enough we would.

The life was tough on the kids. They had to leave old friends to go off and make new ones, which you knew eventually you'd have to leave again. The Army tried to make it easier on the families, making the big rotation times around Christmas and in June to coincide with school terms. Even that had its drawbacks. I remember one time riding the school bus in Belgium listening to one of the kids, whose dad had just come down on orders, giving away the toys he'd just gotten for Christmas because his family was over their weight allowance.

Mom and Dad learned to "reschedule" holidays if necessary. The year Dad came home from Nam we had a late Christmas so we could all enjoy it in Colorado and not have to worry about giving things away. We told the younger kids that we'd made a deal with Santa Claus for a late delivery.

I knew every move meant heartbreak for Mom. It seems like every time we moved something she loved got lost or stolen. China, porcelain figurines, nothing seemed sacred. The worst incident was when the chairs to Mom's pride and joy, her antique cherry wood dining room suit, were destroyed during the move from Ft. Carson, Colorado to Illinois, on our way to Germany. The adjuster tried to give her a few bucks replacement because the chairs were "old and used" – eighty years old. Mom raised a fit, threatened to go up the chain and finally got a couple hundred dollars. But she never was able to replace those chairs – or the memories that went with them.

After that, Mom decided to leave everything in the house in Illinois and use Army issued furniture rather than have her things destroyed until she found a place she could "homestead." She thought she'd found it in Alabama. She'd moved everything into the house they bought outside Ft. Rucker. Then Dad came down on orders for Alaska.

So I considered any career move I made such as a change in specialty, which might require more transfers as much Debbie's decision as mine, as she and the kids would be affected.

Right before I was due to return to work I got caught on a surprise weigh-in. I was two pounds over my allowable weight. I about killed myself but was able to drop the pounds with a few to spare before I had to report back to duty.

I found out a few days before I was due back to work I was being transferred back to headquarters. S-3 needed a new Schools and Training NCO. I was told later the new Battalion Commander, now LTC Reynolds, had been S-3 back when I worked there the last time, had mentioned my name. I have to admit I greeted this news with mixed emotions. I hated leaving Bravo, the guns, and the guys I'd served with the past two years. But I had to admit I would not miss not playing games with "No Slack!"

He had the last laugh.

I discovered one of the last things he did before letting me go was put my name on the Division weight control (lifestyle) program. I had no sooner reported into HSB (Headquarters and Service Battery) than I had to go be evaluated.

At the aid station it was found I was right within my weight limits. It was up to my new BC, CPT Green, to decide what to do with me. He let me go, with a friendly reminder not to throw away a promising career over a few pounds. I was trying hard not to.

I had gotten away this time. I breathed a prayer of thanksgiving. I didn't know how long I could keep on like this. I could feel eyes on me now.

In my new job I was in charge of keeping all the training records for the battalion and coordinating the administration of getting qualified soldiers to the various military schools on post. In the field, I helped in the battalion TOC (Tactical Operations Center), which was the battalion's field headquarters.

For a while I was chalking up "Atta boys!" left and right. I was in a high visibility position with the schools and was able to shine. At the same time, I had managed to put all our battalion training records on computer, which greatly enhanced our keeping of training statistics, which were used as a barometer of unit readiness.

Little did I know that less than a year my world would be turned completely upside-down.

Chapter 25
AR 600-9

I don't like it, no way!
'Up in the morning, 'fore the break of day!
Eat my breakfast, too soon,
'Hungry as a Ranger, before noon!

I went to the mess sergeant on my knees,
'Said, "Mess sergeant, mess sergeant, feed me please!"
He looked at me with a big old grin,
"If you wanna be airborne, you gotta be thin!"
(Anonymous Airborne Running Cadence)

Military life in general places stress on a marriage that is unimaginable for folks who've never been there. The life is a good life - a great life in so many ways; but it is not a lifestyle for everyone. I have nothing but admiration for the husband and wife who can endure a career and make it into the twilight years together. My marriage, which I realize now, was shaky to begin with, fell apart. After Gallant Eagle, my wife saw every jump as a potential "Death Drop." After Grenada, alerts were no longer just a nuisance to be tolerated. And the rumors that were in constant circulation about invading Nicaragua and the flyaways the Division conducted to keep bad guys down there nervous didn't help, either.

I don't think anyone is really interested in the gory details, but we separated and I moved in to Spring Lake, closer to Post. I didn't feel like hitting the bars any more. So I spent a lot of my off time alone – either at the house or exercising to lose weight. Some nights I would run/jog six or eight miles.

I guess it was sitting alone one night in my little shack it was like I had a flashback to my childhood in East St. Louis. I was in the 3rd or 4th Grade; Mom was trying to raise us kids alone and often didn't know where our next meal was coming from. I remember my older brother and I figuring out among ourselves what to leave on our plates without her catching us so Mom could eat.

One day I remember coming home from school and seeing my mother standing at the kitchen sink washing dishes and singing the old hymn, "Where Could I go but to the Lord?"

That was often how she prayed.

Now, we weren't always in church, but I was always aware of my mother's great faith. How else could she have raised us older boys and later keep her house together while her men were at war the way she did?

Yeah, I figured Someone was talking to me. I also had an idea of a church I could attend.

When I moved in to my house my landlady invited me to her church. I'd never heard of her denomination before so I was a bit skeptical. Then, while running at night, Barbara, the woman who worked at the local convenience store I stopped at for coffee after finishing my run invited me to the same church. Again, was Someone talking to me?

I'd passed the church so many times over the years on my way out of Spring Lake toward the trailer park where we had lived. Never did I dream that I would one day be walking through its doors.

I've heard a lot of preachers come down against the old song "All I Want is a Cabin in the Corner of Glory!" But that song means a lot to me. I know we've got a mansion waiting for us that Jesus has prepared for us. I know God wants the best for His children. But on that November morning in 1985, as I made my way up the stairs of that church I would have been happy with just a lean-to on the far side of heaven. I had blown it with my life. I figured I had blown it for God. Now, I prayed God would show a little mercy on me and let me into heaven.

I was a little late getting to church that morning, when I walked in the service had already begun. They were singing the opening hymn. This was okay by me. I'd sit on the back pew and be inconspicuous. I could get up with Barbara later and tell her I'd made it. Boy, was I wrong!

As soon as the song was finished, the preacher (he must have been the youngest looking preacher I had ever seen) was smiling. He got up in the pulpit and shouted, "How many of ya'll are happy to be in the house of the Lord today, say 'Amen!'"

The congregation answered him with a hearty "Amen!"

"Now reach over and give somebody a hug and tell them you're happy to see them in the house of the Lord?"

The next thing I knew, I was being overwhelmed by a bunch of little old ladies who were hugging my neck, introducing themselves, and telling how much they loved me. I looked into their eyes and saw they were telling the truth. If anyone ever needed a hug that day it was me. It was all I could do to keep from crying; it had been a long time since someone had told me they loved me. I had come home.

Over the next two or three years that church and its people were a sanctuary for me as my entire life was turned upside down and inside out.

The first time I shook his hand, I knew Pastor Billy was going to be a friend. He baptized me in February, after nearly four years of looking for someone to do it. After I dried off, he allowed me to give a testimony of Gallant Eagle 82. As I took the pulpit I spoke with a new boldness I had hitherto not known. Folks don't realize it to look at me now, but I am basically a shy person until I get to know someone.

If anyone had suggested the idea of my getting up in front of a crowd and talking years before, I'd have said they were crazy. Much less if they said I was to talk about Jesus. My relationship with God was always too personal to share with anyone, in my mind. Maybe that was because I'd never had much to share about.

As I spoke that Sunday evening though, the words came forth naturally. I felt I was at home.

The desire to play music began to come back. I began singing specials in church and writing Christian songs.

There were a couple times during this period I wondered whether there was a hope of restoring my marriage. Each time I went to visit I realized she was going in her direction and I was going in a completely opposite path.

Folks have told me I did everything I could to save my marriage; that it wasn't my fault. Maybe it looked that way to them. In my heart though, I know I failed my family in one big way.

I had failed to be the priest in my family as God had intended. Oh, I know I'd had good intentions and wanted to go to church. But, except for a very brief time when we first got married, I had never followed through on that. On all those mornings when the alarm didn't ring, or I heard we didn't have nice enough clothes, I should have said, "We'll wear what we've got, then." and gone.

Maybe it wouldn't have saved my marriage, but it was the one – the most important thing- I hadn't tried.

As the year wore on I struggled with less success to lose weight. The best I could do was maintain it around my maximum body fat limit by the calipers test then in use. I believed my current problem was somehow related to my injuries at Gallant Eagle 82. I reviewed my history. I had always been stocky but had never had a problem maintaining my weight or meeting a goal weight until that drop.

The problem was proving it. The medics were skeptical because all the tests they ran on me – the usual for detecting medical causes for obesity: thyroid, adrenal, pituitary, etc. – came back in the normal ranges. The general consensus of my chain of command seemed to be I wasn't taking my weight problem seriously and needed help in losing enough pounds to take below the borderline I was constantly treading. Looking back, at least some of them meant well enough, at the time I resented what I perceived was a lack of trust or a questioning of my integrity when I told them I was doing everything I knew to do to lose the weight.

Looking back, I have to admit part of the problem in convincing people I was still suffering the after-effects of my jump injuries might have been due to my success in convincing the docs (and my chain of command) I had fully recovered so I continue to soldier.

Then, in March 1986, I busted weight for the second time in a year. I had been nailed once and finally on the Division Lifestyle Program, which was their program for fat boys and girls.

We had been out in the field preparing for an ARTEP prior to going on Mission Cycle. I always had a hard time maintaining weight in the field – even in Bravo – because I couldn't run out in the field.

Before we could go on Mission Cycle we had to POR. This time we were conducting our POR over three days. As usual, I had put on a few pounds out in the field and was trying to take them off before I went over.

The POR began Wednesday. On Thursday, I stood on my bathroom scale at home and was right at my goal weight. One more day and I should lose another pound or two to be on the safe side in case the medics' scales were calibrated differently than mine. But the officers I worked for seemed all concerned that I POR (weigh in). I told the major I was going to wait till Friday to POR. He ordered me to go on over.

"Here goes nothing, Lord." I said.

I came in two pounds overweight. I knew something unpleasant was about to hit the fan.

I was right.

The next morning when I came into work it was as if I had

contracted a deadly, contagious disease.

No one answered or even looked up at me when I came in the office. I knew it had something to do with the weigh-in the day before. I hadn't expected this drastic a reaction so soon.

I was called in to the Major's office and given the news, "Sergeant Wood, you know you came in overweight yesterday at the POR."

"Yes, sir." what else was there to say?

"I hate to be the one to tell you this but we are beginning proceedings to have you chaptered out of the Army for being overweight. According to AR 600-9, this is the next step when one comes in overweight twice within a year."

"Sir, doesn't the commander have the right to waive that option in certain cases?"

"I wouldn't worry about that, sergeant. The thing you've got to worry about is saving your career. How long do you have in service, Sergeant Wood?"

"Counting my reserve time, eleven years total."

"It's a shame to throw that down the drain over a few measly pounds. I'd hate to see the Army lose a good NCO over two pounds. I know we'll probably get a replacement who'll do your job half as well as you..." *Then why throw me out?* "So your only hope is to get hot and lose those two extra pounds before you have to see the doctor over at Womack."[159]

"Sir, I've tried to lose the weight, it won't come off."

"There must be something you're not doing right."

There followed a discussion of everything I was doing to try and lose weight. It boiled down a second-guessing session. No matter what I did or said I did, the major could find something wrong.

I knew the major meant well, but all I knew was I had been on a weight control program of my own since December, I had tried everything I knew to lose weight and was doing good to stabilize my weight.

Finally, I made what was to me, a statement of my newfound faith in the Lord, "Sir, I've put it all in God's hands."

"Faith is a good thing, Sergeant Wood," the Major said. I sensed that, in his own way, he was actually trying to help me, "but we've got to do something to help ourselves..."

---

[159] According to AR 600-9 as written then, a medical officer had to confirm a soldiers' excess weight and sign off on the paperwork before the soldier could be discharged. I never met a medical officer who approved of the program when you got them off the record.

"Well, sir, I've done all I can do. All I know how to do. These last few pounds won't come off. I've given it over to the Lord. I've come to the realization that if He wants me out of the Army there is absolutely nothing I can do to stay in. I'll have to accept that He has something better for me on the outside. By the same token, if He wants me in the Army there's nothing anyone can do to throw me out."

Now, I said it as a statement of faith. I was merely saying how I felt. I said it in all innocence. But, when I said it, I realized the Major took offense. His face drained of all color, his nostrils flared, his lips quivered in rage. I was looking in the face of Pilate.

"Very well," he said, "you are to report to the First Sergeant. You'll no longer be working in S-3."

That morning it was as if the last shoe had dropped. I drove to my place just off post to change from my PT uniform to BDUs. I remember sitting there overwhelmed by everything – particularly the dread of what was facing me when I reported to my unit. What now?

It was one thing to make a declaration of faith, no matter how sincere. It was quite another to endure the consequences of that declaration, to learn complete submission.

Suddenly, I felt a warmth flow through me. It was as if someone had taken a bottle of warm oil and poured it over me. It started from the very crown of my head and flowed over me until my entire body was bathed in its warmth. It was the same comfort I felt on Silver DZ in California, when the Lord reached down and took me up in His arms and heard my cry for mercy. As He cradled me in His arms I heard in my head someone say in an almost audible voice, "You can't serve two masters."

Top Franco, my old Chief of Firing Battery and First Sergeant of Bravo Battery, was by now the First Sergeant of HSB (Headquarters and Service Battery). He seemed empathetic. He didn't like the way I had been done by the S-3 and told me so.

"Those people couldn't wait to put a knife in your back. Right's right and wrong's wrong. Let's see what we can do to get that flab off you."

I was allowed to run PT on my own in the mornings. I would run farther and actually exercise better. After all, I had been a martial arts instructor and coach for years, I knew how to train and get weight off. I just had to make it work for me. After running, I would go over to Towle Courts and lift weights and sit in the sauna for a while before showering and going to work. If I couldn't get my weight off, perhaps I could increase muscle content to bring down my body fat percentage.

A few weeks later, I was sent over to Womack Army Hospital for the doctor's evaluation of my case. On the hospital scales I was still one pound overweight. I had weighed in on our unit scales before going over to the hospital. On them, I had been two pounds below weight. I was hanged by the different calibration of the scales. "All things work to together for the good of those who love the Lord..." I kept repeating to myself.

As it turned out, the doctor in charge of the clinic refused to sign off on my paperwork. It was his contention I had not been treated fairly according to AR 600-9 and, until my unit followed *AR* (Army Regulation) 600-9 instead of *Division* (82nd Airborne Division) Regulation 600-9, to the letter, he would not approve my discharge.[160] I was temporarily saved! Praise the Lord!

The BC appeared visibly upset that I wasn't going to slide down the chute easily. He put me on the lifestyle program again. If the doctor said I'd have to have at least six months of dietary counseling to satisfy the Army regulation he'd give me six months on the program and move from there. I discovered it was his plan to leave me on the program whether I met my goal weight or not. This, I later learned was a violation of regulations in effect at the time, both the AR and the Division regulation. I would keep this as an "ace in the hole."

The weight control program was (and still is) touted as the Army's attempt to have a "leaner, fit to fight Army." However, fitness seems to have very little to do with the weight control program. Though I had problems with some of the speed runs we did in the Division, I had time, and time again, passed PT tests and physicals with flying colors. I even met Division standards for running four miles in under thirty-two minutes.

I am not talking about obesity. Obesity is not necessarily a matter of appearance, but rather how much one's weight interferes

---

[160] As in civilian government, where there are federal, State, and local laws and ordinances, in the military there are different levels of regulations. The Army might issue a regulation such as AR (Army Regulation) 600-9, dealing with weight control. At a more local level, say at Corps level, there might be an XVIII Airborne Corps supplement to that regulation, then, on down further, at the Division level, there would be a Division Regulation. This is what happened with AR 600-9. There was the AR 600-9, which outlined an Army wide policy for weight control. It was supplemented in the 82nd Airborne with Division Regulation 600-9, which went a little further and was a bit stricter than the Army regulation (which was typical of the 82nd). The doctors at Womack, who appeared to be no fans of the weight control program in the first place, were upset that the Division was throwing good men out of the service with their own program and refused to cooperate with it.

with one's activity. Ironically, the Army's own *Quartermaster Journal* mentioned in an article on the Falklands War that the British discovered during the campaign that soldiers who were slightly overweight fared better than their leaner buddies in the campaign. The Brits suffered from supply problems during the battle and many of the paratroopers didn't get rations for days. The heavier troopers had more reserve energy upon which to draw and actually functioned better, having better endurance.

But ours was not to reason why. I endured a month of the 82nd's Lifestyle program.

Those of us on the program had our weekends taken. We had to go in every Saturday morning for a weekly weigh-in to "determine our progress." On Sunday afternoons we had to report to a designated classroom for our weekly diet class. Our Separate Rations, the allowance married soldiers and others authorized to live off post get for not eating in the mess hall, were pulled. We were to eat in a special mess hall that prepared special low fat meals. Though designed and touted as an aid to assist soldiers in learning how to eat leaner and healthier, in actual practice it also served as harassment to motivate folks to lose weight. It was an added trial to guys trying to save their careers.

I was amazed when I reported into the first Lifestyle weigh-in and saw the men (occasionally there was a woman) the Army considered fat. Most of these guys were heavy, but muscular. However, they didn't pass their pinch test and stood to lose the years they had invested in the Army. There were some young guys; they were usually built like professional wrestlers. Most of the men, though, had at least ten to fifteen years in the Army. The women I saw in the program may have been big, but usually, they were well proportioned. Did the Army not take into account the physiological differences between men and women?[161]

I was put to work over at S-4 (Battalion level supply and logistics section) as Support Platoon Sergeant. This was actually a promotion of sorts. It was a position for a Sergeant First Class (E-7), one rank higher than the one I held. If my career survived the Lifestyle Program it would at least look good on my record if I did a good job there. Top was trying to help me.

[161]I recently had a female student who wanted to enlist in the Army. She was one of the best female athletes we'd ever had at our high school, playing basketball, softball, volley ball, and running track. Again, she was a full figured girl, with little extra fat on her. She was told she'd have to lose weight to enlist. The Army lost a good one on this case, she was working on losing weight when a local junior college offered her an athletic scholarship.

In the meantime I had a job to do. The Army was trying to work the kinks out of TUFMIS (Tactical Unit Financial Management Information System), a new computerized system to help control the purchase and accountability of spare parts for vehicle maintenance. It would eventually help control costs and cut waste. Many units were being overcharged for spare parts they had neither ordered nor received. 1LT Stewart, my new boss, the Assistant S-4 (AS-4), told me they were working to fix the program. Until then, we were being overcharged.[162]

The battalion was in a bind. Actually most of the units in all branches were in a bind. In the mid 80s, we went through a series of budget cuts, which were attributed to the Gramm-Rudmann-Hollings Act. [163]

We all knew we were going to get a hosing in Fiscal Year 1986. I remember being in S-3 trying to plan for training back at the beginning of the period, not knowing how much money we would have to spend on ammunition and gasoline. We didn't have a budget because Division HQs hadn't gotten their budget from Corps, who hadn't gotten *their* budget from FORSCOM,[164] who hadn't gotten *their* budget from Department of the Army, because Department of the Army hadn't gotten their budget from Congress, because Congress was wrestling with President Reagan over how to spend the money they had to spend with Gramm-Rudman-Hollings looming over their head forbidding them to spend more than they took in.

So, while we waited for Congress to stop wrestling with the President, Division Headquarters told us to go ahead and plan as though we were being given ammunition and gasoline and parts at FY84 levels.

So we did. After all, the new Fiscal Year was upon us and we had to train. Then, in March or April, almost halfway into the year, we discovered our annual budget had been cut by almost half. We had almost completely exhausted our training ammunition. We looked at the ammunition we had left for the year and figured we had

---

[162] The problem was the computer was charging each purchase by unit rather than by actual amount of a part used. For instance, if a unit needed a bolt and the bolt came in dozens they were charged the cost of a dozen bolts instead of the one they actually received and used. That kind of thing adds up after awhile. Particularly with more expensive parts.

[163] The Gramm-Rudmann-Hollings Act was an attempt to balance the budget by forbidding deficit spending. Whenever the government was exceeding the amount of money taken in, government programs had to stop spending money. The consequences of this act could be quite severe.

[164] FORSCOM- FORceS COMmand- the major controlling unit of all operational tactical units in the U.S. Army in the Continental United States.

just enough left to do the minimum requirements, such as evaluations (ARTEPS, etc.). We didn't even have ammo to practice.

The year before, FY84, I guess it was, we ran short on ammo after coming back from Grenada trying to do all our required training in the winter and spring of 1984.[165] We finished up our ARTEP and then got hit with a Division Artillery Readiness Test, or DART (it used to be called the Field Artillery Readiness Test but someone didn't like the acronym that formed). By the time it came to the test all we had left for ammo to shoot it was leftover rounds from previous trips. There were all sorts of mixed lots – using mixed lots of ammo has an adverse effect on the accuracy of the rounds. When we came in from the field from that we sat in garrison for at least eight months letting our skills rust. To the best of my knowledge there simply was no more money to train with. That was two years before – now we had even less ammunition.

Our maintenance section was in worse shape. When I reported into S-4, 1LT Stewart told me we were out of money for spare parts for our vehicles. This meant if any of our vehicles broke down, they'd have to stay broke down until October, when we'd get more money. This was unthinkable in a unit with a mission such as the 82nd's. It was 1981 all over again.

My primary job was to pore over the records and find where we'd been overcharged for parts. Any money I could recover would be all our maintenance shop would have to operate on until October. I had to learn the system and how to read the codes for the printouts. It was a tedious task, but I could see the importance of it.

After I'd finish PT in the mornings and did my chores as platoon sergeant, I went down to the Battalion Motor Pool. I'd spend hours each day pouring over the last several months' parts requests and vouchers. I'd compare them with the computer printouts and receipts. In two or three weeks I was able to find well over eighty thousand dollars that had been erroneously charged to our battalion's account.

According to 1LT Stewart, I had found enough money to keep our battalion rolling for the rest of the fiscal year. I felt pretty good about that. One day I was walking through the battalion area when the Battalion XO, Major Reasoner, stopped me. He told me what a great job I was doing and to keep it up. I thanked him for the good word and was about to move on when he spoke again.

"I'll tell you, I was really sweating it out how we were going

---

[165] I couldn't tell you if it was due to budge contraints, the ammo we'd sent to Grenada and couldn't bring back, or both.

to keep rolling for another four months," his face fell in sadness, "You deserve an ARCOM for the job you're doing..."

"Thank you, Sir." I said. We both knew I'd never get the medal. Soldiers on the fat man program aren't allowed to get medals. Or promotions. Or any favorable actions. I couldn't even get a "thank you" note or an "Atta boy!" from my battalion commander. This was supposed to be an incentive for fat soldiers to lose weight.

Chapter 26
A New Job and an Unexpected Trip

Look to my left and what do I see?
A nasty old leg looking straight at me
He can't make it no sirreee!
He can't be Airborne like me!

Two kind of people I can't stand
It's a bowl-legged woman and a straight-legged man!
If I were the President and had my way
There wouldn't be a leg in the Army today!
(Anonymous UnPC Airborne Running Cadence)

In June I was told I was going up to XVIII Airborne Corps Headquarters on a Special Duty Assignment. At first I was relieved. Our battalion had ROTC Support again. I'd started out as one of three Staff Sergeants (E-6s) on rotation as Sergeant of the Guard for our field sites on OP (Observation Post) 5 at MacRidge Impact Area, working 24 on and 48 off. That didn't last long and soon I was one of three chosen E-6s pulling the duty while the rest of the battalion jumped through hoops supporting ROTC.

It could have been worse; I reflected philosophically, I could have been made NCOIC of Toilet Paper in the latrine.

I do have an amusing story to tell from this period, though. One afternoon I had just assumed my duty on the desk guarding the front entrance of the battalion headquarters. The SDNCO desk was facing the front doorway to battalion headquarters, one could look out and see Ardennes Street and, across it Towle Courts and Stadium and to the right the Old Division Chapel. To the left of the front entrance was the Battalion Commander, LTC Reynold's office. When his door was open I could look through it and see his desk, facing out to the foyer.

I guess I'd been there an hour or so, it was getting on to about 1800 hours (6 pm). The colonel had been doing paperwork behind his desk. I remember him deliberately finishing his last report or whatever, taking a deep breath, and looking up from his work at me.

"Well, Woody," he said to me. He had been S-3 when I came back from Gallant Eagle 82. "'Guess I'll take a stroll…"

He rose from his desk and walked down the hall, checking out the junior officers slaving away at their desks into the late afternoon and early evening.

He returned to the front of the building, went into his office, and grabbed his beret. He paused at the door to put it on, "Woody, I'm going home; you can tell them it's safe to leave now."

With that, he was gone.

I gave him a moment to pull out of his parking spot. I think I saw his little red sports car at the corner of Carentan and Ardennes before I stuck my head down the hall and hollered, "The Colonel's gone!"

It was an Exodus. Within a few minutes I and my runner were alone in the building.

In taking over this job I was replacing a friend of mine, another Staff Sergeant, from the battery who had been working there a couple of months. He had been a chief at Bravo, gone to HSB, and run afoul of the Army's weight control program and was being discharged from the Army. The unit had put him in this assignment while waiting for his papers to come through. They were pulling him back to the battery to clear post. As I recall, he was an older guy who'd had a break in service. I think he had a few years to his retirement when he was given the boot. I was to replace him. I figured they'd keep me on hold until my paperwork was ready and then they'd pull me back, too.

Of course, the doctor had stopped my discharge action. My hope was I could get down below my goal weight and stay there; maybe they'd leave me alone long enough so I could finish my hitch and leave with honor. I felt I had the "go" sign in this battle from the trouble my chain of command was having throwing me out.

In the meantime, I was still on the Division weight control program and required to play their games on the weekends. I got a release from eating at their mess hall, as I was now working across post and my meal hours were irregular. It would be too much of an inconvenience for me to go across post to eat. My separate rations[166] weren't reinstated, however.

Perhaps this new assignment, away from the Division, was the closest thing I could get to a new start. At least it would be a change of environment.

---

[166] "Separate Rations" is the money the Army pays certain personnel for not eating in the mess hall – excuse me- dining facility. The Army promises its troops "three hots and a cot." When a soldier marries or is authorized to live off post he/she is reimbursed for their meals.

To my dismay, upon reporting to my new workplace I discovered the guy I was replacing was under orders to go TDY[167] for forty-five days. I only had three days before I would be on a freight train bound west for Twenty-nine Palms, California. I was to be the Sergeant of the railway guard for XVIII Airborne Corps' vehicles. We were to participate in Joint Training Exercise Gallant Eagle 86. Talk about weird, this was where it all began some four years before. At least I wasn't going to have to jump in.

I didn't have much time to prepare for the trip. I received only the most cursory briefing as to my duties. I really didn't want to go. This was a complete disruption of the new life I was building for myself in my church. My previous schedule had given me plenty of time to go visiting with Pastor Billy. I didn't realize it at the time but Billy was discipling me in the ministry.

Billy had hit me with a zinger during our revival in April. It was one night after a service; we were sitting in his car talking. We'd often do that, talking about different things, usually pertaining to the Bible. I don't know how many times Billy got in trouble with his wife for coming home late because he'd get tied up talking Bible or discussing the direction of the church with me. I had done some special singing and testifying that night. I had really cut loose. We were basking in the afterglow of a good service. Out of the blue, Billy said to me, "Woody, have you ever felt the call to preach?"

I told Billy how I had felt the call in high school. I told him since I had come back to the church and gotten involved in the work the call kept coming back stronger and stronger. I told him about how the only time I really felt alive was when I was up teaching the Bible in Sunday school or to the youth, when I was singing about Jesus, or testifying for Him, or witnessing.

"Yep," he said, "that's the call."

"But, I figure I've blown that, brother. After all, I don't reckon I'm ever going to get my marriage back together. Even if I do, Deb's been divorced before. Either way, I guess I've missed it."

"Not necessarily," he said, "the gifts and callings of God are without repentance. God called you once. You ran but you're still called. All God's been waiting on is for you to get yourself straightened out so He can use you."

"But my divorce..."

"That may not be such a problem. I know of several men in the denomination who got divorced years ago, before they got their lives straight. The Bible says if any man be in Christ he is a new

---

[167] **TDY** – Temporary Duty Assignment

creation, the old man is passed away. The fellows on the Ordination Committee will look at the circumstances surrounding your divorce. I don't think they'll hold it against you any more than God does. Remember, the Blood of Jesus washes away all sins. And sometimes, Woody, divorced people aren't so much the sinners as the sinned against...

"I'd better go now, it's getting late. You just think about it for now, we'll take it slow."

Since that night I had been getting more and more involved in the work of the church. I realized Billy was building up my accountability with the people of the church, whose recommendation I would need to appear before the Ordination Committee.

This excursion to California would keep me away from home almost two months. It would be the longest I had been away from my church family. It would truly test my newfound walk with Jesus.

I reported to the railhead on the evening of departure and got my first look at my guard force. I found out I would actually be the ranking man of two guard forces which would make most of the trip west on the same train. We would split up at a place called Bagdad, California which was about seventy miles from the Marine Base at Twenty-Nine Palms, my crew's destination; the other crew, headed by a Sergeant (E-5), would travel on to Yermo Marine Corps Depot.

I was at a loss to explain much of our mission to my troops. They actually knew more about it than I. I had missed all the briefings concerning our part of the mission. I wasn't too worried about it though; most of it seemed to be common military sense. Our job was to safeguard the equipment until the main body of the Corps element would arrive. All I had to do was follow my three general orders.[168]

The trip out there was fairly uneventful. I had a great opportunity to do some reading, as there was nothing much else to do while we were moving. I had gone to the Christian bookstore and spent some of my TDY pay on a stack of Christian books covering a gamut of different subjects. Plus, I brought along a couple old favorites such as C. S. Lewis' *Mere Christianity*. I realized they would mean more to me now than they did the first time I had read them years before.

---

[168] The three general orders in effect when I was in (Condensed from ten) 1) I will guard everything within the limits of my post and quit my post only when properly relieved. 2) I will obey all special orders and perform all my duties in a military manner. 3) I will report any violation of my special orders, emergencies, or anything not covered in my special orders to the commander of the relief. Basic soldiering.

But it turned out the trip offered many opportunities to exercise my spiritual muscles than had I stayed at home. On the train, the troops saw me reading my Bible, or other Christian books. It didn't take long for some of them to come to me and ask me questions. The guys asked me to have a worship service and devotion on the train on Sunday, our last full day on the train together. A couple of the troopers were Catholic and they wanted to have Communion.

I didn't have a Communion set with me, of course, but I'd just have to make do with what I had. I got one of the railroad men to get us a bottle of grape juice for the wine and used C-ration crackers for the bread. I figured God would understand.

We had a nice service that morning. I took the scripture passages from the Last Supper for my text and explained the meaning of Communion and the importance of being right with Christ before taking Communion (I Cor: 11).

After the service was over, one of the soldiers came over to me, "I really enjoyed that, Sergeant Wood. You know, I've never had the Communion explained to me like that."

That made me feel good. But, at the same time I felt sad, this young man had taken Communion at his church every week practically all his life, but he had never known what he was doing. What good had it done him? At the same time, I wondered how many others like him were out there.

Now, the Army had (and still has) strict regulations concerning how a superior deals with his/her subordinates in areas of faith and politics. As an NCO I had to be careful not to be coercive or even be perceived as coercive when I shared my faith – that was a tough line to walk for someone as enthusiastic as I was. But if the troops asked me about my faith and what I believed I could answer them honestly. This is what I tried to do.

We had one guy on the train who had been detailed as a punishment. He was a good worker but he had a drinking problem. Both of us NCOs had to keep an eye on him because he kept having liquor smuggled aboard the train by the railroad workers. I might have looked the other way if he had been able to handle it, but the guy got crazy when he got drunk.

We were in two cabooses at the end of the train, both were close enough together that we could cross between them at will. This was frowned upon by the railroad personnel as being unsafe at speeds of sixty to seventy miles per hour. The cars often would bunch up and spread apart along their coupling. Step at the wrong time when the cars were bunching and one could get his foot crushed. So our timing had to be exact, but it was necessary for us to communicate between the troops and to keep an eye on them. After all, there wasn't enough room in one caboose for seven troops. I remember one of the train conductors warning us about how dangerous it was for us to jump between cars on a moving train.

I looked at him with a grin, "Chief," I said. "You're talking to a bunch of guys who jump out of airplanes for a living!" He just shook his head.

One night, Sergeant Reese, my second in command, and I were sitting in the observation seats of the rear caboose with the conductor when we saw our problem child lean out the window of the observation compartment of the front caboose and hang by one arm like a monkey. We were moving at close to seventy miles per hour, it would have been funny if it hadn't been so dangerous.

"He shouldn't do that, boys," the conductor said so drily it was funny. "He might get hurt." By this time the guy had changed position and was hanging out the window by his knees.

I looked over at Sergeant Reese. Like we needed him to tell us that? We scampered down the little ladder and jumped the gap between the two rail cars and managed to get the guy inside. Then, we searched his gear for the contraband,

I scolded him for lying to me. Earlier, I had caught him with some beer he had gotten some of the rail personnel to smuggle on board, "Didn't I tell you I didn't want you smuggling any more beer on board the train? And you promised me, didn't you?"

"Yes, Sergeant Wood, I promised." he said apologetically, "But I didn't break my promise."

Digging through his gear I discovered the guy hadn't lied to me. He hadn't smuggled beer aboard. This time it was whiskey. I was reminded of Sheriff Andy confronting Ernest T about throwing rocks, "I ain't going to throw no more rocks, Sheriff," Ernest T promises earnestly. Then, as Andy walks off, he reaches in his bag and mutters, "This time I've got a brick!"

There wasn't much I could do about it now, in the middle of the country, away from any contact with the rest of the Army. He was going with SGT Reese to Yermo. Reese would have to deal with it when the rest of the unit arrived.

We had another guy who was having severe problems with claustrophobia. He paced his caboose all day playing the same tune on his harmonica. Finally, I had to confiscate his harmonica. He was driving the other troops crazy.

We were told it would take us fifteen days to get out to California. We got there in five. In one way, that was a good thing, I don't know if my two problem children could have survived the confinement any longer.

At the same time, it was a major hassle. We had arrived at a place called Bagdad, California ten days early with no one from Corps there to meet us. Bagdad was seventy miles from Twenty-nine Palms, in the middle of the Mojave Desert. All there was to Bagdad were five rail sidings where freight could be loaded or unloaded. A single forlorn palm tree rose from the ground between the railroad tracks. There were no leaves on the thing. I was later told there had once been two palm trees at Bagdad once. The other died. We discussed this and concluded it died of boredom.

There was a detachment of personnel from Ft. Bragg's 1st COSCOM (1st Corps Support Command) at the railhead. They were encamped in two medium sized general-purpose tents (known as GP mediums). Each was capable of comfortably housing between fifteen and twenty troops. I reported to the NCOIC (Non Commissioned Officer in Charge) and was officially relieved of my responsibility for the equipment.

"We'll take it from here." he said.

"What do my men and I do now?" I asked, looking warily at the surrounding countryside

"I guess you just wait till your unit shows up."

Great. The nearest town was some twenty miles down the road. It had a restaurant, motel, and a population of twenty. I commandeered one of the jeeps and drove into the town to call Ft. Bragg. Unfortunately, I couldn't get through on the pay phone outside the restaurant and everything in town was closed up tighter than a drum. That town gave me the creeps. It wasn't anything you could put your finger on; it was the feel of the place. The motel and restaurant reminded me of the Bate's Motel from the movie *Psycho* without the house in back.

The one living soul we saw in the town, an elderly female who lived at the motel told us of a store about twenty more miles down the road where we could get some food and maybe make a call. Water would cost us two dollars a gallon.

My unease was intensified by a large hill just outside of town. On the crest of the hill were four crosses. The ground around the crosses was scorched. Like I said - weird.

Later on I did some research on the area and discovered the

"hill" was an extinct volcano.

By the time we got to the store and I could make my call it was too late to talk to anyone who knew anything, they had all gone home for the day. After all, there was a three-hour time difference between California and the East Coast. So the next day my two troops and I loaded up in our jeep and, having received directions and a map from the NCOIC of the transportation detachment, made the seventy plus mile trip into Twenty-nine Palms.

I must say I was impressed by the facilities there. I found a headquarters unit that let me use their AUTOVON (military long distance line), and I was able to talk to my point of contact at Bragg. I told him the situation and that things were pretty rough. He told me to hang in there as best I could.

So we went back out to Bagdad. On our first day there, the NCOIC had told me my troops and I could sleep in one of their tents if we could find the room. After a look into the sleeping tent, I discovered the folks already there were cramped. I talked one of the railroad guys into letting us keep our caboose for a few more days.

We had it fairly good for a few days. Then the power in the battery went down. The electricity on the old cabooses was generated by the rolling of the wheels. Well, we could live with that, but we began to run short of food, there had been miscounting in distributing MREs when the two guard contingents separated. Again, the transportation folks offered to help us as best as they could. They were living off MREs, but often their unit was slow in getting out and resupplying them. They let us use their water as well, but again, they had to be careful with their supply. The final straw was when we got word the railroad was about to take their caboose back.

This would leave us without any shelter. I had not been briefed to come prepared for a tactical field environment. Our role in the exercise would be administrative; we were to act as the umpires for the field units. Besides, I had accomplished my mission of escorting the vehicles to California. I had been relieved of my responsibility. My first concern now was to take care of the men under my charge.

On our fifth day in California we loaded all our gear on our jeep and headed into Twenty-nine Palms. I told the transportation people where I was in case anyone from Corps happened to try and get hold of me.

I also called back to Bragg and told them where I could be reached. We spent the rest of our time in relative ease. I got a room at the BEQs (Bachelor Enlisted persons Quarters) Guest House on post. I regretted I hadn't done this earlier.

While we were at the base, my men got acquainted with some of marines at the enlisted men's club. They heard about the town we had visited.

"Hey Sergeant Wood, guess what?" they hollered as they busted into the room one night, "That town we were at? It's full of devil worshippers!"

"No wonder it was so weird!" said one,

"Yeah, one of the jarheads (slang for marines) at the club said a buddy of his and his girlfriend were driving out there one Saturday night and caught about twenty people out there in the middle of the desert dancing naked around a big bonfire!"

"You want to have a hamburger in that cafe now?" the other guy asked, "No telling what they put in the meat!"

When the day finally came for us to meet up with the troops coning as advance party for the Corps element we passed the town again, "Hey, Sergeant Wood, you want to get a hamburger?"

I realized they were playfully challenging me. We had some time before we were to meet the unit at Bagdad, "Sure, why not? Greater is He that is in me than He that is in this world."

So on the way back out to the railhead we stopped and had a pretty tasty hamburger at the café. My guys freaked when I took my Bible in with me.

Now, I can't say for sure whether these folks were all devil worshippers or not but it was deathly quiet in that café. Whether it was the Bible or us being paratroopers who knows?

We finished our meal. I left a tip on the table and went to the cashier to pay my bill. I made sure I was last out. As I paid for my lunch, I complimented the waitress on the meal. Then, before leaving, I said, "Ya'll have a nice day, and God bless ya!"

I discovered on my return to Bagdad the Corps Special Troops Battalion Commander wanted to speak to me. The COSCOM element had used several of the vehicles left in their care and wrecked several of them "four-wheeling" in the desert.

I was required to submit a statement of my part in the mess. It looked for a while as if the folks at XVIII Corps Special Troops Battalion were going to try and hang this one on me, even though I had been relieved of my responsibility for the vehicles. I was grilled several times by the Headquarters, Special Troops Battalion Commander.

Finally, I looked the colonel in the eye and said, "Look, sir, we've been through this several times. I've put it all in my report. I stayed with the equipment as long as I could, but here I was with two troops out in the desert and no support whatsoever. Finally, I said to myself, 'What on earth am I doing here? I've been relieved.'

"I believe I did what any other NCO or officer in my situation would have done, having accomplished my mission, I took care of my troops. Do I need to see a lawyer?"

"A lawyer?" he asked me, a bit surprised.

"Yes, sir. If ya'll are going to try and hang this one on me I want to see a lawyer."

"No, Sergeant Wood, it looks like you're in the clear," he said, dropping his eyes to the floor, "We-uh- just wanted to get the facts straight. It looks like they'll hang the guys from COSCOM."

"Thank you, sir, that's all I wanted to know."

That was over, praise the Lord! But I still had to live with the guys on the advance party.

Everything started out okay at first. There were about fifteen of us, mostly NCOs, with a job to do. The operation would be controlled from our location. We had to set up the Administrative Tactical Operations Center (Admin TOC) for the operation. All the umpires would be quartered with us and report to our headquarters. Over two hundred personnel would be coming to our location in a week. We had to set up their living tents, the actual headquarters tent and other tents, which would be used, by the control cell during the operation.

As I said, we all got along well at first. Then, after a few days, the NCOIC, Sergeant First Class Foster began taking a dislike to me. It was a personal thing. It seemed like he'd get great pleasure out of getting me in front of the men and saying something to humiliate me. I really didn't know how to react at first, I was still fairly new in the Lord and had quite a few rough edges left (I still do, really), and my first inclination was to drop kick him right up side the head.

But I couldn't do that, even if I weren't a Christian. He was my superior and it would cost me my career, which was already on the skids due to my weight. And I would remember that night in Germany when I had almost gone a step too far and promised I would never again hit someone in anger. And then, of course, there was Jesus. Everyone around knew I was a Christian and had their eyes on me. This was the first time since I began seriously living for Christ that I was completely alone without any other Christians to lean on for support. I thought I had felt alone before, when Debbie and I separated. This was loneliness of a deeper kind, spiritual loneliness.

I would go out into the desert at night and pray before going to bed. Sitting out there in the dark, away from the camp and all human contact, with the night desert sky seeming so close you'd think you could reach out and touch a star, I felt closer to God than I remembered in a while. I can now understand why Jesus would withdraw to the wilderness at night to pray and be refreshed.

Another practice that became a blessing to me was to climb one of the hills which surrounded our encampment at sunset. There, I would watch the sun sink below the mountains in the distance and pray. During these prayer periods Psalms 46:10 would become real to me. If it hadn't been for these prayer periods, I don't know that I wouldn't have gone off on SFC Foster.

This is not to say I didn't make some friends out there. There was Lieutenant Butler, who took a liking to me. It seemed he enjoyed the company of NCOs more than his fellow officers. And there was SSG Smith, Smitty. Smitty was from the XVIII Field Artillery Brigade, my old unit. We hit it off. It was Smitty who told me what SFC Foster's problem with me was.

"You know, Woody," he said one evening as we were walking back from chow, "Sergeant Foster hasn't liked you since he found out you were a Christian and going to be a preacher."

I had suspected something like that, but it can become a copout to say everyone who dislikes you is merely reacting to the fact you're a Christian. It can be a great excuse for obnoxious personalities. We can hide behind our Christianity when we offend someone and say, "It's the Holy Spirit in me offending him." when actually we may have acted like a jerk.

But when Smitty said this, it all made sense. I had been wracking my brains trying to figure out what it was that had changed his attitude toward me. I first thought it might have had something to do with the vehicles getting messed up. He might have prejudged me as a dud. But after I was absolved of any responsibility in the matter (Lt. Butler, who had been assigned as the investigating officer made sure word got around that I was cleared) it seemed as if his attitude had gotten worse. Of course, there was always the possibility that the findings of the investigation might have had nothing to do with Foster's opinion of my responsibility in the matter.

I remember one Sunday while the investigation was ongoing Lt. Butler, SFC Foster, and I were detailed to go back out to Bagdad.

We had to get statements from some of the personnel out there. We were also supposed to talk to the detachment's company commander, who was to meet us out there. All the way out there, SFC Foster harped about my driving. Lt. Butler thought it was all funny. My patience was wearing thin with Foster. It seemed as if I could do nothing right in his book. I finally stopped the vehicle and told him if he didn't like my driving he could drive. He did. Lt. Butler began needling him about his driving. It was all I could do to keep from laughing out loud, though I would grin appreciatively when Lt. Butler would glance back at me occasionally.

It made matters worse that I was missing church to come out here. We had gotten word one of the chaplains was coming down to hold church services at our location. This was my first chance to go to church in almost a month and I was going to have to miss it to come out to Bagdad and spend the day with a guy who hated my guts.

When we got out to Bagdad the CO hadn't arrived yet. So we sat in their operations tent and waited. I had brought my Bible along, much to SFC Foster's annoyance, and began to read.

A young PFC came up and began asking me about what I was reading. I was in the gospel of Luke by this time. He began asking me questions about salvation and Jesus. As I answered his questions, other soldiers began to gather and pretty soon we had a Bible study going with almost twenty young soldiers gathered round.

Finally, it came time to leave. We had been out there for over an hour and the captain hadn't shown up yet. We had work to do back at Twenty-nine Palms. As we got into our jeep to go, a female soldier came up to me, "You know, Sergeant, they told us the chaplain was going to come out here and have church. He didn't make it; some of us were real disappointed about that. But God sent you. Thank you."

"No, thank God." I said, trying to keep my eyes dry. I apologized to God for being so selfish. I thanked Him for showing me a valuable lesson about what the Church actually is.

"Hey hey, Chaplain Woody!" Lt. Butler said as we drove off. Somehow, I didn't mind SFC Foster's bad temper so much.

Things got better once the main body arrived. I moved into a tent away from Foster and his buddies with some of the guys from HHC. HHC's XO was my point of contact while I was on the train. I was assigned to the Assistant G-3 for Exercises, Colonel Ramirez during the operation. I did what he and his NCO, MSG Faulkner, told me to do. I was basically relegated to the status of being a gofer.

It wasn't a bad job, overall. It was better than being under the gun with Foster.

In the years I'd been in the Army I had served in varied positions at different levels of command. I believe I had seen military leadership at its best and at its worst. Working for Colonel Ramirez I saw leadership at its best. There were times during the exercise when emergencies would crop up and the lower ranking officers would be in a panic. Col. Ramirez would enter the TOC, be informed of the situation, ask a few pointed questions, and then make a decision, which solved the problem. Never did the smile leave his face. More than once he reminded us of the importance of our mission to the exercise, "We're the folks who make it happen. If we don't do it, it won't get done."

I turned thirty out there in the desert. It was our last day at Twenty-nine Palms, Gallant Eagle 86 was over, and we were tearing down the camp. I had planned to spend my birthday at the beach that year. How nice of the Army, I reflected wryly, to send me on an all-expense paid trip to almost fifty thousand square miles of beach. I was just having trouble finding the surf.

That evening, after all the work was done, I climbed my hill to pray and say goodbye to the desert sunset. All we had to do was get up the next morning and drive to Edwards Air Force Base where we would link up with the Corps tactical element. There, I would round up my guard force. We were to board our train for North Carolina at Yermo Marine Corps Depot.

As I sat on the crest of my hill, watching the splendor of the sunset, once more I was swept by the Presence of God. It was somehow fitting that I spent this birthday where my journey started. It was time to go home.

We convoyed up to March Air Force Base (kind of poetic, wish I'd visited the hospital to see if anyone was still there from my visit) where the "tactical" element of the Corps Control Element had been based. I found it ironic, the tactical element had been camped on the main base within walking distance of the Main PX, theater and other amenities, while my section, the "Evaluator" or "Admin" element had been quartered in field conditions, having to be bussed to a field shower facility down the road from our camp. By the time we got back to camp from our shower we were often dirtier than when we left from the dust on the road. It was good to see my Assistant NCOIC, SGT Reese again after almost a month. But I learned our problem child was still with us.

From March AFB my men and I found ourselves dumped at Yermo Marine Depot to await the departure of our train. We were there three days. The rail movement detachment folks from COSCOM were helpful, and I was thankful, if it hadn't been for them, we wouldn't have had water. They allowed us to use the showers at their barracks facilities, and even offered us a place to sleep. Our orders were to stay with our equipment though, so we slept in the vehicles at night. During the day we used huge cardboard packing boxes to shield us from the glaring desert sun until we finally got a train.

The entire post was closed at night and we found ourselves locked in the deserted depot. Of course, we found ways to get in and out of the fence. Sergeant Reese and I found a little cafe across the street from the depot where we could get a hot meal.

Once we were on the road, things went little better. The equipment kept coming loose and my troops and I had to get out and tighten the tie-downs and the trucks and equipment, using tools borrowed from the railroad. It was hot, dirty work. I'd try to get the railroad personnel to hold the train long enough to let my men clean up. I often met resistance from the dispatchers, who were concerned about their schedules. I often had to argue and threaten to get them to stop the train long enough to tighten the tie-downs. I didn't understand it; the guys had cooperated with us on the way out. You would have thought the managers or whatever you called the guys who ran the schedules and rail yards would have cooperated. After all, it was their company that would be held liable for any equipment damaged on the trip back.

I almost got in a fist fight with a yard master in Nashville over his refusal to swap out cabooses when the toilets in our cabooses broke down. Boy was my walk being tested that trip. The toilets overflowed and we had feces washed on the floor of the car where my troops had to live. The guy and his buddies thought it was funny and told me he thought we soldier boys were supposed to be tough. I hadn't felt so much anger in years. But the train was pulling out and I was older and wiser and hopefully could recognize a stacked deck when I saw one. I had to swallow my pride and run to catch the train as it took off from the yard.

I took notes and names and determined to write an after-action report to keep this sort of travesty from happening again.

Chapter 27
My Last Jump

Colonel, colonel, have you heard?
I'm gonna jump from a big iron bird.
Colonel, Colonel, don't you cry
I've got a main that opens wide
If that main don't open wide
I've got a reserve by my side
If that chute should fail me, too
Look out below I'm coming through!
(Anonymous Airborne Running Cadence)

It took us less than five days to get out to California, over two weeks getting back. No one was happier to see North Carolina. That is, until I reported back to my unit to discover what had happened while I was gone. I had come down on orders for recruiting duty. This was an honor, though a dubious one. Recruiting duty has been known to wreck many a promising career.[169] On the other hand, the Army only chose its best as recruiters (and drill sergeants), as recruiters represented the Army on the street. If I did well as a recruiter it might have been a fast track to early promotion.

I didn't have to worry about it, though. My unit had flagged, or killed my orders for recruiter duty. I was on the Lifestyle Program and was therefore ineligible for any favorable personnel action, including a transfer. I spoke with my BC about this, and he told me he was keeping me on the program until October, six full months. If I made my goal weight by then, he would consider taking me off the program.

By then the fact I had been flagged from recruiter duty because I was a "fatman" and not allowed to attend the school would have been noted in my personnel file. Say what you will, this would be a "rock in my rucksack," an unfavorable action which would slow my advancement throughout my career, no matter what I did, from

---

[169] Recruiters are under constant pressure to meet their quota of enlistments each quarter (three months). I've knew one recruiter who received honors as recruiter of the quarter for exceeding her quota and even setting records for her district. She still received a letter of reprimand because she missed her quota one time in over three years of recruiting. If a recruiter misses too many quotas, it can ruin a career.

here on out. For the first time, my weight problem had caused permanent, perhaps irreparable, damage to my career.

This was in spite of the fact I had met my goal weight for body fat content during most of my time on the program. I was even several pounds below my goal weight right before leaving for California, though it killed me to get there.

I said most of the time. I had gained about ten pounds back during my trip to California. Even though I had tried to watch my diet and exercise as much as possible, I had been cooped up in a railroad caboose for over twenty days, and there was little chance to run while out in the field.

I put myself on an excruciating regimen to lose weight. I reduced my caloric content drastically. I stepped up my running program. It was becoming increasingly more painful to run due to Baker's cysts – a symptom of osteo-arthritis - which had developed on the backs of my knees.

I was referred to orthopedics. I got to see a physician's assistant. He had the worst attitude of any of the medical personnel I had ever seen. I later learned why. He had been passed over for promotion and was being forced out of service himself. His diagnosis was painfully blunt.

"You're fat, Sarge. Lose weight. It'll take the pressure off your knees and ease the pain."

Once back at Bragg I found I enjoyed my work at Corps. SFC Foster worked in another section of G-3, his office was across post and I seldom saw him. When I did see him, his attitude seemed to have changed from California. He was even friendly. It was as if nothing had happened. I decided not to hold a grudge. In the new path I was walking I wasn't allowed grudges anyway. Besides, the folks I worked with seemed to like me – as we used to say in the Army: "If you don't rate me and you don't pay me – get out of my face!"

For a period out in the desert, when I had been afraid I was going to be the scapegoat for the vehicles, I had definite concern about something adverse happening to my record, on top of the troubles I was having with the Division over my weight. However, the overall supervisor for Gallant Eagle 86, Colonel Ramirez, made sure I received an Army Achievement Medal for my performance. He told the audience (one of whom was SFC Foster)[170] gathered at

---

[170] Pardon me if I sound like I'm gloating. But God *does* take care of his children. As Jesus said, "Wisdom is justified of her children." This award may not sound like much to

the awards ceremony that he was particularly impressed with the fact I always had a smile on my face whenever he saw me.

It was then I realized what God had been doing for me personally out in the desert. Without my church family to lean on, I had to increasingly depend on my relationship with Him. Even with the troubles I encountered out there, my time alone with Him in the desert gave me a peace and a joy so that I could smile. I had found what Paul called that "peace that passeth all understanding." God was granting me favor with those over me. I thought of Joseph.

I wondered at how I could receive a medal being on the Lifestyle Program. I was told it had been arranged for the award to be given as an "impact," or immediate, on-the-spot award. There were special exceptions which allowed "fat boys" to be given impact awards. Thus I could be decorated. I thought of what Major Reasoner had said about all the operating money I'd found for my battalion. I wondered why my battalion didn't do that for me then.

I believed I knew the answer. My chain of command had put me on the lifestyle program. It might have been embarrassing to give me a medal.

I had to fight to keep the bitterness from creeping in.

As I got into the swing of things at my new job, I discovered the people I worked for were behind me all the way. I told them my situation and they didn't like the way I was being done. They hadn't liked the way my predecessor had been done, either. The Major, Lieutenant Colonel, and his NCOIC, SFC Lillard, told me they'd do anything they could to help me. Over the next months their support and the support of Pastor Billy would be a blessing.

One October morning I was wakened by a phone call at about 4:30 a.m. It was Top Franco. He told me to report into his office at 0630 in PT trunks. We were having a weigh-in. I had been expecting this; the Army had just again revised its weight control program. There were new, stricter standards to meet. On October 1, everyone was going to have to re-weigh and undergo a new type of body fat test.

I was almost looking forward to it. The BC had told me if I made weight I'd be taken off the program. My exercising and dieting program had paid off. I had managed to get down to size. I had another year and a half on my enlistment. I wanted to do my time in peace.

the reader, but to me, at that time it was a sort of vindication, it was a way of telling me I wasn't a total failure, in spite of what everyone around me had seemed to be saying.

I figured my only hope was to get off the Lifestyle Program and put in for a transfer. By this time my buddies at Corps told me they'd file a request for me to "move upstairs." If that failed I was prepared to put in a request for overseas transfer. As much as I hated to leave my church and jump status, I believed I needed a new start. If that meant leaving the 82nd and Ft. Bragg, well, so be it.

All I wanted out of the Army now was to be allowed to at least finish my enlistment. I loved the Army. I loved being a soldier, even though I didn't like all the things that went with it. I guess you could say being a soldier was a job I loved to hate. With my family gone, now all I hoped to do as to pay off my numerous bills and go to Bible College or into full-time ministry. I think now, as the years have passed, there was still a part of me that hoped God would let me stay in the Army somehow.

I knew I had more than one IG complaint over regulations that had been violated in the handling of my case. But I was waiting until the time was right to play that card.

I went into Top's office. When I stood on the scales, even in PT trunks, which were lighter than the full uniform in which we used to weigh in, I was still three pounds below the goal weight set by the earlier "pinch" test. Elated, I reported to the BC.

"Well, Sergeant Wood," he said. "As you probably know, the Army's got a new body fat test, the tape test. You're going to have to meet the new standards."

The new test, I discovered, consisted of taking a regular tape measure and measuring the width of one's neck at the Adam's apple, and comparing it to the width of one's waist at the navel. Somehow, through a mathematical formula, the guru's had figured out a way to calculate one's body fat from these measurements. It sounded like some sort of voodoo to me. Of course, I might have been a little biased.

Is it turned out that I was considered to have 2% too much body fat to meet the new standards. Therefore, the BC was going to have me separated (kicked out) from the Army for being overweight. As I had been on the weight control program for six months, he no longer had to go through the hospital, so the doctors couldn't interfere. My next stop would be the Separation Physicals Section at Womack Army Hospital.

My only hope now was to somehow meet the new standard before my physical. The problem here was that now my goal was no longer a matter of losing a few pounds, but of losing inches. And I had to lose the inches in the right places. Somehow, I had to lose two inches off my waist without losing any inches off my neck. How does one do that?

I had a picture of our soldiers in the gyms at night doing sit-ups and trunk twisters to shrink their waists and neck bridging exercises to build up their necks. I had this picture of bull necked, trim waisted soldiers hulking their way into combat. Then I remembered the "goons" on "Goon Island" from old "Popeye" cartoons. They weren't too smart, but they would have met the body fat standards.

I began doing all sorts of exercises to reduce my waistline and build up my neck. One night, while I was out running, my knees gave out on me. I went to take a step and it was as if a balloon in my knee had popped and I had nothing to stand on. I fell flat on my face in the middle of the street. I lay there in pain trying to get up. Finally, I was able to make it home on a knee that felt like a sponge.

I managed to get an emergency appointment at Ortho a few days later. The PA[171] I had seen before heard me out and said, "Well, Sarge, it's like I said, 'You're fat, you've got to lose weight.'" He gave me a prescription for Motrin and that was that.

The question now was how to lose weight when I couldn't run?

About two weeks later, I got a phone call from my First Sergeant. I was to meet SFC Molina at the Separation Physicals Branch of Womack Army Hospital. My stomach fell at the news.

I had known it was coming, of course. I had planned on taking my case to the IG, with all the documentation I had on how I had been kept on the program even though I had made weight. At the same time, I wondered if there was something in there because the standards had been changed at the last minute. Didn't I get some time to meet the new standards before they tossed me? If I got no satisfaction from the IG there was always a letter to my Congressman. But that took time. Time I didn't have. The way things were moving, by the time my Congressman got my letter I'd be out on my ear.

I had told myself again and again it was all in the hands of God and I would trust Him. Still, when the moment hits you, you can't help feeling the emotional impact of having your life shattered. I supposed the Christians in the Coliseum felt butterflies in their stomach when they stared the lions in the eye and saw the big cats grinning back at them, even though they were willing to die for the Lord.

---

[171]Physician's Assistant.

Then, as I was passing McFadden Pond off Butner Road, the words to a song returned to me. I had written it as a personal testimony of Gallant Eagle 82. The chorus came to me:

Hang on child, you know I've got you covered.
Hang on child, you know I'd never lie.
Hang on child, just make it through this valley.
I'll be your companion till you reach the other side.

Again, I felt the presence of my Lord. It was as if I could hear Jesus say to me in His still, small voice in the back of my head, "I never let you down before, what makes you think I've forsaken you now?"

"But Lord-"

"Trust in Me, My, child. Do you really think I brought you back from Gallant Eagle to let you go now?"

"It's not fair to use my song against me, Lord."

"I gave you the song."

"Yes, You did, Lord,"

Again, I was reassured. Somehow, it was going to turn out all right. I didn't know quite how, I just knew Jesus was in control of my life and had me covered.

When I got to the physicals section SFC Molina was waiting for me.

According to regulations, anyone being discharged from the Army for disciplinary reasons (such as overweight) must be accompanied by an NCO at least one rank higher than the individual being separated from service. Molina had just been promoted and was chosen to accompany me. It was humiliating for me to be led around as if I couldn't be trusted.

At least Top had given me the liberty of meeting Ken instead of having him drive me over. There wasn't much for him to do except wait while I took the physical.

Everyone stared at me when I walked into the clinic and identified myself. I wondered what the problem was. It was only after we finished the preliminary questionnaire that I figured out what the mix-up was. Someone had typed the wrong chapter under which I was being separated from service. My paperwork designated me as being separated for homosexuality. It took a phone call to my unit to straighten the mess out. In spite of my bad mood I had to laugh at that.

At the end of an Army physical, after they have poked and

prodded, taken blood and other bodily fluids, measured most of your bodily functions and vital signs, there is a consultation with a physician with the preliminary questionnaire, on which you have listed any medical abnormalities or complaints are discussed at length.

During this consultation the doctor decides whether any of the complaints you have listed require any further medical attention. I figured this was it, my last stand. Here I'd make my final try to get someone to pay attention to me.

After we went over the form, I told the doctor about the trouble I had been having with my weight and how the most drastic measures I had taken had done little or nothing to help. I told her about how I had never had any problem controlling my weight before my head injury. I told her there had to be something wrong with me because of my injuries. I explained they had run thyroid and pituitary function tests on me and the results had all come back normal. But I knew my weight problem began with my head injury and they had to be related, no matter what the medics said.

As I spoke, she looked through my medical records, pausing every now and then to ask me a question or two about a particular symptom I might have felt. There were things she asked me about that I had experienced but didn't think were related to my weight problems.

Finally, she said, "Sergeant, we're going to run some tests on you. I'm referring you to the Neurology Clinic. I'll inform your unit that your physical's on hold until we finish running these tests. If they confirm what I suspect, they'll either leave you alone or the Army's going to have to pay you some money."

"Thank you, Ma'am," I said. He had told me he had me covered!

When I returned to EPG the folks were astonished when I told them what happened. They listened in silence. Then grins broke out all around and I about got a rib busted with them slapping me on my back.

"Boy, Sergeant Wood," CPT Banner, our Operations Officer said with a grin. "You were born under one lucky star. You keep falling into sewers and come out smelling like a rose!"

"No Ma'am," I replied. "I just reckon I've got a big angel in my pocket who looks out for me!"

"You know, you're a very lucky young man."
The head of neurology at Womack, Colonel Shipman, said,

with a gleam in his eye. "*JAMA*, the *Journal of the American Medical Association*, just happened to publish an article on your condition the very month you were being processed out of the service. The doctor had just read the article the night before you walked in to her clinic displaying the exact symptoms the article describes... a freak chance of fate." he said.

More like Divine Providence, I thought, "What exactly is wrong with me, Sir?"

"I believe you suffer from what is known as 'post traumatic hypothalamic obesity' secondary to you head injury."

"Just what is hypothalamic obesity?" I asked. Of course, I knew what obesity was, but what was this hypothalamic stuff?

"Your hypothalamus is a gland which lies at the base of your skull on your cranial shelf, where the spinal cord meets the skull. Right about where you took your bump on the head. Evidently, what happened was when you took your crack on the head your helmet or something crashed into the base of your skull and 'tore' the gland, causing it to malfunction.

"We don't know too much about the hypothalamus right now, but we're learning more every day. We do know that it controls the entire endocrine system: your pancreas, thyroid gland, adrenal gland, pituitary...

"When it's messed up everything goes haywire. That's why all your thyroid and pituitary tests came back negative. They're functioning just fine. They're just doing what the hypothalamus is telling them to do and it's sending out messed up signals."

It all began to make sense to me now. "That's why my body temperature is so low."

He nodded with an approving smile. I felt like a bright student with my own private tutor. "The hypothalamus is like your thermostat. You see, they've just discovered the link between head injuries such as yours and the hypothalamus. That's what that article was all about.

"You're quite a medical rarity," he continued, still smiling. "According to *JAMA*, you're the twelfth person in the world to he diagnosed with hypothalamic obesity secondary to a head injury."

Lucky me.

"We're going to refer you to internal medicine and they'll run their tests on you. We'll probably confer with the gurus at Walter Reed. We don't have a resident endocrinologist here. I bet they'll be dying to get their hands on you..."

Like I said, lucky me!

The next few months were spent making several appointments at Womack Army Hospital. I had to cut a Christmas leave short to make an appointment for another EEG. I had gone home to Alabama and visited my family for the first time in over three years. I was under orders from my First Sergeant to make every appointment without postponement.

I took it with a grain of salt. This was the second time since I stood in that major's office and made my declaration of faith that my unit had tried to toss me out of the Army. It was the second time they had been stopped.

While all this was going on with the Army, my name was mentioned for nomination to deacon at church. There were some reservations by several of the board members as to whether they knew me well enough to make me a deacon or not. After all, I'd only been at the church a little over a year.

My name was placed, removed, and replaced on the ballot several times. It wasn't really a big thing to me. As I told Pastor Billy the first time my name was brought up that all I really wanted to do was preach, but I'd be a deacon if God wanted me to be a deacon.

On the night of the election I was nominated again off the floor and elected. I reckoned God wanted me to be a deacon. It turned out okay, too, after some furor died down. By the end of the year, I was one of two members left on the board; the others had died or been forced to retire due to health reasons. As the only other deacon(ess) was a seventy-two year old widow who didn't drive, most of the "deacing" was up to me.

I can't help but think God knew what was going to happen and used this as an opportunity for me to prove myself to a skeptical congregation.

Everything came to a head over a misunderstanding on the physicals process in February 1987. My physical had been put on hold for over 90 days, the ETS Physicals Section wanted to know if my unit wanted the thing dropped or continue. I was sent over to my doctors at Womack to find out what was taking so long to finish my physical.

I went to see my internal specialist at Womack, Major Post. As head of the department of Internal Medicine at Womack he had been supervising the tests to determine what, if anything was wrong with me. He had been skeptical at first – something I've encountered over the years – after all, the tests were apparently normal. Unable to find anything at Womack, he sent my records to Walter Reed Army hospital at Washington DC for the experts to look at. Everything had been on hold for the last several weeks while they studied the results. I was half expecting to be sent up there for them to examine personally.

I explained what was going on and he got on the phone with Walter Reed. A short conversation with someone up there who was apparently an expert settled it, "The gurus confirm it, Sarge, hypothalamic obesity. I'm having orders cut transferring you to the Medical Holding Company while we board you for a disability hearing. "

A letter was typed up along with orders for me to take back to my unit. It explained my medical condition and basically told everyone to get off my back. Along with the letter came orders transferring me out of the Division within the week. I felt like an accused felon who had been exonerated. I went back to my battery and showed Top the letter.

Top read the letter, then up at me with sadness. We had once been friends. We had served together five years, which is a long time in the Army. We had come up through the ranks together. I would have gone to hell and back for him.

"I didn't know..." he said, sadly. At that moment I forgave him. After all, it must have looked bad to him.

At first he had supported me. It was only after months went by and I still didn't lose the weight be began to think I was playing him for a sucker. Then there was the struggle with the folks at EPG over getting me back to the unit. I could understand why he thought I was lying to him. The one thing you didn't do to Top was lie to him. There had been others for whom he had gone down to the wire and they had failed him. Who could blame him for thinking I was but one

By Friday, I was out of the 82d Airborne Division after five years- almost to the day. It was March 1, 1987. I had signed into the Division on February 16, 1982. I recalled it had been a week less than a year before that I had stood in the major's office and made my declaration of faith.

Let me tell you how neatly things worked out. I made my last jump in December 1986. I didn't know at the time it was my last jump, of course. We (EPG) had managed to "strap hang" with our buddies at Special Forces in a Hollywood out on Sicily DZ at about

10:30 AM. We were dropping from an altitude of three to five thousand feet. It doesn't get much better than that.

It was a clear, crisp December day. The weather was unseasonably warm. The sun was shining. I was having a blast with my MC1-1B parachute. I had the sky to myself.

Then, at about five hundred feet, I noticed another jumper getting uncomfortably close to me. As I was the high jumper, the other jumper had the right away. She didn't seem to have noticed me, so I called out, "Slip away!"

At about that time the other jumper kicked her legs in the air and shouted, "Whoopee!"

She steered her chute directly toward me. She wasn't paying attention to anything in the sky or around her.

I remember saying to myself, *She's going to get us both killed. I'm getting away from her - now!* I slipped off to my right to escape her.

By the time I got away from her, I had lost about three hundred feet, which put me at two hundred or so feet. This is the time you're supposed to be preparing to land. I was oscillating badly (swinging from side to side).

I was trying to stabilize myself. At the same time, I noticed I had the wind to my back. In the MC1-1B parachute, I was "running with the wind." I was going to hit like a hundred tons of bricks.

Oh well, nothing for it but to suck it up and drive on...

I was still oscillating when I hit the ground. I had just swung up and was on the way back down when I hit. I got slapped into the DZ like a rock on a string. Believe me, I was rattled.

I got up from the ground still dazed. As I staggered around gathering up my chute and packing it away, I looked up into the sky. There were tracers flashing by overhead. Why on earth was somebody shooting tracers over a drop zone during a jump? Someone was going to fry for this.

On the walk back to the rally point I met Major Schlicter, my boss at EPG. I told him what had happened. I looked up in the sky, "Who's firing tracers over the DZ? That's about stupid!"

He looked up, "What tracers?"

I looked up at the sky again. Sure enough, I could see the streams of light cross the sky. "Oh man, I'm not seeing tracers, I'm seeing stars! Lord, I'm getting too old for this."

Maybe that's what the Lord as waiting for. I always figured when God wanted me to quit jumping, He'd bring me out. Perhaps God was waiting for me to realize it was time to quit.

As it turned out, God's timing was perfect. When I cleared S-3, I got my DA Form 1307 (Individual Jump Log), and they closed it out. SFC Harmon, who had been my supervisor when I worked at S-3, looked at the log, "Uh-oh, Sergeant Wood, it looks like you're going to lose jump pay.[172] "

I looked at him in disbelief, "But I'm current."

"No, Sergeant Wood, it's been three months since you jumped."

"But I was jumping ahead when I jumped. I'm covered until tomorrow."

I'd been through this a couple times since going to EPG. We often jumped and "Strap-hanged" with various units and sometimes a DA Form 1306, manifest of personnel didn't make it down to my battalion. After all, I would often be listed as being with Corps. As a result some of my jumps never made my main log. At the time I had other things to worry about. As long as I was on the Weight program I wasn't going to get to Jumpmaster School or Senior Wings anyway. As long as I got my pay, I was okay. I did have to make a couple unnecessary "Pay Hurt" jumps my unit put me on, though. It was better than having your pay docked then having to get it back.

He looked at a log again checked the dates I jumped and counted the months, "You know, you're right. You're getting out of here just in time. If you'd have waited one more day you'd have owed the Army a month of jump pay."

In the midst of all the sadness I was feeling, I found a reason to smile. Ain't God good?

---

[172] If a trooper doesn't jump at least once during a three-month period he/she loses jump pay until a jump is made. A person who is "current" "jumps forward" that is, the jump counts ahead three months. Someone who isn't current, "jumps back." I had been current when I jumped in December, so I was covered for December, January, and February. Had I signed out a day later I would have been paid for March and had to pay that money back because I was no longer on Jump Status.

Chapter 28
To Jump and Run No More...

Here we go again, same old thing again
Marching down the avenue, won't be long and we'll be through
I'll be glad and so will you
Won't be long and I'll be home, drinking beer and spitting foam
Won't be long and free at last, all this crap will soon be past.
Won't be long and I'll be free, this will all be history
(Anonymous Army Marching Cadence)

I spent four months waiting for the decision of the board. While I was waiting I was assigned to the Medical Holding Company (MHC). Normally, soldiers assigned to MHC are used as support personnel in the hospital, doing odd jobs for the various clinics.

My buddies at EPG called my First Sergeant at MHC and arranged to have me work for Corps while I waited for my orders. I had turned in all my field gear and would not be able to participate in field operations. I had to be available for any appointments that might come up at Bragg. Major Schlicter tried to take me with him to Honduras once – I'd gotten a special issue of a helmet and some gear for the trip. The bird no sooner hit the ground than there was a message waiting for me at Palmerola Air Base in Honduras telling me I had to get back to Bragg. I had to turn all the stuff back in.

There was a part of me that missed the excitement of flying off to places not knowing what was waiting; even if the occasion was supposed to be just a training exercise in Honduras. We were real busy in Central America at the time, it seemed we were always sending someone down to Honduras, El Salvador or somewhere, either for training or "real world" stuff often the one served as a smokescreen for the other. I had to accept that my days of "running in the jungle with a knife in my teeth" were over – even in practice. I could at least still work on planning.   I was thankful I was able to finish my career as a soldier with dignity, doing a soldier's job up to my last day in the Army. Actually, I was called in a couple times after getting out to answer a question or two on an operation in which I had been involved as the "action officer."[173]

---

[173] To some of you reading this who have been in the military, you may be thinking,

I worked until the last day before I started "clearing" or out processing from the Army. And I went out in style.

It started out in an ordinary enough way.

The previous September, Major Schlicter, my boss at EPG had wanted to improve the appearance of the office. We were in a rundown section of post between Butner Road and Longstreet Avenue filled with old World War II barracks whose paint was peeling. As we officially didn't exist on the TO&E[174] and therefore had no budget we had been outfitted with leftovers from other "authorized" units. The office looked shabby with old pea green paint on the walls, faded tiles, and dilapidated metal desks and file cabinets. We were representing XVIII Airborne Corps and Ft. Bragg and often had representatives not only from different major commands and the four branches of service, but from foreign armies who were involved in our activities. It made a bad impression.

Major Schlicter asked me to look into whether or not I could get some new furniture for the office and see what I could do about maybe getting some work done on the building. One morning I decided to go over to Corps G-4 (supply and logistics) to see if there was any I could get some new stuff for our office.

It turned out the Master Sergeant in charge of that sort of thing had been the S-4 (supply) Sergeant in my battalion in Germany. I had brought some donuts along. Of course he had some coffee, I watched him eat my donuts (I was abstaining, I was still trying to lose that lousy pound or two) while we sat down chewed the fat (sorry – in the new Army should I say "lean?") about old times and talked about the fishing on the Cape Fear River.

After a while he came to the point, "So what can I do for you, Sergeant Wood?"

"Well, Major Schlicter wants to know if we can get some new officer furniture. The place looks kind of shabby and it presents a poor impression, you know? The problem is we don't really have a budget of our own."

He leaned back in his chair, pursing his lips in thought. "You're in luck!"

I brightened. "Really?"

---

action officers are usually captains. I know, but at EPG, everyone had to do everything, and I, a Staff Sergeant (E-6) in a Master Sergeant's (E-8) slot often found myself doing the job of a captain on some operations. I had a captain and a major and across at Main Post, a Colonel to back me up if I needed it.

[174] TO&E or TOE – Table of Organization and Equipment. Categorized list of authorized units and authorized personnel (by MOS) and equipment for each unit down to the last bolt or nut.

"Yep!" He leaned over, reached into a drawer in his desk, "We're at the end of the fiscal year and we've got fifty thousand dollars left over in our operating fund we haven't spent. And you know-"

"Yeah, use it or lose it." I finished the sentence.[175]

"Well, we've been trying to figure out what to spend it on and there's only so many pencils and ink pens you can buy... So what do you want?"

Well, I had a ball spending money. We got new desks, managed to get the downstairs part of our building carpeted, new blinds were installed in the windows. He even told me how I could get new computers for our office. The final touch was the Major's desk. I wanted my boss to have the best.

We were looking through a catalog of desks.

"Which one do you want?" he asked.

I looked into the G-4 officer, Colonel Orr's office. I saw the beautiful oak executive desk he had. "I want one like that."

"You've got it."

It took a couple of months, then after the first of the year the stuff started coming in. It was like Christmas. Workers began coming in and renovating our office. By the time it was over, we had an office to be proud of. Then came the *piece de la resistance* - the major's desk. I was getting short, by that time my orders for discharge were due to come through. I had been concerned I wouldn't be there to see him get it. As it was, it came in a few days before I was to start clearing post. It did my heart good to see him beam as he sat behind his desk. I figured it was the least I could do to repay him for all he had done for me.

Everything was great until he noticed a knick at on the bottom corner of the desk.

"Look at this!" he said, calling us all in to the office. "A scratch. They must have dinged it bringing it in." He picked up the phone and began dialing.

"What are you doing, sir?" I asked nervously.

"I'm calling the warehouse to get them to give me a new desk."

"Well, Sir," SFC Lillard chimed in, picking up on my

---

[175] Under the old operating rules (maybe it's still that way) if a unit didn't spend all the money allocated to it for supplies or vehicle parts or whatever, it usually found its budget cut by the amount of money left over in the next year's budget. This usually led to an orgy of spending in September at the end of the fiscal year in an effort to avoid losing money the next year. The practice has been criticized since I was a kid as being wasteful, but was still in effect when I left the service.

unease. "It's not that big a scratch, maybe we ought to let it go…"

"Not on your life."

Let me condense the conversation for you. What followed was Major Schlicter getting into it with a female civilian employee who was more than willing to exchange the desk provided we brought it back to the warehouse. When Major Schlicter protested that we had no way to get the desk back to the warehouse and that was the job of the civilian employees at the warehouse anyway things began to get nasty. The Commanding General of Ft. Bragg and XVIII Airborne Corps had just issued a directive about such a thing; stating that soldiers' jobs were to train, not do menial chores the government was paying civilians for. The lady pulled an ace from the deck.

"Who's that desk for, anyway?" She demanded.

"It's for me," the major retorted.

"How'd you get it?"

"What do you mean how I got it? My sergeant got it for me."

"That style of desk is reserved for colonels 0-5 and above, how did a major get it?"

"Wait a minute," the major turned to me, "Sergeant Wood, how'd you get this desk?"

"I asked for it."

"He asked for it," he repeated into the phone.

"Well, you're not supposed to have it."

"What do you mean I'm not supposed to have it, I'm filling a colonel's slot."

"When they promote you, then you can get the desk."

Well, finally the major and the lady reached a compromise. She'd allow him to keep the scratched desk if he didn't insist on them coming to pick it up. After he hung up, he looked at the desk with new eyes, "After all, the scratch isn't that big. I think we can cover it with some polish."

He looked around the office, at all the furniture and equipment as if seeing it for the first time.

"Sergeant Wood," he finally said, breaking a poignant silence. "Am I going to go to jail for all this?"

I paused a moment, wondering what to say. As far as I knew, we'd broken no regulations; I'd just asked for the stuff and gotten it; and I had spent money that would have been otherwise wasted on things our office needed to do an important job and present a professional face.

Finally I answered, "No sir." I sneaked a wink at SFC

Lillard, "You're name's not on any paperwork." I paused a beat, "And by the time anyone thinks to look I'll be long gone."

Later that day we got a call from a Captain Duesenberg, the Assistant Corps G-4. Actually, CPT Duesenberg was more accurately the assistant to the assistant G-4. No one in the office actually liked CPT Duesenberg. He'd given us reason. He had turned out to be a real cutthroat kind of guy. He'd tried to get our captain in trouble more than once after she'd tried to help him.

One time we were working on an exercise called Solid Shield 88, which turned out to be a practice run on our invasion of Panama a couple years later (though I don't think it was specifically on anyone's mind at the time). One of our jobs was to issue Operations Orders (OpOrders) that told everyone what their responsibilities were for this particular exercise. I had been assigned to work on it at the last minute and had submitted a draft, which had yet to be approved.

CPT Duesenberg had dropped by the office wanting something to work with so he could get a start on G-4s' part of the operation. CPT Banner, who was the actual Operations Officer for this party let him look at our draft, telling him it wasn't final yet.

"Can I make a copy of this, Julie?"

CPT Banner nodded.

The captain came downstairs to where SFC Lillard and my desk were and began copying the OpOrder draft, which was a no-no because it was classified and hadn't been finalized. While he was using our copying machine to do this he asked if he could use our phone to call his office. When he got on the phone he asked to talk with Colonel Orr, the G-4. Then he began telling his boss how messed up the plan was and how there was going to be trouble and this plan wasn't going to work and the colonel needed to talk to the general to get it all straightened out...

SFC Lillard gave me a nod and I hotfooted it upstairs to tell CPT Banner and her assistant, SFC Gaines what was going on. There ensued a ruckus over him being a jerk.

About a month later, Major Schlicter got to meet CPT Duesenberg for the first time to iron out the difficulties we were having over another operation we were working on. Some five thousand commanders and their staff were descending on Ft. Bragg for a major Command Post Exercise (CPX), that is, a war game done on maps or computers.

Now, Major Schlicter had never had the pleasure of having to work with the captain personally before so we were all looking forward to this meeting of military minds. We were all eavesdropping through the open office door to hear what happened.

After the formalities were settled, Major Schlicter, always a no-nonsense, get-the-job-done-come-hell-or-high-water Infantry officer began going over the problems, "First, Captain, we've got to deal with billeting for the several thousand officers and troops coming. We need you to-"

"I'm sorry, sir," CPT Duesenberg interrupted, "I'm afraid we won't be able to handle billeting for this operation."

"Why not?" Major Schlicter, a bit irritated, asked. "No" wasn't usually a word in his vocabulary and he didn't have much use for those who used it in theirs.

"Well, sir, you see we have these conflicting demands with Solid Shield and we're short handed-"

"But we're all dealing with these problems, Captain." Major Schlicter said patiently. "You've got to walk and chew gum at the same time..." He waved it away, "Okay, that'll wait, let's move on to the next point. Can you guys handle messing facilities?[176] We've got to feed these guys coming in."

"Well, sir." CPT Duesenberg replied, "Wouldn't it be better if your office handled it seeing as you're the point of contact on all this and tasking is your ball of wax?"

There was a moment of silence then. In the other room, I could picture Major Schlicter's face flushing red. When he spoke again, it was slowly, every sound measured. He was struggling to control his temper.

"Well, Captain, do you think you might be able to arrange for POL[177] points to be set up convenient to the billet areas."

"I don't see how, Sir. We-"

"You are the most negative individual I have ever seen wear a uniform, Captain." Schlicter burst out. "I have nothing more to say to you. Tell Colonel Orr to send me someone who can find his behind with two hands and a compass!"

Captain Duesenberg left the office in a hurry.

A few days later we were having a skull session trying to figure out how we were going to billet, feed, and provide for the needs of the soldiers coming when our contact at G-4 seemed unwilling to co-operate in any way we came up with an idea. I think it was mine.

---

[176] Messing is the old Army term for feeding the troops. Troops ate in Mess Halls. Sometime in the 80s, some guru up at the Pentagon decided to start calling them "Dining Facilities." Political Correctness strikes again.

[177] POL- Petroleum, Oil, and Lubrication. Military gas stations.

"Why don't we just send them a tasking letter and tell them to handle it?" I said. A tasking letter was basically an order written on a generic Department of the Army form, called a Disposition Form 2496, which said, "This needs to be done - handle it." "It would make our request official so they'd have to explain why they weren't complying."

That was the beauty of the stroke. Prior to this we had been trying to deal with the issues on an interpersonal basis, one professional to another. Captain Duesenberg had been refusing to go along. By putting our requests on a Disposition Form we were making an official request that would be logged through channels. G-4 would have to explain why they weren't cooperating to the Commanding General – if it got that far without them cooperating with us beforehand.

Major Schlicter grinned. "That would surely cut through a lot of nonsense, wouldn't it? Type it up and I'll sign it."

That meeting had been the previous week. So now, here I was, my last day on the job. We'd just settled the furniture crisis and the phone rang. SFC Lillard answered it.

"Corps Exercise Planning Group, SFC Lillard speaking, this line is not secure, may I help you, sir?"

Pause.

"Oh, Captain *Duesenberg*. You want to speak to Major Schlicter? Could you hold one, Sir?

"Major Schlicter? You have a call on line seven."

"Who is it?"

"Captain Duesenberg."

"I don't want to talk to that schmuck!"

About that time I got a bright idea. "Do you want me to talk to him, Sir?"

There was a pause, then Major Schlicter came out of his office grinning, "Sure, Sergeant Wood, handle him."

I picked up the phone, ensuring I had a wide smile on my face and in my voice when I spoke, "Sergeant Wood, Sir. May I help you?"

There was a moment of confused silence, "Sergeant Wood," he stammered, "I need to speak with Major Schlicter."

"Well, I'm sorry, Sir. He doesn't want to talk to you," I said as politely as possible. I allowed this to sink in for a moment, "May *I* help you, Sir? *I'll* talk to you."

There was another moment of silence. Then, "Okay- It's about this tasking letter, Sergeant Wood-"

"Oh, you got it! Good! I'm so glad. You know how these things get lost in channels..."

"But Sergeant Wood, this is all wrong!"

"What's all wrong, Sir?"

"This letter is tasking us to handle billeting, messing, and POL for the operation. That's not our job."

"It isn't?"

"No, Sergeant Wood, this isn't our job!"

"Well, Sir," I said in as soothing a voice as I could while struggling not to break down laughing. By this time everyone in the office was gathered around to see the show. We had him on the speaker, "Let me see if I have this right. G-1 is personnel; they make sure we have the people to go kill the enemy- right?"

"Right..."

"And G-2 is intelligence; they tell us where the enemy is so we can go kill them, right?"

"Right..."

"G-3 is Operations and Planning, that's us, we figure out how to go kill the enemy, right?"

"Right... but-"

"-and G-4 is logistics, they make sure we have the bullets, gas, and food so we can kill the enemy, right?"

"Right!" he was getting flustered again, "But-"

"So it sounds to me like billeting, mess, and POL are right up your alley-"

"But tasking is a G-3 function, not a G-4 function!" he sputtered.

"That's right, Sir, and we've tasked G-4 to handle it."

"But you can't do that!"

"Sir, we just did."

"Well, I'm going to talk to Colonel Orr about this..."

"Sir, I suggest you do, Major Schlicter would *love* to talk to Colonel Orr, but he doesn't want to talk to you. Good day, Sir."

The whole office burst out laughing as I hung up. It was my last official phone call and it was a good way to go out. I remember thinking how much I was going to miss it all.

I would have to say my time at EPG, in spite of all the flak coming at me from other quarters, was one of the best times of my military career.

A few days before my discharge, they had held a going away lunch for me at which I was presented a plaque. I was asked to say a few words at the luncheon. For the first time since the Lord had filled me with His Spirit, I was speechless. I looked at these men and women who had stood by me and was overwhelmed by emotion. I managed to choke out a few words thanking them for believing in me when no one else cared and for helping me finish my career as a soldier, doing a soldier's job with dignity. I thanked God for giving me friends and comrades like them.

Even after I left the Army their friendship didn't end. They had two surprises for me. The day after I signed out I was asked if I could stop by the office. They said they needed my help with an operation on which I had been working. When I showed up at the office I discovered they'd arranged an informal awards ceremony to award me a Meritorious Service Medal. Captain Banner and Major Schlicter apologized for not having gotten the orders pushed through before I left service, but they'd had so little time between my MRB results and my discharge – they only had a week to get it processed, and a medal that high took time. SFC Gaines, one of my buddies, had walked the award through the entire chain of command to get it in spite of the current XVIII Abn Corps Commander's prohibition of awarding any medal above an Army Commendation Medal to anyone below SFC/E-7.

There was a motto I first read at Ft. Sill, Oklahoma while at artillery school. It said, "Mission First, People Always." I always felt that was what the Army was supposed to be about. Ultimately, though our mission is to protect our country by killing people and breaking things if need be, we are in the people business. It is our soldiers who accomplish the mission. If you take care of your people and they know you will, they'll accomplish the mission. The folks at EPG helped me see that idea was still there.

I was so thankful to God who had fought my battles. I was leaving the Army with honor and dignity instead of shame and disgrace. As he told me that day in the car and many times since, He hadn't brought me back from California to let go of me now. If I just stayed the course.

On July 24, 1987, I reported to the Separation Transfer Point at Ft. Bragg and signed out of the Army, giving them my military ID card. For the first time since I was old enough to carry one, I was without any type of military ID. I was a true civilian, without any attachments to the Army.[178]

---

[178] Twenty-three years later – again, almost to the day, interestingly, I was given military ID Card after being classified as 100% service-connected medically disabled. I felt as if I'd been let back into the family.

I took my check, which was more money than I'd ever had at one time in my life, to the bank. I asked the clerk if I could hold the cash for a few minutes before depositing it. She gave it to me in fifty and hundred dollar bills. To the amusement of all around, after holding and smelling the bills, and letting anyone around who wanted to hold it, I put it in the bank.

I drove around post after I signed out, taking a last look at all the familiar sights. I suppose I was prolonging the moment. I would be staying in the area, at least for a while and I would visit Post and see them again, but I knew it wouldn't be the same. From now on I would be an outsider.

I visited the 82nd museum that afternoon. There was a retirement ceremony going on outside. It was for CSM Clarke, "Daddy Clarke" from HHB, 18th FA, my first jump assignment. He saw me after the formal ceremony was over and broke away from the crowd to talk to me. We talked for a moment about how the Army had changed and about the good days at HHB before he had to return to the crowd to shake hands and do the social thing.

I went inside the museum, and walked through the displays as I had dozens of times before. I came to the Grenada display; saw the familiar pictures of the battle. There was our famous trooper, sleeping behind the wheel of his goat, waiting to be deployed. There was the now famous "Magic" helmet exhibit; the Kevlar helmet that had stopped a bullet during the battle and saved a trooper's life. As I looked at the helmet a thousand memories, both good and bad swept over me. And then, softy over the speaker system, which constantly played a tape of the 82nd Airborne Division Chorus singing airborne songs, came "The All American Fight Song," the anthem of the 82nd Airborne Division. Tears welled in my eyes. I left the place quickly.

I drove home and took my uniform off for what I knew now would be the last time. Unlike the first time I left, there was now no going back. All my bridges had been burned. A major chapter in my life had been closed. A new one was about to begin.

Reflections

I'm a big believer in miracles; the fact I'm able to sit here and type this is a miracle to me. Several of the doctors who treated me after the accident in California would agree.

It's hard to believe as I write this it's been almost thirty-five years since I jumped in to California. A few years ago a bunch of Grenada vets returned to the island for the thirtieth anniversary. It's even harder to believe I've been out of the Army longer than I was in. Time flies when you're having fun. Well, time flies. But, in spite of everything, life is good and I am a blessed man in so many ways.

After leaving the Army I hung around the Ft. Bragg/Fayetteville area finishing my Bachelor's degree in History and earning my minister's license. Then I returned home to Alabama, to continue with my education, earning a Masters degree and teacher's certificate in Social Science. I thought it would be a good way to "make tents" to support my ministry. And it was.

The fact I eventually found a full-time job teaching school not only gave me a great outlet to work with young people on a daily basis, but enabled my new wife and me to work in ministries that would have been impossible had we been dependent on the ministry for our support. It hasn't been a typical ministry, but it has had its rewards.

It seems like each year researchers discover something new about bumps on the noggin and the unfortunate side effects of what was called "Post Closed Head Injury" in 1982 but is now referred to as Traumatic Brain Injury (TBI). As I watched news broadcasts from the wars in Afghanistan and Iraq I realized many of the troops who were victims of IEDs and diagnosed with TBI had suffered trauma to the primitive brain (where dwells the hypothalamus) similar to mine. I know the services and VA are making great shows of doing research and treating the behavioral and cognitive side effects of TBI but wonder how many troops have had their bells rang by an IED have come home apparently okay, but have noticed drastic decreases in energy levels and have run afoul of AR 600-9?

I wonder how many troops, male and female, are being "put out" of service for being overweight, who should be receiving treatment instead. There are so many doctors unaware of Post-traumatic Hypothalamic Obesity – even endocrinologists, under whose specialty the condition falls. Just recently, I saw a VA endo guru. In our first meeting, after asking and hearing my problem, he first denied there was such a thing as Post-traumatic Hypothalamic Obesity as he had never heard of it. After "Googling" it and proving it existed, he admitted, okay, there *is* such a thing as Post-traumatic Hypothalamic Obesity but I didn't have it. And he hadn't even done so much yet as taken my pulse or blood pressure! What a medical genius!

Again, I wonder how many troops are facing what I faced, not knowing. If I could keep one vet from going through what I went through finding out what was wrong with me, it would be worth it. So I write letters and make phone calls to anyone I hope will listen trying to make folks aware. As of the time I type this the VA still doesn't have a rating scale for my condition. Instead I am rated according to the scale for hypothyroidism – kind of equating skin cancer to acne, in my humble opinion...

My wife sees me dealing with the residual effects of my injuries on a daily basis as I wait for God to heal me one way or another. I taught school nineteen years after leaving the service and finishing my education (if one can truly finish one's education). My kids would see me deal with some of the physical problems; they would hear a story I would tell of something that happened to me or a buddy which could be used as an illustration, to teach a lesson I've learned about life, or just to relieve the tedium of school, and always to thank God for what He's done for me. I am often asked if it was all worth it.

Ronald Reagan once said, "Some people go through their entire lives wondering if they ever made a difference. A Marine doesn't have to worry about that."

I believe he was speaking at the memorial service for the Marines killed in the Beirut bombing the weekend before we went in to Grenada. I don't think he'd mind, and I hope the Marine Corps doesn't mind if I say that statement could apply to anyone who wears a uniform - Army, Navy, Air Force, Marines, and even Coast Guard (a much neglected branch). You could go on and say that about police, firemen, and EMTs.

I am humbly aware that the things I did and experienced pale when compared to those generations who went before – and came after. I served - as did an entire generation who served -between the fall of Saigon in 1975 and Desert Storm.

I think it can safely be said they made a difference.

When I think of my own career, I think of the freezing nights in Germany on the border peering across the 1K Zone at Soviet border checkpoints on the "Iron Curtain" as one of the 350,000 – 500,000 troops the US had in Western Europe at various times during the Cold War. I think of the German school children running out to wave "V" signs for victory at us as we made our way east on trips to the border. Then I remember the sight of delirious mobs as Germans tore down the Berlin Wall and the Iron Curtain tumbled. Communism was defeated. I take some satisfaction that I had a tiny part in that. We, the Cold Warriors, the so-called "peacetime soldiers" helped Ronald Reagan defeat the "Evil Empire."

When people make fun of our operation in Grenada, or criticize it as an illegal operation, I think of the Grenadian people dancing in the streets and singing "God Bless America!" I remember my younger brother, who later served in the Navy telling me about the reactions of the Grenadian people on the tenth anniversary of their liberation. When they found out his brother had been with the invasion force, they treated him like a hero. He was almost ashamed to tell them he didn't drink when they wanted to treat him. I remember I had a small part in that, too.

"Peacetime soldiers" invaded Panama and conducted numerous operations in Central America and other regions, not only furthering US interests and thwarting Soviet expansion in the Cold War, but maybe giving folks in those countries a shot at self-determination. They made a difference.

As I said before, as I watched the US buildup in the First Gulf War in 1990 I recognized the deployment plan we worked on back in 1982 when I was with 18th FA Bde Headquarters. I have to admit satisfaction in having even a microscopic part in that.

Even Gallant Eagle 82 had its positive impact. As a result of that catastrophe the Army re-examined its jump procedures to prevent another catastrophe from happening. The issue of the Kevlar helmet was stepped up to ensure no other trooper was ever killed by his parachutist's helmet. To be sure, troopers have died in parachute accidents since then; parachuting is an inherently dangerous occupation. Maybe our sacrifices saved lives. And, on a personal level, I met Jesus Christ in a direct personal way on that drop zone.[179]

Was it worth it? Is it worth it?

Yeah, for me, it was all worth it. A word from an old trooper to the men and women sacrificing today; yes, it's worth it.

---

[179] I should note here that parachute catastrophes continued to happen. In late 1985 the 82nd Commanding General, Major General Bobby B. Porter was seriously injured in an airborne operation in Turkey. Again, high winds wrought havoc on the jumpers, causing some thirty or so injuries. General Porter, in true airborne tradition, was the first out the door sustaining severe head injuries which eventually forced him to retire early.

The U.S. Army, the 82nd Airborne Division and all the folks I served with will always be a part of me. Often, the principal at the school at which I worked would refer to me as an ex-paratrooper. There is no thing as an ex-paratrooper. If you've jumped your wings – served in an airborne unit – you will always be a paratrooper. As the man said, "Airborne is more than wings or a patch – it's a state of mind."

When I tell folks about Gallant Eagle, I like to open with the story of Private Tuffy. I am often asked if I am Private Tuffy. I smile. There is a little bit of Private Tuffy in everyone who has weathered the Jump School at Ft. Benning and earned those coveted wings.

I may never jump again, probably never will, but I will always be Airborne in my heart. With the life I have now, for which I am thankful, I could never imagine going back into the Division, or even the Army. At the same time, there isn't a day I don't miss it.

There are nights I dream of jumping again, feel the wind in my face, the sensation of total weightlessness. There are other nights I dream of being out in the bush, running down a trail, or "chiefing" a fire mission, sometimes the dreams are so real I can smell the gun powder. Then I wake up and sadly realize it was all a dream.

Now, as we are engaged in a world wide war against terrorists. I watch our young men and women in uniform performing their duties in such a superb manner I am filled with pride in our youth, in our nation. I see the next generation of my family "stepping up." One of my sons served his hitch in the Navy, my youngest as I type is serving as an AIRBORNE Infantry officer, fulfilling one of his old man's ambitions. He scares his Mom as he wants to go "all the way" to Ranger School. My nephew did two tours in Afghanistan as an infantryman – he was approached to sign up for Special Forces. Not bragging (well, maybe a little), but my family has skin in this "game."

No one knows the evils of war and hates war more than a veteran. My brief taste of combat has convinced me it is evil. In this fallen world though, it remains a necessary evil.

As a veteran and a parent I can only ask of our leaders (most of whom I remember sadly have never served) before they send OUR kids to war is this:

1) Do not send our kids to war unless they intend to WIN it. I am sick and tired of hearing about "exit strategies." The only exit is VICTORY. If you cannot give a clear definition of what

constitutes victory then perhaps we don't need to be sending our most precious resource – our children – into a meat grinder.

2) Do not keep our troops in harm's way any longer than absolutely necessary. A soldier is not a cop. If you want to build nations, maybe send the Peace Corps with security. Too often we risk snatching defeat out of the jaws of victory by staying after the military mission has been accomplished.

3) Do not bind our troops' hands with impossible Rules of Engagement that prevent them from defending themselves after putting them in harm's way.

4) And please, please, don't use these kids up and toss them away in your hurry to "downsize" after the war is over. When will politicians learn it is cheaper – not only in dollars and cents – but in blood – to maintain a strong military than to be constantly in the process of dismantling and rebuilding our military in every war?

The first three are lessons we should have learned from Vietnam. The last one is a lesson every war we ever fought should have taught us.

As one who worked with our young people daily I am always filled with amazement at our young people. In my opinion, what's amazing is not that there are so many "bad" kids out there. It's that there are so many good kids still out there with so much against them in this world.

I believe that point is proven by the current generation of warriors. There is a part of me that is wistful. There is a part of me that believes I should be out there with those kids, giving them the benefit of my experience, sharing their deprivations. But I know at my age and in my condition I'd be a hindrance. I've done my part, however small it was. It's their turn to do – to fight, it's my turn to pray for our troops, and pray for our leaders and people that they don't repeat the mistakes of the past and fail another generation of warriors.

As my wife reminds me, I'm no longer in the Army. Maybe not; but I'll always be a soldier. I'm in a different Army now, a different war, different rules of engagement, a different enemy. There are really no uniforms, it's often hard to tell friend from foe, and sometimes the pay isn't so great. But, as they say, you can't beat the retirement plan,

AIRBORNE!

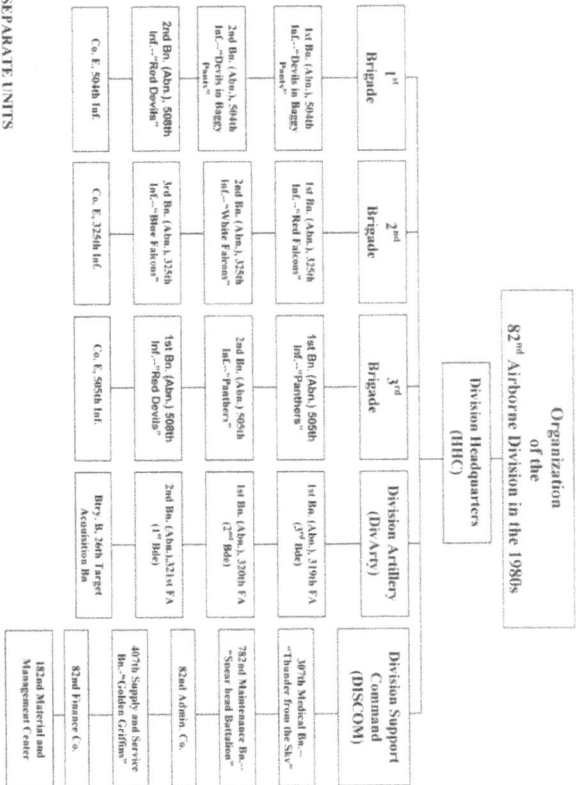

**Organization
of the
82nd Airborne Division in the 1980s**

Division Headquarters
(HHC)

1st Brigade
- 1st Bn. (Abn.), 504th Inf.—"Devils in Baggy Pants"
- 2nd Bn. (Abn.), 504th Inf.—"Devils in Baggy Pants"
- 2nd Bn. (Abn.), 508th Inf.—"Red Devils"
- Co. E, 504th Inf.

2nd Brigade
- 1st Bn. (Abn.), 325th Inf.—"Red Falcons"
- 2nd Bn. (Abn.), 325th Inf.—"White Falcons"
- 3rd Bn. (Abn.), 325th Inf.—"Blue Falcons"
- Co. E, 325th Inf.

3rd Brigade
- 1st Bn. (Abn.), 505th Inf.—"Panthers"
- 2nd Bn. (Abn.), 505th Inf.—"Panthers"
- 1st Bn. 508th Inf.—"Red Devils"
- Co. E, 505th Inf.

Division Artillery (Div Arty)
- 1st Bn. (Abn.), 319th FA (3rd Bde)
- 1st Bn. (Abn.), 320th FA (2nd Bde)
- 2nd Bn. (Abn.), 321st FA (1st Bde)
- Btry. B, 26th Target Acquisition Bn

Division Support Command (DISCOM)
- 307th Medical Bn.—"Thunder from the Sky"
- 782nd Maintenance Bn.—"Spearhead Battalion"
- 82nd Admin. Co.
- 407th Supply and Service Bn.—"Golden Griffin"
- 82nd Finance Co.
- 182nd Material and Management Center

SEPARATE UNITS
307th Engineer Bn.—"Injuners"
82nd Signal Bn.—"Commander's Voice"
82nd Military Police Co.
1st Squadron, 17th Cavalry
4th Bn. (Abn.), 68th Armor—"Thunderbolts"

3rd Bn. (Abn.), 4th Air Defense Arty.
82nd Combat Aviation Bn.—"Wolfpack"
313th Military Intelligence Bn. (Combat Electronic Warfare Intelligence)
14th Chemical Detachment

APPENDIX A

Organization
of the
3rd Armored Division in the 1970s*

Division Headquarters (HHC) (Frankfurt)

1st Brigade (Kirchgoens)
- 3rd Bn 32nd Armored
- 2nd Bn 33rd Armored
- 3rd Bn 33rd Armored
- 2nd Bn 32nd Infantry
- 3rd Bn 32nd Infantry

2nd Brigade (Gelnhausen)
- 1st Bn 33rd Armored
- 1st Bn 48th Infantry
- 2nd Bn 48th Infantry

3rd Brigade (Friedburg)
- 1st Bn 32nd Armored
- 3rd Bn 32nd Armored
- 1st Bn 36th Infantry

Division Artillery (Div Arty) (Hanau)
- 2nd Bn 3rd FA (1st Bde) (*155mm SP)
- 2nd Bn 6th FA (2nd Bde) (*155mm SP)
- 2nd Bn 27th FA (3rd Bde) (*155mm SP)
- 1st Bn 40th FA General Support 8 - inch SP

Division Support Command (DISCOM)
- 45th Medical Bn
- 122nd Ordinance Bn
- 503rd Supply & Transport Bn

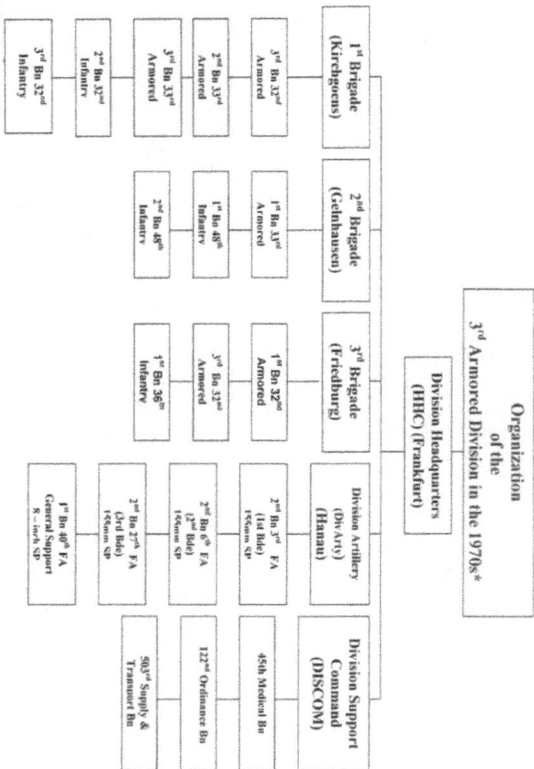

SEPARATE UNITS
3rd Bn 12th Cavalry
143rd Signal Battalion
503rd Replacement Co.
503rd Military Intelligence Co.
503rd Aviation Bn
3rd Bn 61st Air Defense Bn

23rd Engineer Battalion
503rd MP Company
503rd Admin Company
503rd CIC Detachment
856th ASA Co.

*Locations of major units are given in parenthesis below the unit according to my best recollections and information available.

APPENDIX B

390

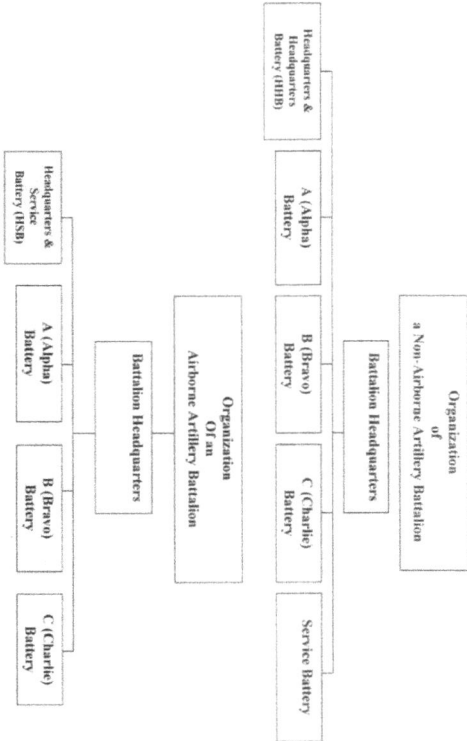

APPENDIX C

Organization of a Non-Airborne Artillery Battalion

- Battalion Headquarters
  - Headquarters & Headquarters Battery (HHB)
  - A (Alpha) Battery
  - B (Bravo) Battery
  - C (Charlie) Battery
  - Service Battery

Organization Of an Airborne Artillery Battalion

- Battalion Headquarters
  - Headquarters & Service Battery (HSB)
  - A (Alpha) Battery
  - B (Bravo) Battery
  - C (Charlie) Battery

Appendix D
82nd AIRBORNE DIVISION ORDER OF BATTLE
OPERATION URGENT FURY
LIBERATION OF GRENADA

HHC, 82d Airborne Division

HHC, 1st Brigade, 82nd Airborne Division
Company A, 2d Battalion, 504th Infantry (replaced Co C 2/325)
1st Battalion, 508th Infantry
2d Battalion, 508th Infantry

HHC, 2d Brigade, 82nd Airborne Division
2d Battalion, 325th Infantry (minus Company C)
3d Battalion, 325th Infantry

HHC, 3d Brigade, 82nd Airborne Division
1st Battalion, 505th Infantry
2d Battalion, 505th Infantry

HHB, 82d Airborne Division Artillery
Battery A, 1st Battalion, 319th Field Artillery (3nd Bde)
1st Battalion (-Battery A), 320th Field Artillery (2rd Bde)

HHC, 82d Airborne Division Support Command
182d Airborne Division Materiel Management Center

Independent 82nd Units Deployed
1st Squadron (- Troop C), 17th Cavalry
3d Battalion (-Battery D), 4th Air Defense Artillery
82d Aviation Battalion
82d Signal Battalion (- Companies A and B)
307th Engineer Battalion (-Company B)
307th Medical Battalion (-Company B)
313th Military Intelligence Battalion
407th Supply and Service Battalion (-Detachment B and Company E)
782d Maintenance Battalion (-Companies B and E)
82d Military Police Company
101st Chemical Company

Appendix E
Glossary of Terms

The following glossary is provided to assist the reader in understanding Army Talk. I've provided definitions in the text and in notes, but hopefully, this will compliment those notes.

AIT – Advanced Individual Training – School after Basic Training where soldiers are taught their MOS – or jobs.

Aiming Circle – Device used to "lay" or orient an artillery firing battery for azimuth (direction) of fire.

Airborne – Refers to military tactic of "vertical insertion" – that of landing troops behind enemy lines to seize vital points and cause confusion in enemy rear areas to assist the main ground force in its advance. Though at the concept's birth "Airborne Operations" consisted of both gliderborne and parachute troops (paratroopers) today, the idea primarily conveys dropping troops and equipment by parachute.

Airland – The landing of troops transported by aircraft instead of dropping them by parachute.

Airmobile – The rapid transportation of troops and equipment from part of the battlefield to another by helicopter.

ALICE- All Purpose, Lightweight, Individual Combat Equipment – A fancy acronym and name to describe the individual equipment and load bearing gear such as pistol belts, ammo pouches and field packs after Vietnam.

ANGLICO – Air, Naval Gun Liaison Company; Airborne qualified Marine Forward Observers.

APERS – Anti-Personnel Rounds. They were designed to be fired with either VT or Proximity fuses set to explode approximately fifty meters above the target scattering their contents on enemy troops. There were two types: 1) APERS/Flechettes – Scattered sharp needle-like shards of metal on the target; 2) APERS/Beehive – Scattered small grenade-like explosive devices on the target.

ARTEP – Army Readiness Training Evaluation Program – a lengthy name and nifty acronym for unit test. ARTEPs consist of established sets of tasks according to the type of unit (Infantry, Artillery, Armored, etc) that the Army has decided are necessary for that unit to function in combat. When I was in ARTEPs were officially conducted at company/battery level and battalion level. Larger unit ARTEPs sometimes were conducted. I remember one time doing a "Division ARTEP" in the 82nd.

Article 15 - Non-judicial (or administrative) punishment rendered either at company or field grade (Major through Colonel) level offered in lieu of a courts martial.

ARVN - Army of the Republic of Vietnam, or South Vietnamese Army. They were on our side, more or less.

ASOP - Air Standing Operating Procedures. The rules governing all airborne operations.

AWOL – Absent Without Leave - Being away from your place of duty for any period (technically) up to thirty days, after which, when I first came in the Army, you were listed as a deserter.

Bn - Battalion – the subordinate unit between company and brigade. In the 70s and 80s, a battalion consisted of three "line" battalions, a Headquarters Company (or Battery), and a Support or Service Company. Two or more battalions made up a brigade. Usually commanded by a lieutenant colonel.

BC – In Field Artillery, usually Battery Commander; in other types of units is also Battalion Commander.

BDU – Battle Dress Uniform – camouflaged uniform the Army adopted to replace fatigues as the work and field uniform.

Blackhat – NCO instructors at either the Basic Airborne Course (Jump School) or Advanced Airborne Course (Jumpmaster School). They get their nickname from the black baseball caps with their wings and rank insignia pinned on them they wear. Blackhats must be Jumpmaster qualified.

Boocoo – Very much; from the French *Beaucoup*. Vietnam term.

Brass, the – High ranking officers and civilian officials.

Bde - Brigade – the subordinate unit between battalion and division, usually consisting of two or more battalions. In the 70s and 80s two or more brigades made up a division. Usually commanded by a colonel.

Canopy Release Assembly/Capewell - Buckle that attaches risers to the parachute harness. Releasing a capewell after landing frees the chute to flow away from the jumper and collapse in all but the highest of winds.

CAPEX - Capabilities Exercise; a dog and pony show where guests were given an idea of a unit's capabilities. The 82nd's annual CAPEX was a highly anticipated event at Bragg.

CARP - Computed Air Release Point – The calculated (or computed) point where parachute-dropped loads (personnel or equipment) are released to land on the objective (or DZ).

CIF – Central Issue Facility; issued soldiers combat, or field gear.

CESO – Communications-Electronics Staff Officer

Chain of Command – or "Chain"- the direct hierarchy, or "pecking order" in a military unit, from the lowest private to the highest ranking general officer.

Chalk - A number given an aircraft and its load (either personnel or equipment) to ensure the right folks or cargo get on the right aircraft and that aircraft is its proper order.

Chaptered - To be "chaptered" out of service means you left under circumstances other than the normal expiration of your enlistment – usually under less than desirable circumstances.

CQ – Charge of Quarters - NCO (usually SGT/E-5) assigned to sit up at night to answer the phone and watch over barracks and personnel. He is assisted by an enlisted person, a "CQ Runner."

Charlie – Nickname for Viet Cong. Derived from phonetic alphabet: VC translates Victor Charlie. Charlie for short.

CFB/"Smoke" – **Chief of Firing Battery/Chief of Smoke - SFC** who is senior NCO in a Field Artillery firing battery. Has been called the "Field First Sergeant" of the battery.

Chief/Chief of Section – Senior ranking NCO on a gun. Chief is an informal term of respect among artillerymen. It can also be used as a friendly term to a lower ranking troop in the artillery by a superior NCO.

Combat Arms - Refers to the three basic fighting branches of the Army: Infantry, Armor, and Field Artillery; sometimes Combat Engineers are also considered Combat Arms.

CG – Commanding General.

CP – Command Post.

CPX – Command Post Exercise - An exercise of command and staff without (usually) the deployment of troops and/or possible battle plans in response to various scenarios – often real-world contingency operations. In the "old days" commanders and staff of involved units would set up their Command Posts and maneuver their units on maps while umpires would use complex formulas to calculate casualties on both sides. Toward the end of my career, the military was moving to computer simulators.

Commissary – Grocery store on post.

COSCOM – Corps Support Command; provides logistical support for an Army corps. XVIII Abn Corps was supported by 1st COSCOM.

C-rations- or C-rats, or C's. Field rations used for decades by the US military, came in 12 meals with three sets of accessories or condiments. The main "courses" were in cans. Some thought the "C" stood for "Combat." However, the "C" stood for the type ration. "A" rations were hot fresh food, "B" were canned or otherwise packaged but cooked by mess section, "C"s were meant to be eaten straight out of the can and issued individually to troops. There were three different categories or types of C-rations: B-1, B-2, and B-3 which varied on the mixture of entrees (B-1s & B-3s had meats like chicken loaf, or beef with spiced sauce; B-2s had entrees like pork and beans, Spaghetti...) , deserts" (B-1s and B-3s had canned fruits, B-2s had cakes), and candy bars (depended on the meal – see "John Wayne Bar."

CID – Criminal Investigative Division - The Army's criminal detectives.

D-Ring – As its name implies, a "D" shaped metal device sewn into the parachute harness used to attach the reserve, pack, and other individual equipment to the jumper in a combat equipment jump.

D-Bag - In parachute parlance, the bag, or cover of the parachute when packed. In a static line jump the D-bag is pulled off the parachute by the static line allowing the chute to deploy.

DA - Department of the Army

Dinky Dau – Vietnamese for crazy.

Division – A major organizational unit between a brigade and a corps. A division in the 1970s and 80s consisted of two to three maneuver brigades, a Division Artillery (an artillery brigade), along with Division Support Command (DISCOM) consisting of various support units. Usually commanded by a Major General.

DivArty – Division Artillery - Administrative control headquarters/unit for a division's field artillery battalions. Usually one battalion per maneuver brigade with a heavier general support battalion. The 82nd did not have a general support battalion when I served with it.

DRF – Division Ready (or Reaction) Force. This is part of the 82nd's continuing role as the United States' rapid response force. When I was in, the Division's nine infantry battalions were always in a readiness posture numbered 1 through 9. With DRF1 being on call 24/7.

DISCOM- Division Support Command. Brigade – sized units made up of individual supply and support companies and maintenance units in a division to provide the materiel and maintenance support for the division's subordinate units the units are unable to provide for themselves.

DZ – Drop Zone – Field or area where paratroopers are dropped in an airborne operation.

DZSO – Drop Zone Safety Officer – Jumpmaster qualified officer responsible for taking wind readings and ensuring the wind speeds on the DZ are safe to jump.

ETS – End of Term of Service. Date one's enlistment expires.

Executive Officer – XO – Second in command of a unit from company level on up.

Fatigues – Basic OD work and field uniform from the 1950s through the 1980s.

FSOP – Field Standard Operating Procedures

FDC – Fire Direction Control – Section that converts and calculates firing data it receives from the front to the guns.

FDO – Fire Direction Officer – Officer in charge of FDC in the field. In a firing battery he's usually a lieutenant. At Battalion level, a captain.

FSO – Fire Support Officer – Officer (usually a lieutenant) assigned as a leader to a FIST.

FIST – Fire Support Team – Forward Observer Team who travels with the infantry to call in field artillery when needed.

FO – Forward Observer – Troop assigned to a FIST, nicknamed "FIST dog."

FTX – Field Training Exercise – As the name implies, an exercise involving troops maneuvering in the field, sharpening their field survival skills, individual soldier skills and MOS skills while the unit trains and sharpens its ability to function as a team.

FORSCOM – Forces Command – Major command established at the same time as TRADOC (1973) as the major supervising command for all combat units in the Army.

Fourth Point of Contact - Airborne Term used for butt, as in "Get your head out of your Fourth Point of Contact!"

Fuse – Device screwed into the nose of an artillery round. Fuses activate and detonate the round on target. In my time we used several different types of fuses, depending on the mission: 1) Point Detonating (PD): Usually exploded upon impact after activating. Could be set to delay a few seconds after hitting target to maximize impact; 2) Time Fuze: Could be set to explode at a precise time after leaving the tube. 3) Variable Time (VT): Set to explode after coming within a certain distance of a target after set time has expired.

Gamma Goat (or "Goat"), M561 – Six-wheeled 1 ¼ Ton cargo truck used across the Army but extensively by the 82nd Abn Division Artillery to haul its guns and provide other transportation. It was alleged to be water-proof and therefore amphibious.

Green Ramp – Staging area of Pope AFB where troops from Ft Bragg loaded equipment and jumpers onto aircraft for our airborne operations.

"Gunny"/Gunnery Sergeant - In the Army, Gunnery Sergeants are assistants to the Chief of Firing Battery, or "Smokes." It is also a Sergeant First Class slot.
HHB or HHC – Headquarters and Headquarters Battery or Company

HALO – High Altitude, Low Opening jump. Military skydiving. HALO school is one of the toughest courses in the Army.

HE – High Explosive round

Hip Shoot – Emergency Mission; called when a battery is travelling. The battery has to pull off in the nearest convenient location, lay and fire.

Hollywood Jump - Jumping with only main parachute, reserve, and helmet.

Impact Area – Designated area on a military post for target practice.

JRDTF – Joint Rapid Deployment Task Force, also known as RDF or Rapid Deployment Force.

JTX – Joint Training Exercise – Usually an inter-service Field Training Exercise (FTX)

JM - Jumpmaster – Paratroopers who have passed the Advanced Airborne Course (Jumpmaster School) to become qualified to manage a military parachute jump. Jumpmaster qualified personnel conduct airborne related training from Jump School through period refresher classes required of all paratroopers.

JMPI - Jumpmaster Physical Inspection. A physical inspection of a jumper by a jumpmaster qualified individual to ensure the jumper's equipment is properly rigged and displays no sign of damage or disrepair that might cause the parachute to fail to open or function properly in the air.

John Wayne Bars - Our nickname for C-ration chocolate bars. There was more than one kind of bar in C-rations, depending on the type of meal we had: B-1, B-2, B-3 each had different configurations of entrées (if you could call them that) cakes or canned fruits for desert, or candy bars. B-1s and B-3s contained a smaller bar - chocolate or chocolate with nuts – we'd get two with a meal (I think one of the types had nuts in them.) These were also called "Audie Murphy Bars" after the most decorated soldier in World War II who was nicknamed "Little Texas" by his buddies. B-2s contained a larger – like John Wayne – bar with chocolate covering coconut or mint filling.

JAG – Judge Advocate General – Military lawyers.

Kaserne – German for barracks. Our Army barracks in Germany were called kasernes.

Kevlar – Helmet that replaced the M-1 steel helmet. The 82nd Abn Division was the only major unit to wear the Kelvar in Grenada.

KP – Kitchen Police – Duty in the mess hall. Either punitive or as part of the regular garrison rotations of duties troops pulled.

LAW - Acronym and nickname for M-72 66mm Light Anti-Tank Weapon.

LCE – Load Carrying Equipment – a more modern name for web gear.

Leg- Airborne name for non-airborne personnel. Short for "straight leg." Usually preceded by the adjectives, "dirty (or nasty) stinking.."

Lifer - Term used to describe career soldiers. When used by the lower enlisted it is usually considered derogatory. One acronym I heard made from the word was something like this: Lazy Inefficient [Person] Expecting Retirement.

MAU – Marine Amphibious Unit – now called a "Marine Expeditionary Unit" (MEU); it's the smallest independent Marine unit with air and ground assets – basically the size of an infantry battalion with support elements.

MassTac- (or Masstac) – Mass Tactical Jump. Simulated combat jump with full equipment, jumpers exiting the door at one second intervals per door or half-second intervals from alternating doors.

"Master Blaster" - One who has earned a Master Parachutist Badge.

MHC – Medical Holding Company. The unit where soldiers are sent while they heal from serious injuries, to await the results of their Medical Review Board, or discharge after the decision is made.

MRB – Medical Review Board – Board that reviews medical records of injured soldiers to determine whether they should be reclassified and retained in service or are unfit to serve.

MRE – Meal, Ready to Eat – the replacement for C-rations. They were packaged in soft pouches making them lighter to carry.

MAC – Military Airlift Command – the major Air Force command responsible for transporting cargo and troops around the world and in to combat. They put the "air" in airborne.

Million Dollar Minute, the – The climatic moment of the Division's annual CAPEX where every weapon available to the Division was brought to bear on a target. The "million dollars" was just a way of saying it cost a lot to do.

MOS – Military Occupational Specialty. The classification for a soldier's assigned job.

"Mox Nix" – GI German for unimportant or it doesn't matter. From German *"Machts Nichts."* Literally - "Makes Nothing."

NBC – Nuclear, Chemical, and Biological

NCO – Non-Commissioned Officer - Corporal through Sergeant.

NCOIC – Non-Commissioned Officer in Charge – The highest ranking sergeant in a unit who supervises others. A gun chief is NCOIC of a gun section; a squad leader is NCOIC of an infantry squad. A platoon sergeant is NCOIC of a platoon.

NVA – North Vietnamese Army - The regular army of Communist North Vietnam. They were always our enemy.

OPORDER – Operations Order – Should be self-explanatory. It basically gives a general outline of the plan and unit responsibilities for a given operation.

OP – Observation Post. In peacetime OP's are located around impact areas for Forward Observers to use in calling fire missions.

OPT – Off-Post Training Exercise – As the name implies, a training exercise requiring a unit to go off their assigned post to conduct training in an unfamiliar environment.

One and Two Gun Raids – When one or a pair of gun sling load (hook up) to a helicopter and are flown away from the battery to a remote location to fire a mission, either by direct or indirect fire.

1K Zone – One Kilometer Zone. Buffer area or de-militarized zone established between West Germany and Czechoslovakia during the Cold War.

OPFOR – Opposing Forces. The enemy.

Parachute - During my time in service we used two parachutes:
        T-10 – was an older model parachute requiring tugging on the risers of the chute to steer. The canopy was a full round canopy allowing for a generally slower descent than the MC1-1B steerable chute.
        MC1-1B – was a newer chute. With portions of the rear panels cut out to allow more airflow the chute was steerable – and potentially faster in descent if not controlled properly - by the use of toggles.

PCS – Permanent Change of Station - Transfer.

PLF – Parachute Landing Fall - Consists of five points of contact: 1) Balls of Feet; 2) Calf; 3) Outer thigh; 4) Butt 5) Side of back, or pushup muscle. Too often, it's Feet, Butt, Head.

Paratrooper – Military parachutists.

Phonetic Alphabet - Standardized system to avoid confusion in military transmissions.

A – Alpha	J – Juliet	S – Sierra
B – Bravo	K – Kilo	T – Tango
C – Charlie	L – Lima	U – Uniform
D – Delta	M – Mike	V – Victor
E – Echo	N – November	W – Whiskey
F – Foxtrot	O – Oscar	X – X-ray
G – Golf	P – Papa	Y – Yankee
H – Hotel	Q – Quebec	Z – Zulu
I – India	R – Romeo	

"Prick", the - Nickname for the AN-PRC 77 radio used by troops. Carried on the back. Heavy. Heavier after it was carried for awhile. Under proper conditions it was supposed to be able have a range of about five miles. So I'm told.

PX – Post Exchange – General store on post.

Range Control – The office on an Army base that has administrative control over that post's training areas. If a unit needs to run a weapons qualification range the S-3 has to request that range for the day in question. If a unit wants to go out on a field problem the commander has to submit requests to use the position areas (PAs or Papa Alphas) he will require – usually through the S-3 – to get approval to use them from Range Control, who compares and coordinates requests to ensure there is no conflict in scheduling or training between units in the field. Range Control is also responsible for safety downrange. Any safety violation, such as a round missing the Impact Area (or target zone) is immediately reported to and investigated by Range Control. Until that investigation is complete Range Control can shut the entire range down.

RSOP – 1) In Field Artillery: **Recon, Selection, and Occupation of Position** – Also called a deliberate occupation of position. 2) **Readiness Standard Operation Procedure** – regulations concerning maintaining the Division's readiness in light of its role as the Rapid Response Force.

REMF – Rear Echelon [Individual] – refers to rear area and support personnel. Usually used by combat arms and other field soldiers to describe non-combat personnel.

REFORGER – REturn of FORces to GERmany. Exercises conducted every two years during the Cold War (and maybe after) in which units stationed in the US were deployed to Germany for war games to familiarize themselves with the German geography they would fight in if total war ever broke out.

RIF – Reduction in Force after a war or budget cuts.

Risers - The straps connecting the parachute harness to the suspension lines of a parachute.

"Rock-n-Roll" – nickname for fully automatic fire.

Rucksack (or "Ruck") – Soldier's name for Field Pack or "ALICE" Pack.

Shell Report (Shell Rep) – an investigation of the site of the crater for shell fragments to determine the weapon that caused it – usually after a round misses the Impact Area.

Skin of an aircraft - the outer wall of an aircraft.

"Skycrane" – or "Sky Crane" – CH-54 helicopter specifically designed to carry heavy loads to large for other helicopters – even the CH-47 Chinook.

Snake Mission – Name we used for a tactical nuclear mission.

Staff Duty Officer/NCO – Person assigned to man phone at higher headquarters during off-duty hours and oversee CQs in their functions.

Staff Sections: The offices established at higher headquarters to assist the commander in carrying out his job. At battalion and brigade level each position is designated with an "S", at division and higher the position/section is designated by a "G" to denote "General Staff." The staff sections are as follows:

G-1/S-1   - Personnel
G2/S-2 - Intelligence
G-3/S-3 – Operations & Training
G-4/S-4 – Supply and Logistics
G-5 – Public Affairs (did not exist at battalion or brigade levels when I was in)

Static Line – The fifteen-foot long nylon cord that attached to the bridle at the apex (center top) of the parachute by a tie of ¼ inch cotton webbing (string) by which it pulls the chute out of the tray.

Steel Pot, or Pot – M-1 steel helmet used by US armed forces from World War II up into the 80s.

Suspension Lines – Nylon cords that connected the "skirt" of the parachute canopy to the risers and thus to the jumper through the parachute harness.

TA-50 - Field or Combat Gear. Comes from Table of Allowances – 50 – the list of field issue items for each soldier, depending on his or her MOS.

TO&E – Table of Organization and Equipment. A list of everything – EVERYTHING – a given unit is required to have, from personnel down to the last spare nut or bolt they're supposed to have on hand to do the job.

TDY – Temporary Duty Assignment.

34 – Foot Tower – Used to practice exits from and aircraft.

TOC – Tactical Operations Center - Fancy acronym for the Tactical Field HQ, run by an S-3 or G-3 Section.

TRADOC – Training and Doctrine Command - Major command formed toward the end of the Vietnam War (1973) to standardize and supervise all Army level training, such as Basic Training, etc. TRADOC also established both training and operational doctrine for the Army.

200 – Foot Tower – Used to simulate the actual fall in a parachute.

USAREUR – United States Army EURope – The major US Army command for Army Forces in Europe.

WP - White phosphorous round, also called "Willie Peter."

"Was ist Los?" – GI German for "What's up?"

Web Gear – The Vietnam holdover name for our individual combat gear. Properly, it was the pistol belt, ammo pouches, canteen cover, and shoulder straps a soldier wore. My first hitch we called it "web gear," after my break in service it was called LCE.